My Little Monster

4

Robico

C O N T E N T S

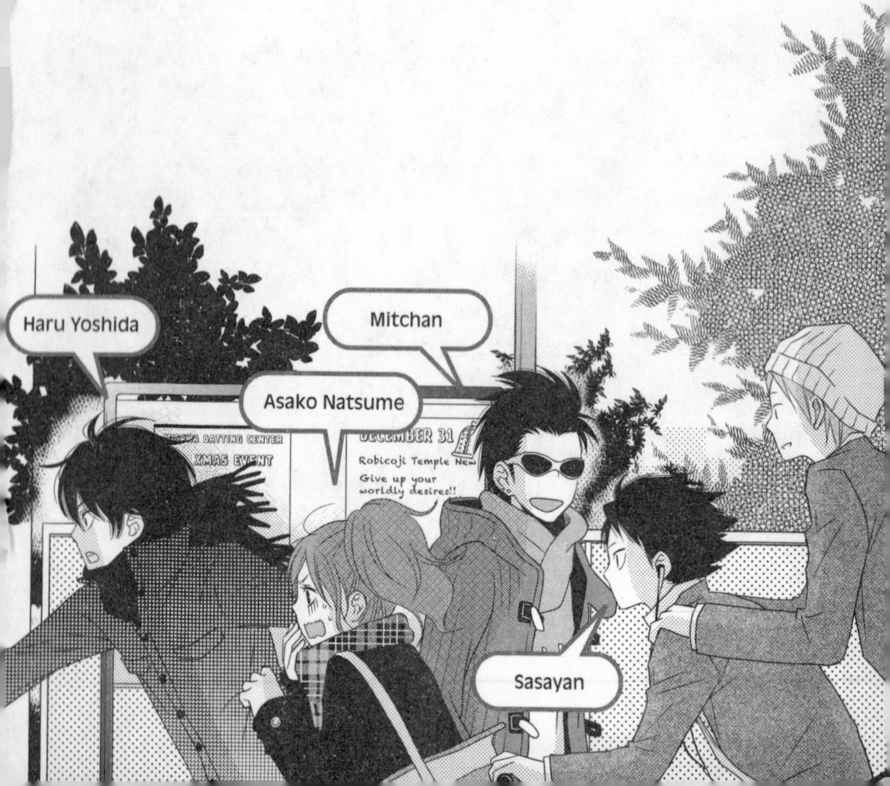
Mitchan
Haru Yoshida
Asako Natsume
DECEMBER 31
Robicoji Temple New
Give up your worldly desires!!
BATTING CENTER
XMAS EVENT
Sasayan

S T O R Y

When Shizuku Mizutani does a favor for problem child Haru Yoshida, who sits next to her in school, he develops a huge crush on her. Attracted to his innocence, she eventually falls for him too, but when she asks him out, he inexplicably turns her down. She determines to win him over and ask him out again, but when she can't figure out how to do that, she locks away her romantic feelings. However, after getting some helpful advice from Haru's friend Yamaken, Shizuku gradually beings to change, and decides to face people more assertively.

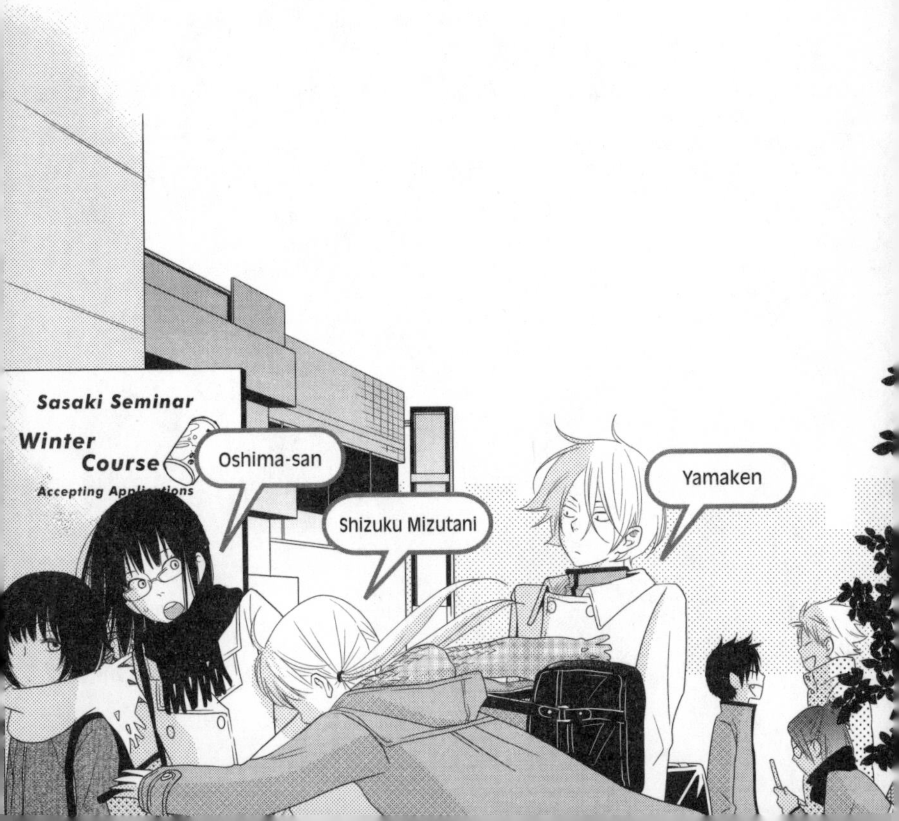
Yamaken
Shizuku Mizutani
Oshima-san
Sasaki Seminar
Winter Course

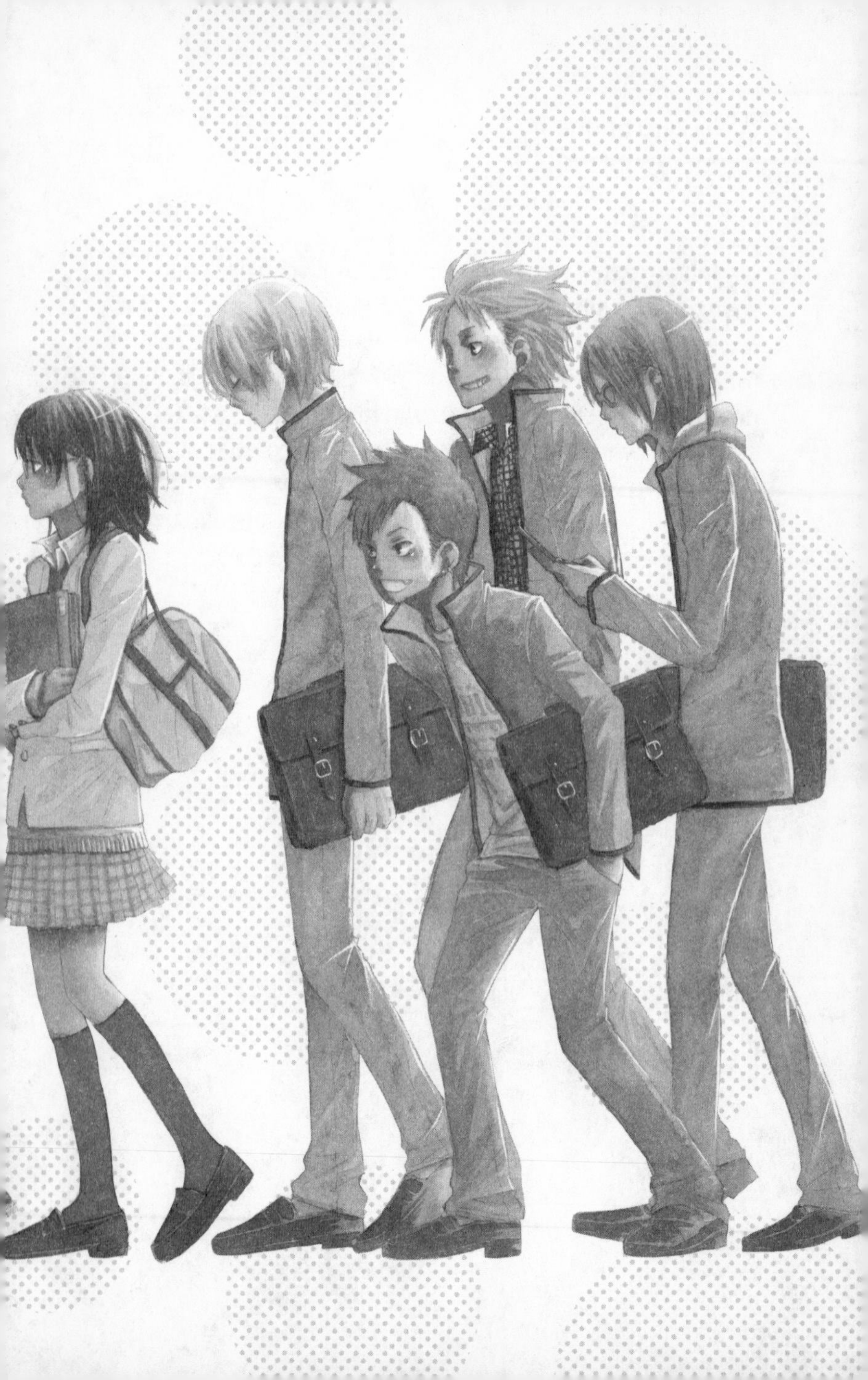

Chapter 13 Zero or One

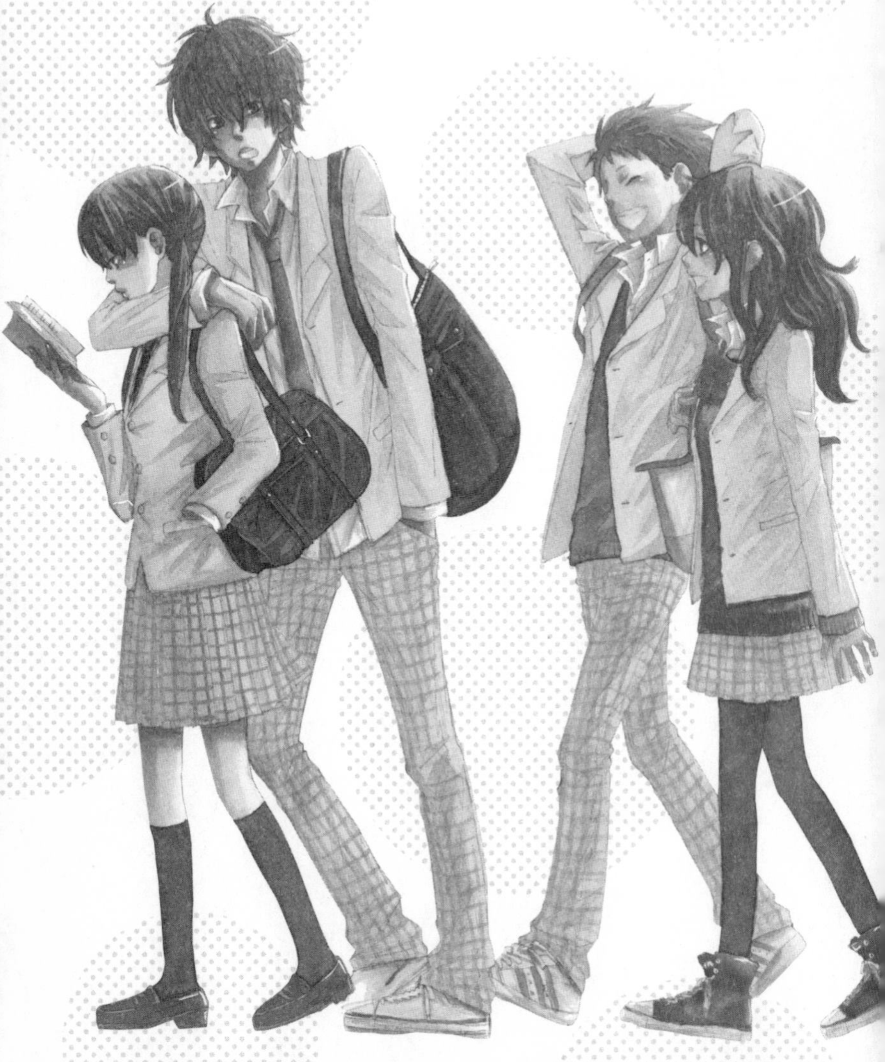

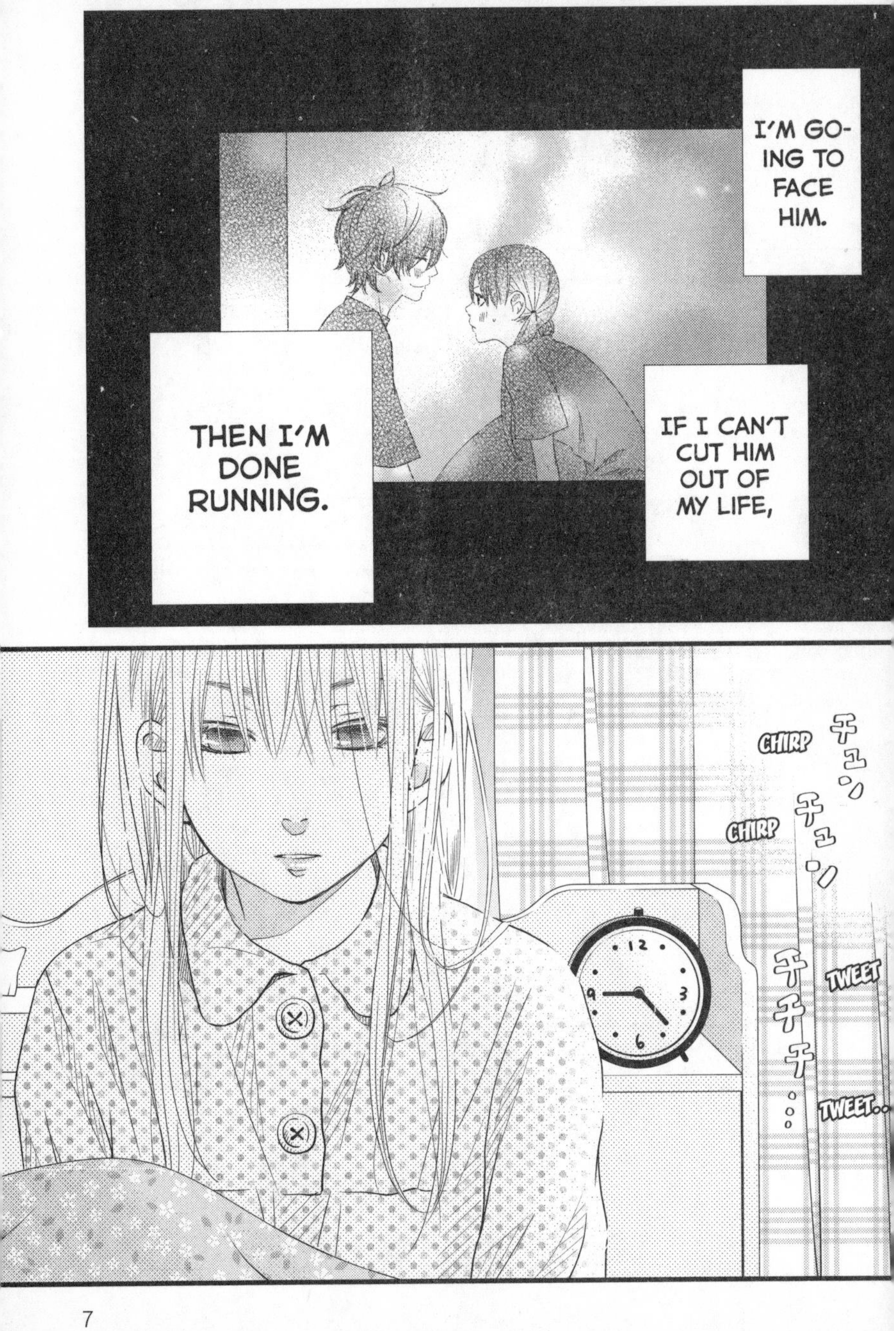
I'M GOING TO FACE HIM.
IF I CAN'T CUT HIM OUT OF MY LIFE,
THEN I'M DONE RUNNING.
チュン
CHIRP
チュン
CHIRP
チチチ…
TWEET
TWEET…

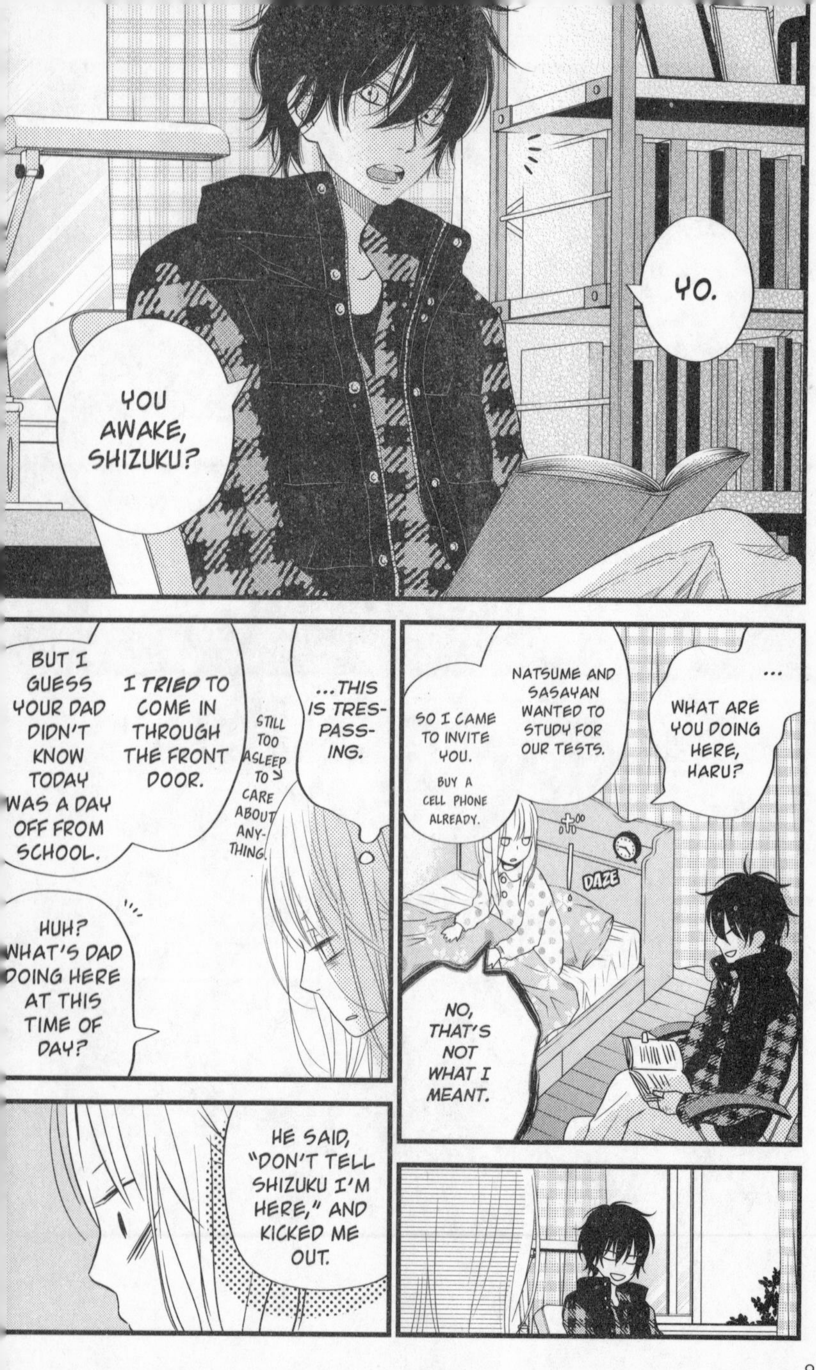
YO.
YOU AWAKE, SHIZUKU?
...WHAT ARE YOU DOING HERE, HARU?
NATSUME AND SASAYAN WANTED TO STUDY FOR OUR TESTS.
SO I CAME TO INVITE YOU.
BUY A CELL PHONE ALREADY.
DAZE
NO, THAT'S NOT WHAT I MEANT.
...THIS IS TRES-PASS-ING.
STILL TOO ASLEEP TO CARE ABOUT ANYTHING.
I TRIED TO COME IN THROUGH THE FRONT DOOR.
BUT I GUESS YOUR DAD DIDN'T KNOW TODAY WAS A DAY OFF FROM SCHOOL.
HUH? WHAT'S DAD DOING HERE AT THIS TIME OF DAY?
HE SAID, "DON'T TELL SHIZUKU I'M HERE," AND KICKED ME OUT.

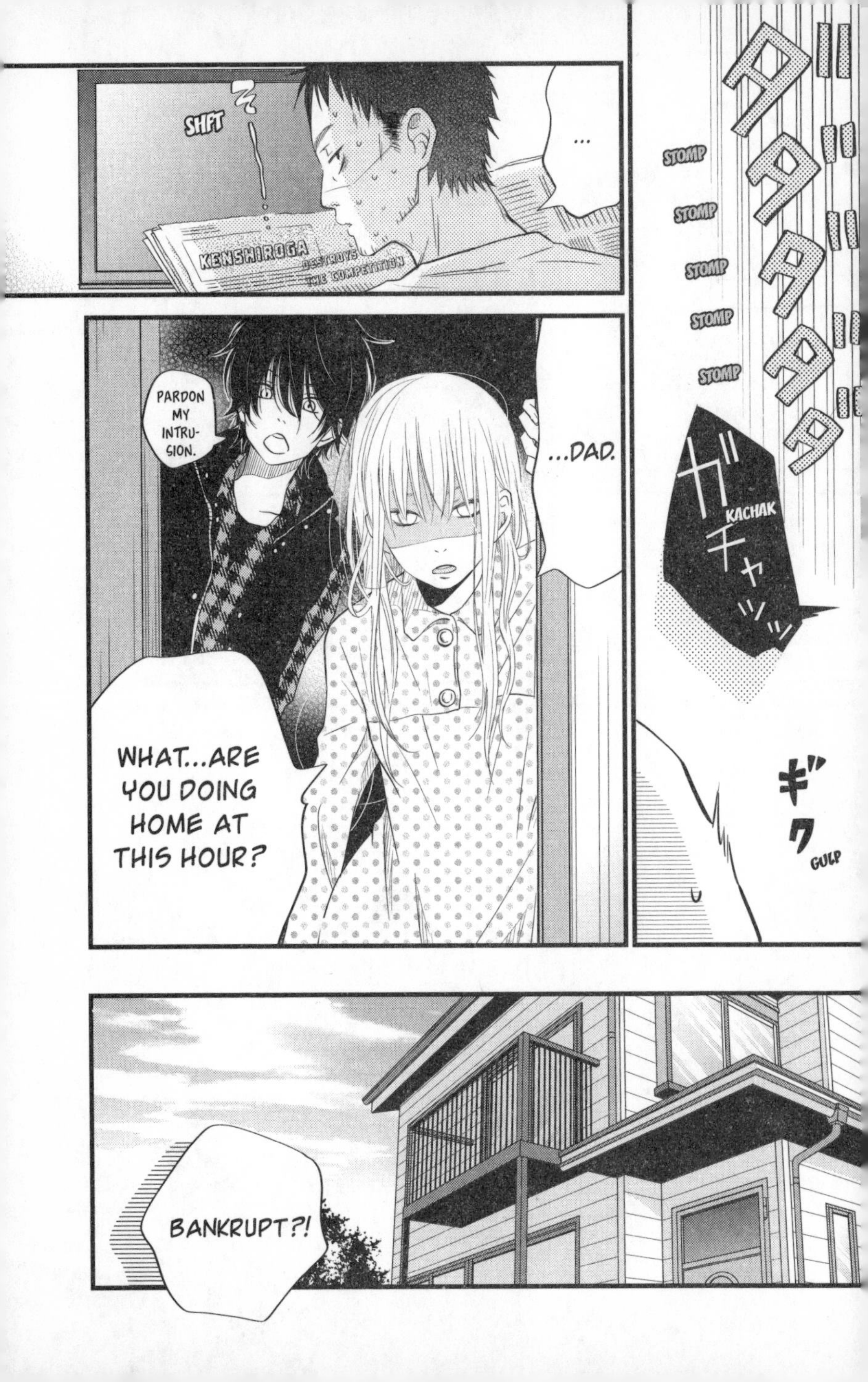

STOMP
STOMP
STOMP
STOMP
STOMP
ガチャッ
KACHAK
ギク
GULP
SHFT
...
KENSHIROGA DESTROYS THE COMPETITION
...DAD.
PARDON MY INTRU-SION.
WHAT...ARE YOU DOING HOME AT THIS HOUR?
BANKRUPT?!

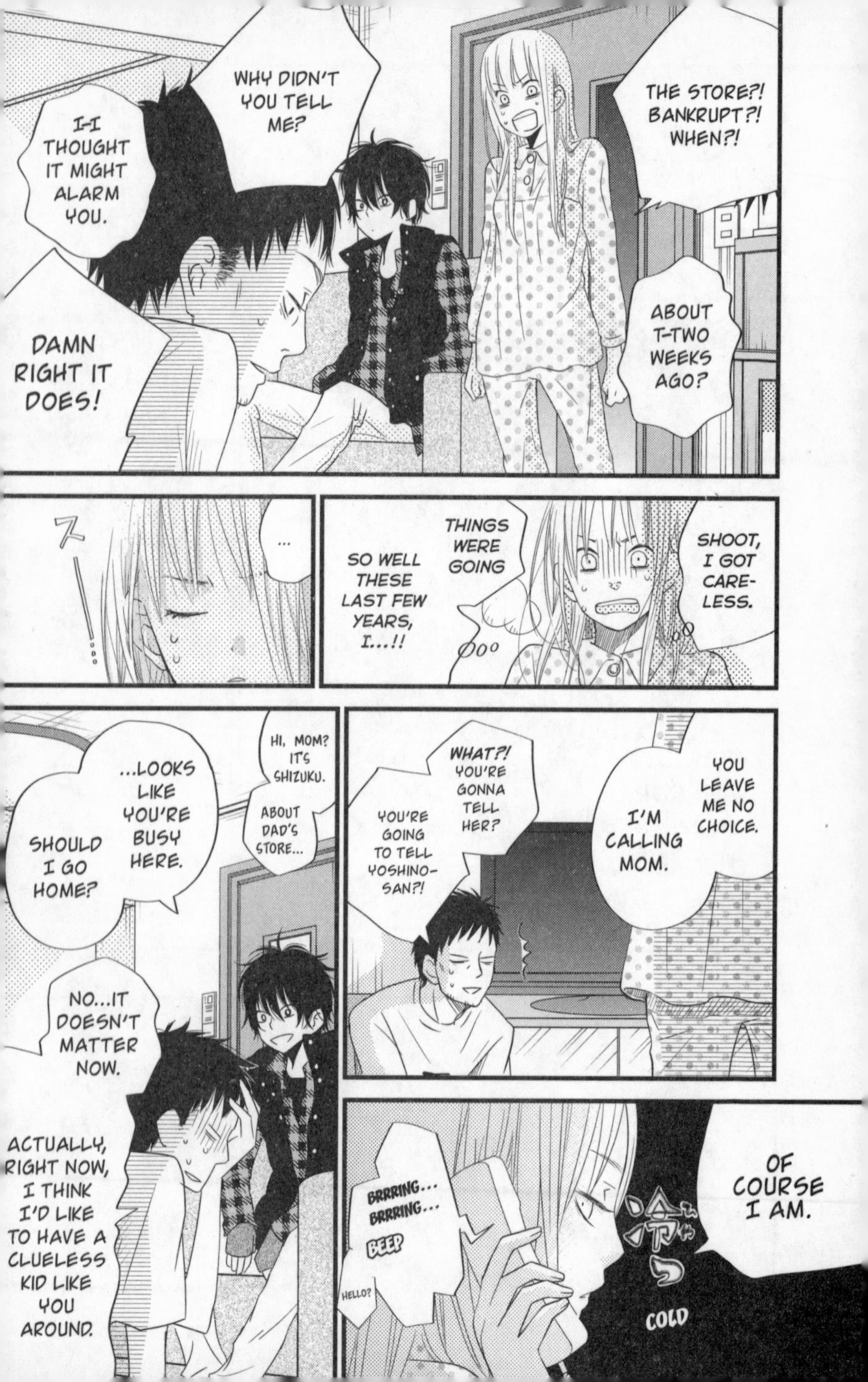
THE STORE?! BANKRUPT?! WHEN?!
ABOUT T-TWO WEEKS AGO?
WHY DIDN'T YOU TELL ME?
I-I THOUGHT IT MIGHT ALARM YOU.
DAMN RIGHT IT DOES!
SHOOT, I GOT CARE-LESS.
THINGS WERE GOING SO WELL THESE LAST FEW YEARS, I...!!
...
ス
YOU LEAVE ME NO CHOICE.
I'M CALLING MOM.
WHAT?! YOU'RE GONNA TELL HER?
YOU'RE GOING TO TELL YOSHINO-SAN?!
OF COURSE I AM.
冷っ
COLD
BRRRING... BRRRING...
BEEP
HELLO?
HI, MOM? IT'S SHIZUKU.
ABOUT DAD'S STORE...
...LOOKS LIKE YOU'RE BUSY HERE.
SHOULD I GO HOME?
NO...IT DOESN'T MATTER NOW.
ACTUALLY, RIGHT NOW, I THINK I'D LIKE TO HAVE A CLUELESS KID LIKE YOU AROUND.

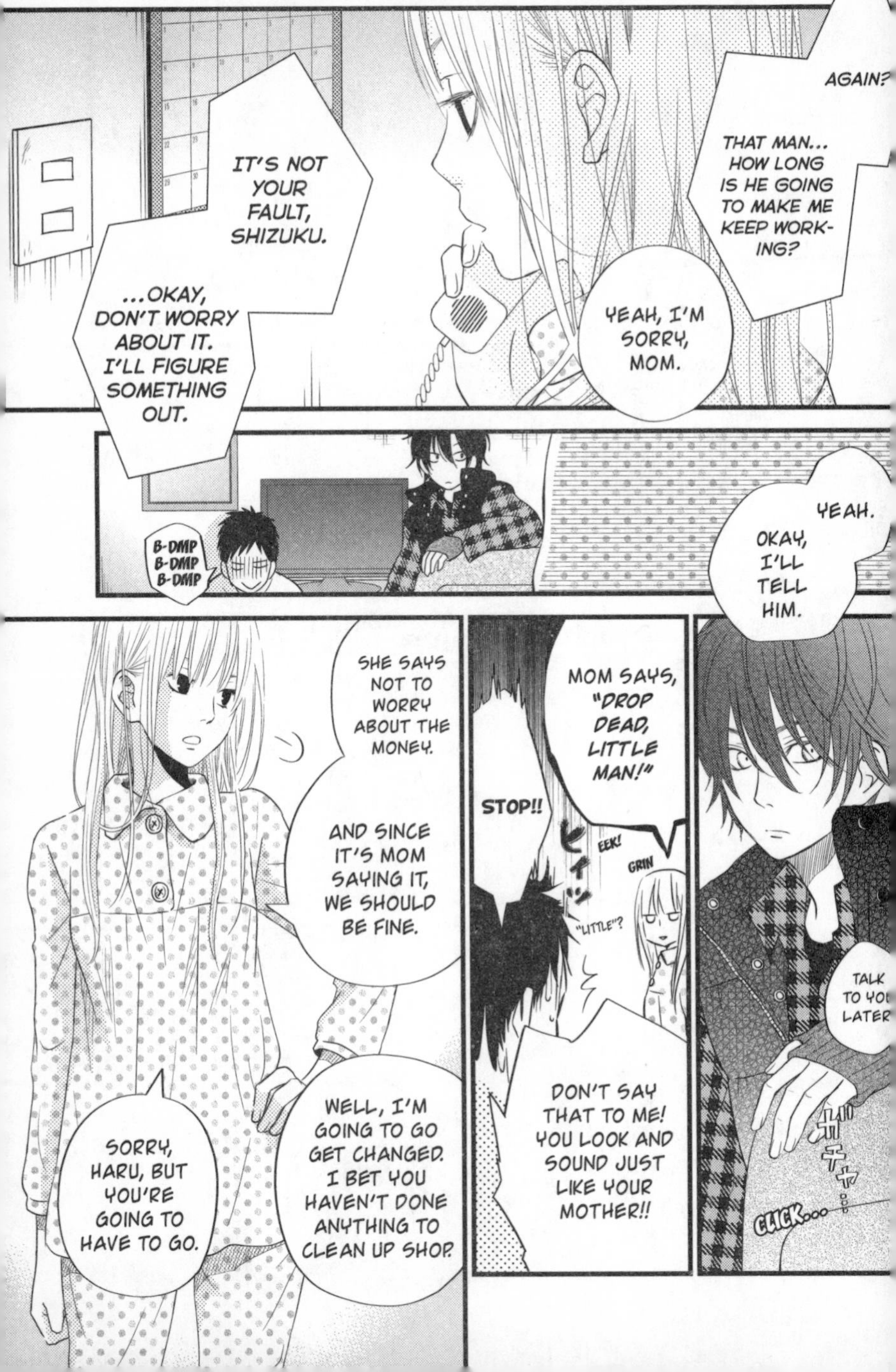
AGAIN?
THAT MAN... HOW LONG IS HE GOING TO MAKE ME KEEP WORKING?
YEAH, I'M SORRY, MOM.
IT'S NOT YOUR FAULT, SHIZUKU.
...OKAY, DON'T WORRY ABOUT IT. I'LL FIGURE SOMETHING OUT.
YEAH. OKAY, I'LL TELL HIM.
B-DMP B-DMP B-DMP
TALK TO YOU LATER
CLICK...
MOM SAYS, "DROP DEAD, LITTLE MAN!"
STOP!!
EEK!
GRIN
"LITTLE"?
DON'T SAY THAT TO ME! YOU LOOK AND SOUND JUST LIKE YOUR MOTHER!!
SHE SAYS NOT TO WORRY ABOUT THE MONEY.
AND SINCE IT'S MOM SAYING IT, WE SHOULD BE FINE.
WELL, I'M GOING TO GO GET CHANGED. I BET YOU HAVEN'T DONE ANYTHING TO CLEAN UP SHOP.
SORRY, HARU, BUT YOU'RE GOING TO HAVE TO GO.

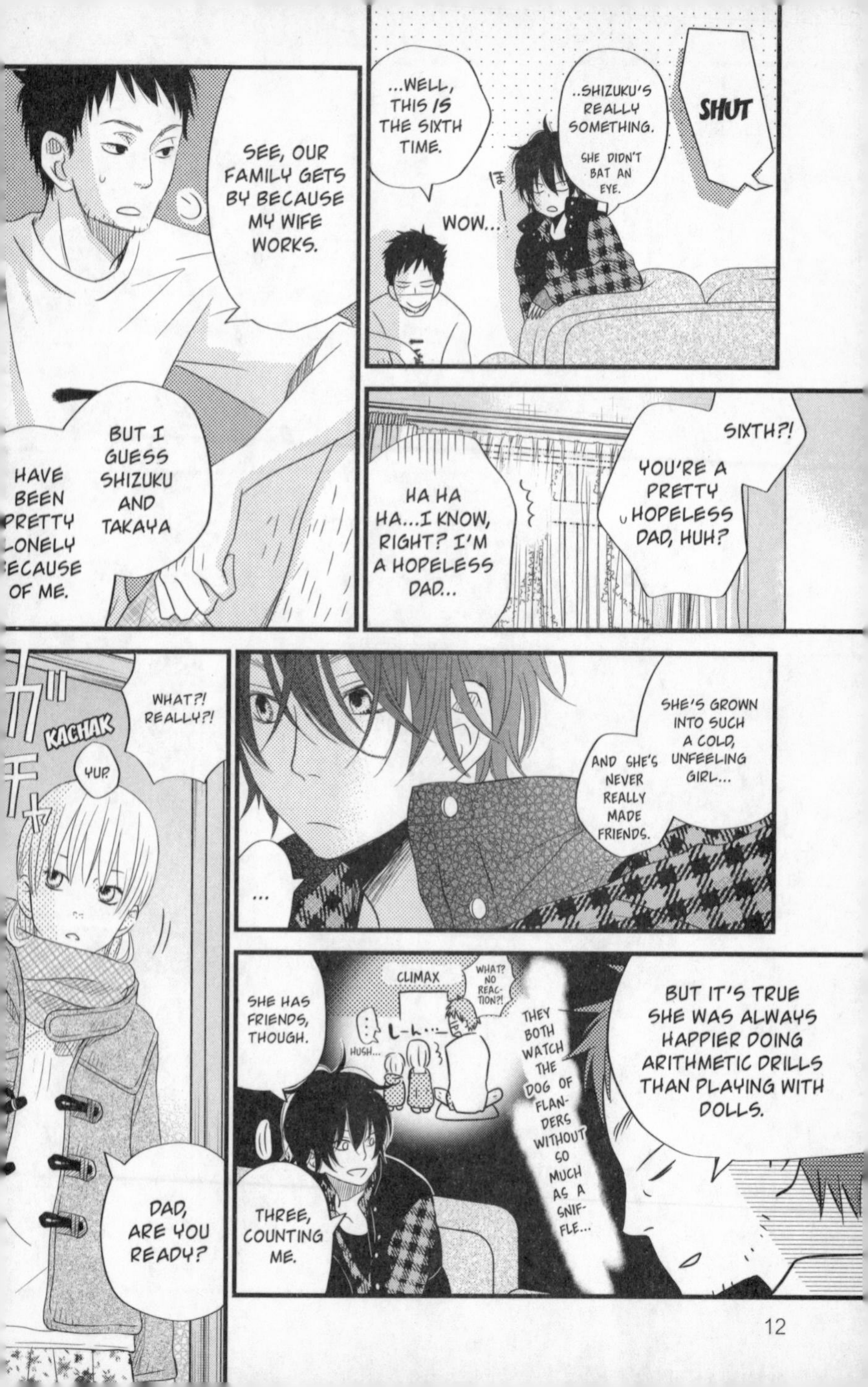
SHUT
..SHIZUKU'S REALLY SOMETHING.
SHE DIDN'T BAT AN EYE.
...WELL, THIS *IS* THE SIXTH TIME.
WOW...
SIXTH?!
YOU'RE A PRETTY HOPELESS DAD, HUH?
HA HA HA...I KNOW, RIGHT? I'M A HOPELESS DAD...
SEE, OUR FAMILY GETS BY BECAUSE MY WIFE WORKS.
BUT I GUESS SHIZUKU AND TAKAYA
HAVE BEEN PRETTY LONELY BECAUSE OF ME.
SHE'S GROWN INTO SUCH A COLD, UNFEELING GIRL...
AND SHE'S NEVER REALLY MADE FRIENDS.
...
BUT IT'S TRUE SHE WAS ALWAYS HAPPIER DOING ARITHMETIC DRILLS THAN PLAYING WITH DOLLS.
THEY BOTH WATCH THE DOG OF FLANDERS WITHOUT SO MUCH AS A SNIFFLE...
WHAT? NO REACTION?!
CLIMAX
HUSH...
SHE HAS FRIENDS, THOUGH.
THREE, COUNTING ME.
WHAT?! REALLY?!
KACHAK
YUP.
DAD, ARE YOU READY?

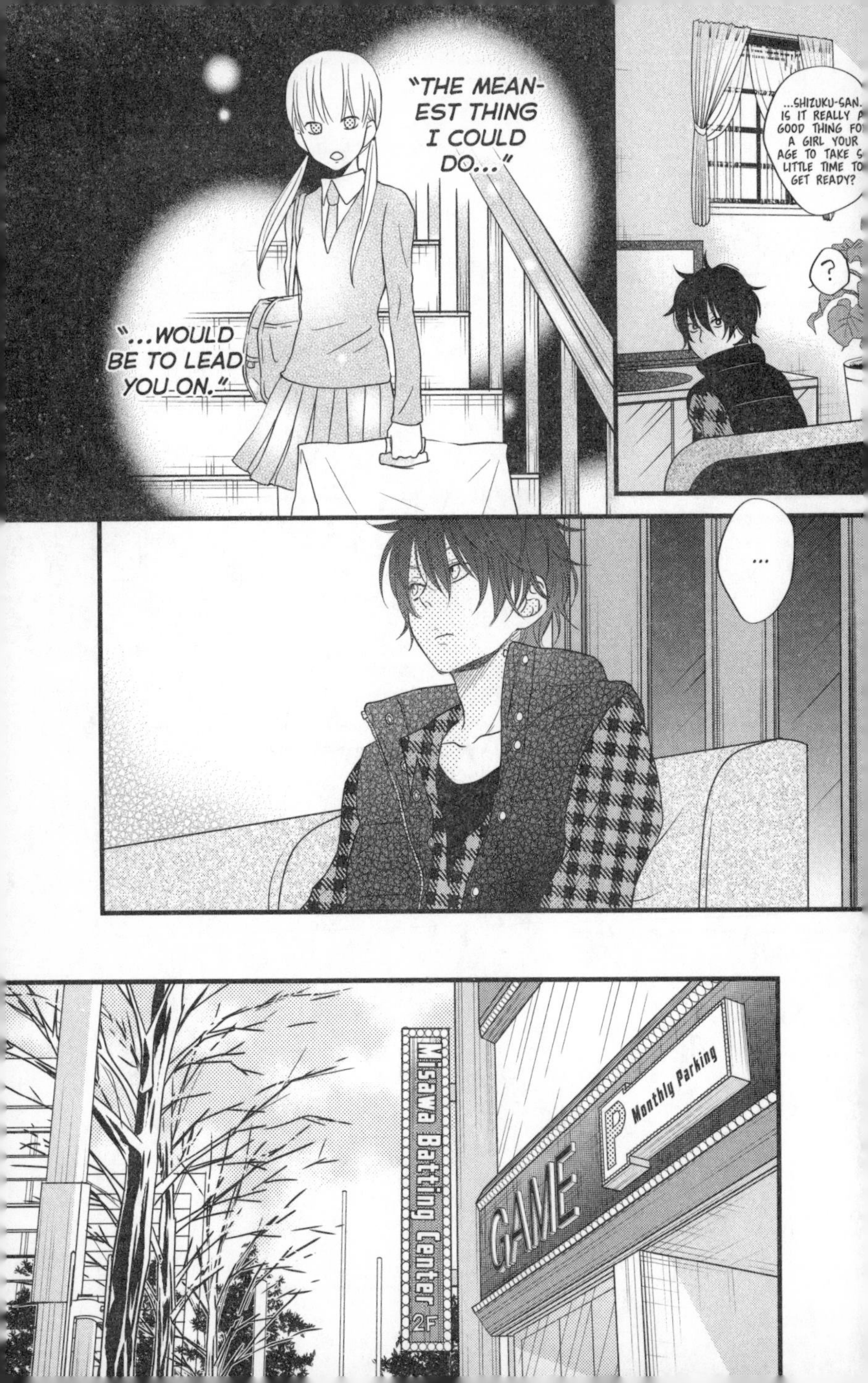
...SHIZUKU-SAN... IS IT REALLY A GOOD THING FOR A GIRL YOUR AGE TO TAKE SO LITTLE TIME TO GET READY?
?
"THE MEAN-EST THING I COULD DO..."
"...WOULD BE TO LEAD YOU ON."
...
Misawa Batting Center 2F
Monthly Parking
P
GAME

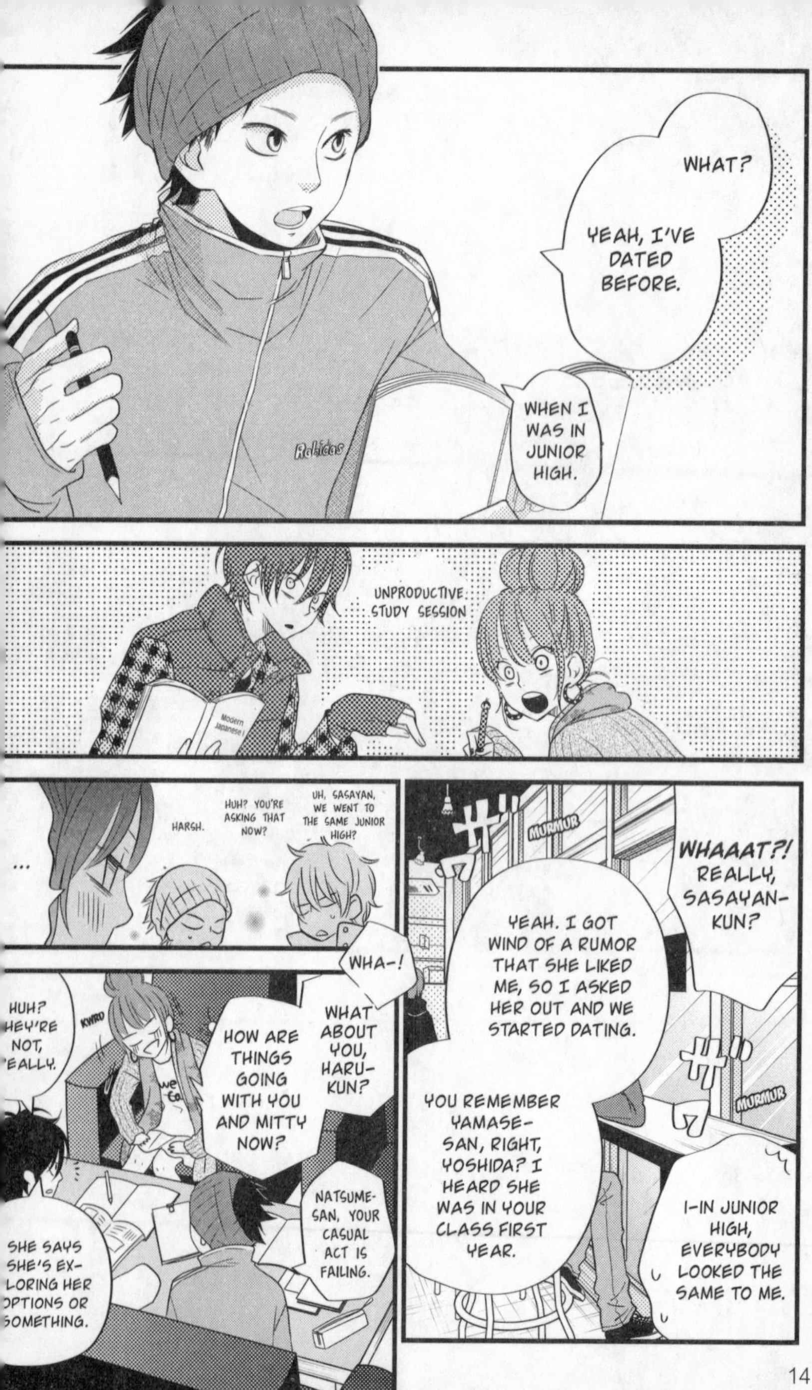
WHAT?
YEAH, I'VE DATED BEFORE.
WHEN I WAS IN JUNIOR HIGH.
UNPRODUCTIVE STUDY SESSION
Modern Japanese I
WHAAAT?! REALLY, SASAYAN-KUN?
MURMUR
YEAH. I GOT WIND OF A RUMOR THAT SHE LIKED ME, SO I ASKED HER OUT AND WE STARTED DATING.
MURMUR
YOU REMEMBER YAMASE-SAN, RIGHT, YOSHIDA? I HEARD SHE WAS IN YOUR CLASS FIRST YEAR.
I-IN JUNIOR HIGH, EVERYBODY LOOKED THE SAME TO ME.
UH, SASAYAN, WE WENT TO THE SAME JUNIOR HIGH?
HUH? YOU'RE ASKING THAT NOW?
HARSH.
...
WHA-!
WHAT ABOUT YOU, HARU-KUN?
HOW ARE THINGS GOING WITH YOU AND MITTY NOW?
KWRD
HUH? HEY'RE NOT, 'EALLY.
NATSUME-SAN, YOUR CASUAL ACT IS FAILING.
SHE SAYS SHE'S EX-LORING HER OPTIONS OR OMETHING.

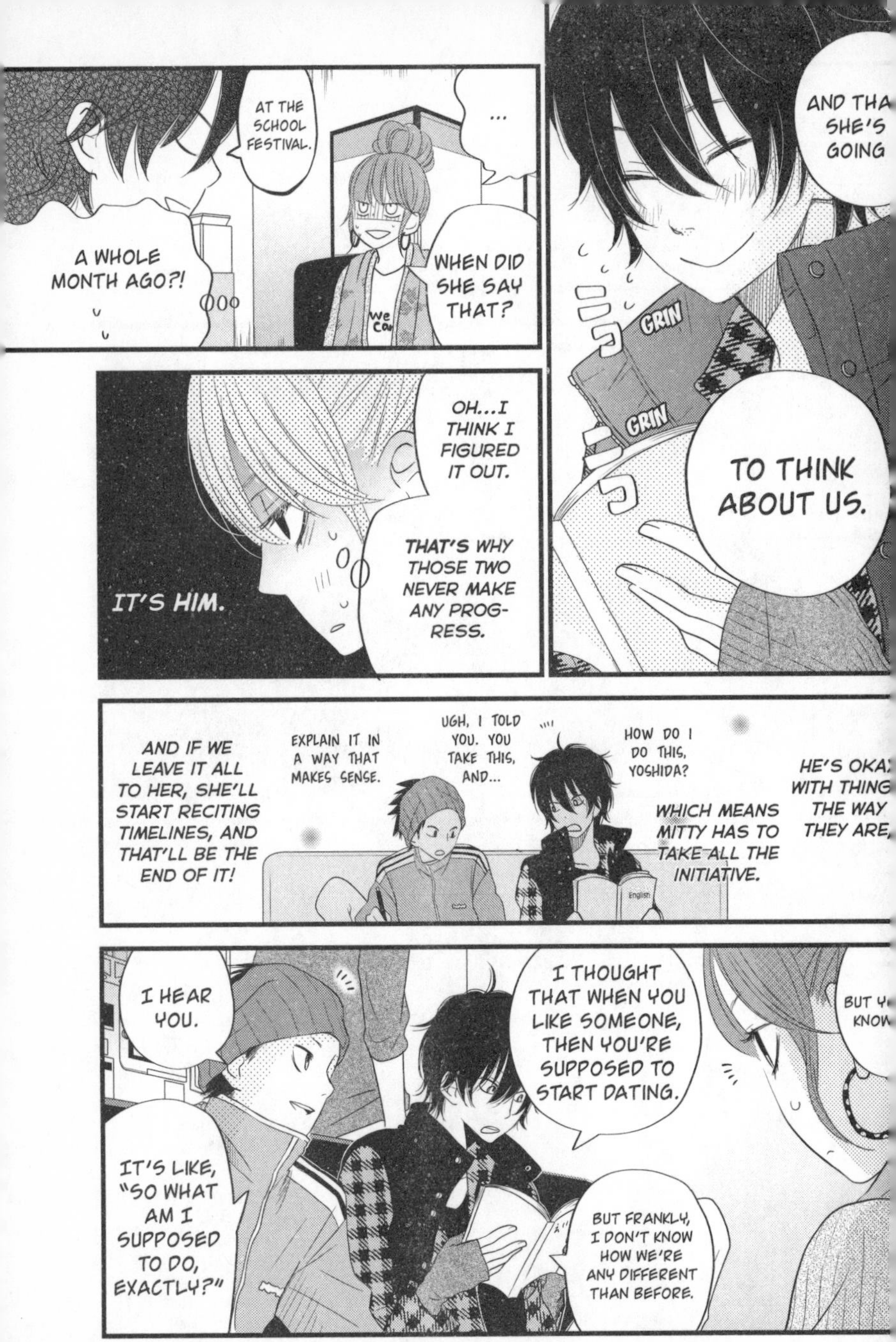
AND THA
SHE'S
GOING
GRIN
GRIN
TO THINK ABOUT US.
...
WHEN DID SHE SAY THAT?
AT THE SCHOOL FESTIVAL.
A WHOLE MONTH AGO?!
OH...I THINK I FIGURED IT OUT.
THAT'S WHY THOSE TWO NEVER MAKE ANY PROG-RESS.
IT'S HIM.
HE'S OKA
WITH THING
THE WAY
THEY ARE,
HOW DO I DO THIS, YOSHIDA?
WHICH MEANS MITTY HAS TO TAKE ALL THE INITIATIVE.
UGH, I TOLD YOU. YOU TAKE THIS, AND...
EXPLAIN IT IN A WAY THAT MAKES SENSE.
AND IF WE LEAVE IT ALL TO HER, SHE'LL START RECITING TIMELINES, AND THAT'LL BE THE END OF IT!
BUT Y
KNOW
I THOUGHT THAT WHEN YOU LIKE SOMEONE, THEN YOU'RE SUPPOSED TO START DATING.
BUT FRANKLY, I DON'T KNOW HOW WE'RE ANY DIFFERENT THAN BEFORE.
I HEAR YOU.
IT'S LIKE, "SO WHAT AM I SUPPOSED TO DO, EXACTLY?"

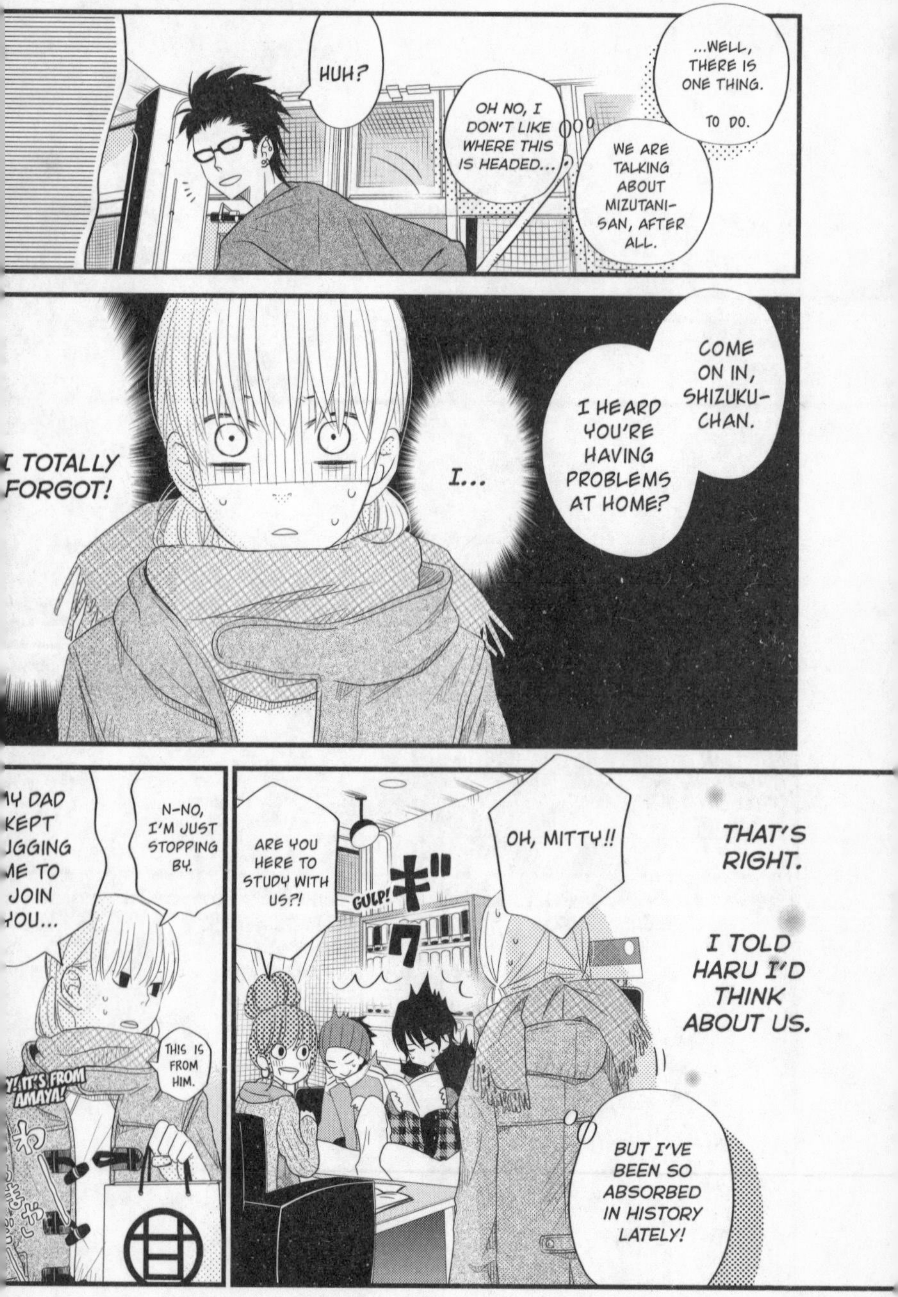
...WELL, THERE IS ONE THING.
TO DO.
WE ARE TALKING ABOUT MIZUTANI-SAN, AFTER ALL.
OH NO, I DON'T LIKE WHERE THIS IS HEADED...
HUH?
COME ON IN, SHIZUKU-CHAN.
I HEARD YOU'RE HAVING PROBLEMS AT HOME?
I...
I TOTALLY FORGOT!
THAT'S RIGHT.
I TOLD HARU I'D THINK ABOUT US.
BUT I'VE BEEN SO ABSORBED IN HISTORY LATELY!
OH, MITTY!!
GULP!
ARE YOU HERE TO STUDY WITH US?!
N-NO, I'M JUST STOPPING BY.
MY DAD KEPT ...UGGING ME TO JOIN YOU...
THIS IS FROM HIM.
...Y! IT'S FROM AMAYA!

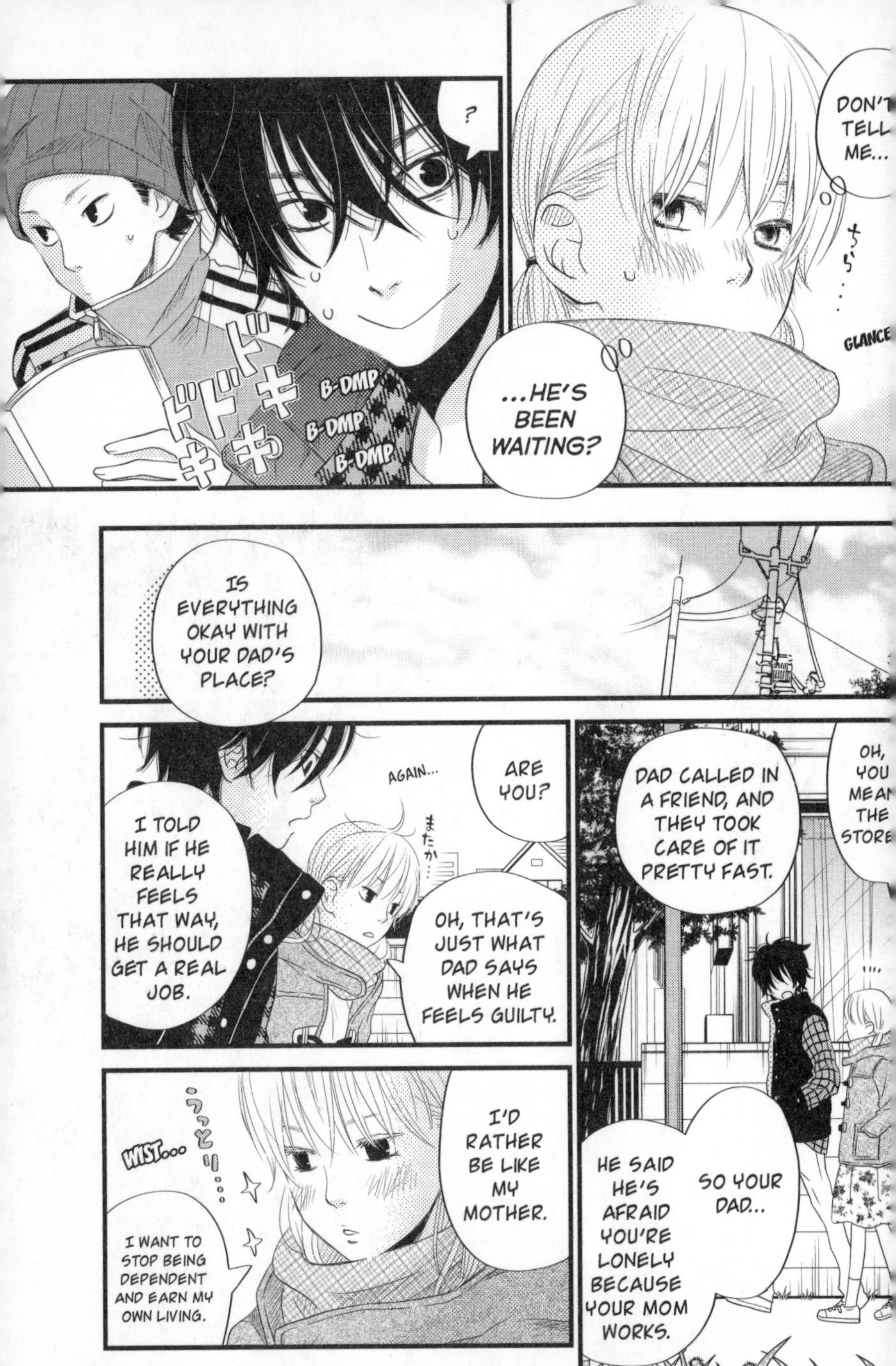
DON'T TELL ME...
ちら...
GLANCE
...HE'S BEEN WAITING?
?
ドキドキ
B-DMP
B-DMP
B-DMP
IS EVERYTHING OKAY WITH YOUR DAD'S PLACE?
OH, YOU MEAN THE STORE
DAD CALLED IN A FRIEND, AND THEY TOOK CARE OF IT PRETTY FAST.
!!!
SO YOUR DAD...
HE SAID HE'S AFRAID YOU'RE LONELY BECAUSE YOUR MOM WORKS.
ARE YOU?
AGAIN...
またか...
OH, THAT'S JUST WHAT DAD SAYS WHEN HE FEELS GUILTY.
I TOLD HIM IF HE REALLY FEELS THAT WAY, HE SHOULD GET A REAL JOB.
I'D RATHER BE LIKE MY MOTHER.
うっとり...
WIST...
I WANT TO STOP BEING DEPENDENT AND EARN MY OWN LIVING.

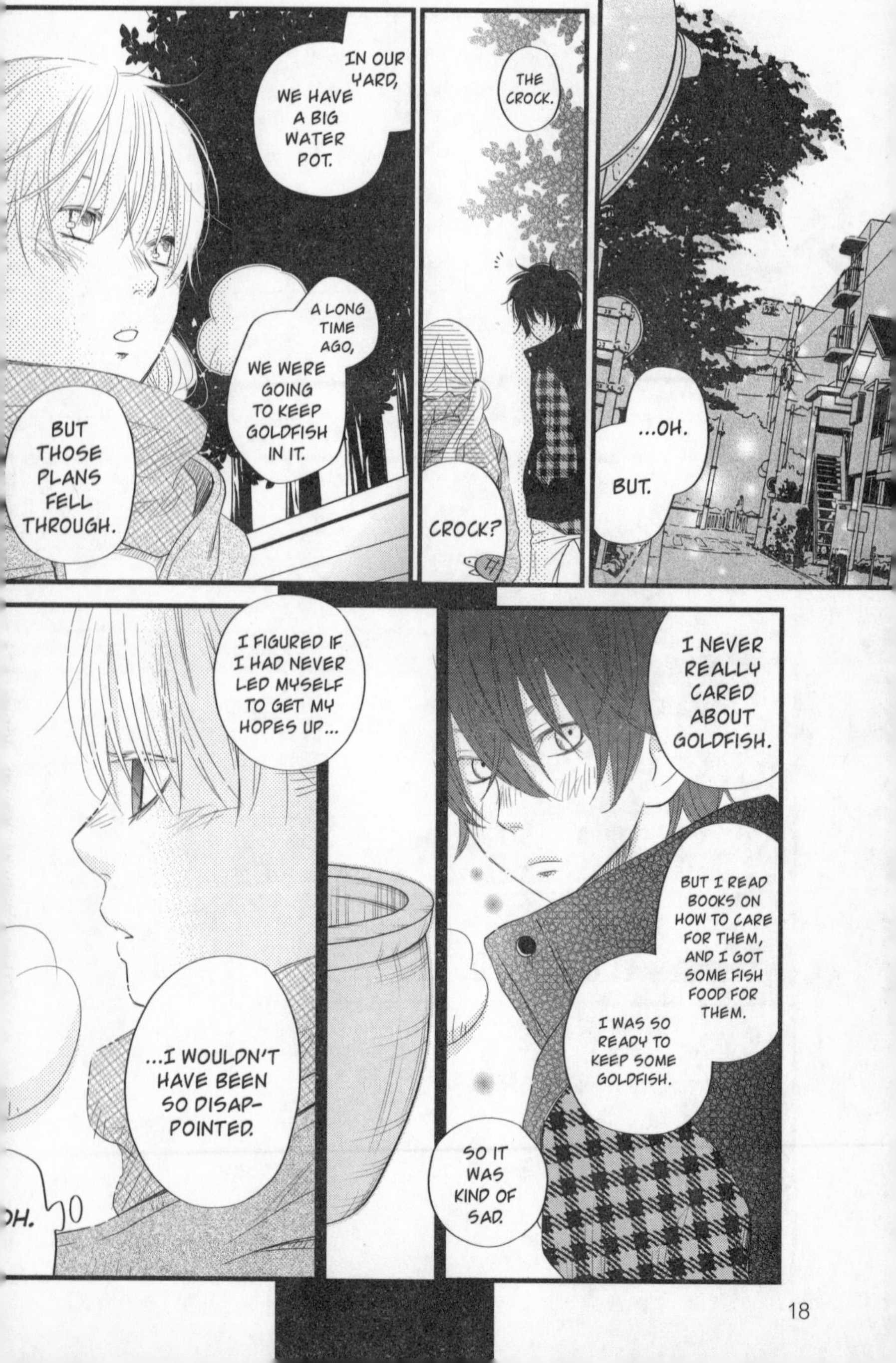

...OH.
BUT.
THE CROCK.
CROCK?
IN OUR YARD, WE HAVE A BIG WATER POT.
A LONG TIME AGO, WE WERE GOING TO KEEP GOLDFISH IN IT.
BUT THOSE PLANS FELL THROUGH.
I NEVER REALLY CARED ABOUT GOLDFISH.
BUT I READ BOOKS ON HOW TO CARE FOR THEM, AND I GOT SOME FISH FOOD FOR THEM.
I WAS SO READY TO KEEP SOME GOLDFISH.
SO IT WAS KIND OF SAD.
I FIGURED IF I HAD NEVER LED MYSELF TO GET MY HOPES UP...
...I WOULDN'T HAVE BEEN SO DISAP-POINTED.
OH.

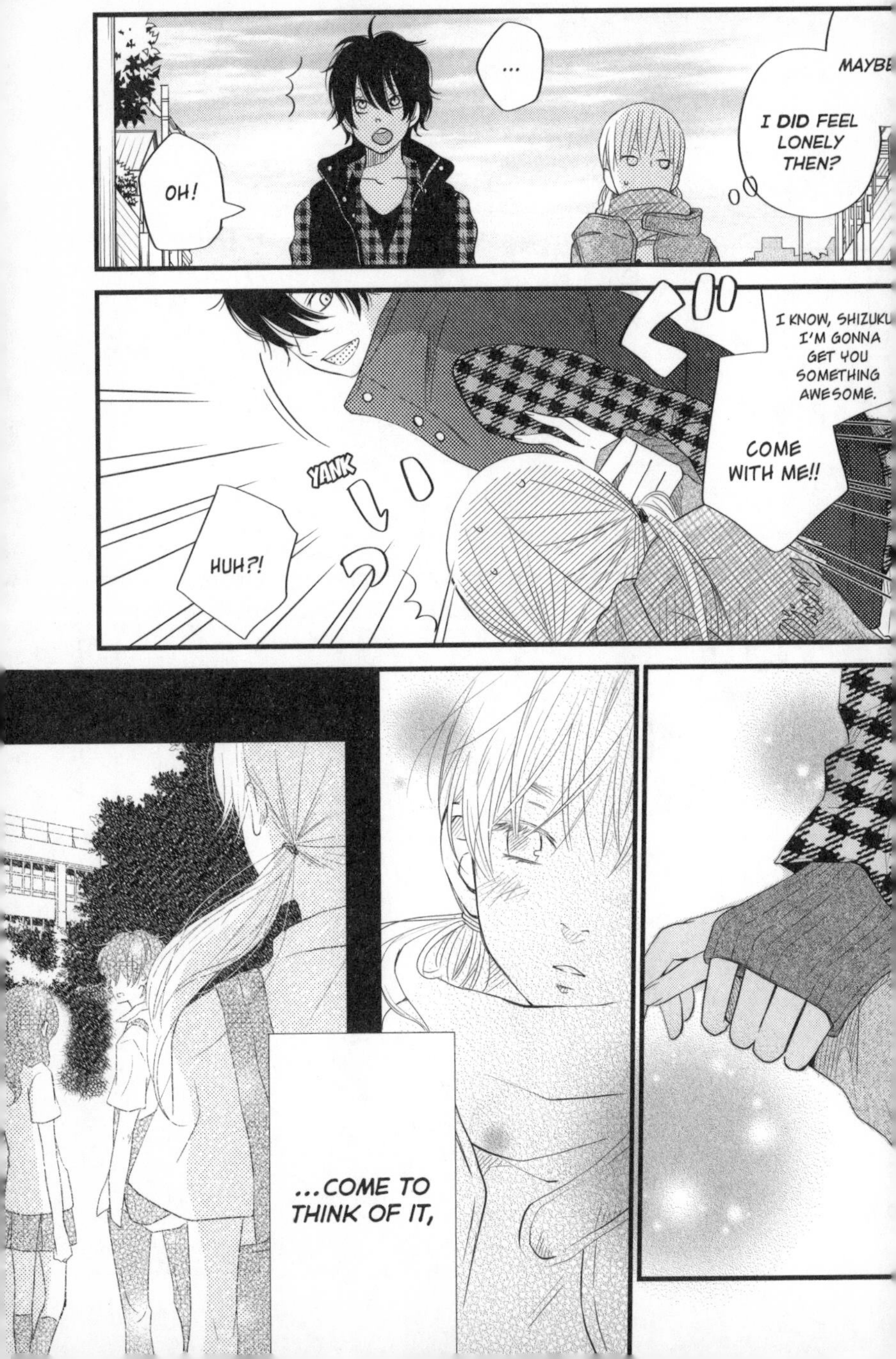
MAYBE I DID FEEL LONELY THEN?
...
OH!
I KNOW, SHIZUKU I'M GONNA GET YOU SOMETHING AWESOME.
COME WITH ME!!
YANK
HUH?!
...COME TO THINK OF IT,

I THINK I THOUGHT THE SAME THING BACK THEN...

...
RUSTLE
HARU...
RUSTLE
NO THANK YOU!
I DON'T WANT ANY CRAYFISH!
WHAT? BUT THEY HAVE **REALLY** BIG ONES HERE.
I WASN'T TRYING TO SAY I WANTED A PET FOR THAT POT!!

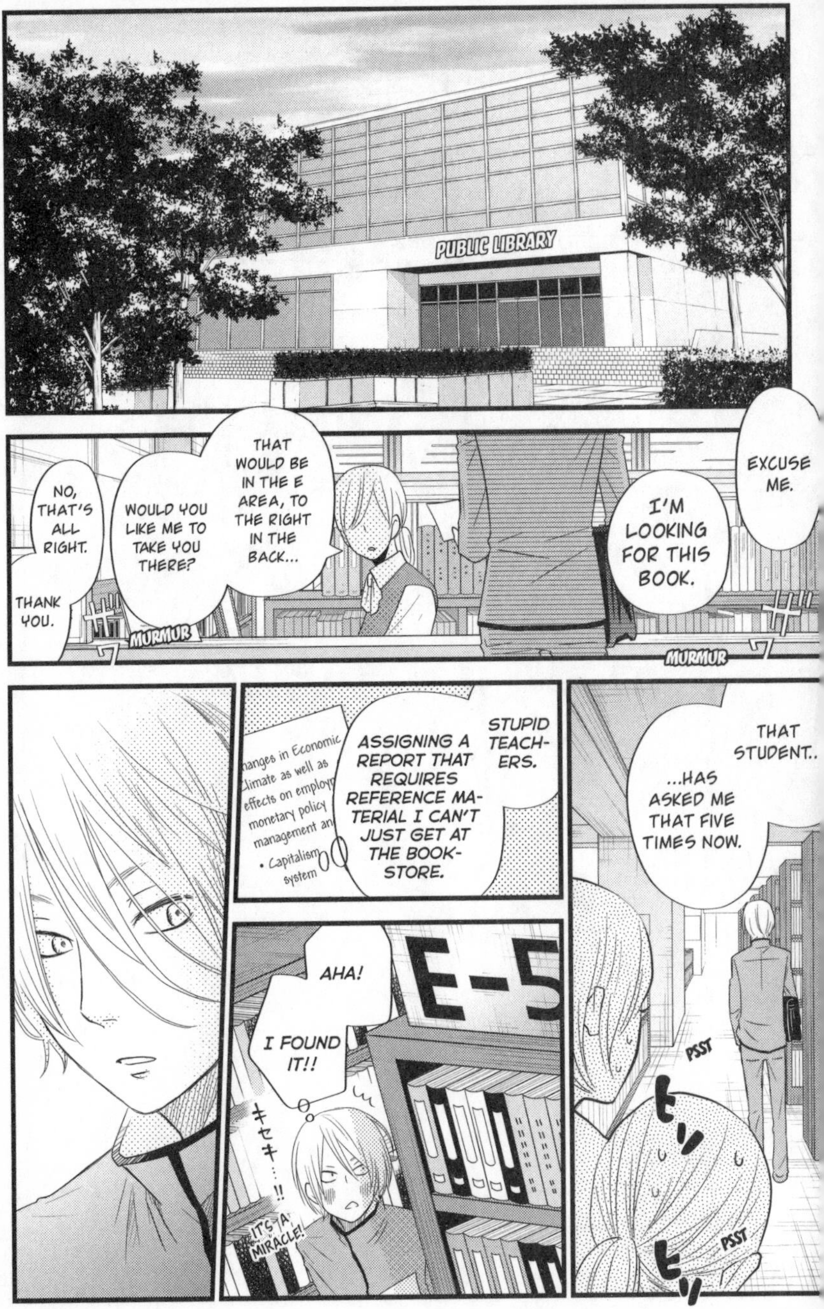
PUBLIC LIBRARY
EXCUSE ME.
I'M LOOKING FOR THIS BOOK.
MURMUR
THAT WOULD BE IN THE E AREA, TO THE RIGHT IN THE BACK...
WOULD YOU LIKE ME TO TAKE YOU THERE?
NO, THAT'S ALL RIGHT.
THANK YOU.
MURMUR
THAT STUDENT..
...HAS ASKED ME THAT FIVE TIMES NOW.
PSST
PSST
STUPID TEACHERS.
ASSIGNING A REPORT THAT REQUIRES REFERENCE MATERIAL I CAN'T JUST GET AT THE BOOKSTORE.
hanges in Economic
limate as well as
effects on employ
monetary policy
management an
• Capitalism
system
E-5
AHA!
I FOUND IT!!
キセキ…!!
IT'S A MIRACLE!

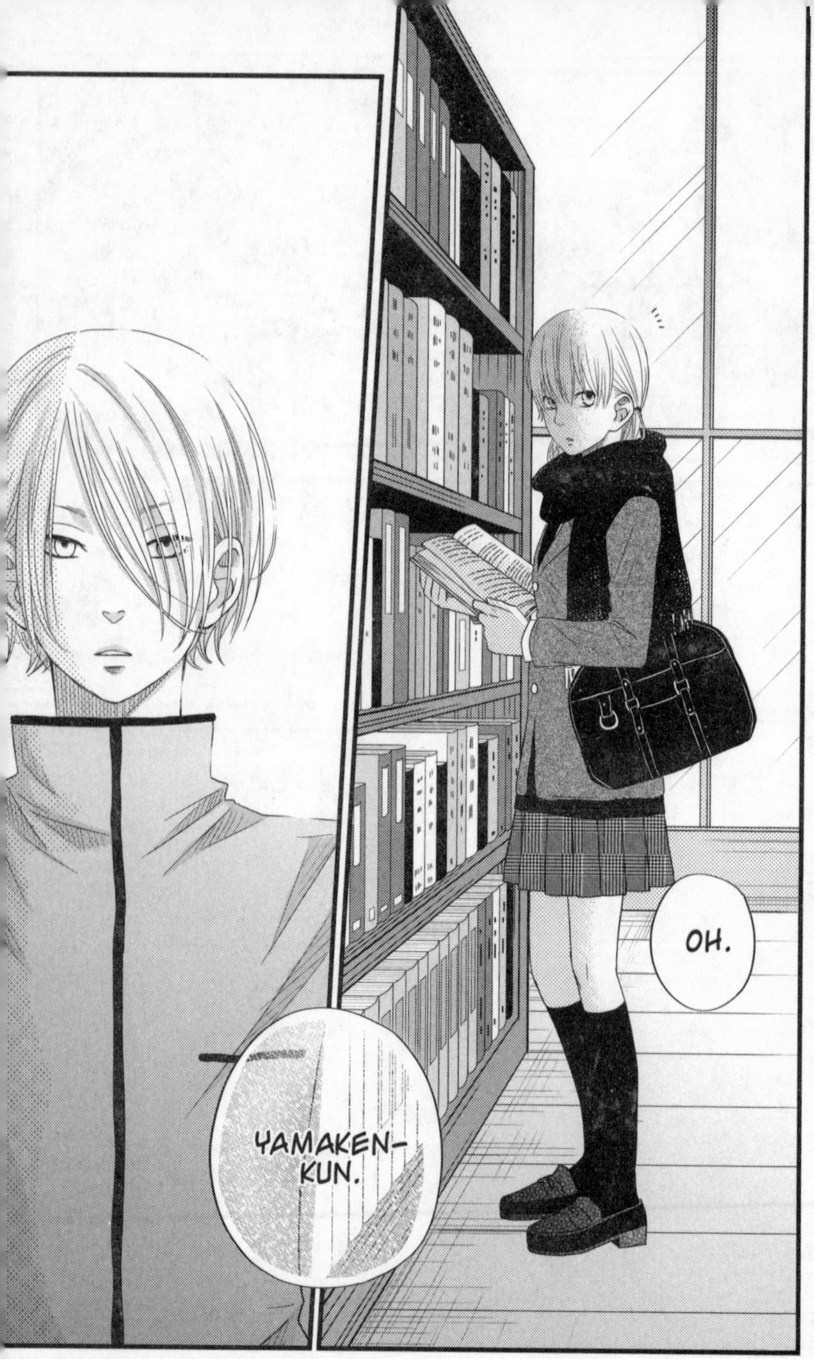
OH.
YAMAKEN-KUN.

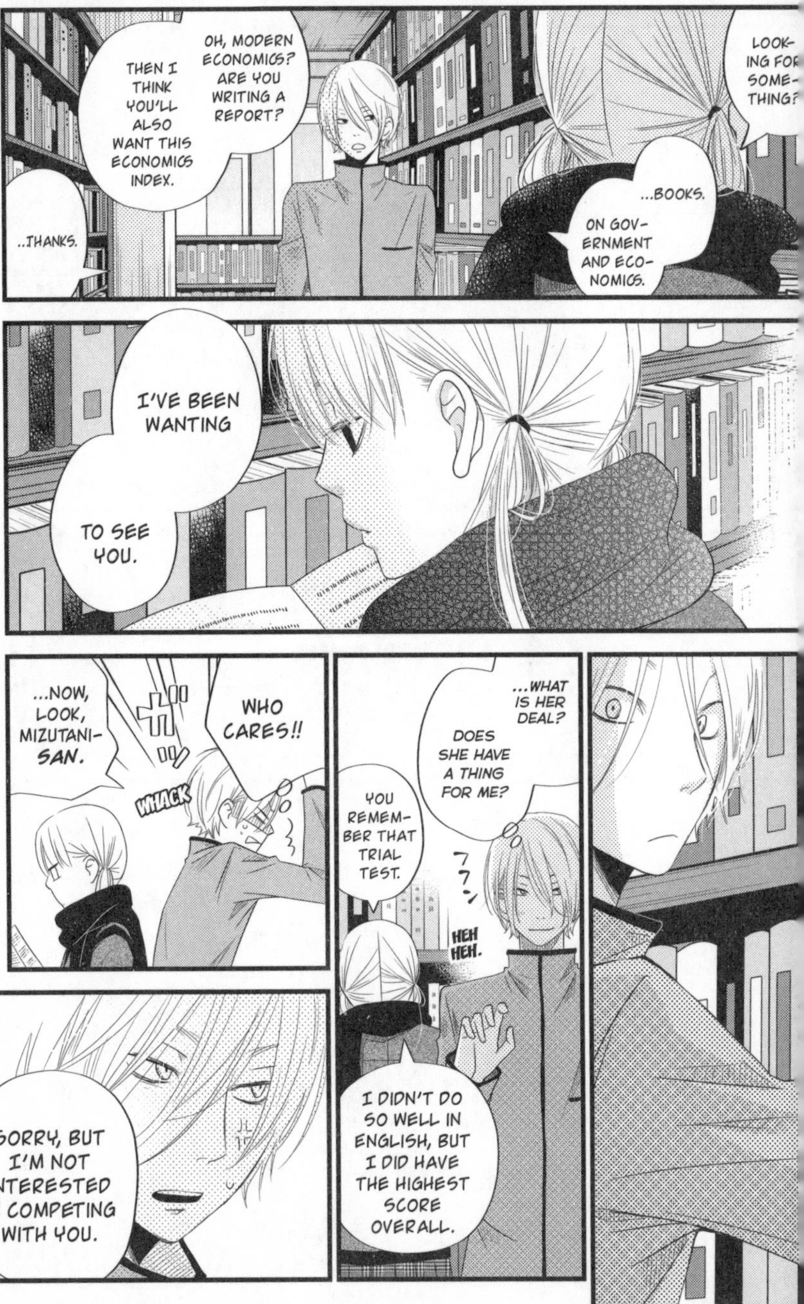

LOOK-ING FOR SOME-THING?
...BOOKS.
ON GOV-ERNMENT AND ECO-NOMICS.
OH, MODERN ECONOMICS? ARE YOU WRITING A REPORT?
THEN I THINK YOU'LL ALSO WANT THIS ECONOMICS INDEX.
..THANKS.
I'VE BEEN WANTING
TO SEE YOU.
...WHAT IS HER DEAL?
DOES SHE HAVE A THING FOR ME?
HEH HEH.
YOU REMEMBER THAT TRIAL TEST.
I DIDN'T DO SO WELL IN ENGLISH, BUT I DID HAVE THE HIGHEST SCORE OVERALL.
WHO CARES!!
WHACK
...NOW, LOOK, MIZUTANI-SAN.
SORRY, BUT I'M NOT INTERESTED IN COMPETING WITH YOU.

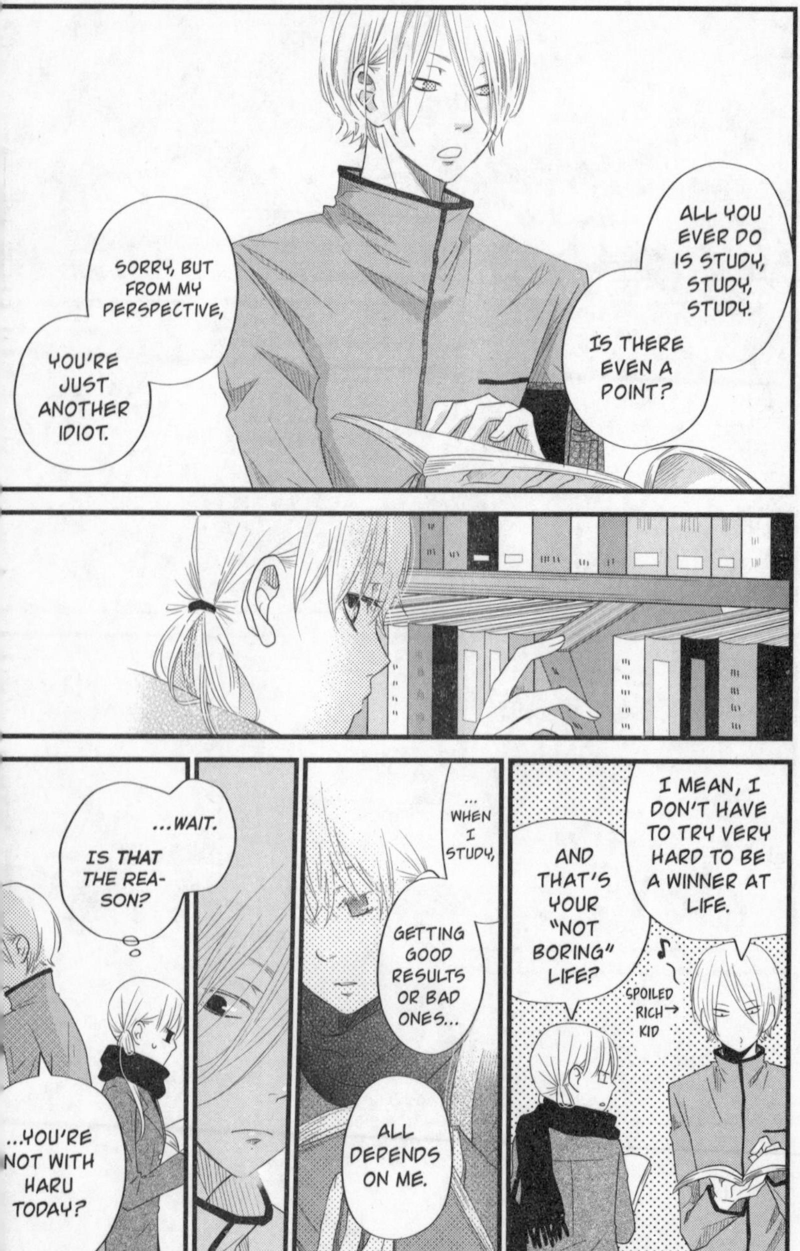
ALL YOU EVER DO IS STUDY, STUDY, STUDY.
IS THERE EVEN A POINT?
SORRY, BUT FROM MY PERSPECTIVE,
YOU'RE JUST ANOTHER IDIOT.
I MEAN, I DON'T HAVE TO TRY VERY HARD TO BE A WINNER AT LIFE.
SPOILED RICH KID
AND THAT'S YOUR "NOT BORING" LIFE?
...WHEN I STUDY,
GETTING GOOD RESULTS OR BAD ONES...
ALL DEPENDS ON ME.
...WAIT. IS THAT THE REASON?
...YOU'RE NOT WITH HARU TODAY?

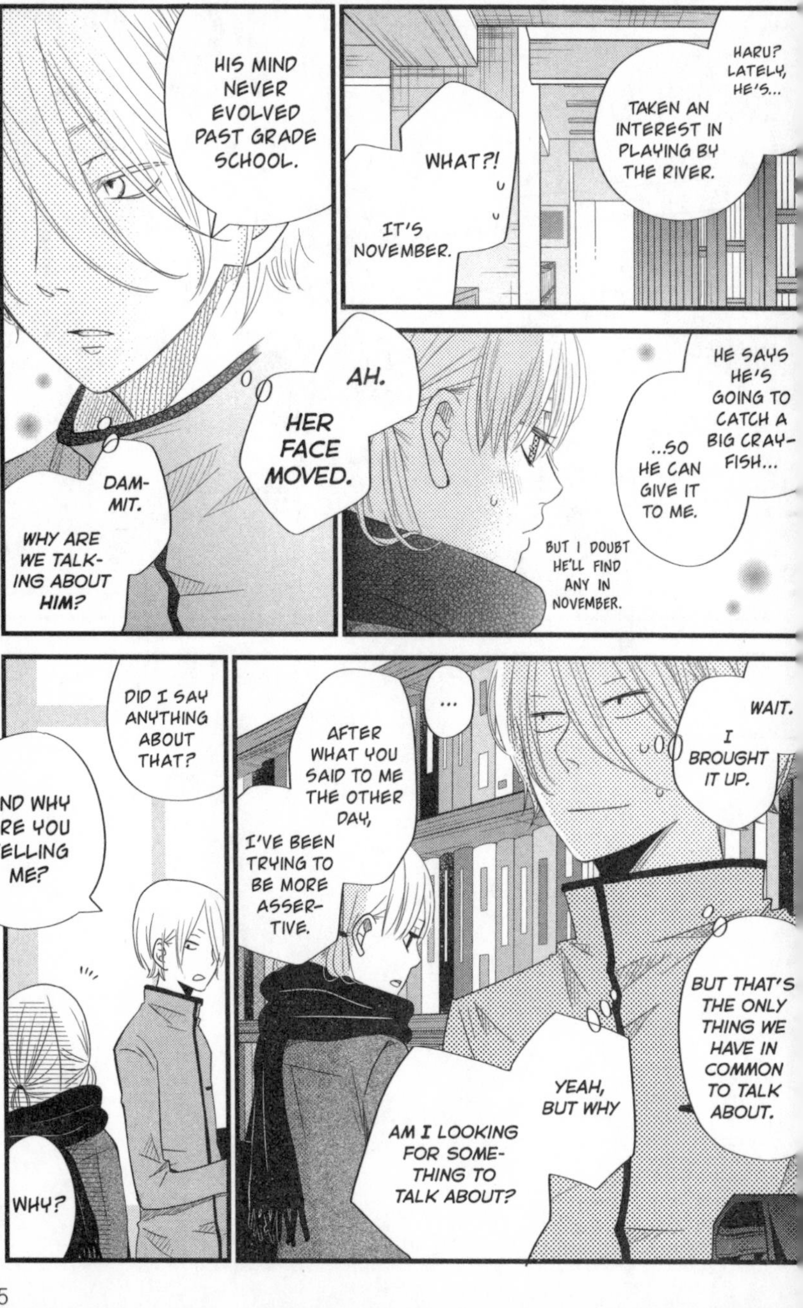

HARU? LATELY, HE'S...
TAKEN AN INTEREST IN PLAYING BY THE RIVER.
WHAT?!
IT'S NOVEMBER.
HE SAYS HE'S GOING TO CATCH A BIG CRAY-FISH...
...SO HE CAN GIVE IT TO ME.
BUT I DOUBT HE'LL FIND ANY IN NOVEMBER.
AH.
HER FACE MOVED.
HIS MIND NEVER EVOLVED PAST GRADE SCHOOL.
DAM-MIT.
WHY ARE WE TALK-ING ABOUT HIM?
WAIT.
I BROUGHT IT UP.
...
AFTER WHAT YOU SAID TO ME THE OTHER DAY,
I'VE BEEN TRYING TO BE MORE ASSER-TIVE.
BUT THAT'S THE ONLY THING WE HAVE IN COMMON TO TALK ABOUT.
YEAH, BUT WHY
AM I LOOKING FOR SOME-THING TO TALK ABOUT?
DID I SAY ANYTHING ABOUT THAT?
AND WHY ARE YOU TELLING ME?
WHY?

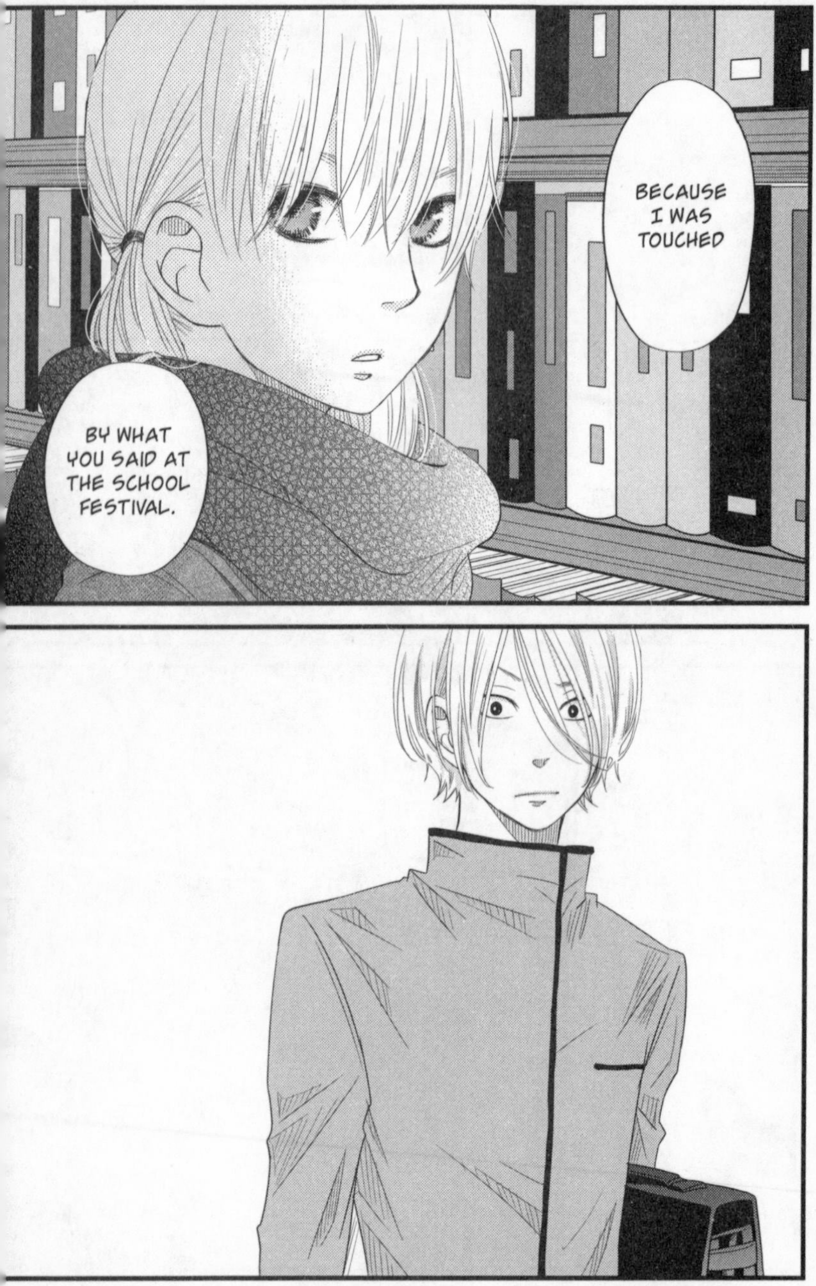
BECAUSE I WAS TOUCHED
BY WHAT YOU SAID AT THE SCHOOL FESTIVAL.

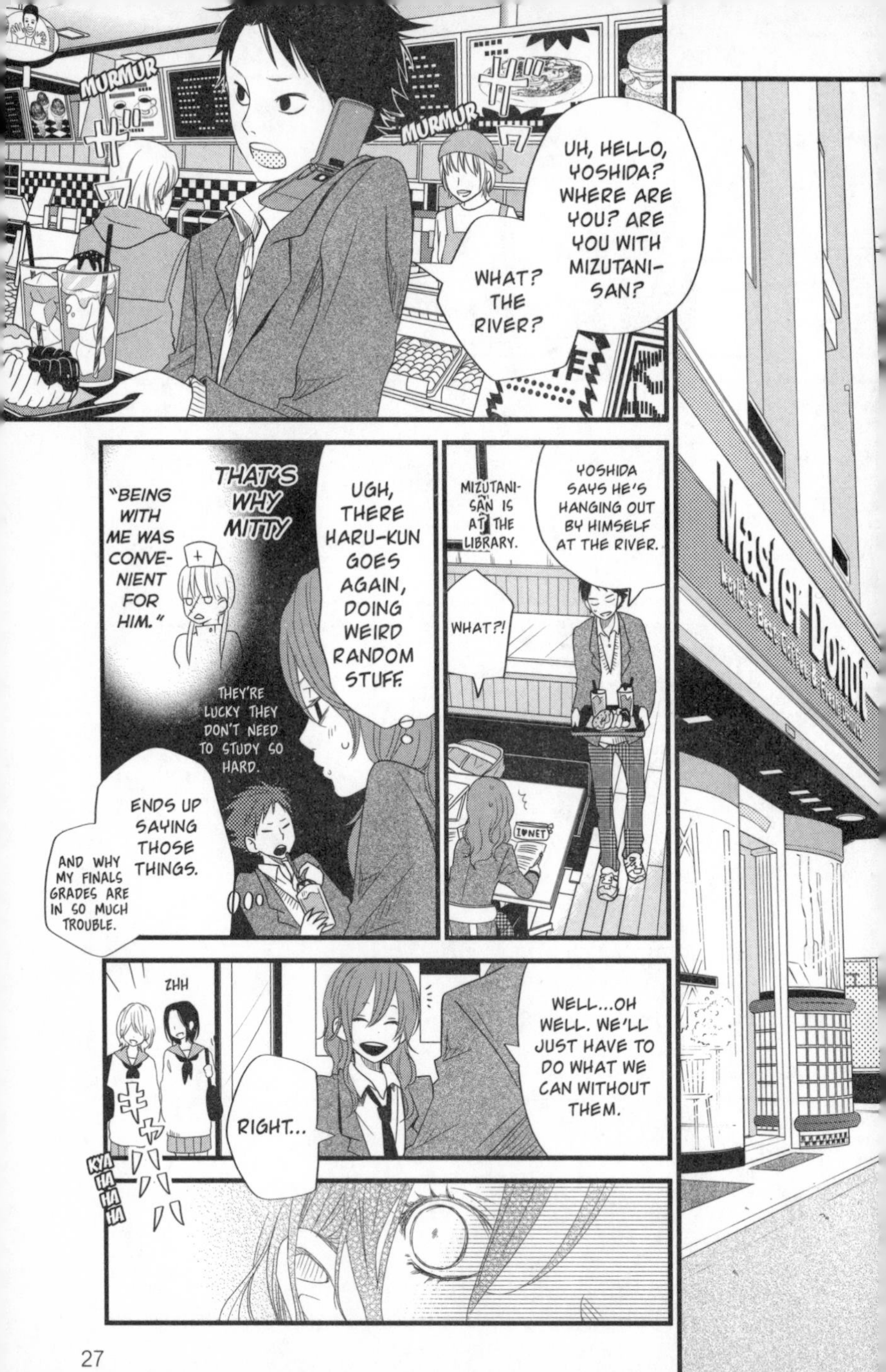
MURMUR
MURMUR
UH, HELLO, YOSHIDA? WHERE ARE YOU? ARE YOU WITH MIZUTANI-SAN?
WHAT? THE RIVER?
Master Donut
YOSHIDA SAYS HE'S HANGING OUT BY HIMSELF AT THE RIVER.
MIZUTANI-SAN IS AT THE LIBRARY.
WHAT?!
UGH, THERE HARU-KUN GOES AGAIN, DOING WEIRD RANDOM STUFF.
THAT'S WHY MITTY
"BEING WITH ME WAS CONVENIENT FOR HIM."
THEY'RE LUCKY THEY DON'T NEED TO STUDY SO HARD.
ENDS UP SAYING THOSE THINGS.
AND WHY MY FINALS GRADES ARE IN SO MUCH TROUBLE.
WELL...OH WELL. WE'LL JUST HAVE TO DO WHAT WE CAN WITHOUT THEM.
RIGHT...
ZHH
KYA HA HA HA

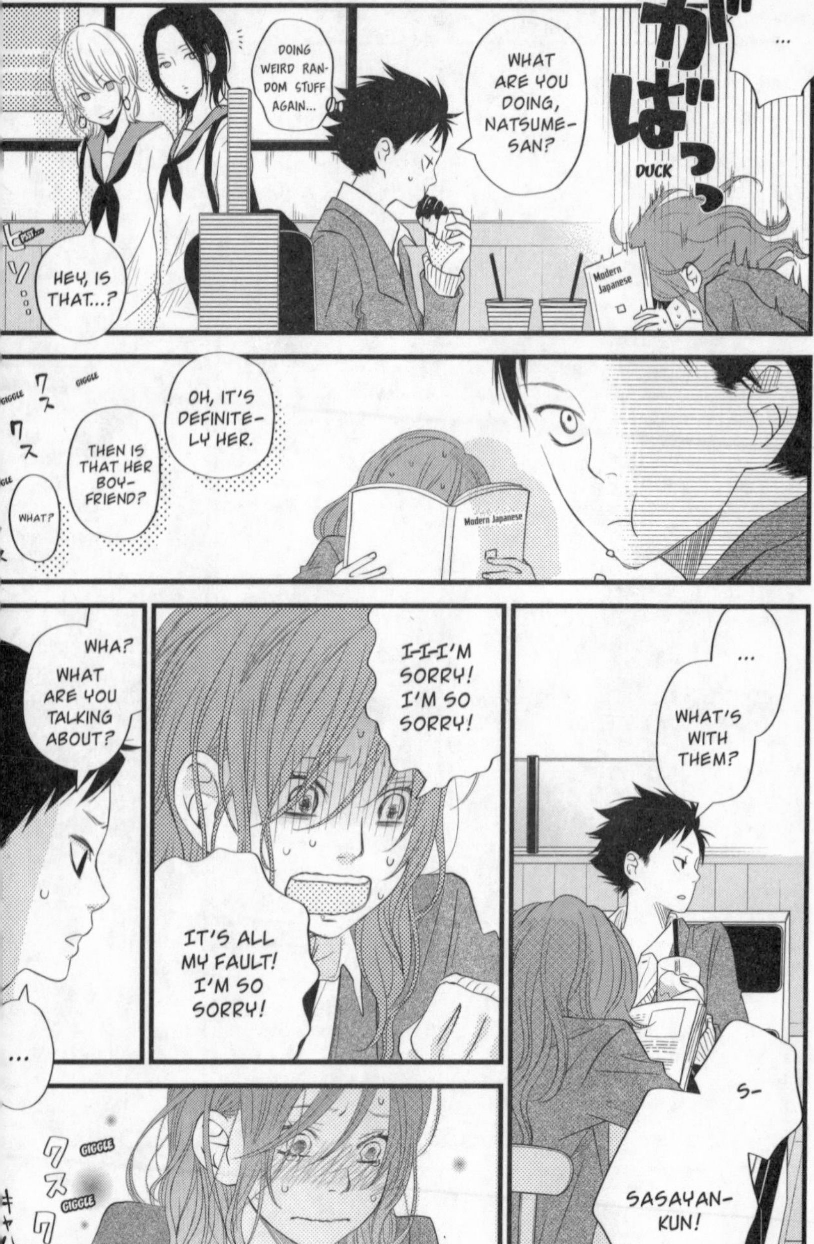
...
がばっ
DUCK
WHAT ARE YOU DOING, NATSUME-SAN?
DOING WEIRD RAN-DOM STUFF AGAIN...
HEY, IS THAT...?
OH, IT'S DEFINITE-LY HER.
THEN IS THAT HER BOY-FRIEND?
WHAT?
GIGGLE
... WHAT'S WITH THEM?
S-
SASAYAN-KUN!
I-I-I'M SORRY! I'M SO SORRY!
IT'S ALL MY FAULT! I'M SO SORRY!
WHA? WHAT ARE YOU TALKING ABOUT?
...
クスクス
GIGGLE
KYA HA HA...

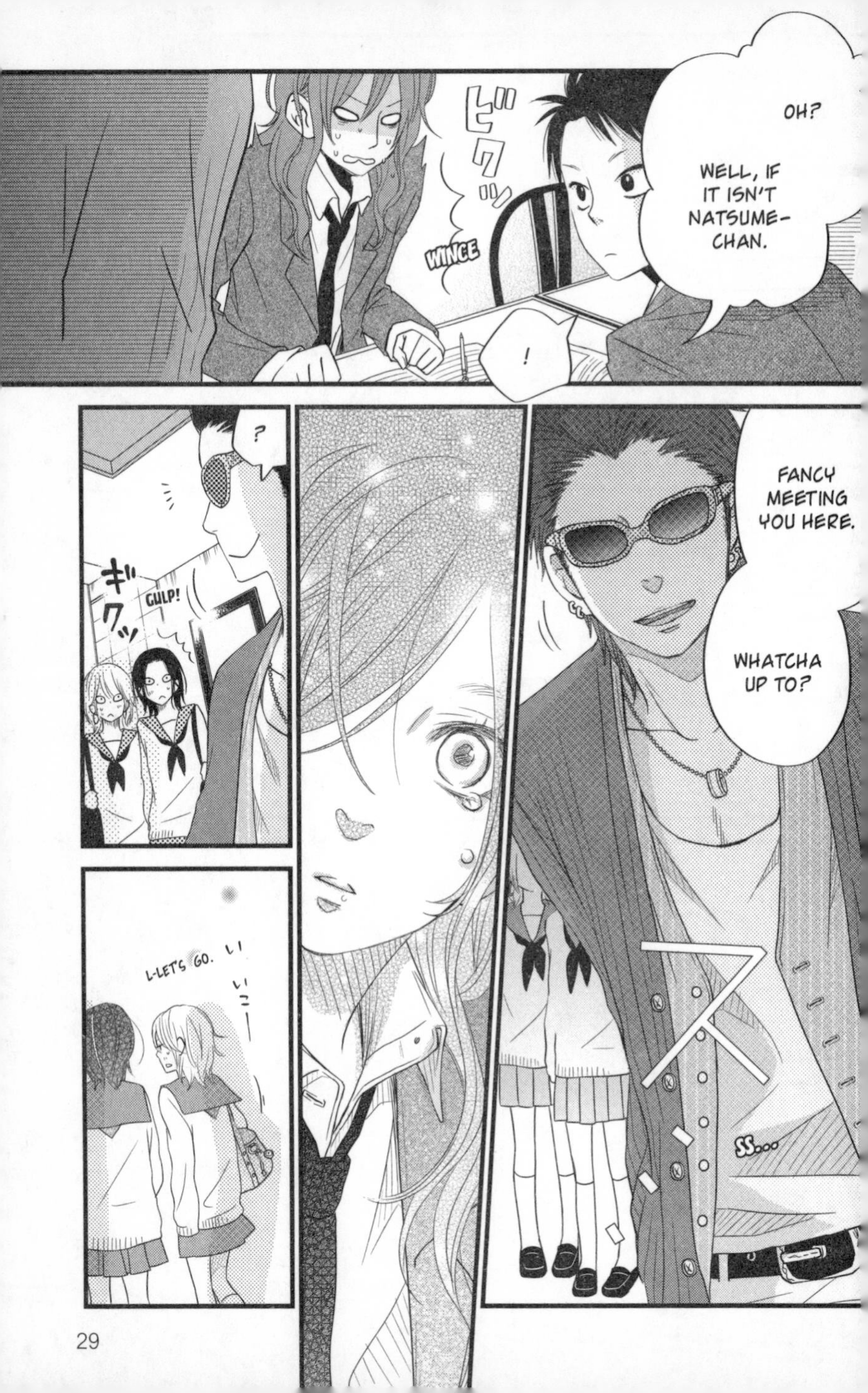
OH?
WELL, IF IT ISN'T NATSUME-CHAN.
!
ビクッ
WINCE
FANCY MEETING YOU HERE.
WHATCHA UP TO?
ス
SSooo
?
ギクッ
GULP!
L-LETS GO.

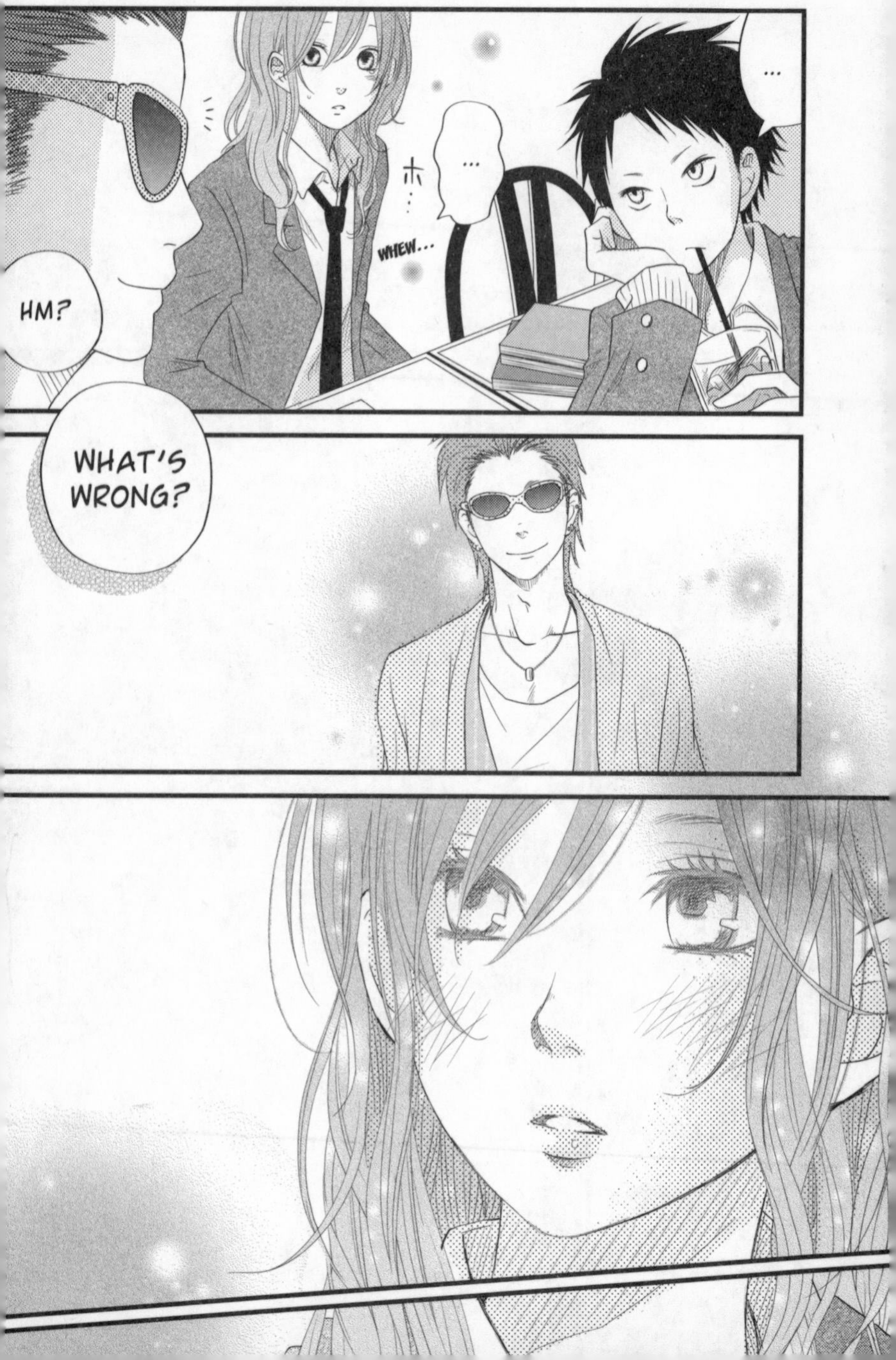
...
...
ホ…
WHEW...
HM?
WHAT'S WRONG?

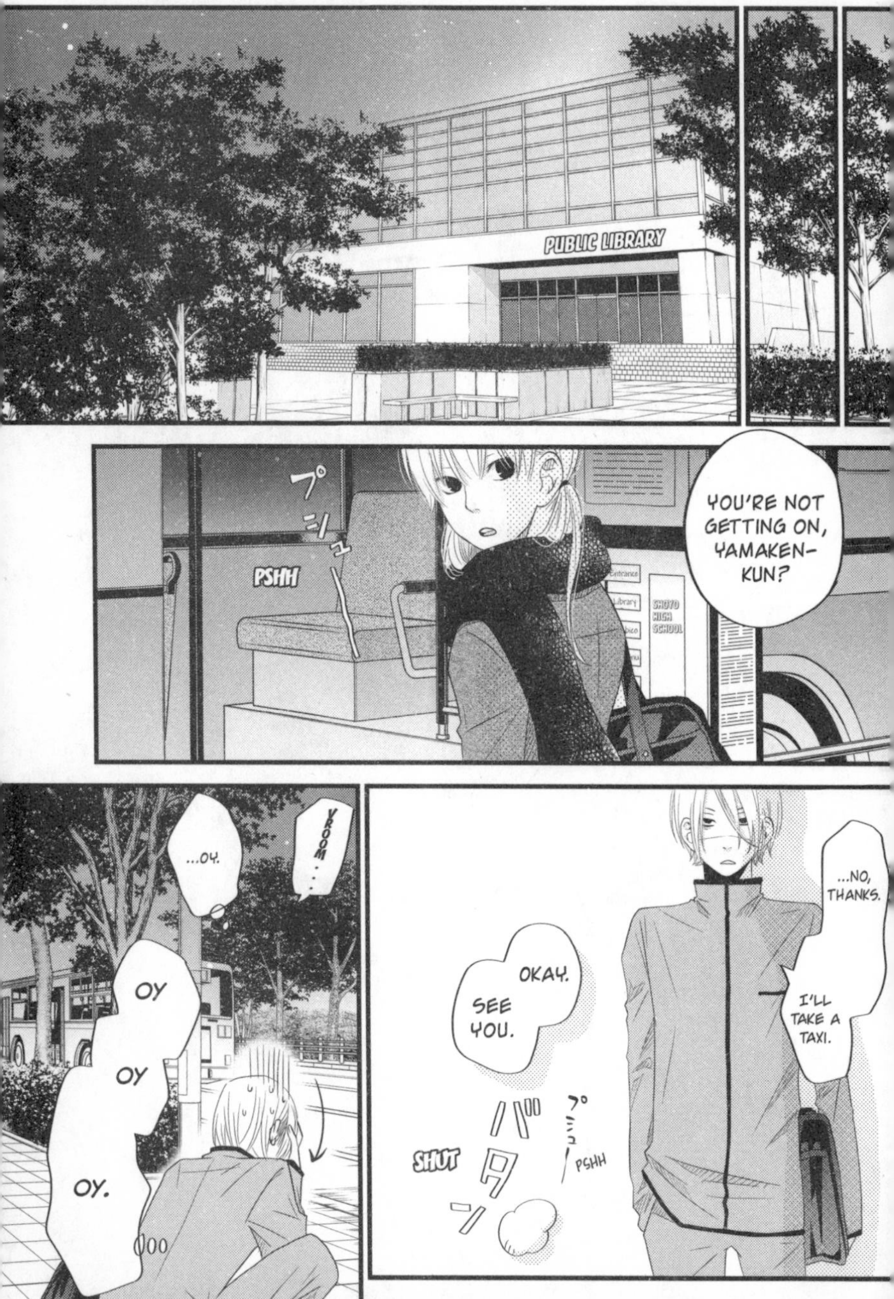
PUBLIC LIBRARY
プシュー
PSHH
YOU'RE NOT GETTING ON, YAMAKEN-KUN?
Entrance
Library
SHOYO HIGH SCHOOL
...NO, THANKS.
I'LL TAKE A TAXI.
OKAY. SEE YOU.
プシュー
PSHH
バタン
SHUT
VROOM...
...OY.
OY
OY
OY.

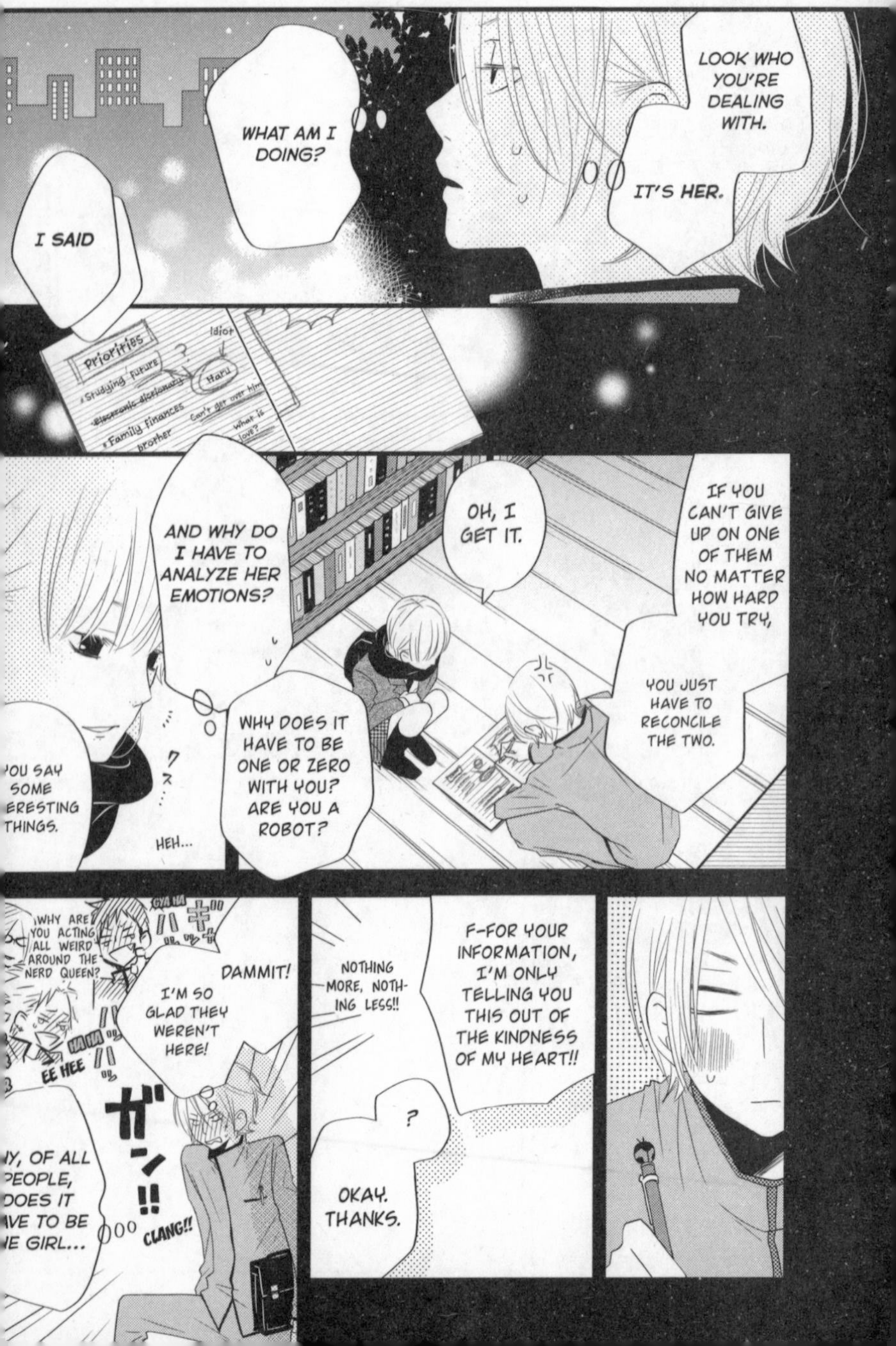
LOOK WHO YOU'RE DEALING WITH.
IT'S HER.
WHAT AM I DOING?
I SAID
Priorities
Idiot
Studying future
Haru
Electronic dictionary
Can't get over him
Family finances
brother
what is love?
IF YOU CAN'T GIVE UP ON ONE OF THEM NO MATTER HOW HARD YOU TRY,
YOU JUST HAVE TO RECONCILE THE TWO.
OH, I GET IT.
AND WHY DO I HAVE TO ANALYZE HER EMOTIONS?
WHY DOES IT HAVE TO BE ONE OR ZERO WITH YOU? ARE YOU A ROBOT?
HEH...
OU SAY SOME ERESTING THINGS.
F-FOR YOUR INFORMATION, I'M ONLY TELLING YOU THIS OUT OF THE KINDNESS OF MY HEART!!
NOTHING MORE, NOTHING LESS!!
?
OKAY. THANKS.
DAMMIT!
I'M SO GLAD THEY WEREN'T HERE!
WHY ARE YOU ACTING ALL WEIRD AROUND THE NERD QUEEN?
GYA HA
HA HA
EE HEE
Y, OF ALL PEOPLE, DOES IT AVE TO BE E GIRL...
ガン!!
CLANG!!

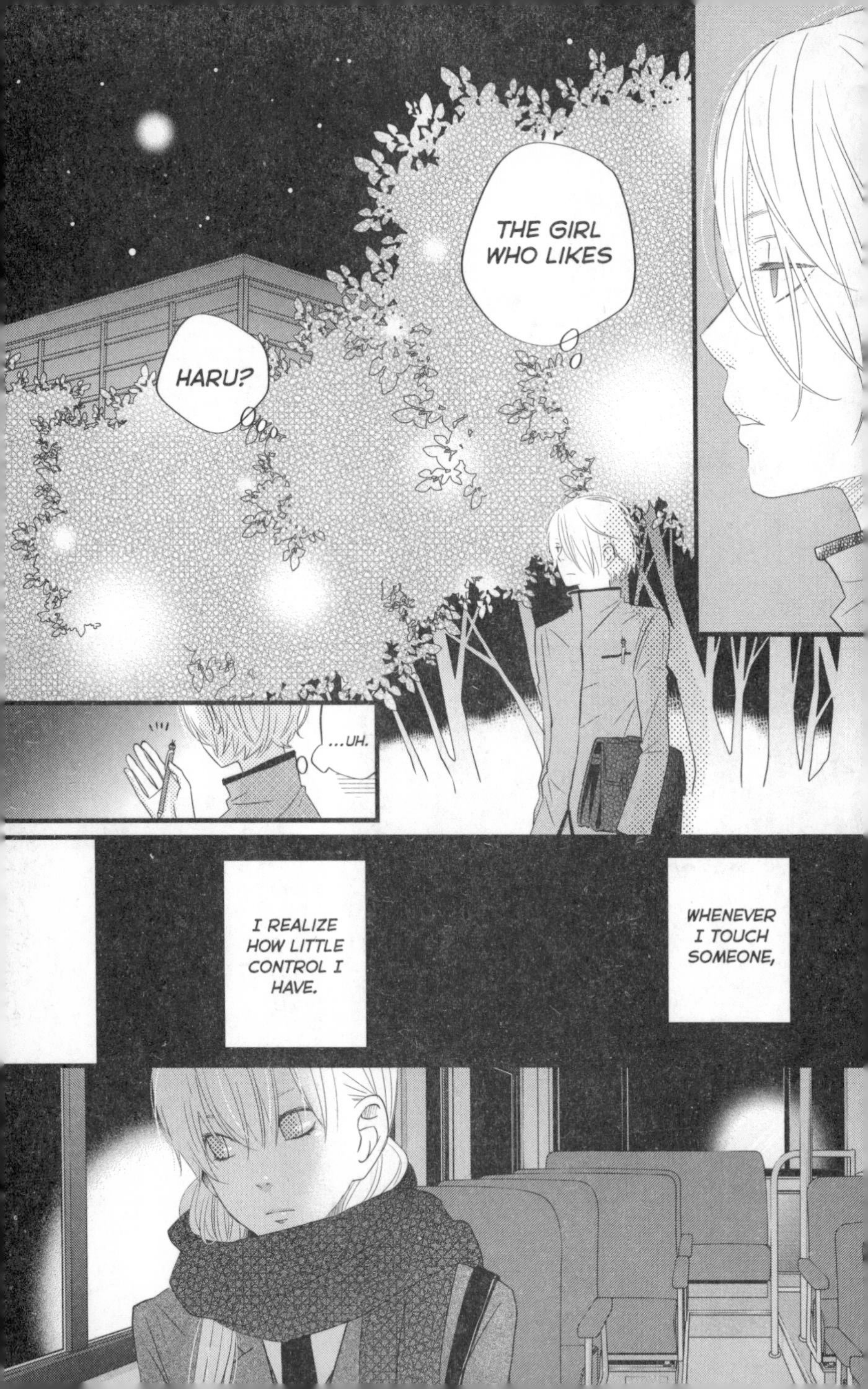
THE GIRL WHO LIKES
HARU?
...UH.
WHENEVER I TOUCH SOMEONE,
I REALIZE HOW LITTLE CONTROL I HAVE.

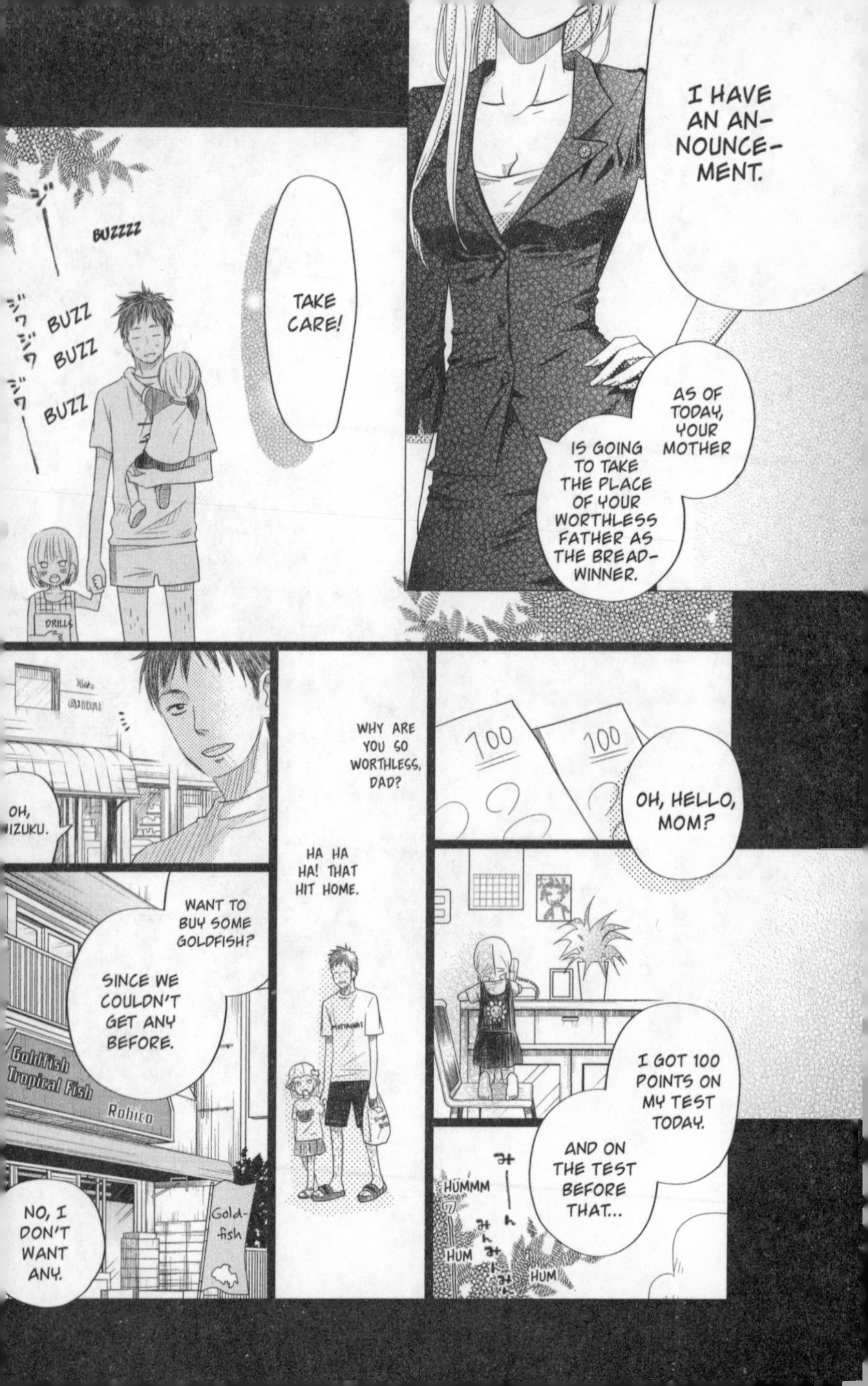
I HAVE AN AN-NOUNCE-MENT.
AS OF TODAY, YOUR MOTHER
IS GOING TO TAKE THE PLACE OF YOUR WORTHLESS FATHER AS THE BREAD-WINNER.
TAKE CARE!
BUZZZZ
BUZZ
BUZZ
BUZZ
DRILLS
OH, HELLO, MOM?
I GOT 100 POINTS ON MY TEST TODAY.
AND ON THE TEST BEFORE THAT...
HUMMM
HUM
HUM
WHY ARE YOU SO WORTHLESS, DAD?
HA HA HA! THAT HIT HOME.
OH,
IZUKU.
WANT TO BUY SOME GOLDFISH?
SINCE WE COULDN'T GET ANY BEFORE.
Goldfish Tropical Fish
Robico
Gold-fish
NO, I DON'T WANT ANY.

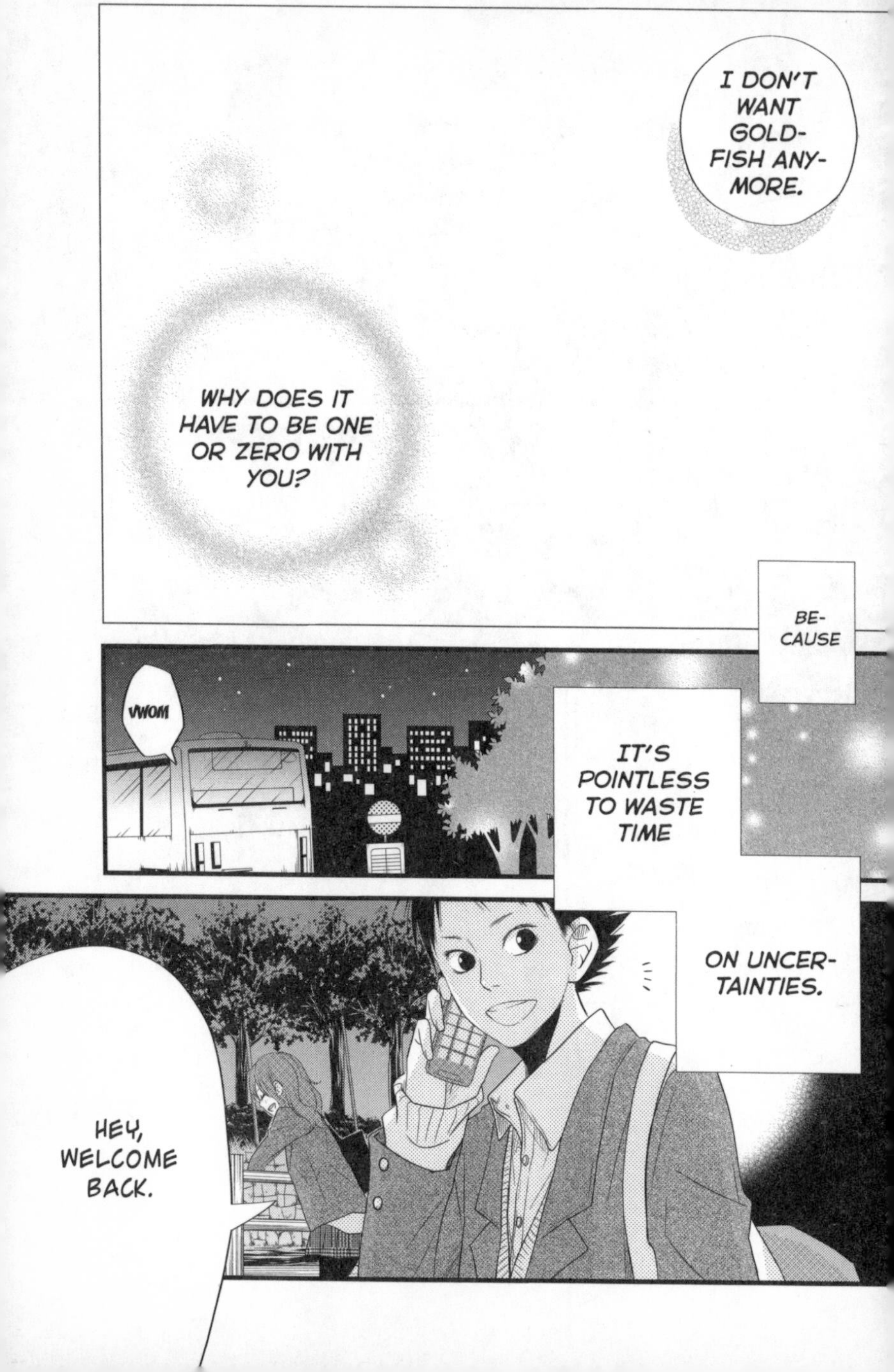
I DON'T WANT GOLD-FISH ANY-MORE.
WHY DOES IT HAVE TO BE ONE OR ZERO WITH YOU?
BE-CAUSE
IT'S POINTLESS TO WASTE TIME
VWOM
ON UNCER-TAINTIES.
HEY, WELCOME BACK.

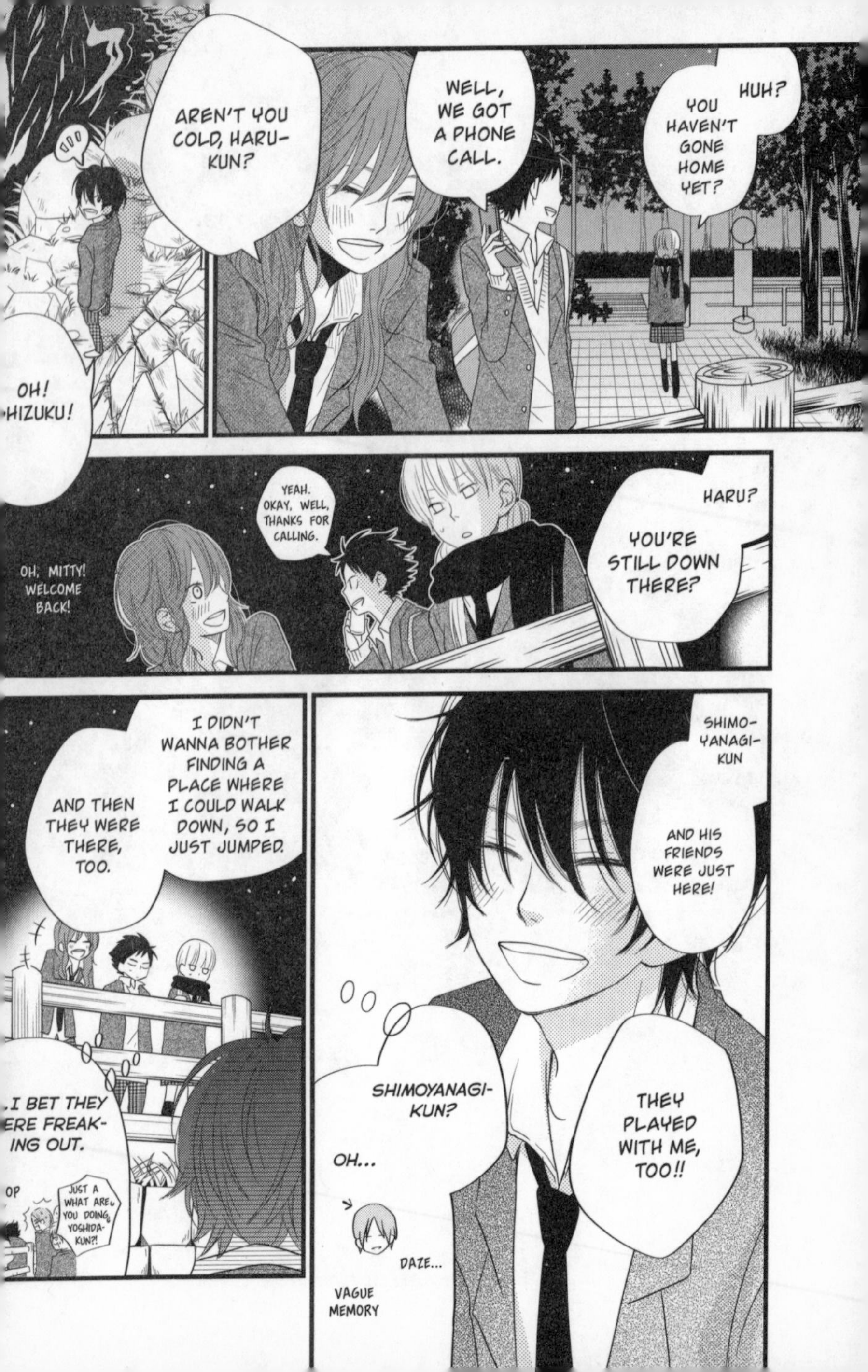
HUH? YOU HAVEN'T GONE HOME YET?
WELL, WE GOT A PHONE CALL.
AREN'T YOU COLD, HARU-KUN?
OH! HIZUKU!
HARU?
YOU'RE STILL DOWN THERE?
YEAH. OKAY, WELL, THANKS FOR CALLING.
OH, MITTY! WELCOME BACK!
SHIMOYANAGI-KUN
AND HIS FRIENDS WERE JUST HERE!
THEY PLAYED WITH ME, TOO!!
SHIMOYANAGI-KUN?
OH...
DAZE...
VAGUE MEMORY
I DIDN'T WANNA BOTHER FINDING A PLACE WHERE I COULD WALK DOWN, SO I JUST JUMPED.
AND THEN THEY WERE THERE, TOO.
I BET THEY ERE FREAK-ING OUT.
OP
JUST A
WHAT ARE YOU DOING, YOSHIDA-KUN?!

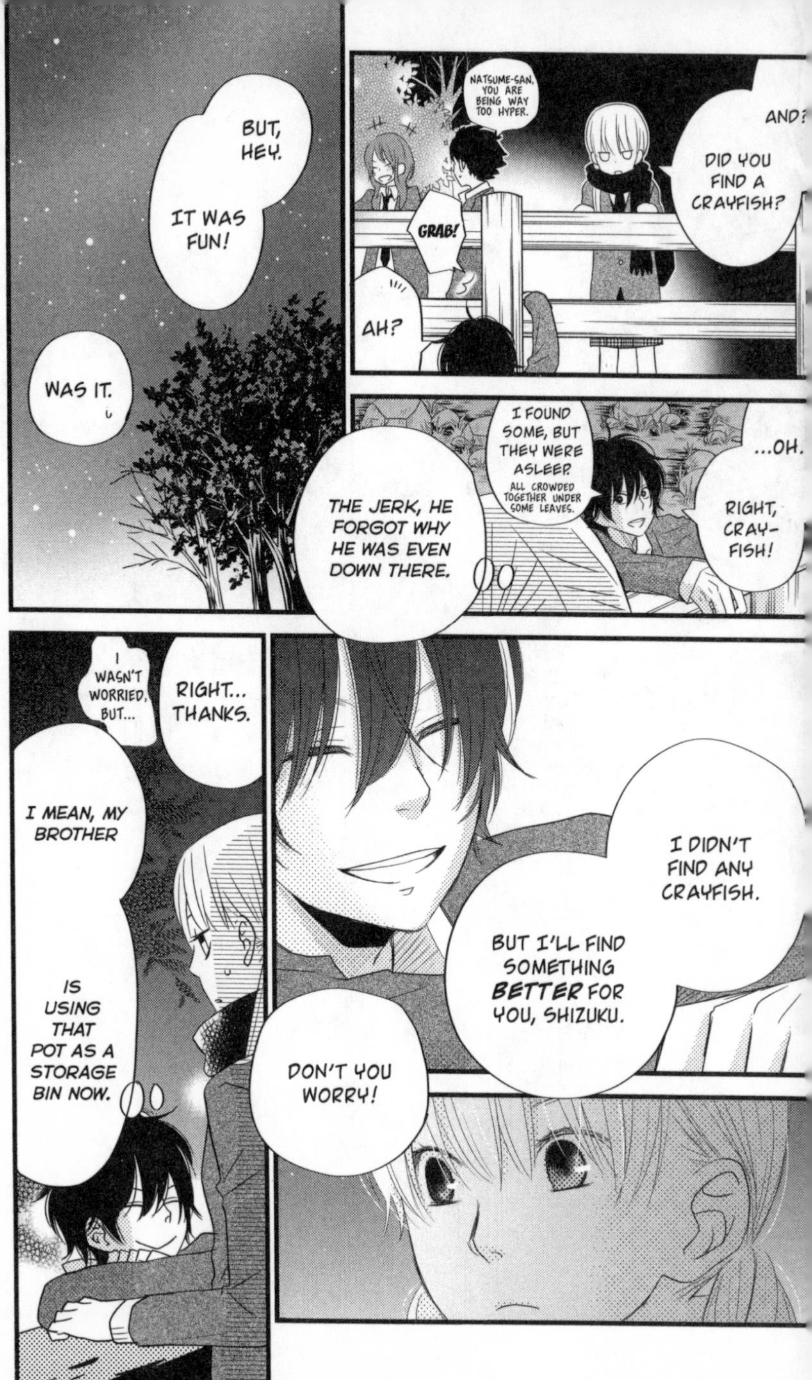
AND? DID YOU FIND A CRAYFISH?
NATSUME-SAN. YOU ARE BEING WAY TOO HYPER.
GRAB!
AH?
...OH. RIGHT, CRAY-FISH!
I FOUND SOME, BUT THEY WERE ASLEEP.
ALL CROWDED TOGETHER UNDER SOME LEAVES.
THE JERK, HE FORGOT WHY HE WAS EVEN DOWN THERE.
BUT, HEY. IT WAS FUN!
WAS IT.
I DIDN'T FIND ANY CRAYFISH.
BUT I'LL FIND SOMETHING BETTER FOR YOU, SHIZUKU.
DON'T YOU WORRY!
RIGHT... THANKS.
I WASN'T WORRIED, BUT...
I MEAN, MY BROTHER IS USING THAT POT AS A STORAGE BIN NOW.

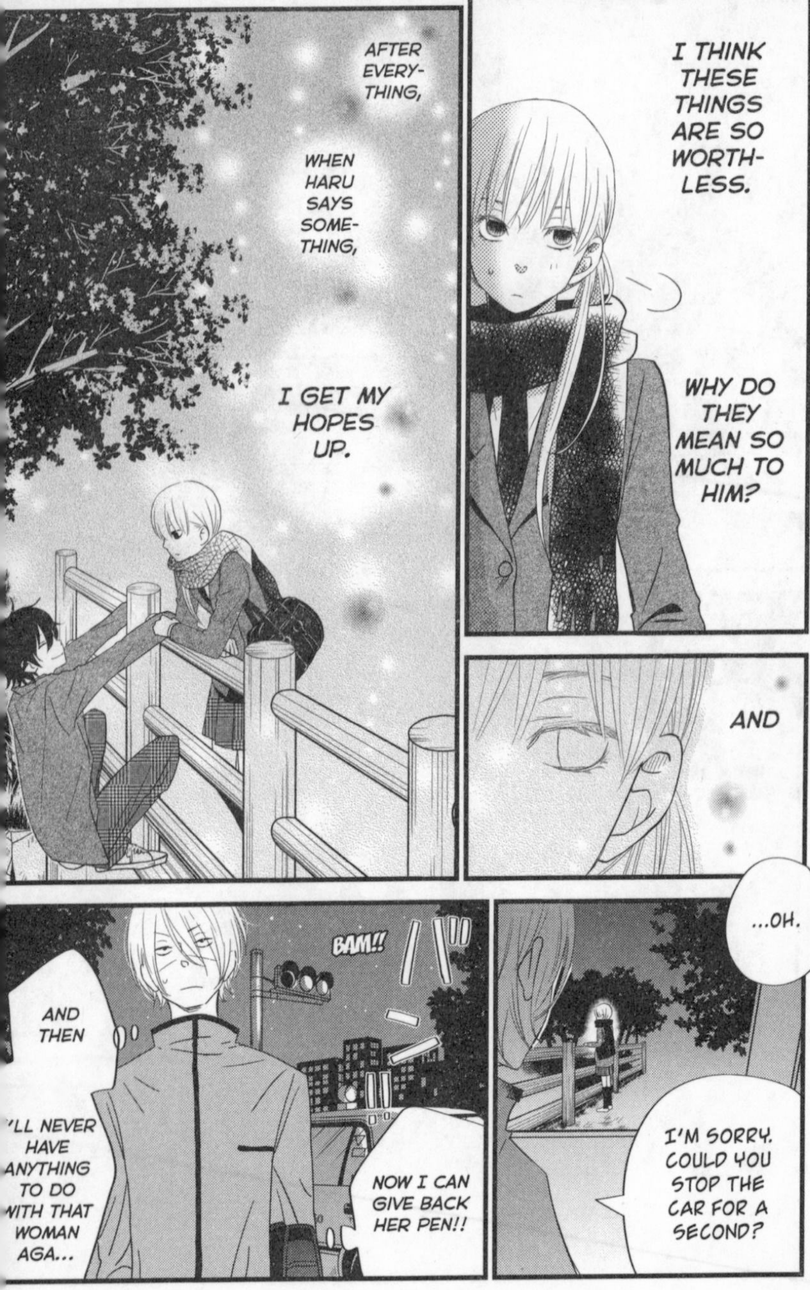
I THINK THESE THINGS ARE SO WORTHLESS.
WHY DO THEY MEAN SO MUCH TO HIM?
AND
AFTER EVERYTHING,
WHEN HARU SAYS SOMETHING,
I GET MY HOPES UP.
...OH.
I'M SORRY. COULD YOU STOP THE CAR FOR A SECOND?
BAM!!
NOW I CAN GIVE BACK HER PEN!!
AND THEN
'LL NEVER HAVE ANYTHING TO DO WITH THAT WOMAN AGA...

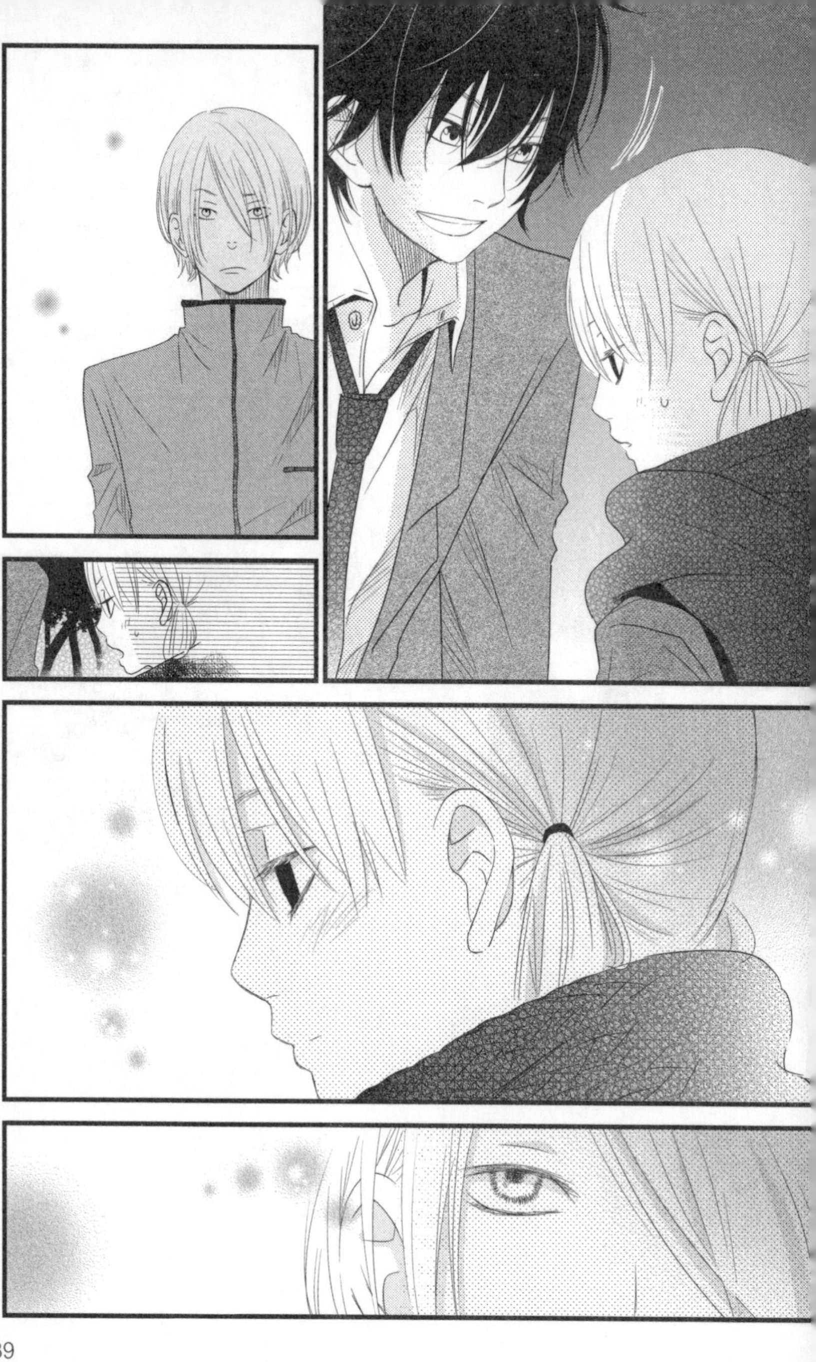

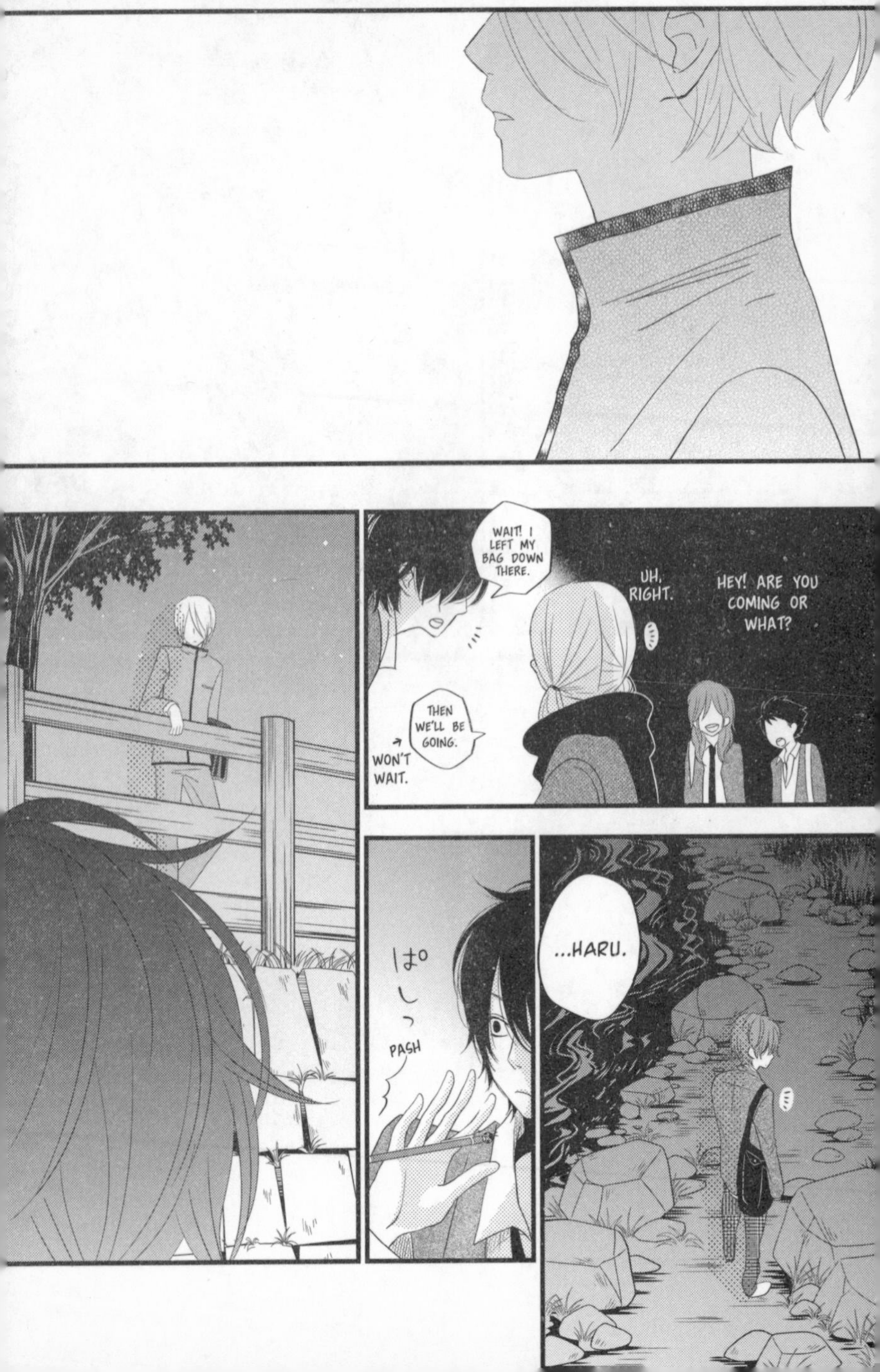
HEY! ARE YOU COMING OR WHAT?
UH, RIGHT.
!
WAIT! I LEFT MY BAG DOWN THERE.
THEN WE'LL BE GOING.
WON'T WAIT.
...HARU.
!
ぱしっ
PASH

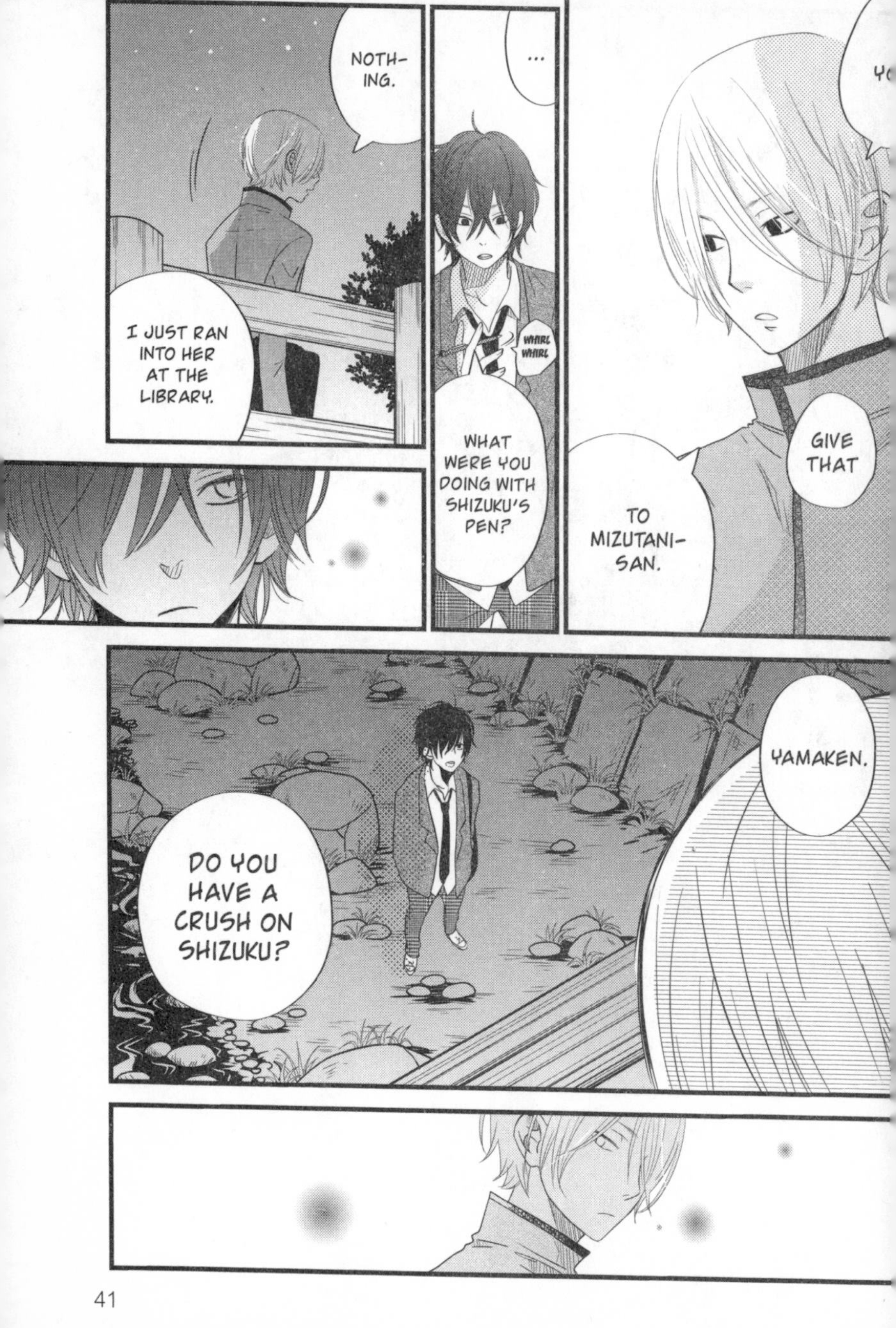
GIVE THAT
TO MIZUTANI-SAN.
...
WHIRL WHIRL
WHAT WERE YOU DOING WITH SHIZUKU'S PEN?
NOTHING.
I JUST RAN INTO HER AT THE LIBRARY.
YAMAKEN.
DO YOU HAVE A CRUSH ON SHIZUKU?

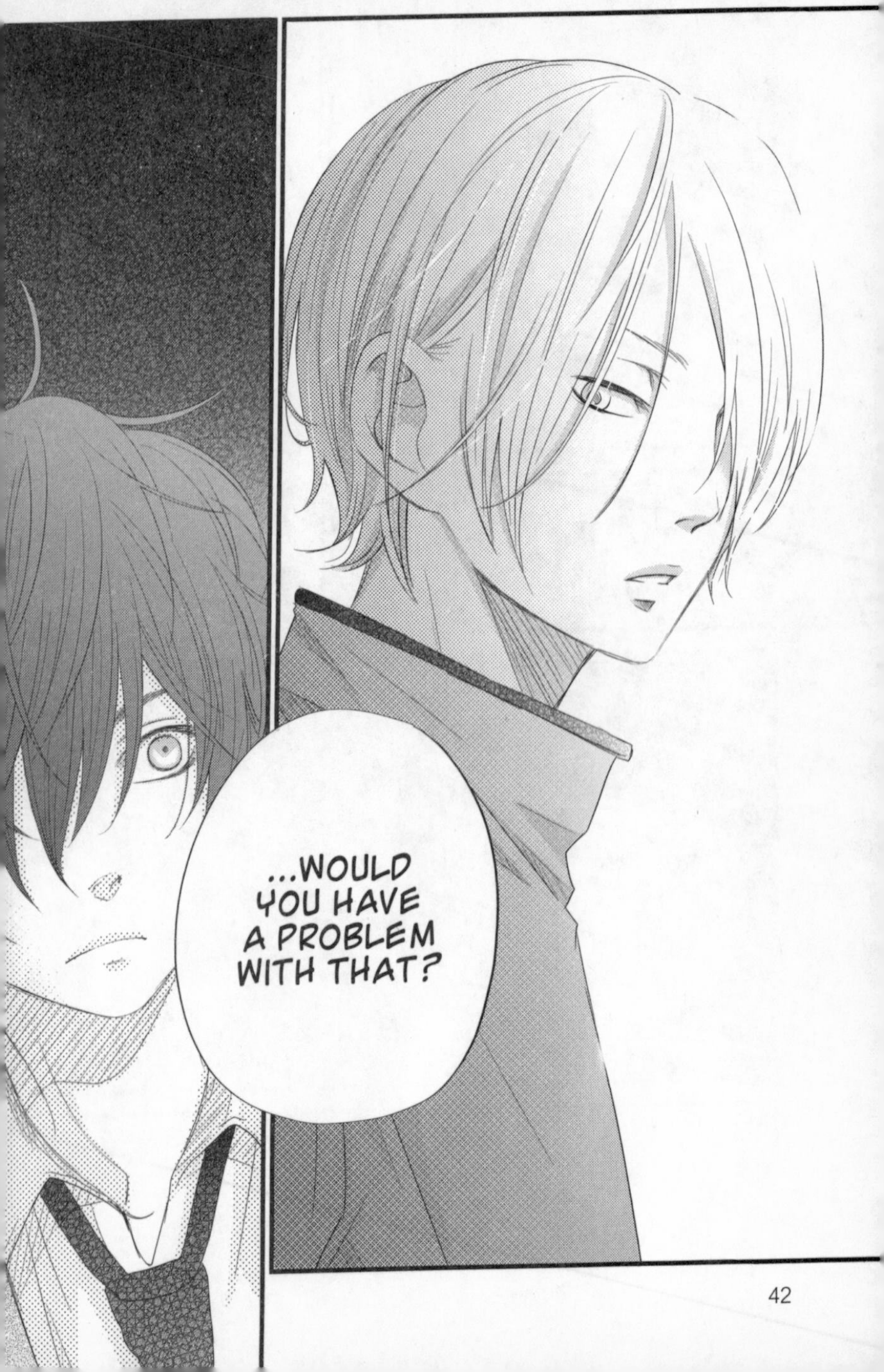
...WOULD YOU HAVE A PROBLEM WITH THAT?

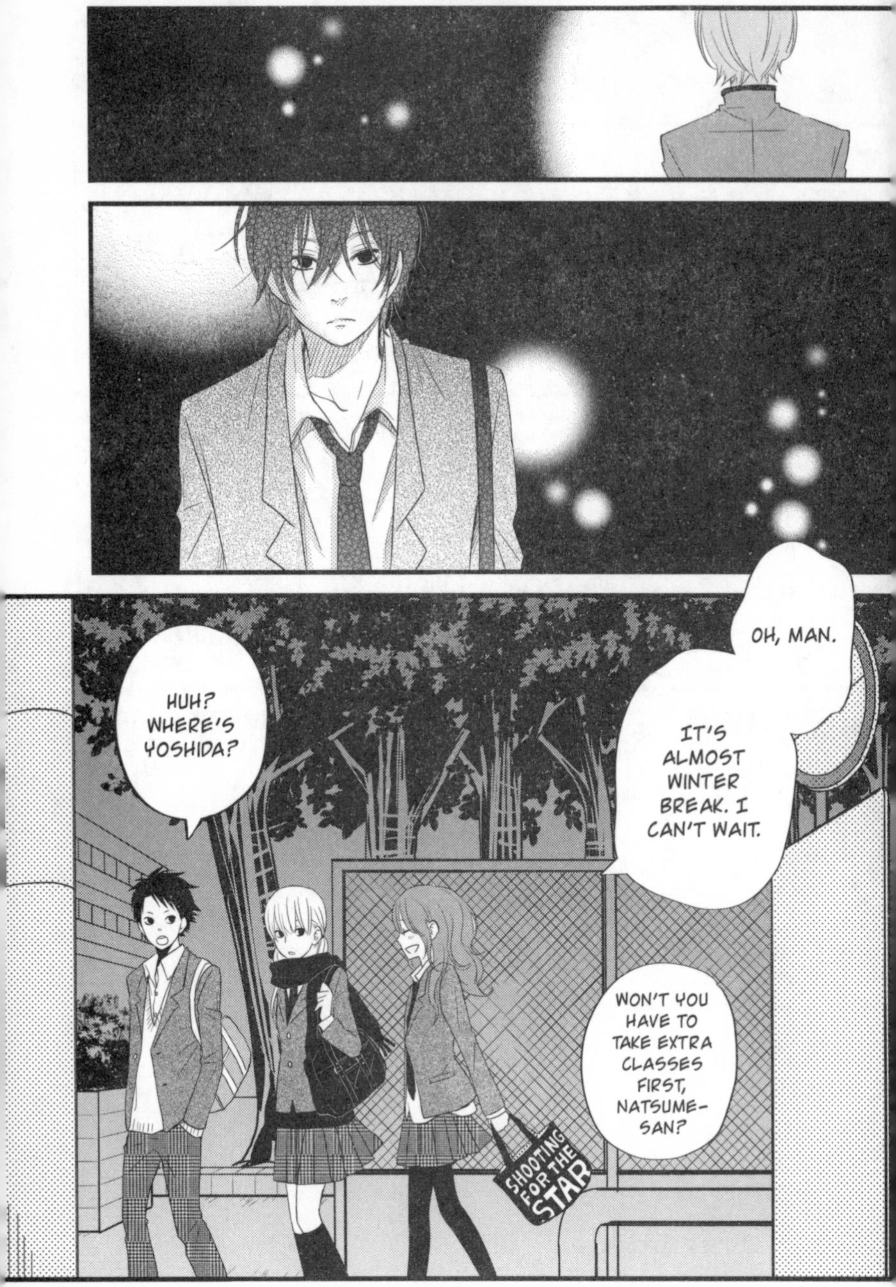
OH, MAN.
IT'S ALMOST WINTER BREAK. I CAN'T WAIT.
WON'T YOU HAVE TO TAKE EXTRA CLASSES FIRST, NATSUME-SAN?
HUH? WHERE'S YOSHIDA?
SHOOTING FOR THE STAR

Studying for Exams 1

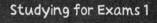

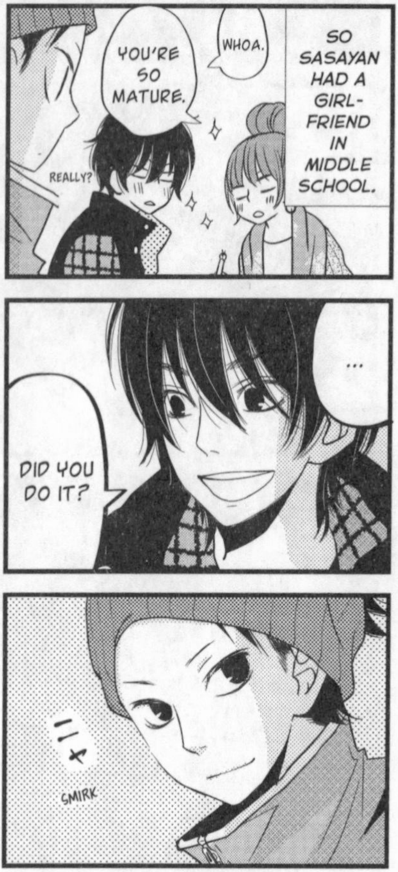
SO SASAYAN HAD A GIRLFRIEND IN MIDDLE SCHOOL.
WHOA.
YOU'RE SO MATURE.
REALLY?
...
DID YOU DO IT?
SMIRK
JUST WHAT ARE YOU TALKING ABOUT?
I'M KIDDING. KIDDING.
WHOA.
SHE DUMPED ME.
'CUZ ALL I EVER DID WAS PLAY BASEBALL.

Studying for Exams 2

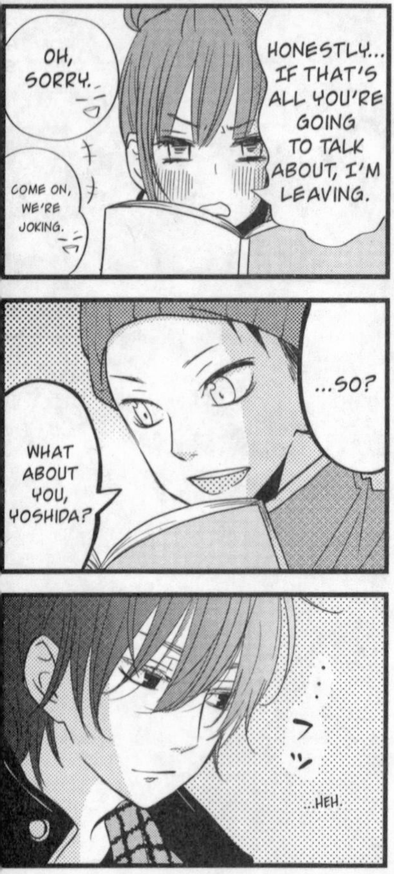
HONESTLY... IF THAT'S ALL YOU'RE GOING TO TALK ABOUT, I'M LEAVING.
OH, SORRY.
COME ON, WE'RE JOKING.
...SO?
WHAT ABOUT YOU, YOSHIDA?
...HEH.
...I REALLY AM GOING TO LEAVE.
GYA HA HA HA

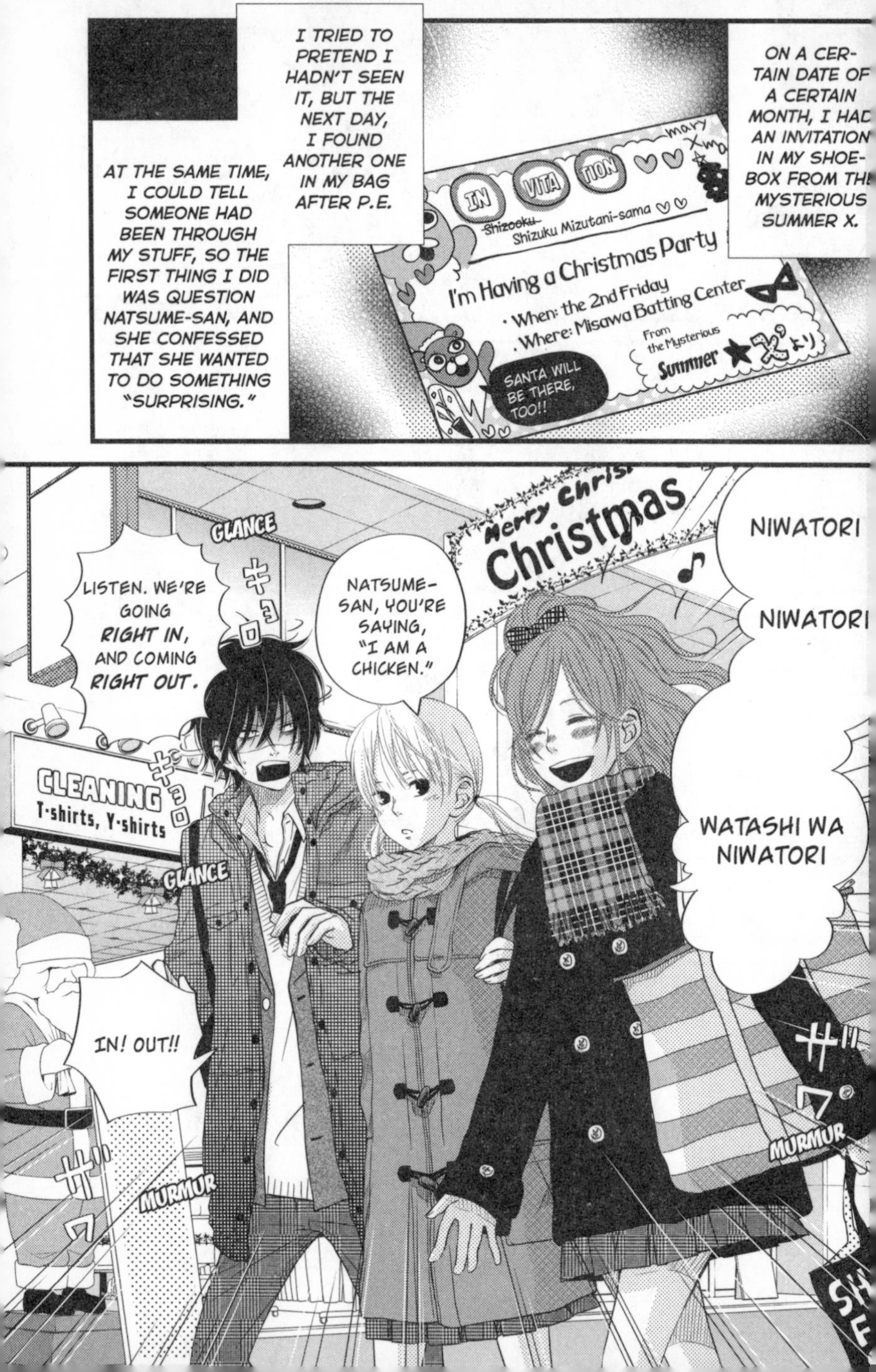
ON A CERTAIN DATE OF A CERTAIN MONTH, I HAD AN INVITATION IN MY SHOEBOX FROM THE MYSTERIOUS SUMMER X.
I TRIED TO PRETEND I HADN'T SEEN IT, BUT THE NEXT DAY, I FOUND ANOTHER ONE IN MY BAG AFTER P.E.
AT THE SAME TIME, I COULD TELL SOMEONE HAD BEEN THROUGH MY STUFF, SO THE FIRST THING I DID WAS QUESTION NATSUME-SAN, AND SHE CONFESSED THAT SHE WANTED TO DO SOMETHING "SURPRISING."
mary Xmas
IN VITA TION
~~Shizooku~~
Shizuku Mizutani-sama
I'm Having a Christmas Party
• When: the 2nd Friday
. Where: Misawa Batting Center
From the Mysterious Summer ★ Xより
SANTA WILL BE THERE, TOO!!
NIWATORI
NIWATORI
WATASHI WA NIWATORI
Merry Christmas
Christmas
NATSUME-SAN, YOU'RE SAYING, "I AM A CHICKEN."
GLANCE
キョロ
LISTEN. WE'RE GOING RIGHT IN, AND COMING RIGHT OUT.
キョロ
GLANCE
CLEANING
T-shirts, Y-shirts
IN! OUT!!
MURMUR
MURMUR

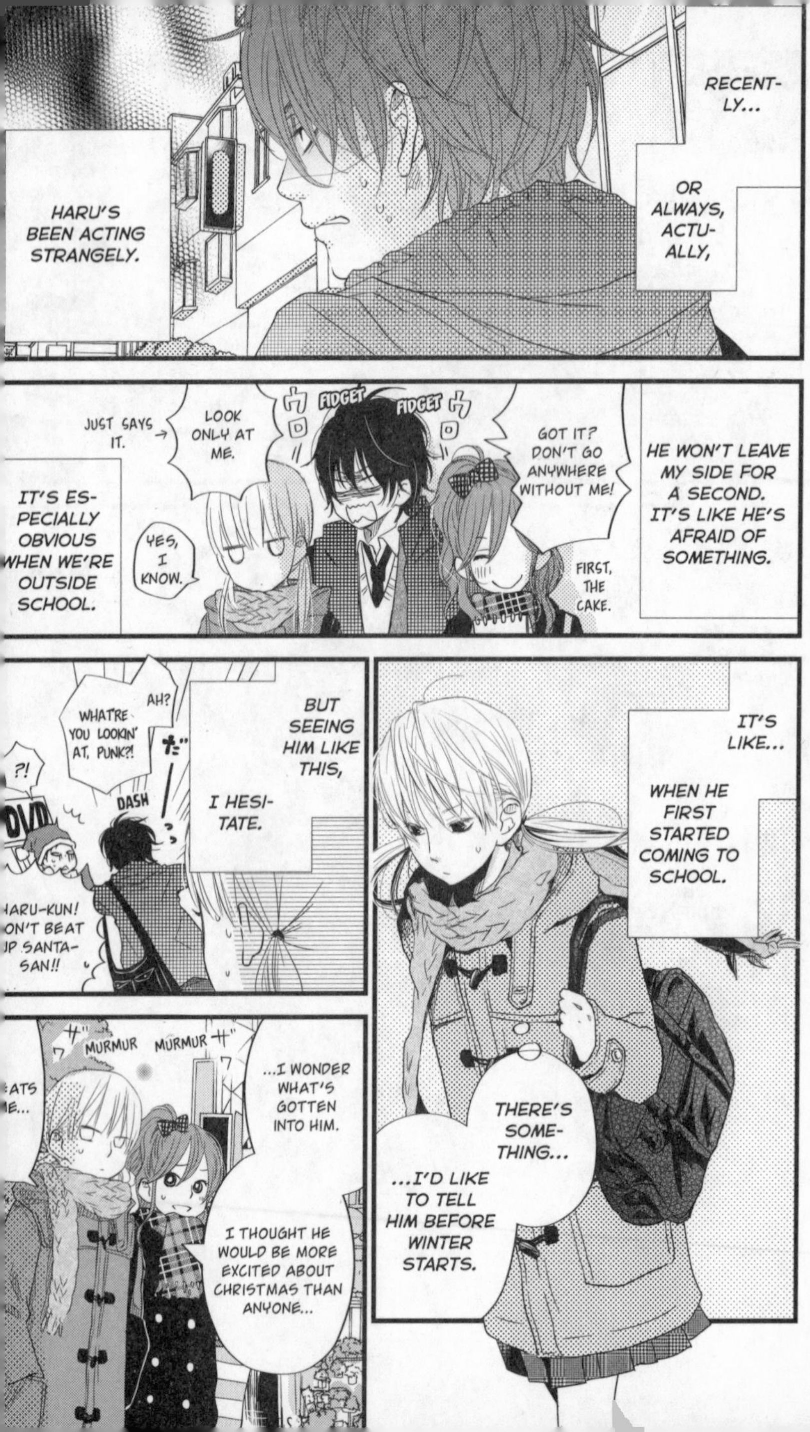
RECENTLY...
OR ALWAYS, ACTUALLY,
HARU'S BEEN ACTING STRANGELY.
HE WON'T LEAVE MY SIDE FOR A SECOND. IT'S LIKE HE'S AFRAID OF SOMETHING.
GOT IT? DON'T GO ANYWHERE WITHOUT ME!
FIRST, THE CAKE.
FIDGET
FIDGET
LOOK ONLY AT ME.
JUST SAYS IT. →
YES, I KNOW.
IT'S ESPECIALLY OBVIOUS WHEN WE'RE OUTSIDE SCHOOL.
IT'S LIKE...
WHEN HE FIRST STARTED COMING TO SCHOOL.
THERE'S SOMETHING...
...I'D LIKE TO TELL HIM BEFORE WINTER STARTS.
BUT SEEING HIM LIKE THIS,
I HESITATE.
AH?
WHATRE YOU LOOKIN' AT, PUNK?!
DASH
?!
DVD
HARU-KUN! ON'T BEAT JP SANTA-SAN!!
...I WONDER WHAT'S GOTTEN INTO HIM.
MURMUR
MURMUR
EATS ME...
I THOUGHT HE WOULD BE MORE EXCITED ABOUT CHRISTMAS THAN ANYONE...

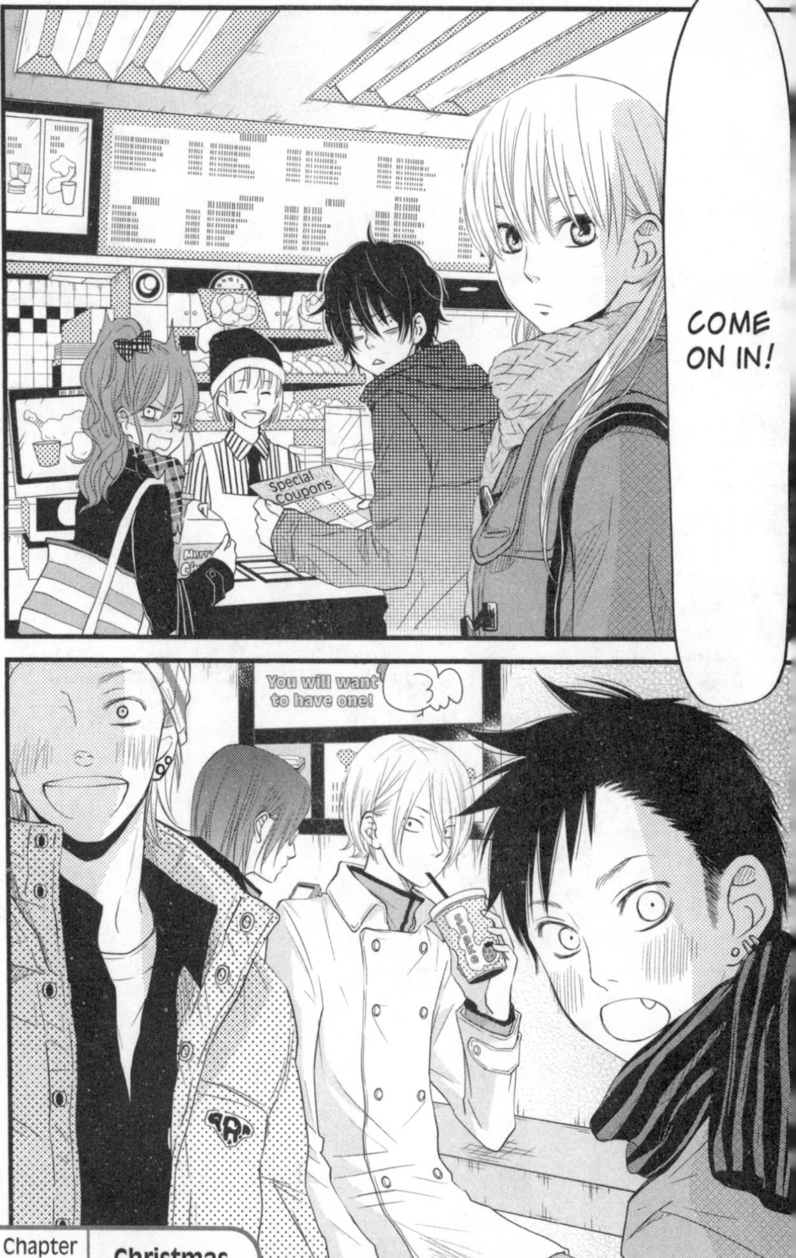
COME ON IN!
Special Coupons
You will want to have one!
Shake

Chapter 14 Christmas

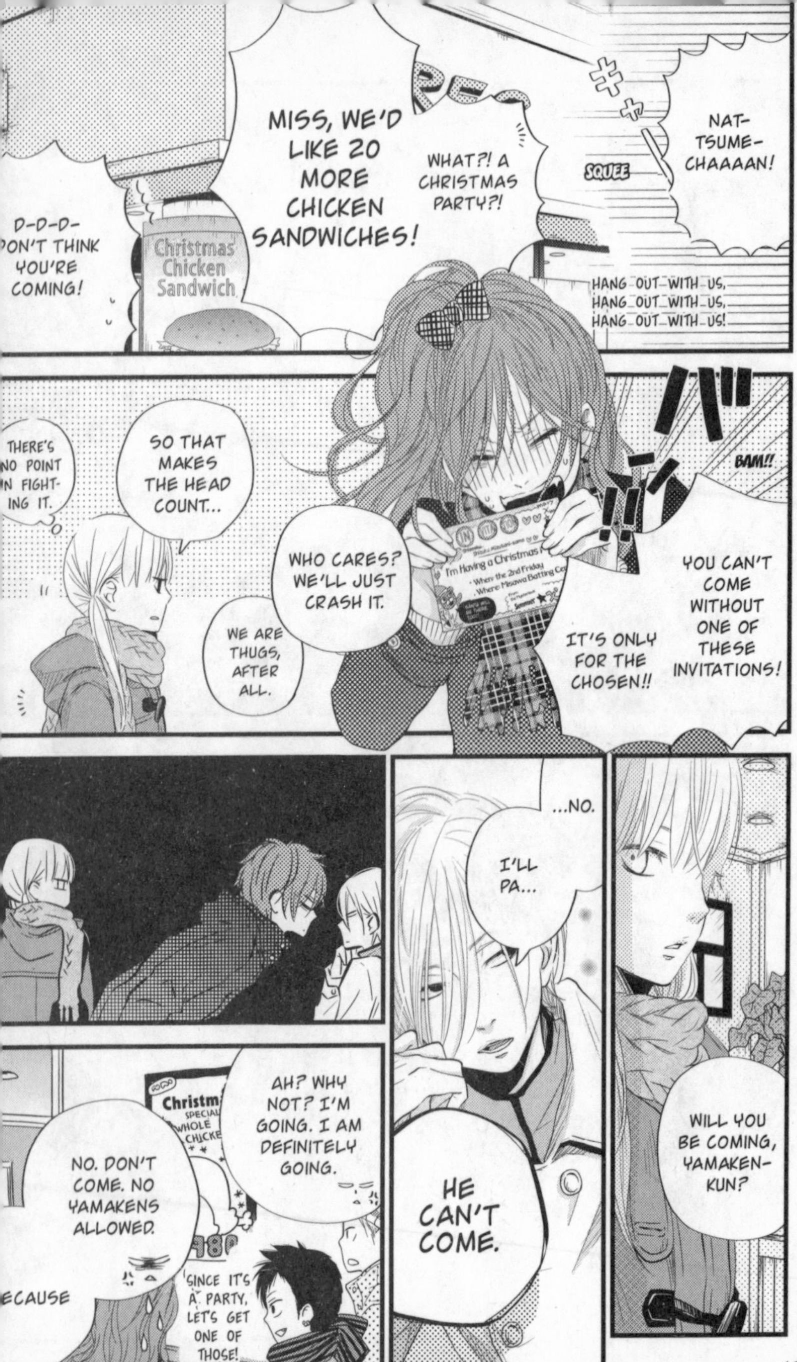

NAT-TSUME-CHAAAAN!
SQUEE
HANG OUT WITH US, HANG OUT WITH US, HANG OUT WITH US!
WHAT?! A CHRISTMAS PARTY?!
MISS, WE'D LIKE 20 MORE CHICKEN SANDWICHES!
Christmas Chicken Sandwich
D-D-D-DON'T THINK YOU'RE COMING!
BAM!!
YOU CAN'T COME WITHOUT ONE OF THESE INVITATIONS!
IT'S ONLY FOR THE CHOSEN!!
I'm Having a Christmas
When the 2nd Friday
Where Misawa Batting Ca
WHO CARES? WE'LL JUST CRASH IT.
WE ARE THUGS, AFTER ALL.
SO THAT MAKES THE HEAD COUNT...
THERE'S NO POINT N FIGHT-ING IT.
WILL YOU BE COMING, YAMAKEN-KUN?
...NO.
I'LL PA...
HE CAN'T COME.
AH? WHY NOT? I'M GOING. I AM DEFINITELY GOING.
Christm SPECIAL WHOLE CHICKE
NO. DON'T COME. NO YAMAKENS ALLOWED.
ECAUSE
SINCE IT'S A PARTY, LET'S GET ONE OF THOSE!
EXPEN-SIVE!!

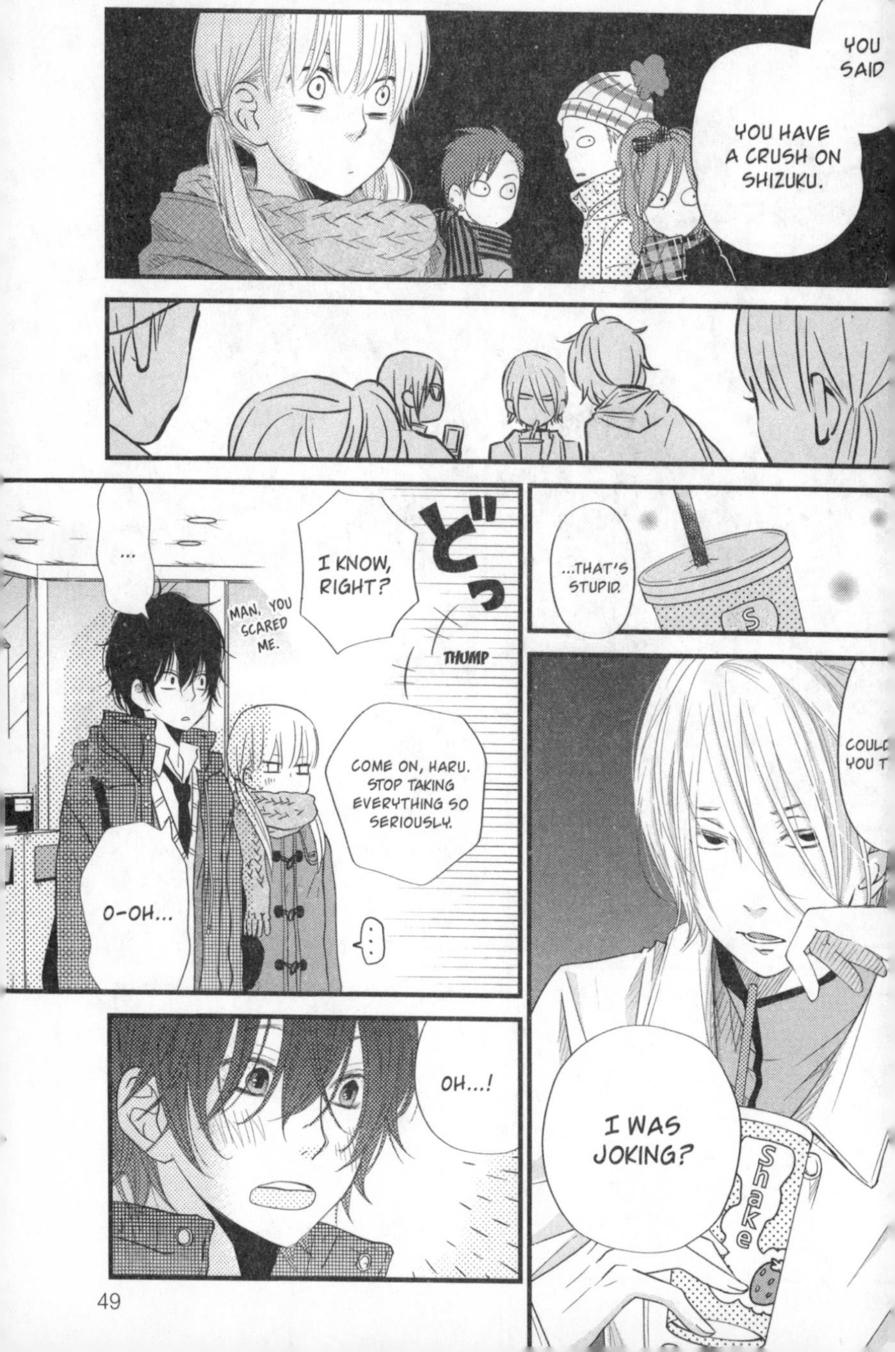
YOU SAID
YOU HAVE A CRUSH ON SHIZUKU.
...THAT'S STUPID.
COULD YOU T
I WAS JOKING?
...
I KNOW, RIGHT?
どっ
THUMP
MAN, YOU SCARED ME.
COME ON, HARU. STOP TAKING EVERYTHING SO SERIOUSLY.
...
O-OH...
OH...!
Shake

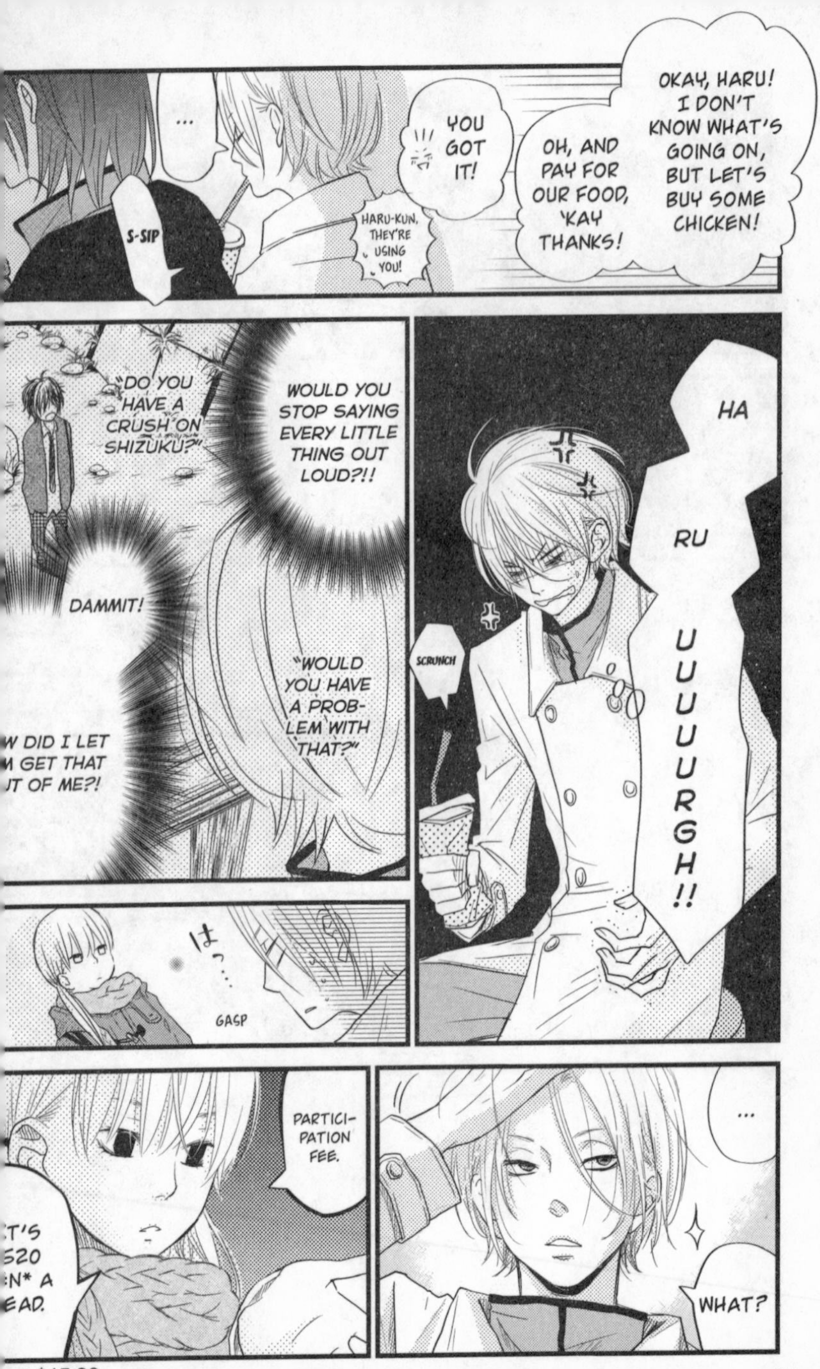
OKAY, HARU! I DON'T KNOW WHAT'S GOING ON, BUT LET'S BUY SOME CHICKEN!
OH, AND PAY FOR OUR FOOD, 'KAY THANKS!
YOU GOT IT!
HARU-KUN, THEY'RE USING YOU!
S-SIP
...
HA
RU
UUUUURGH!!
SCRUNCH
WOULD YOU STOP SAYING EVERY LITTLE THING OUT LOUD?!!
"DO YOU HAVE A CRUSH ON SHIZUKU?"
"WOULD YOU HAVE A PROBLEM WITH THAT?"
DAMMIT!
W DID I LET M GET THAT T OF ME?!
はっ…
GASP
...
WHAT?
PARTICI-PATION FEE.
T'S 520 EN* A EAD.

out $15.20

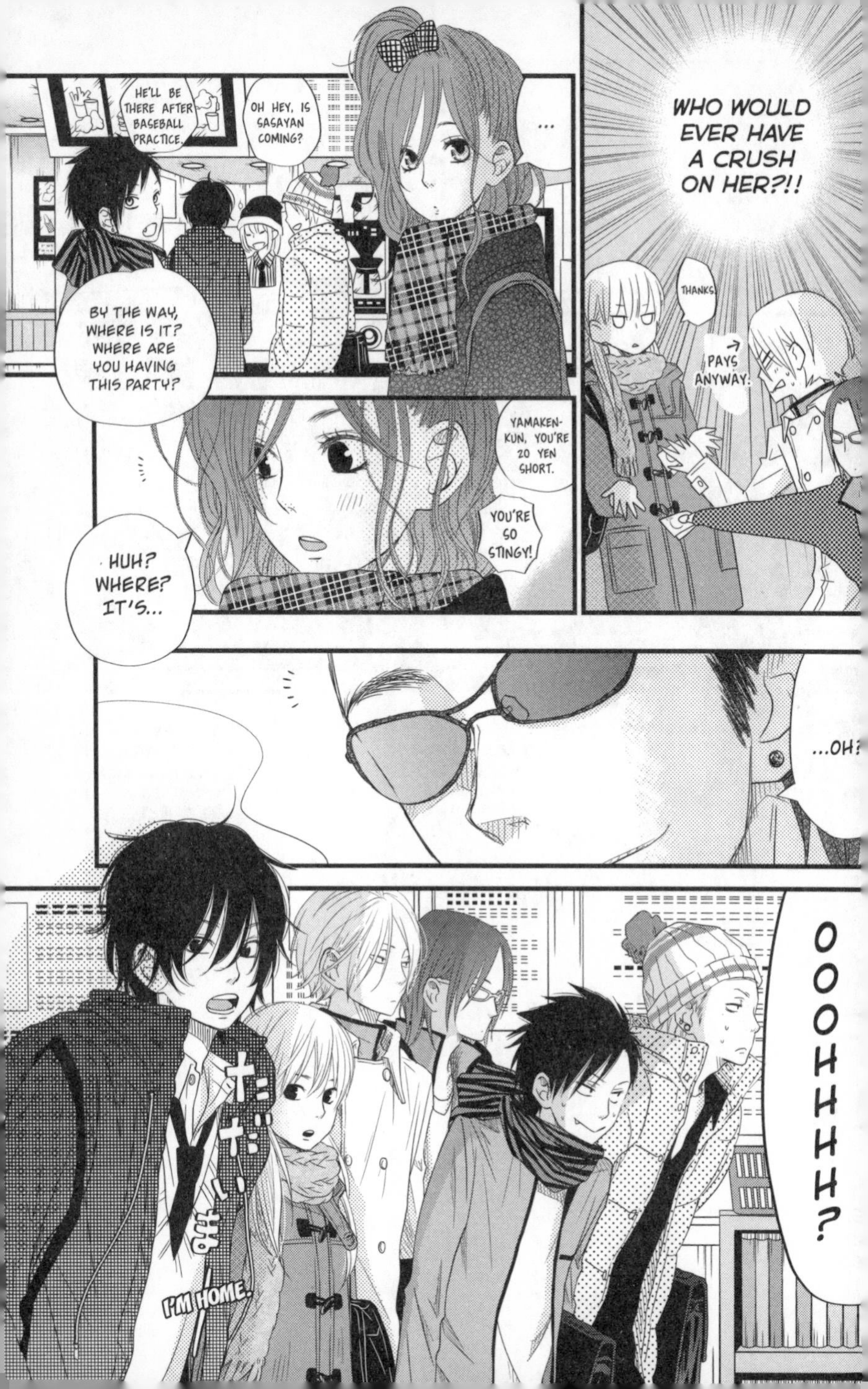
WHO WOULD EVER HAVE A CRUSH ON HER?!!
THANKS.
→ PAYS ANYWAY.
...
OH HEY, IS SASAYAN COMING?
HE'LL BE THERE AFTER BASEBALL PRACTICE.
BY THE WAY, WHERE IS IT? WHERE ARE YOU HAVING THIS PARTY?
YAMAKEN-KUN, YOU'RE 20 YEN SHORT.
YOU'RE SO STINGY!
HUH? WHERE? IT'S...
...OH?
OOOHHHHH?
ただいま
I'M HOME.

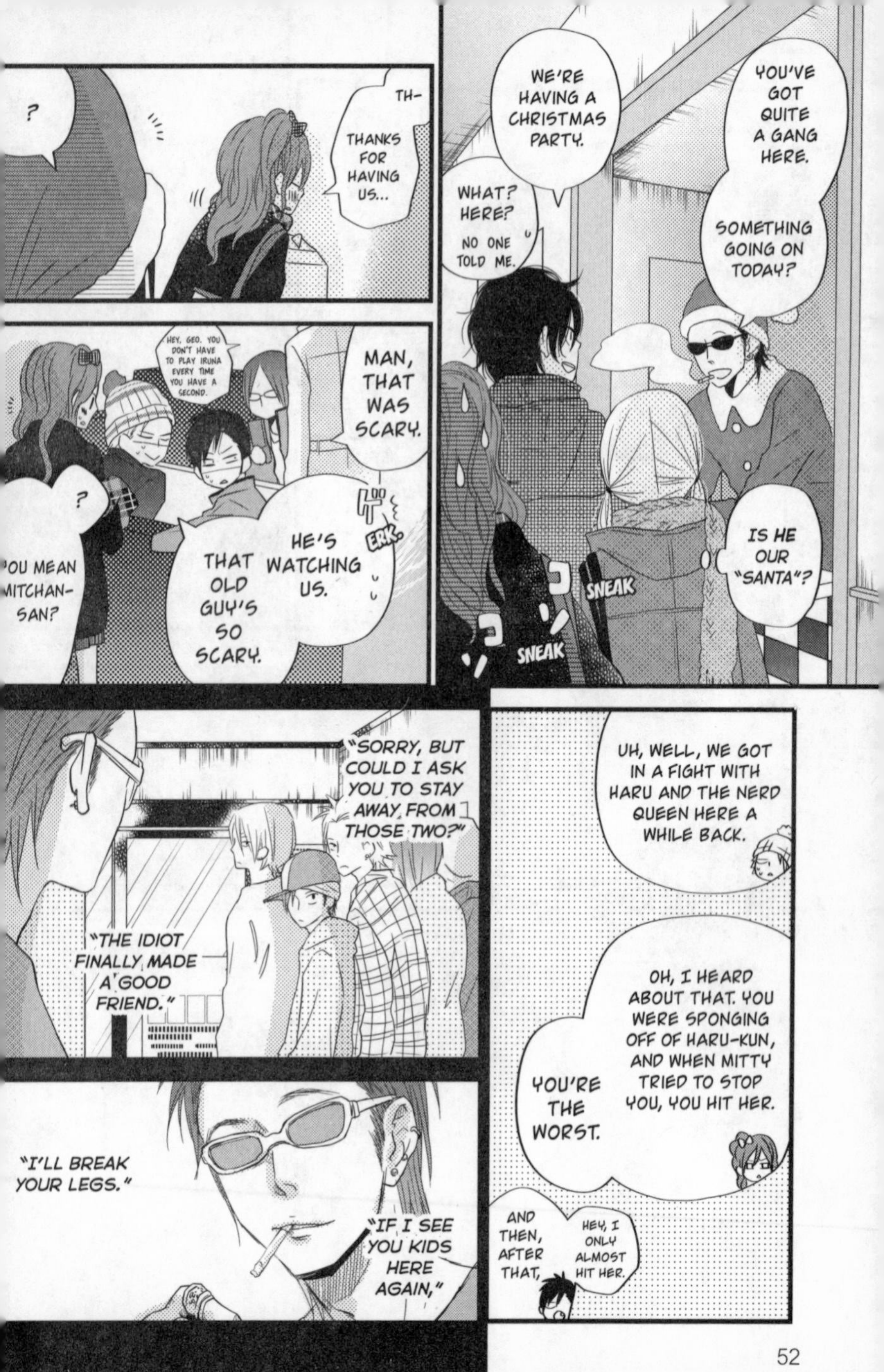
YOU'VE GOT QUITE A GANG HERE.
SOMETHING GOING ON TODAY?
WE'RE HAVING A CHRISTMAS PARTY.
WHAT? HERE?
NO ONE TOLD ME.
IS HE OUR "SANTA"?
SNEAK
SNEAK
TH-
THANKS FOR HAVING US...
?
MAN, THAT WAS SCARY.
HEY, GEO. YOU DON'T HAVE TO PLAY IRUNA EVERY TIME YOU HAVE A SECOND.
ERK.
HE'S WATCHING US.
THAT OLD GUY'S SO SCARY.
?
OU MEAN MITCHAN-SAN?
UH, WELL, WE GOT IN A FIGHT WITH HARU AND THE NERD QUEEN HERE A WHILE BACK.
OH, I HEARD ABOUT THAT. YOU WERE SPONGING OFF OF HARU-KUN, AND WHEN MITTY TRIED TO STOP YOU, YOU HIT HER.
YOU'RE THE WORST.
AND THEN, AFTER THAT,
HEY, I ONLY ALMOST HIT HER.
"SORRY, BUT COULD I ASK YOU TO STAY AWAY FROM THOSE TWO?"
"THE IDIOT FINALLY MADE A GOOD FRIEND."
"IF I SEE YOU KIDS HERE AGAIN,"
"I'LL BREAK YOUR LEGS."

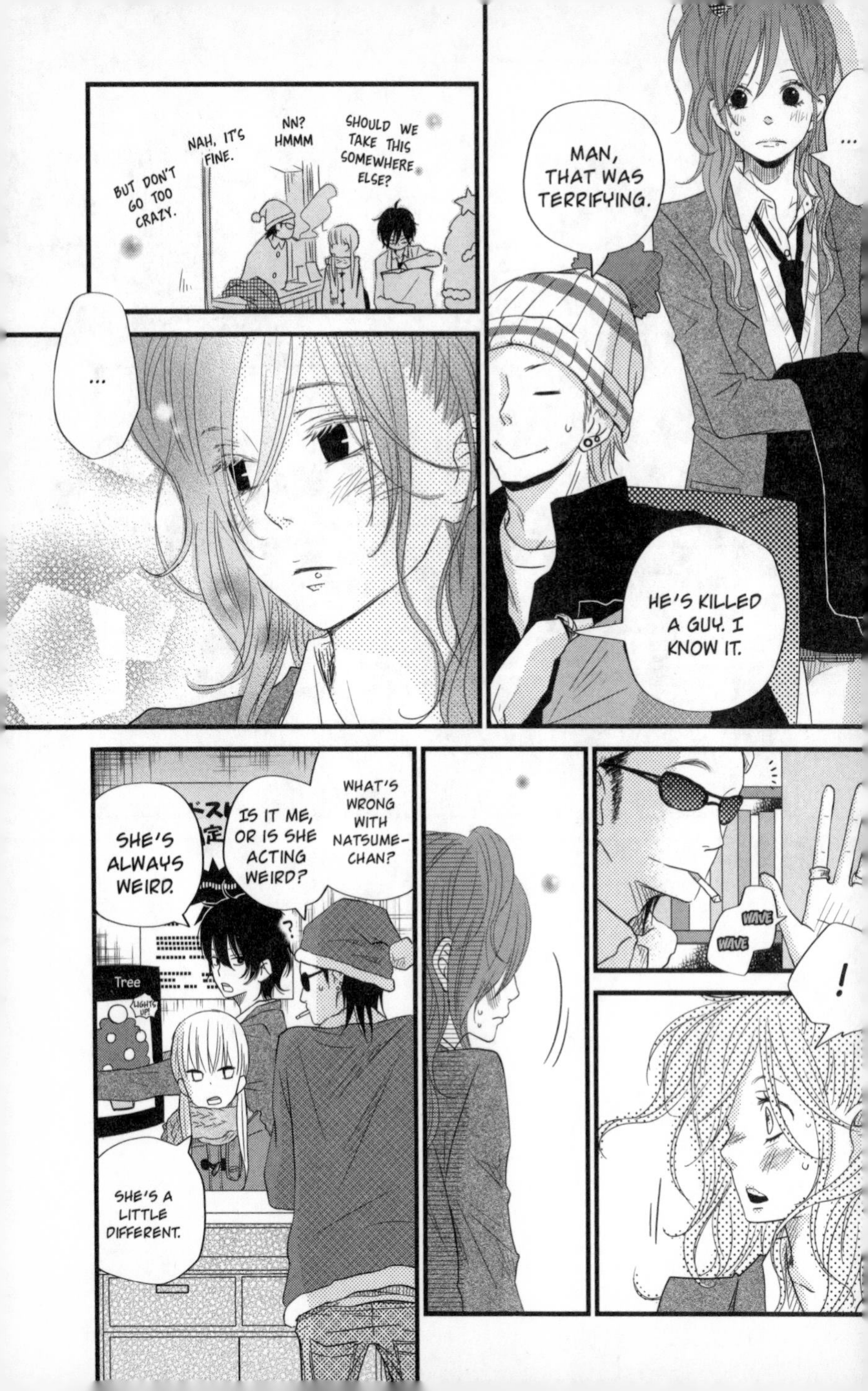
...
MAN, THAT WAS TERRIFYING.
HE'S KILLED A GUY. I KNOW IT.
SHOULD WE TAKE THIS SOMEWHERE ELSE?
NN? HMMM
NAH, IT'S FINE.
BUT DON'T GO TOO CRAZY.
...
WAVE
WAVE
!
WHAT'S WRONG WITH NATSUME-CHAN?
IS IT ME, OR IS SHE ACTING WEIRD?
SHE'S ALWAYS WEIRD.
Tree
LIGHTS UP!
SHE'S A LITTLE DIFFERENT.

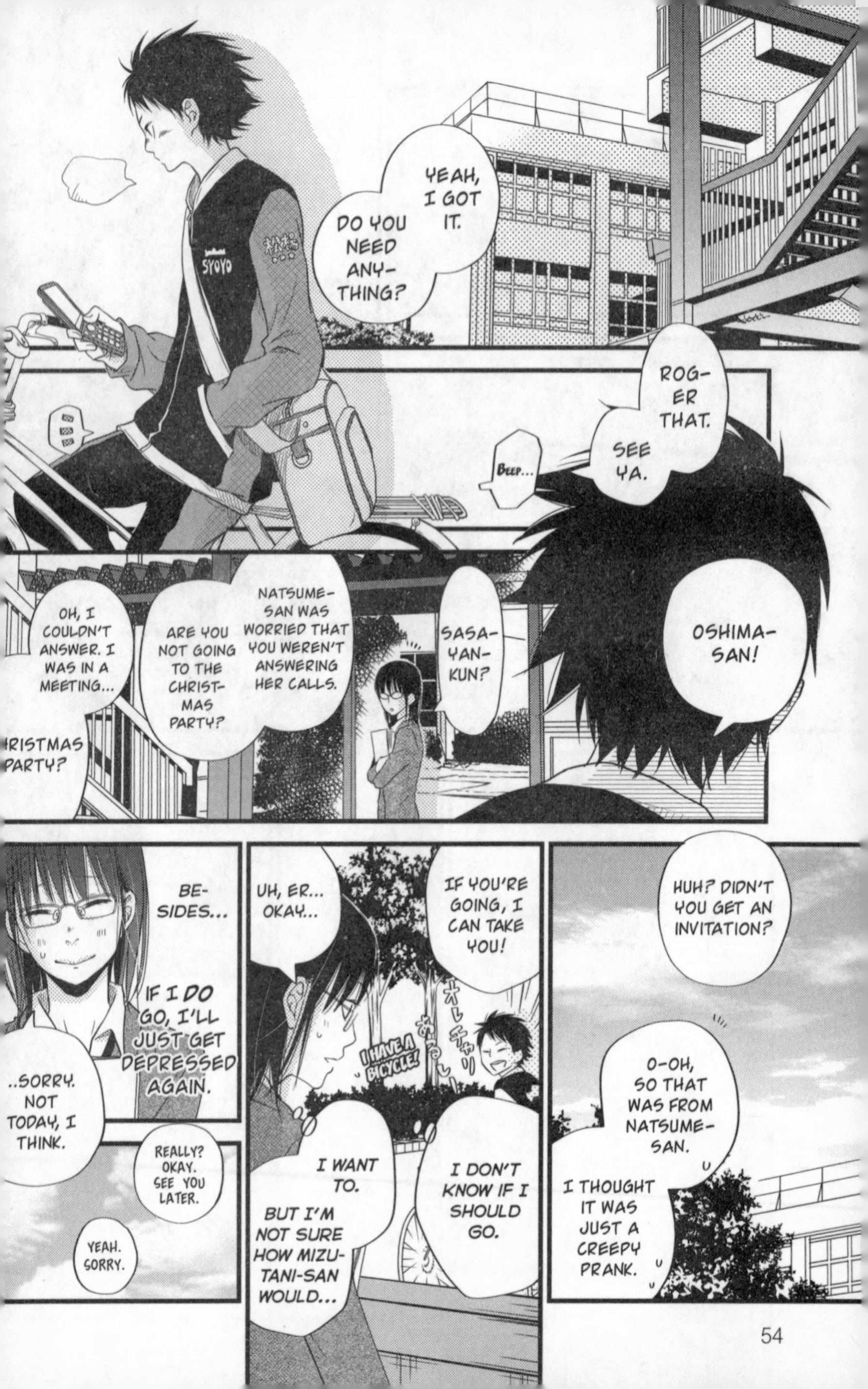
YEAH, I GOT IT.
DO YOU NEED ANYTHING?
ROGER THAT. SEE YA.
BEEP...
OSHIMA-SAN!
SASAYAN-KUN?
NATSUME-SAN WAS WORRIED THAT YOU WEREN'T ANSWERING HER CALLS.
ARE YOU NOT GOING TO THE CHRISTMAS PARTY?
OH, I COULDN'T ANSWER. I WAS IN A MEETING...
RISTMAS PARTY?
HUH? DIDN'T YOU GET AN INVITATION?
O-OH, SO THAT WAS FROM NATSUME-SAN.
I THOUGHT IT WAS JUST A CREEPY PRANK.
IF YOU'RE GOING, I CAN TAKE YOU!
I HAVE A BICYCLE!
UH, ER... OKAY...
I DON'T KNOW IF I SHOULD GO.
I WANT TO.
BUT I'M NOT SURE HOW MIZUTANI-SAN WOULD...
BESIDES...
IF I DO GO, I'LL JUST GET DEPRESSED AGAIN.
...SORRY. NOT TODAY, I THINK.
REALLY? OKAY. SEE YOU LATER.
YEAH. SORRY.

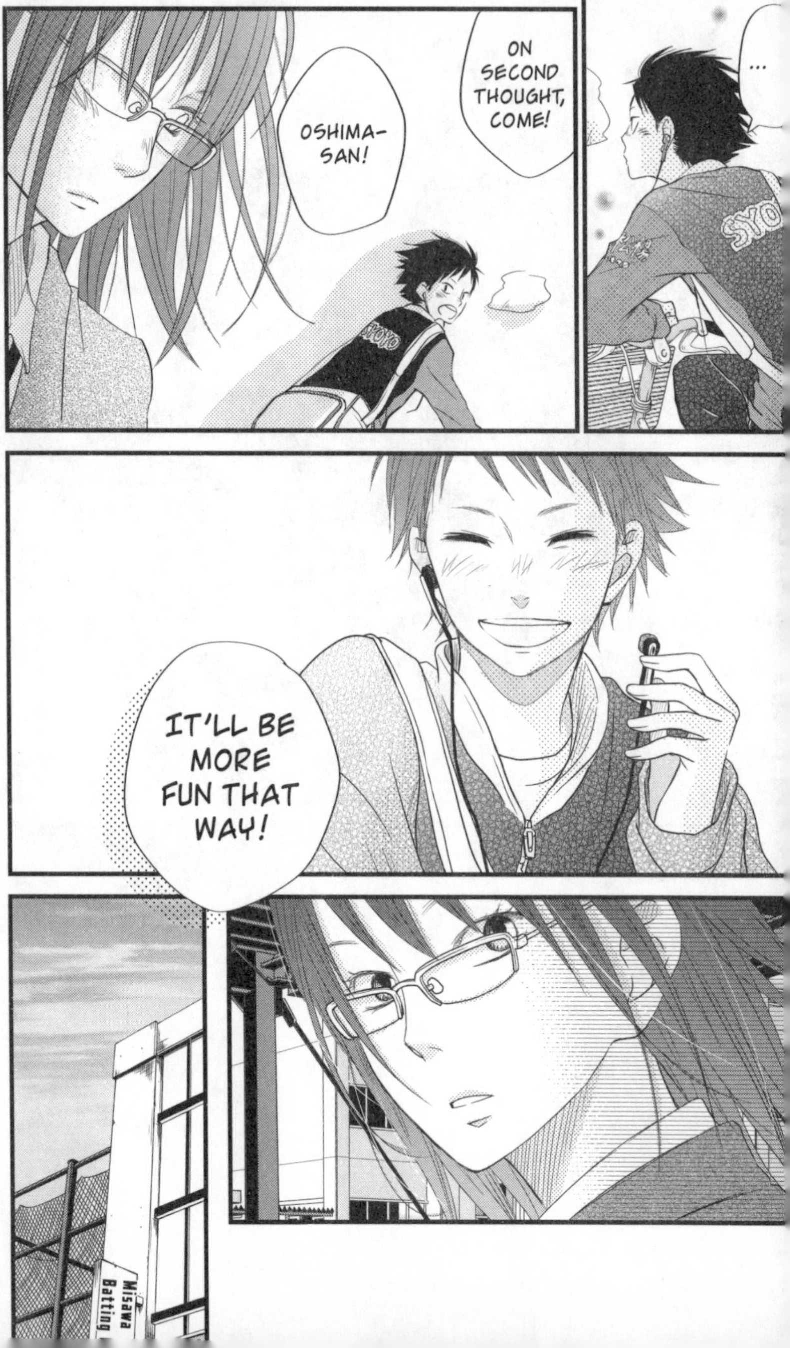
...
ON SECOND THOUGHT, COME!
OSHIMA-SAN!
IT'LL BE MORE FUN THAT WAY!
Misawa Batting

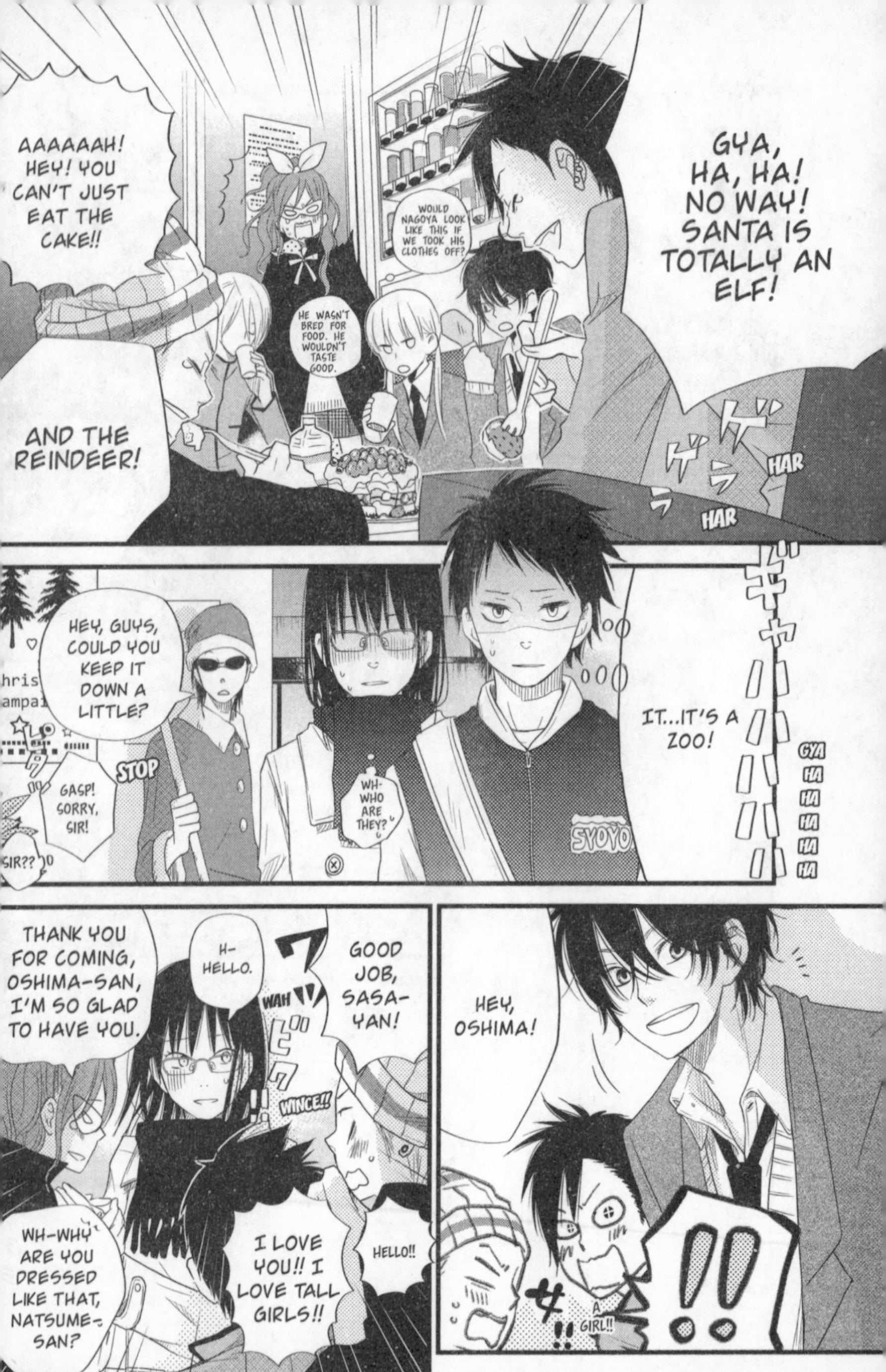
GYA, HA, HA! NO WAY! SANTA IS TOTALLY AN ELF!
WOULD NAGOYA LOOK LIKE THIS IF WE TOOK HIS CLOTHES OFF?
AAAAAAH! HEY! YOU CAN'T JUST EAT THE CAKE!!
HE WASN'T BRED FOR FOOD. HE WOULDN'T TASTE GOOD.
AND THE REINDEER!
HAR
HAR
GYA HA HA HA HA HA
IT...IT'S A ZOO!
WH-WHO ARE THEY?
HEY, GUYS, COULD YOU KEEP IT DOWN A LITTLE?
STOP
GASP! SORRY, SIR!
SIR??
HEY, OSHIMA!
!!
A GIRL!!
GOOD JOB, SASA-YAN!
H-HELLO.
THANK YOU FOR COMING, OSHIMA-SAN, I'M SO GLAD TO HAVE YOU.
WAH
WINCE!!
HELLO!!
I LOVE YOU!! I LOVE TALL GIRLS!!
WH-WHY ARE YOU DRESSED LIKE THAT, NATSUME-SAN?

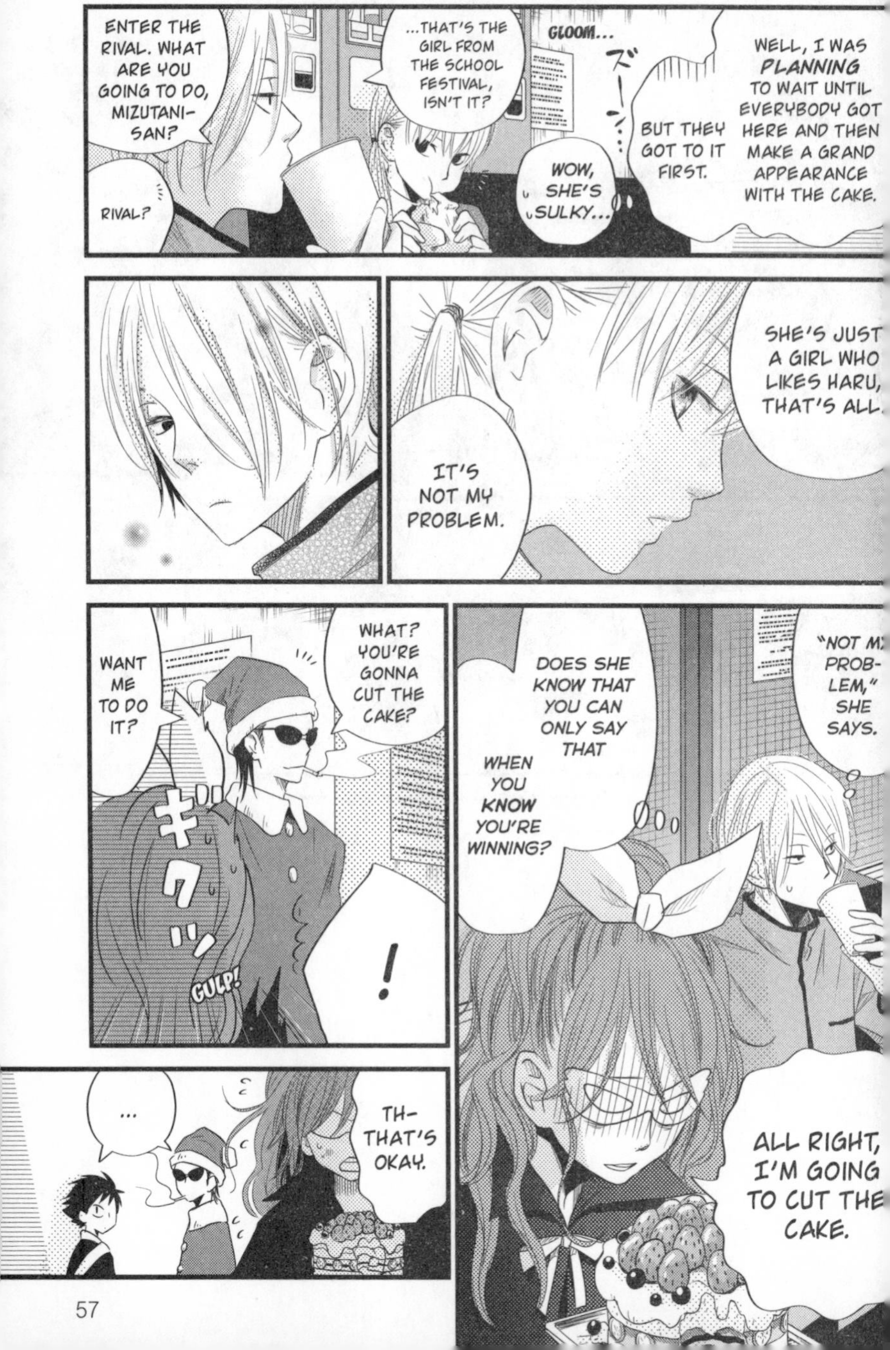
WELL, I WAS PLANNING TO WAIT UNTIL EVERYBODY GOT HERE AND THEN MAKE A GRAND APPEARANCE WITH THE CAKE.
BUT THEY GOT TO IT FIRST.
GLOOM...
WOW, SHE'S SULKY...
...THAT'S THE GIRL FROM THE SCHOOL FESTIVAL, ISN'T IT?
ENTER THE RIVAL. WHAT ARE YOU GOING TO DO, MIZUTANI-SAN?
RIVAL?
SHE'S JUST A GIRL WHO LIKES HARU, THAT'S ALL.
IT'S NOT MY PROBLEM.
"NOT MY PROB-LEM," SHE SAYS.
DOES SHE KNOW THAT YOU CAN ONLY SAY THAT
WHEN YOU KNOW YOU'RE WINNING?
ALL RIGHT, I'M GOING TO CUT THE CAKE.
WHAT? YOU'RE GONNA CUT THE CAKE?
WANT ME TO DO IT?
GULP!
!
TH-THAT'S OKAY.
...

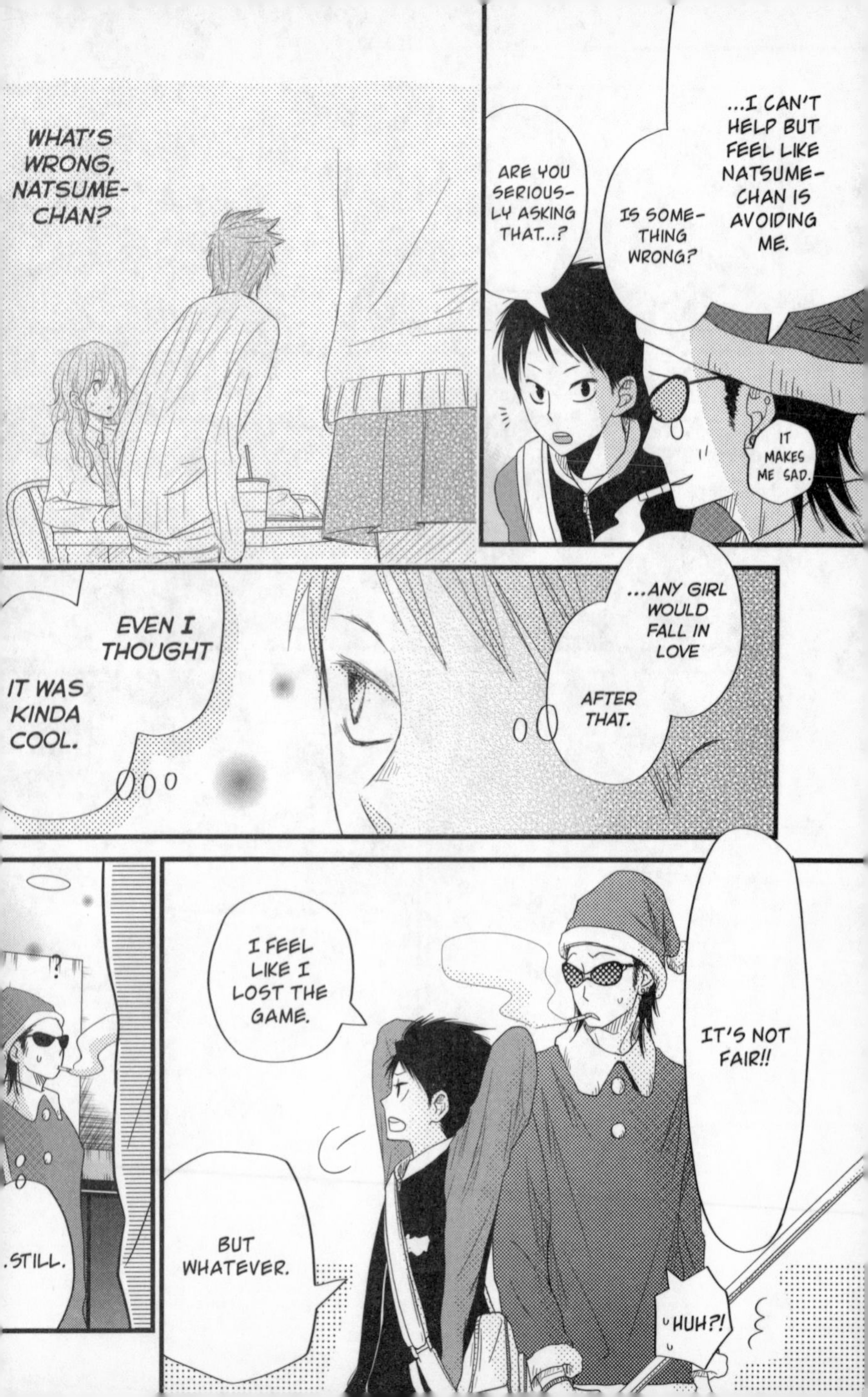
...I CAN'T HELP BUT FEEL LIKE NATSUME-CHAN IS AVOIDING ME.
IS SOME-THING WRONG?
IT MAKES ME SAD.
ARE YOU SERIOUS-LY ASKING THAT...?
WHAT'S WRONG, NATSUME-CHAN?
...ANY GIRL WOULD FALL IN LOVE
AFTER THAT.
EVEN I THOUGHT
IT WAS KINDA COOL.
IT'S NOT FAIR!!
HUH?!
I FEEL LIKE I LOST THE GAME.
BUT WHATEVER.
?
.STILL.

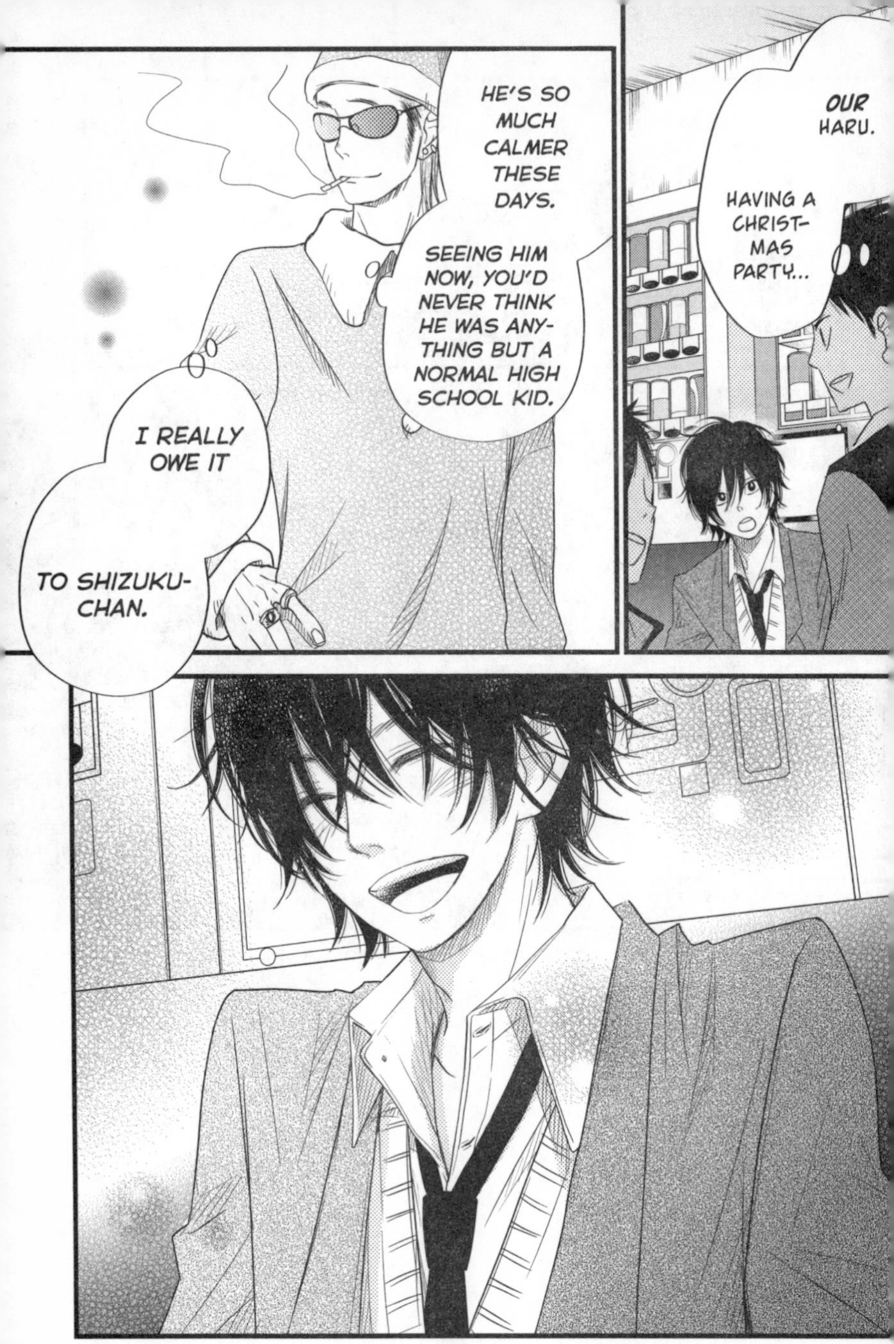
OUR HARU.
HAVING A CHRIST-MAS PARTY...
HE'S SO MUCH CALMER THESE DAYS.
SEEING HIM NOW, YOU'D NEVER THINK HE WAS ANY-THING BUT A NORMAL HIGH SCHOOL KID.
I REALLY OWE IT
TO SHIZUKU-CHAN.

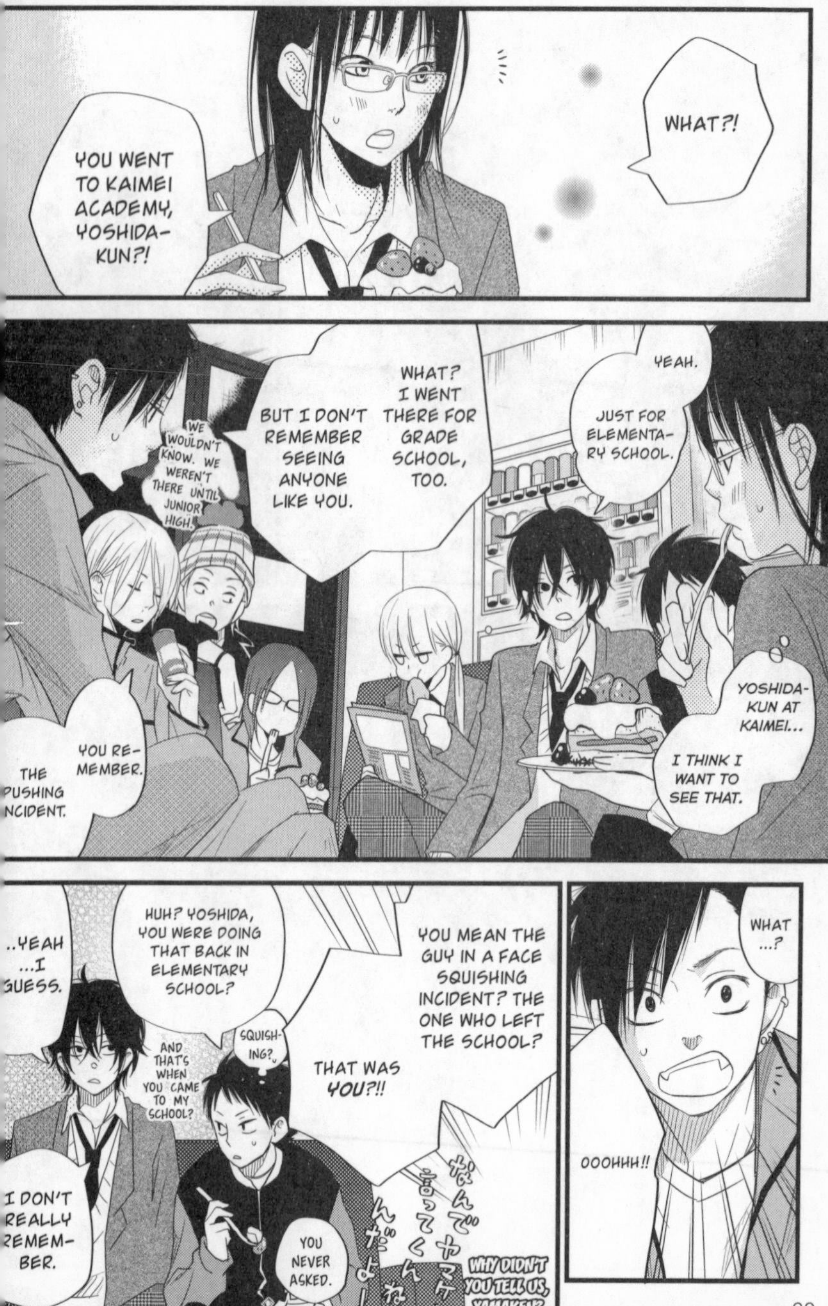
WHAT?!
YOU WENT TO KAIMEI ACADEMY, YOSHIDA-KUN?!
YEAH.
JUST FOR ELEMENTARY SCHOOL.
WHAT? I WENT THERE FOR GRADE SCHOOL, TOO.
BUT I DON'T REMEMBER SEEING ANYONE LIKE YOU.
WE WOULDN'T KNOW. WE WEREN'T THERE UNTIL JUNIOR HIGH.
YOSHIDA-KUN AT KAIMEI...
I THINK I WANT TO SEE THAT.
YOU REMEMBER.
THE PUSHING INCIDENT.
WHAT ...?
OOOHHH!!
YOU MEAN THE GUY IN A FACE SQUISHING INCIDENT? THE ONE WHO LEFT THE SCHOOL?
HUH? YOSHIDA, YOU WERE DOING THAT BACK IN ELEMENTARY SCHOOL?
..YEAH ...I GUESS.
SQUISHING?
AND THAT'S WHEN YOU CAME TO MY SCHOOL?
THAT WAS *YOU*?!!
なんでヤマケン言ってくんねーんだよー
WHY DIDN'T YOU TELL US, YAMAKEN?
YOU NEVER ASKED.
I DON'T REALLY REMEMBER.

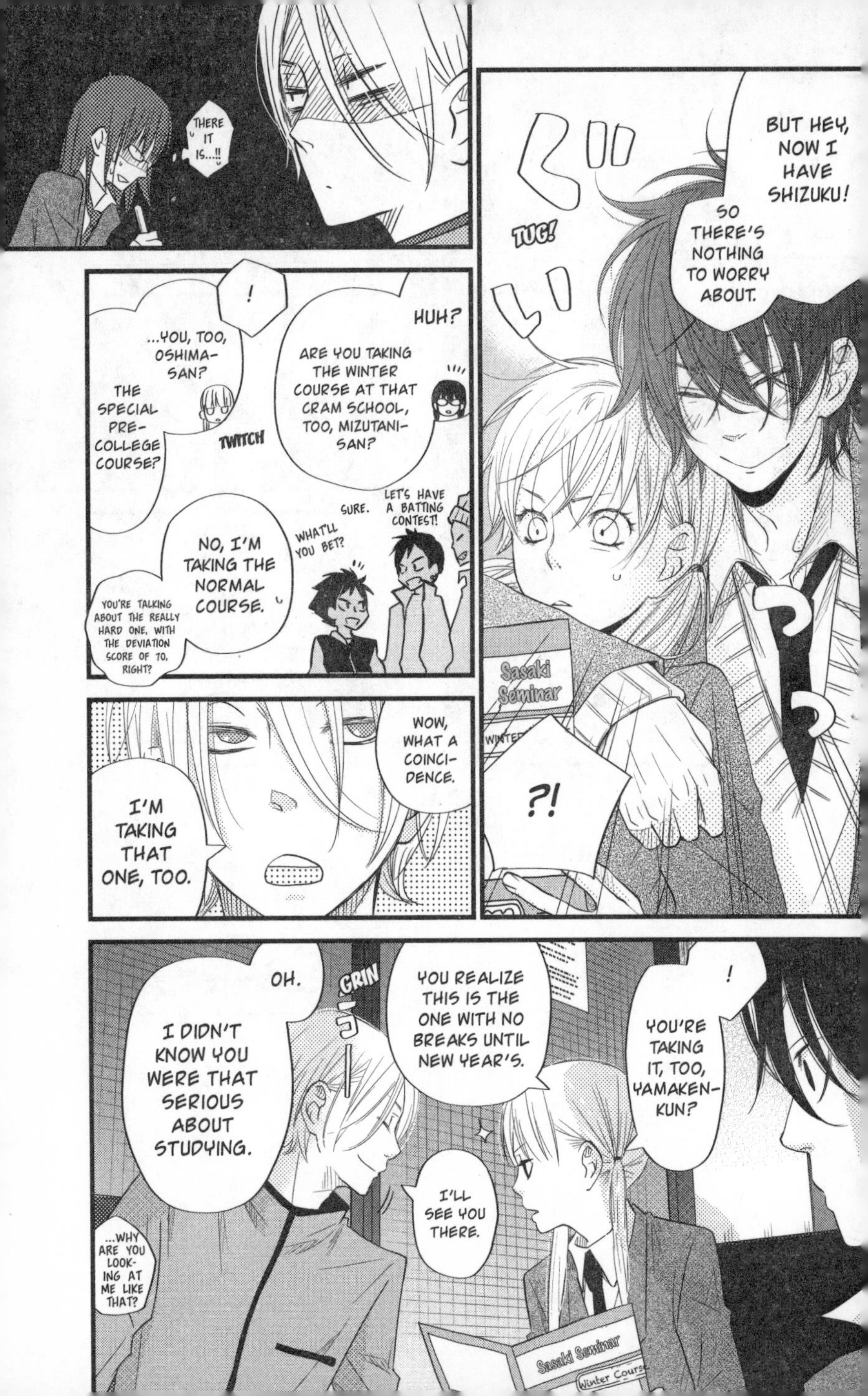
THERE IT IS...!!
BUT HEY, NOW I HAVE SHIZUKU!
SO THERE'S NOTHING TO WORRY ABOUT.
TUG!
Sasaki Seminar
?!
HUH?
ARE YOU TAKING THE WINTER COURSE AT THAT CRAM SCHOOL, TOO, MIZUTANI-SAN?
!
...YOU, TOO, OSHIMA-SAN?
THE SPECIAL PRE-COLLEGE COURSE?
TWITCH
NO, I'M TAKING THE NORMAL COURSE.
YOU'RE TALKING ABOUT THE REALLY HARD ONE, WITH THE DEVIATION SCORE OF 70, RIGHT?
LET'S HAVE A BATTING CONTEST!
SURE.
WHAT'LL YOU BET?
WOW, WHAT A COINCIDENCE.
I'M TAKING THAT ONE, TOO.
!
YOU'RE TAKING IT, TOO, YAMAKEN-KUN?
YOU REALIZE THIS IS THE ONE WITH NO BREAKS UNTIL NEW YEAR'S.
GRIN
OH.
I DIDN'T KNOW YOU WERE THAT SERIOUS ABOUT STUDYING.
I'LL SEE YOU THERE.
...WHY ARE YOU LOOKING AT ME LIKE THAT?
Sasaki Seminar
Winter Course

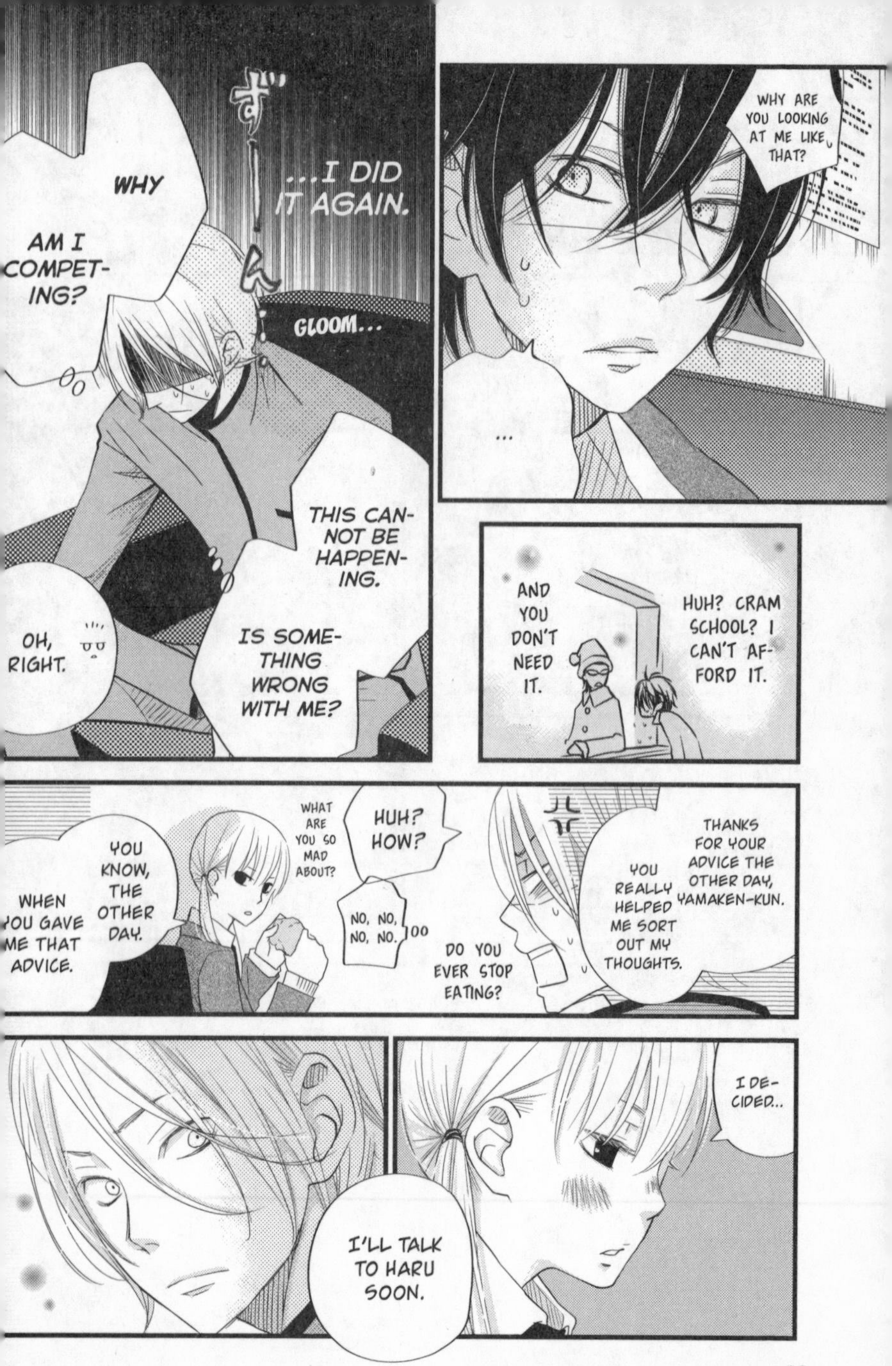
WHY ARE YOU LOOKING AT ME LIKE THAT?
...
HUH? CRAM SCHOOL? I CAN'T AF-FORD IT.
AND YOU DON'T NEED IT.
ずーん
...I DID IT AGAIN.
WHY AM I COMPET-ING?
GLOOM...
THIS CAN-NOT BE HAPPEN-ING.
IS SOME-THING WRONG WITH ME?
OH, RIGHT.
THANKS FOR YOUR ADVICE THE OTHER DAY, YAMAKEN-KUN.
YOU REALLY HELPED ME SORT OUT MY THOUGHTS.
DO YOU EVER STOP EATING?
HUH? HOW?
WHAT ARE YOU SO MAD ABOUT?
NO, NO, NO, NO.
YOU KNOW, THE OTHER DAY.
WHEN YOU GAVE ME THAT ADVICE.
I DE-CIDED...
I'LL TALK TO HARU SOON.

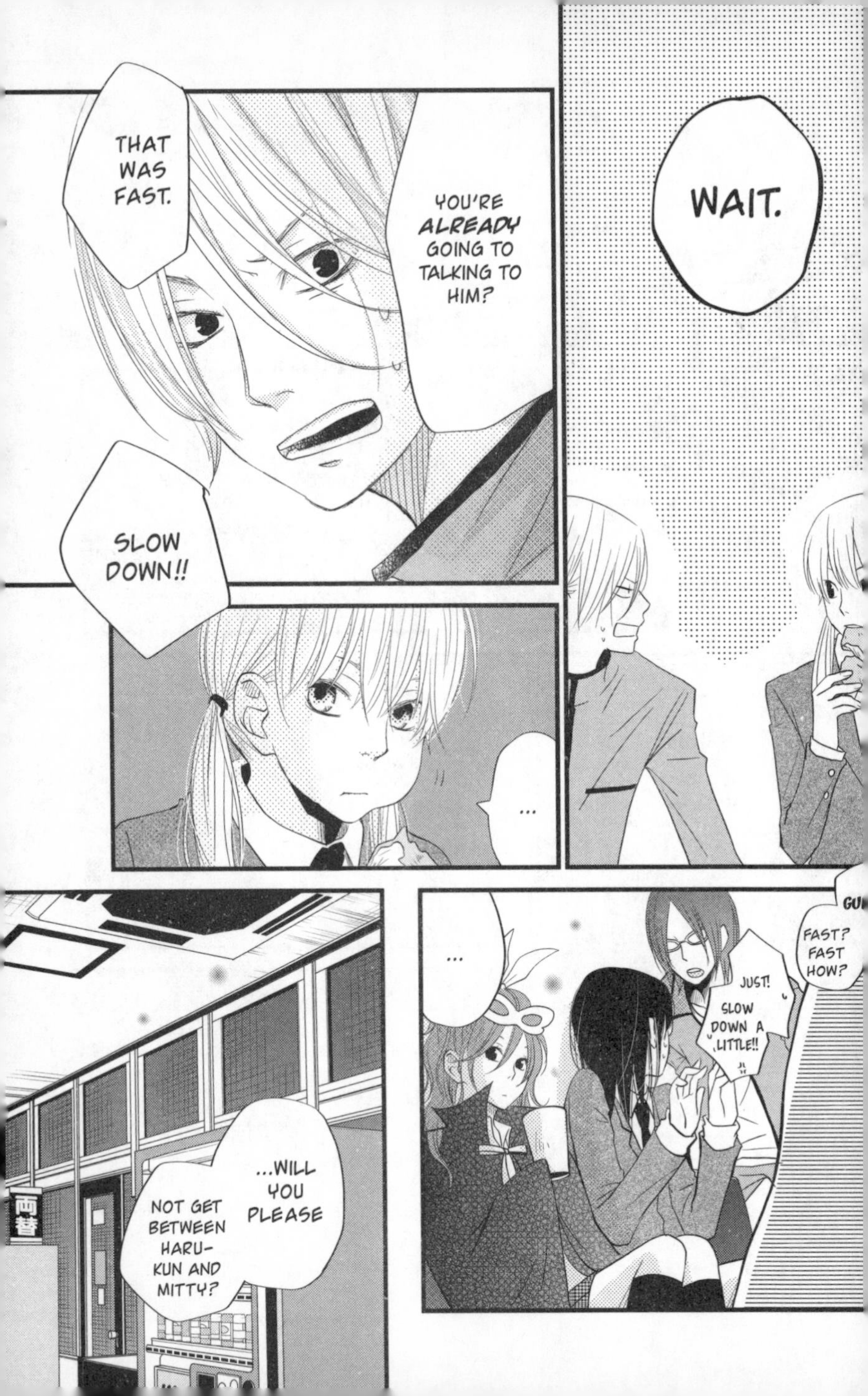
WAIT.
YOU'RE ALREADY GOING TO TALKING TO HIM?
THAT WAS FAST.
SLOW DOWN!!
...
FAST? FAST HOW?
JUST! SLOW DOWN A LITTLE!!
...
...WILL YOU PLEASE
NOT GET BETWEEN HARU-KUN AND MITTY?
両替

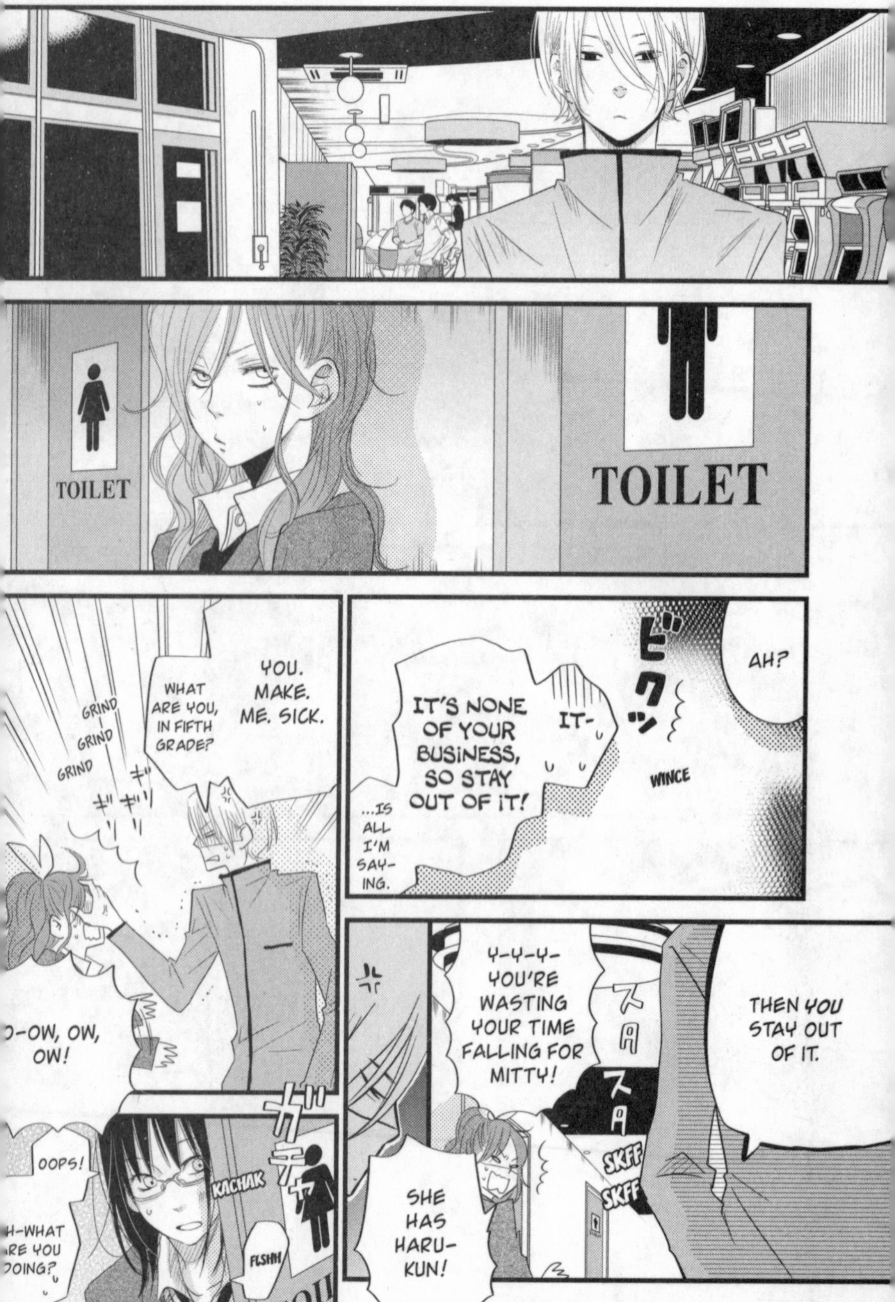
TOILET
TOILET
AH?
ビクッ
WINCE
IT-
IT'S NONE OF YOUR BUSINESS, SO STAY OUT OF IT!
...IS ALL I'M SAYING.
YOU. MAKE. ME. SICK.
WHAT ARE YOU, IN FIFTH GRADE?
GRIND GRIND GRIND
ギギギリ
O-OW, OW, OW!
THEN YOU STAY OUT OF IT.
スタスタ
Y-Y-Y-YOU'RE WASTING YOUR TIME FALLING FOR MITTY!
SKFF SKFF
SHE HAS HARU-KUN!
ガチャ
KACHAK
OOPS!
H-WHAT RE YOU OING?
FLSHH

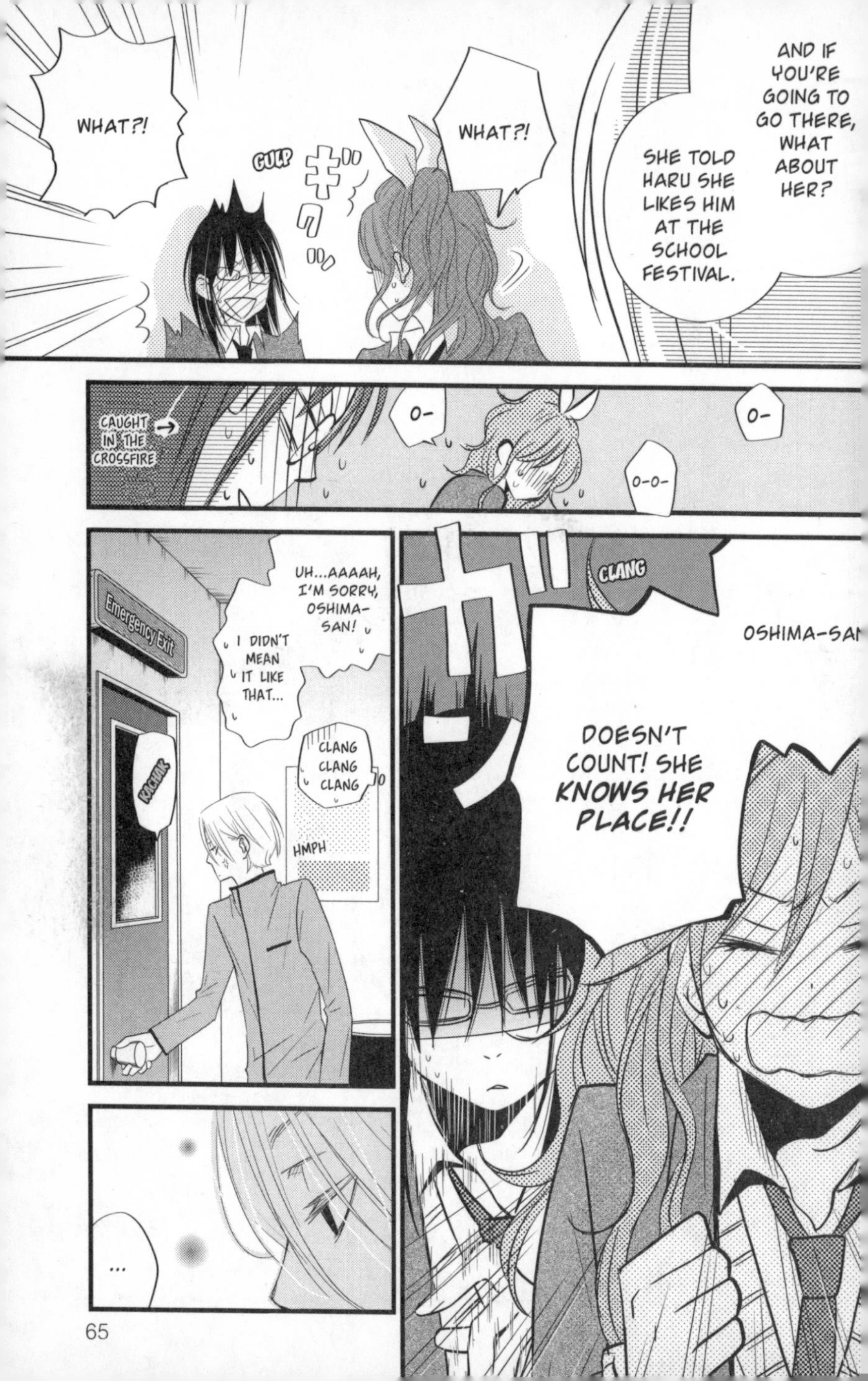
AND IF YOU'RE GOING TO GO THERE, WHAT ABOUT HER?
SHE TOLD HARU SHE LIKES HIM AT THE SCHOOL FESTIVAL.
WHAT?!
GULP
WHAT?!
O-
O-O-
O-
CAUGHT IN THE CROSSFIRE
CLANG
OSHIMA-SAN
DOESN'T COUNT! SHE KNOWS HER PLACE!!
UH...AAAAH, I'M SORRY, OSHIMA-SAN!
I DIDN'T MEAN IT LIKE THAT...
CLANG CLANG CLANG
Emergency Exit
KACHAK
HMPH
...

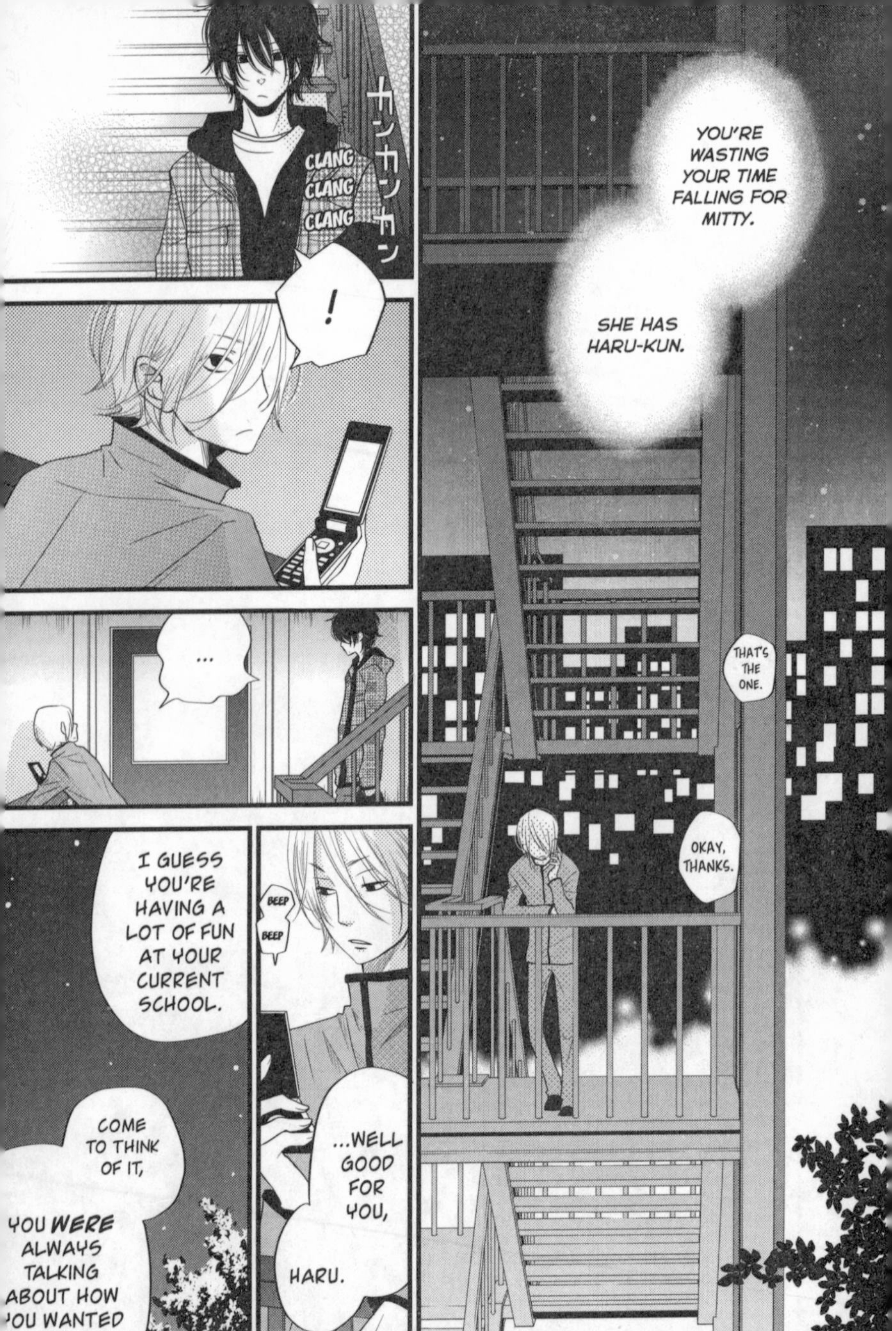
YOU'RE WASTING YOUR TIME FALLING FOR MITTY.
SHE HAS HARU-KUN.
THAT'S THE ONE.
OKAY, THANKS.
カンカンカン
CLANG CLANG CLANG
!
...
BEEP
BEEP
...WELL GOOD FOR YOU,
HARU.
I GUESS YOU'RE HAVING A LOT OF FUN AT YOUR CURRENT SCHOOL.
COME TO THINK OF IT,
YOU *WERE* ALWAYS TALKING ABOUT HOW YOU WANTED FRIENDS.

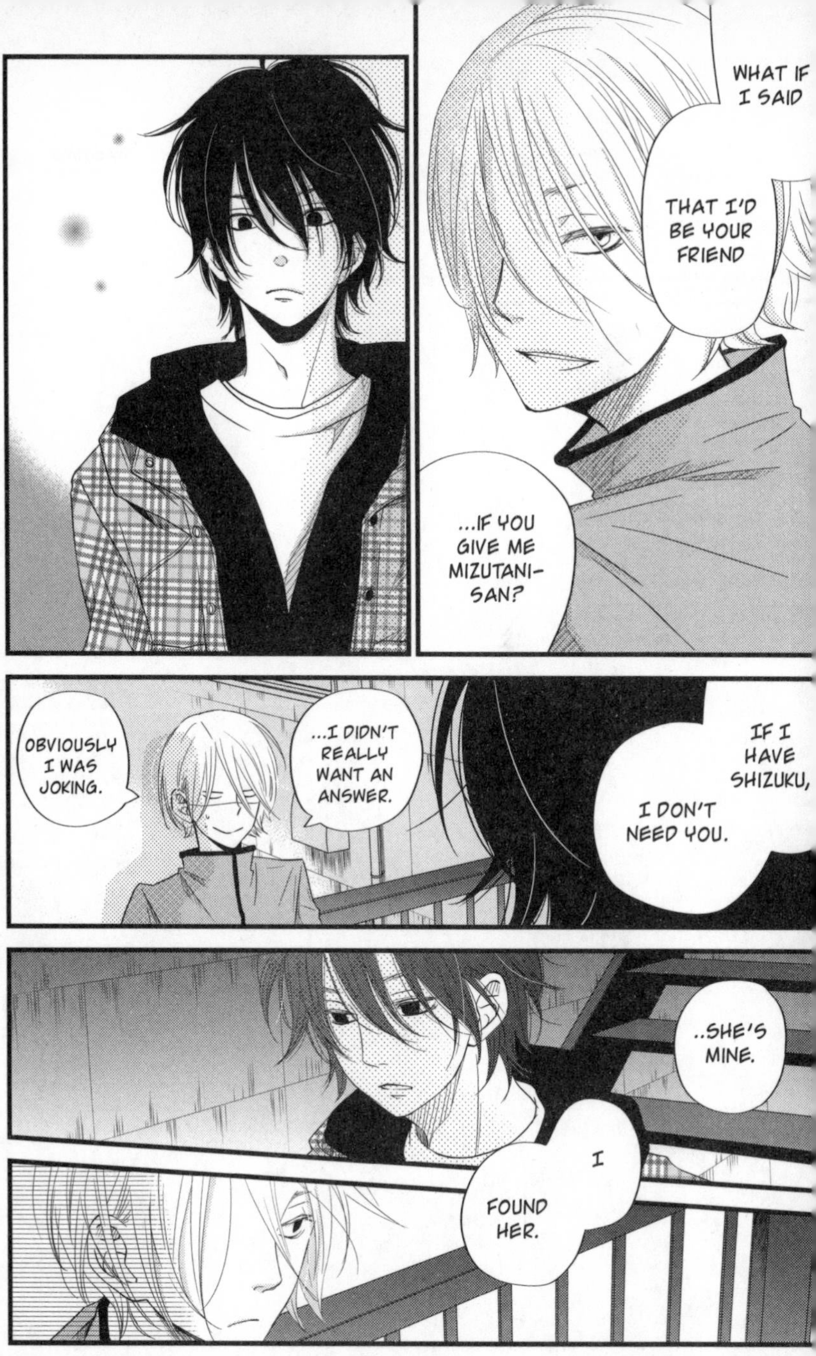
WHAT IF I SAID
THAT I'D BE YOUR FRIEND
...IF YOU GIVE ME MIZUTANI-SAN?
IF I HAVE SHIZUKU,
I DON'T NEED YOU.
...I DIDN'T REALLY WANT AN ANSWER.
OBVIOUSLY I WAS JOKING.
..SHE'S MINE.
I
FOUND HER.

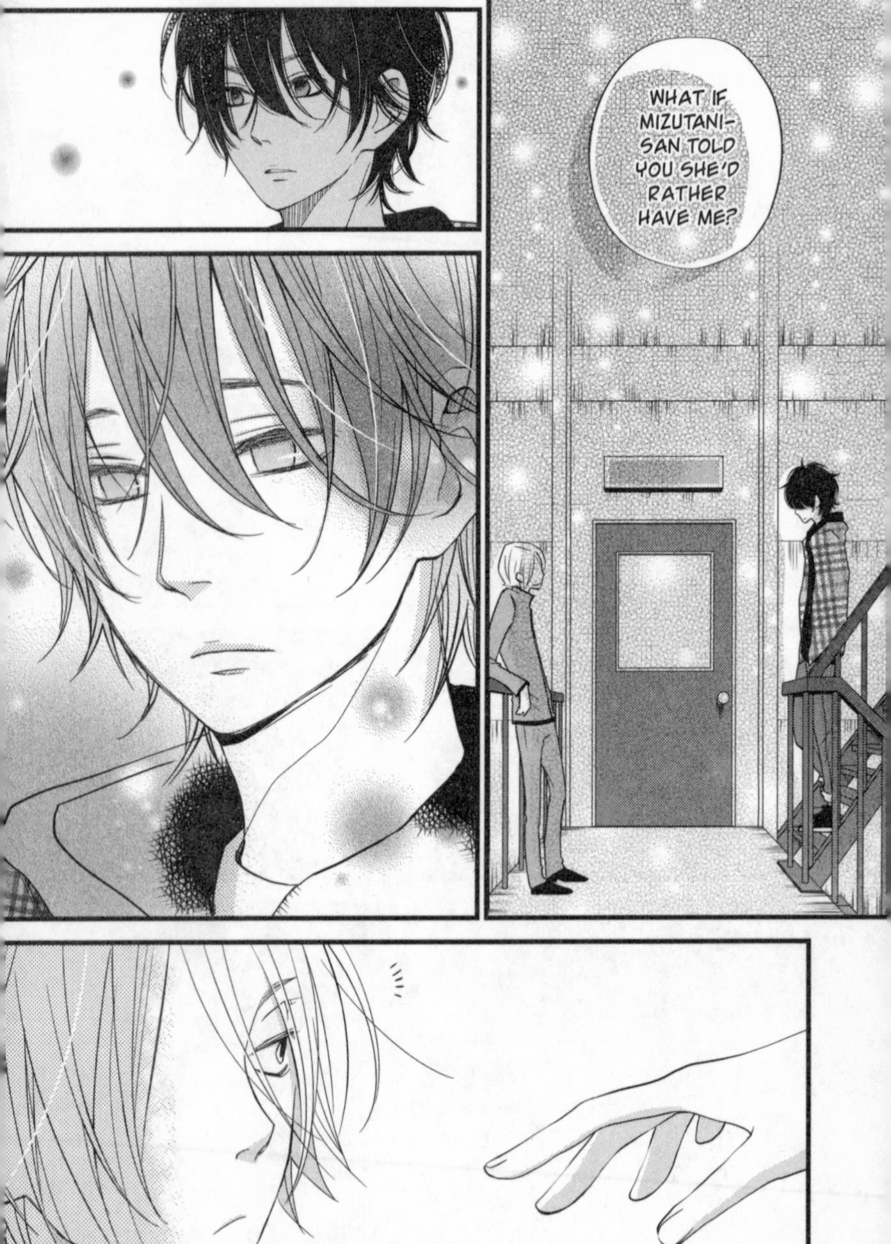
WHAT IF MIZUTANI-SAN TOLD YOU SHE'D RATHER HAVE ME?

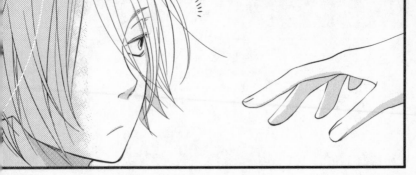

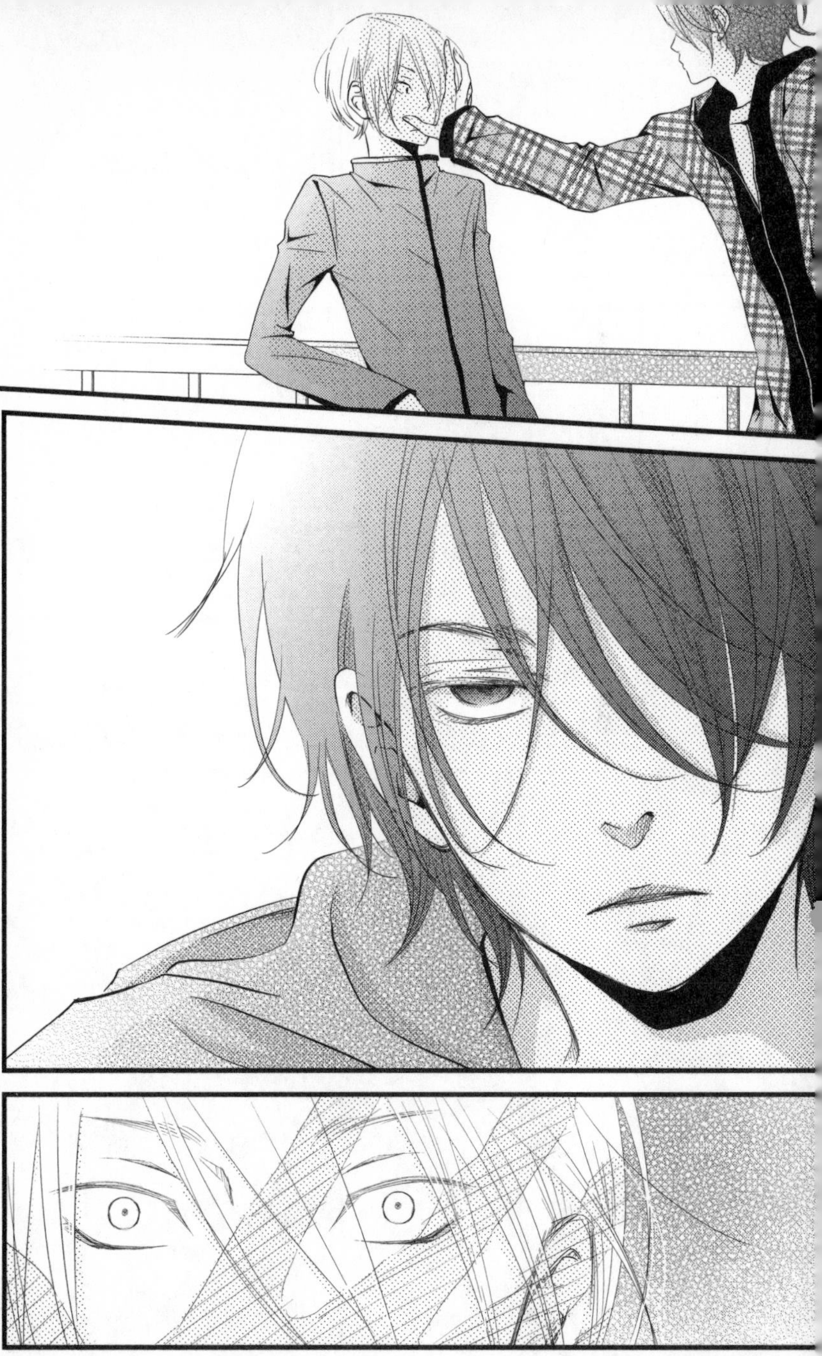

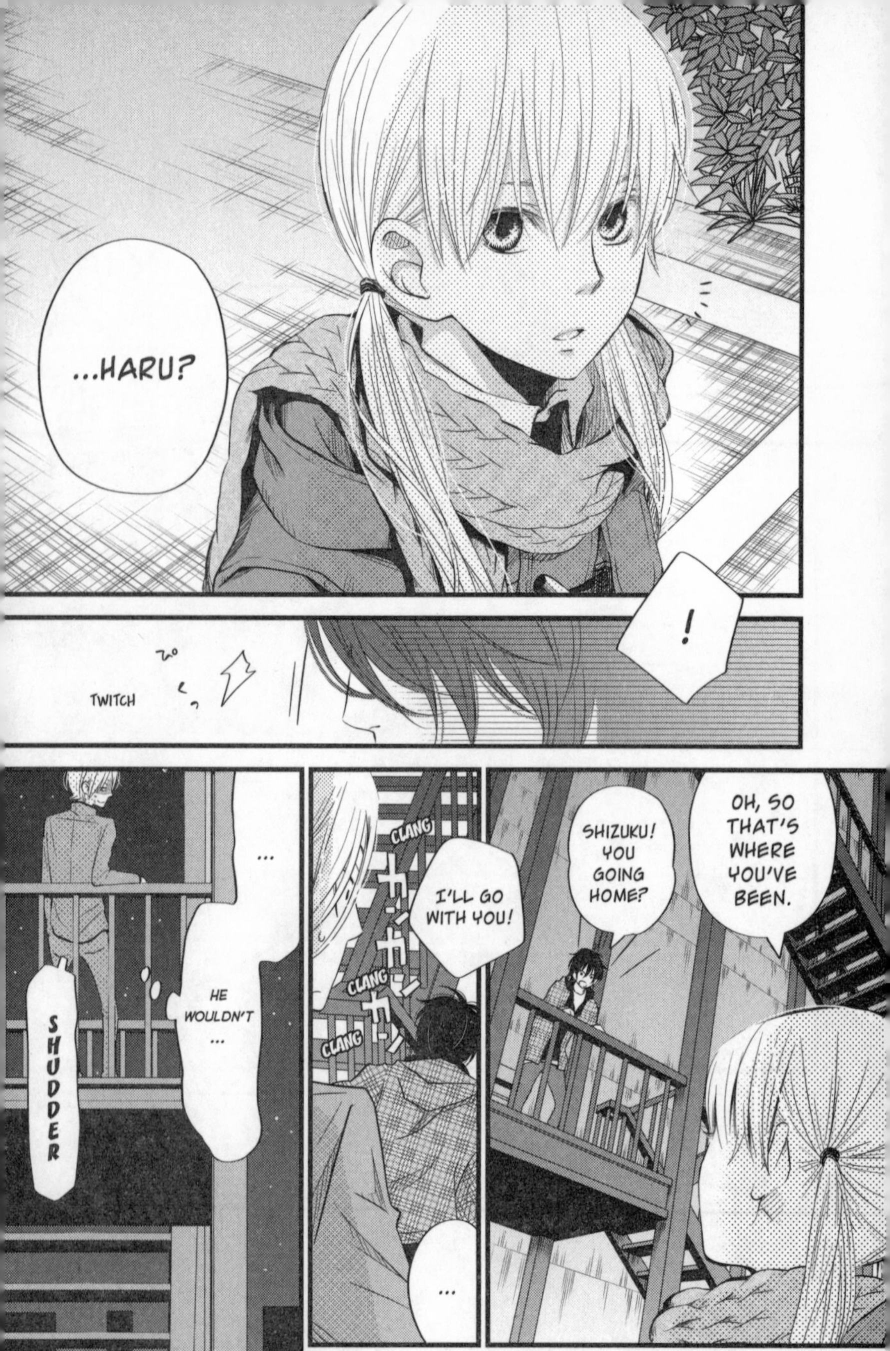
...HARU?
!
TWITCH
OH, SO THAT'S WHERE YOU'VE BEEN.
SHIZUKU! YOU GOING HOME?
CLANG
I'LL GO WITH YOU!
CLANG
CLANG
...
...
HE WOULDN'T ...
SHUDDER

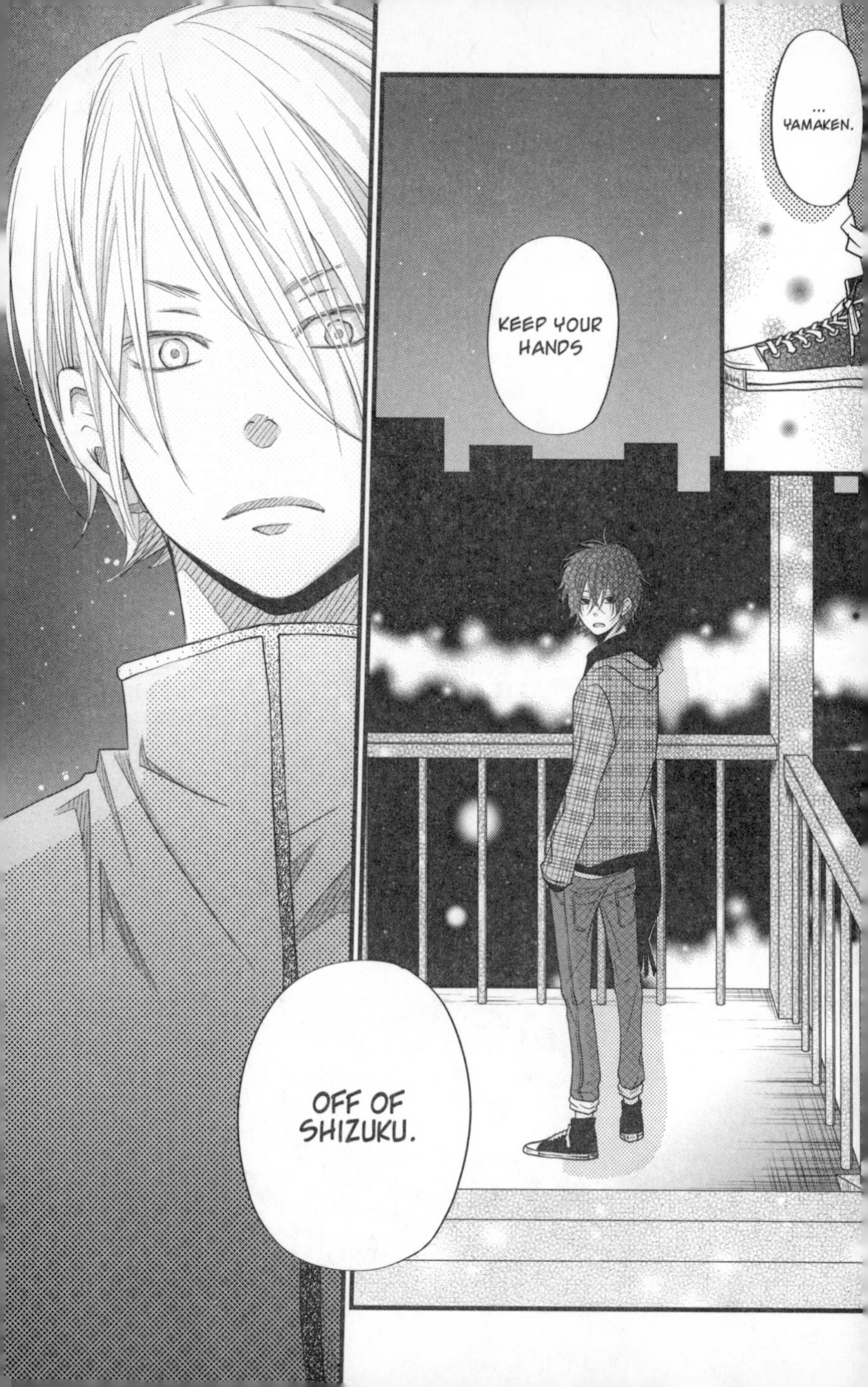

... YAMAKEN.
KEEP YOUR HANDS
OFF OF SHIZUKU.

...

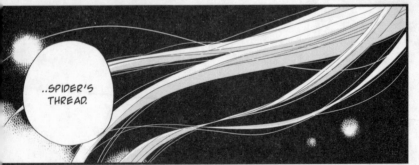

..SPIDER'S
THREAD.

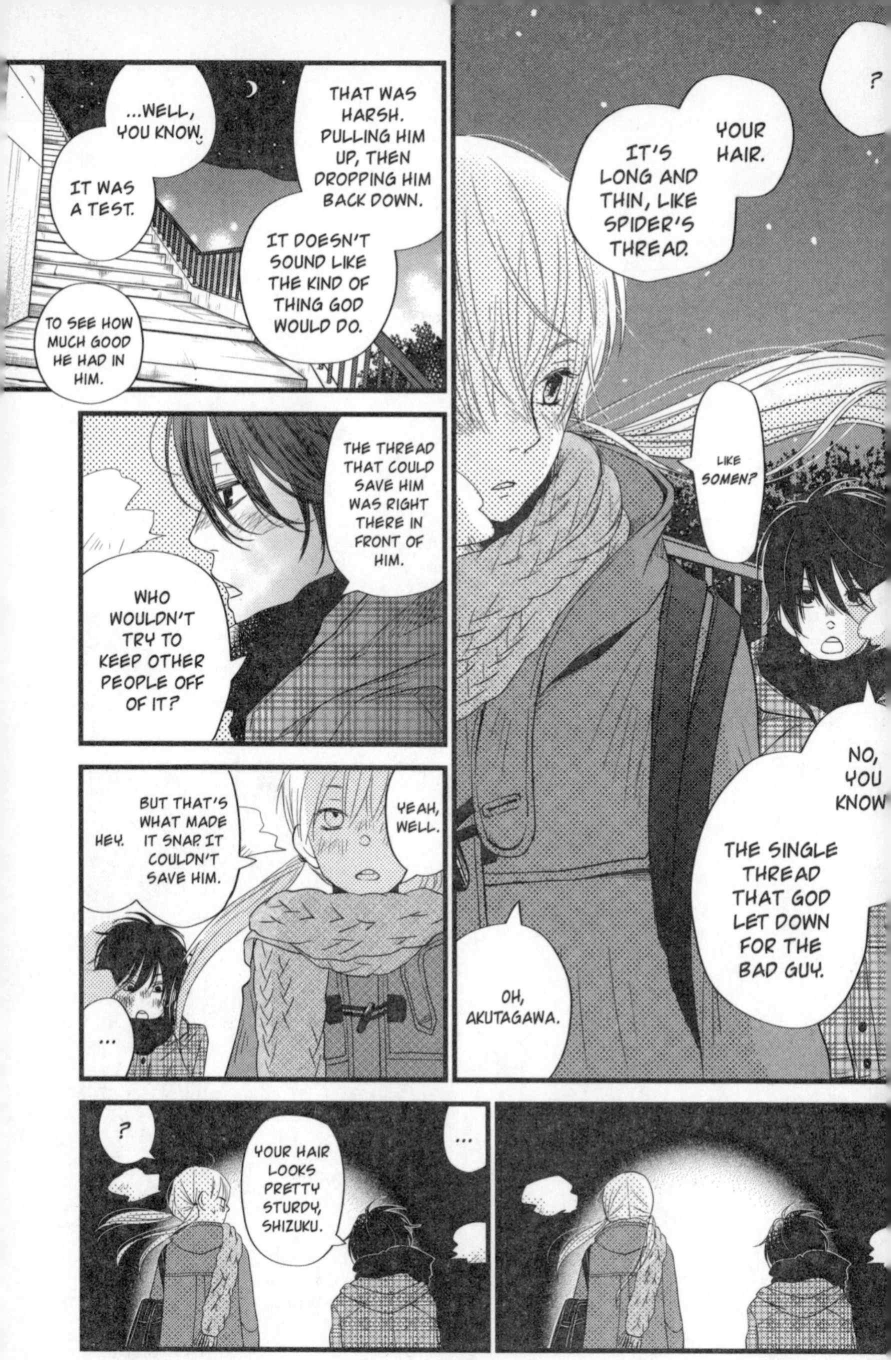
?
YOUR HAIR.
IT'S LONG AND THIN, LIKE SPIDER'S THREAD.
LIKE SOMEN?
NO, YOU KNOW
THE SINGLE THREAD THAT GOD LET DOWN FOR THE BAD GUY.
OH, AKUTAGAWA.
THAT WAS HARSH. PULLING HIM UP, THEN DROPPING HIM BACK DOWN.
...WELL, YOU KNOW.
IT DOESN'T SOUND LIKE THE KIND OF THING GOD WOULD DO.
IT WAS A TEST.
TO SEE HOW MUCH GOOD HE HAD IN HIM.
THE THREAD THAT COULD SAVE HIM WAS RIGHT THERE IN FRONT OF HIM.
WHO WOULDN'T TRY TO KEEP OTHER PEOPLE OFF OF IT?
YEAH, WELL.
BUT THAT'S WHAT MADE IT SNAP. IT COULDN'T SAVE HIM.
HEY.
...
...
YOUR HAIR LOOKS PRETTY STURDY, SHIZUKU.
?

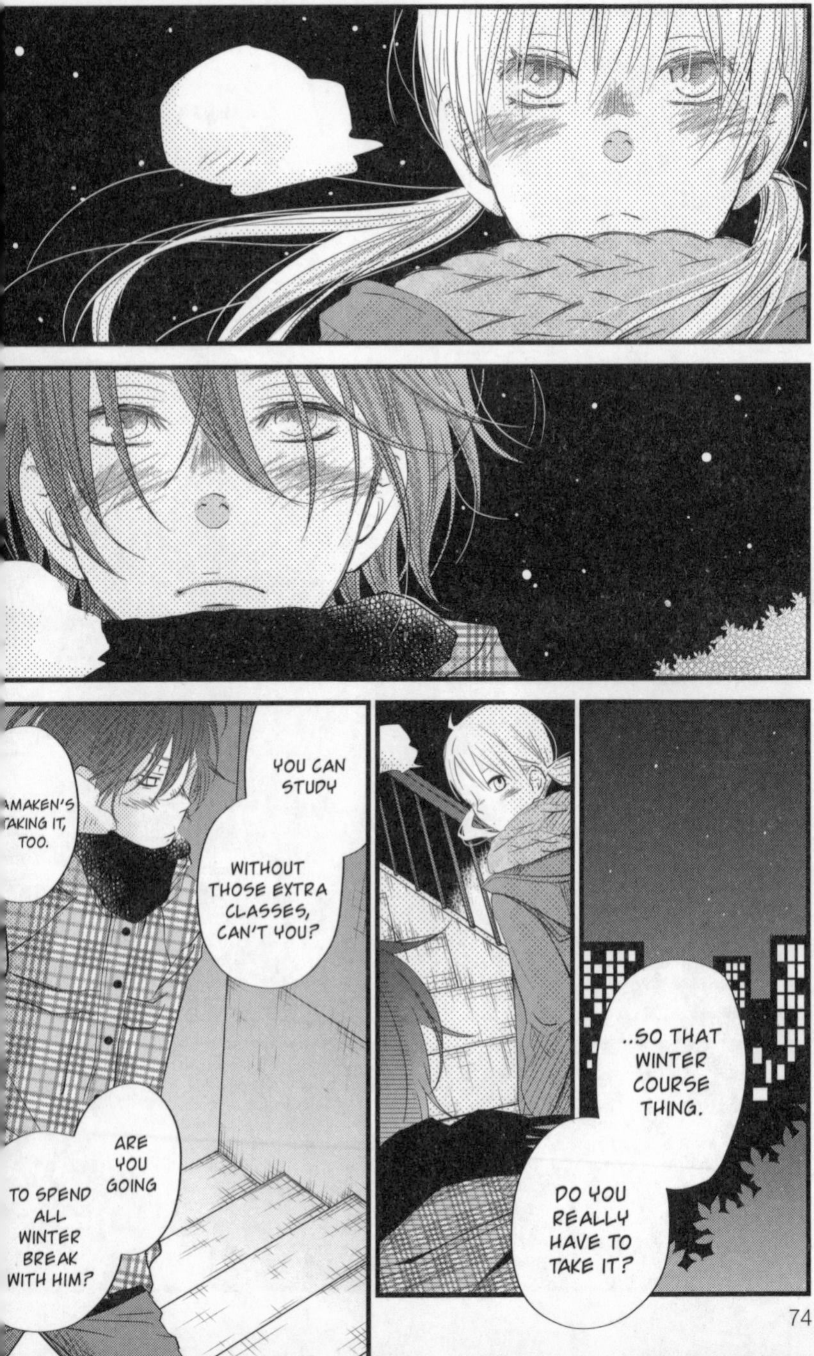
..SO THAT WINTER COURSE THING.
DO YOU REALLY HAVE TO TAKE IT?
YOU CAN STUDY
WITHOUT THOSE EXTRA CLASSES, CAN'T YOU?
AMAKEN'S TAKING IT, TOO.
ARE YOU GOING
TO SPEND ALL WINTER BREAK WITH HIM?

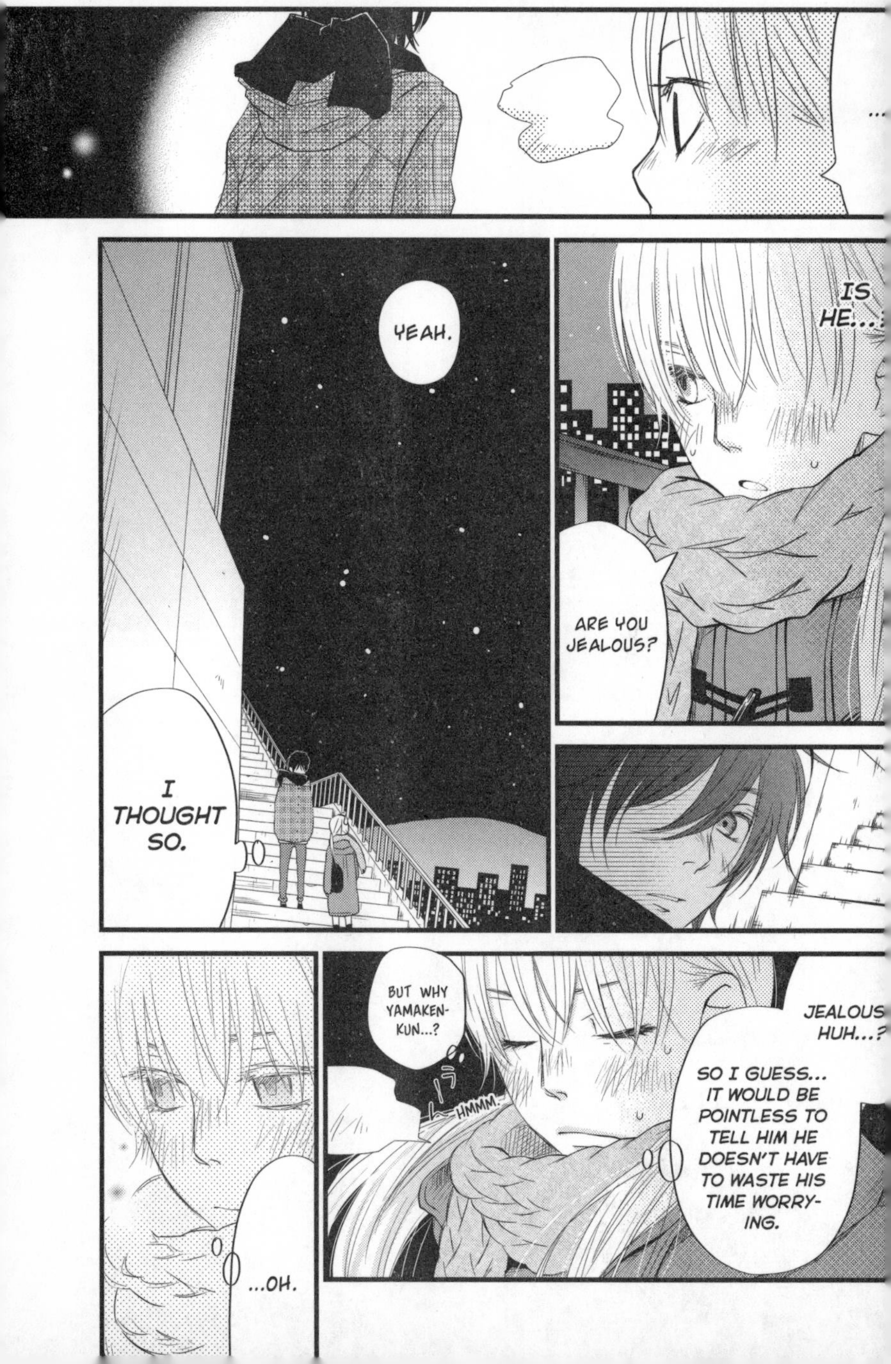
...
IS HE...?
ARE YOU JEALOUS?
YEAH.
I THOUGHT SO.
JEALOUS HUH...?
SO I GUESS... IT WOULD BE POINTLESS TO TELL HIM HE DOESN'T HAVE TO WASTE HIS TIME WORRY-ING.
BUT WHY YAMAKEN-KUN...?
HMMM.
...OH.

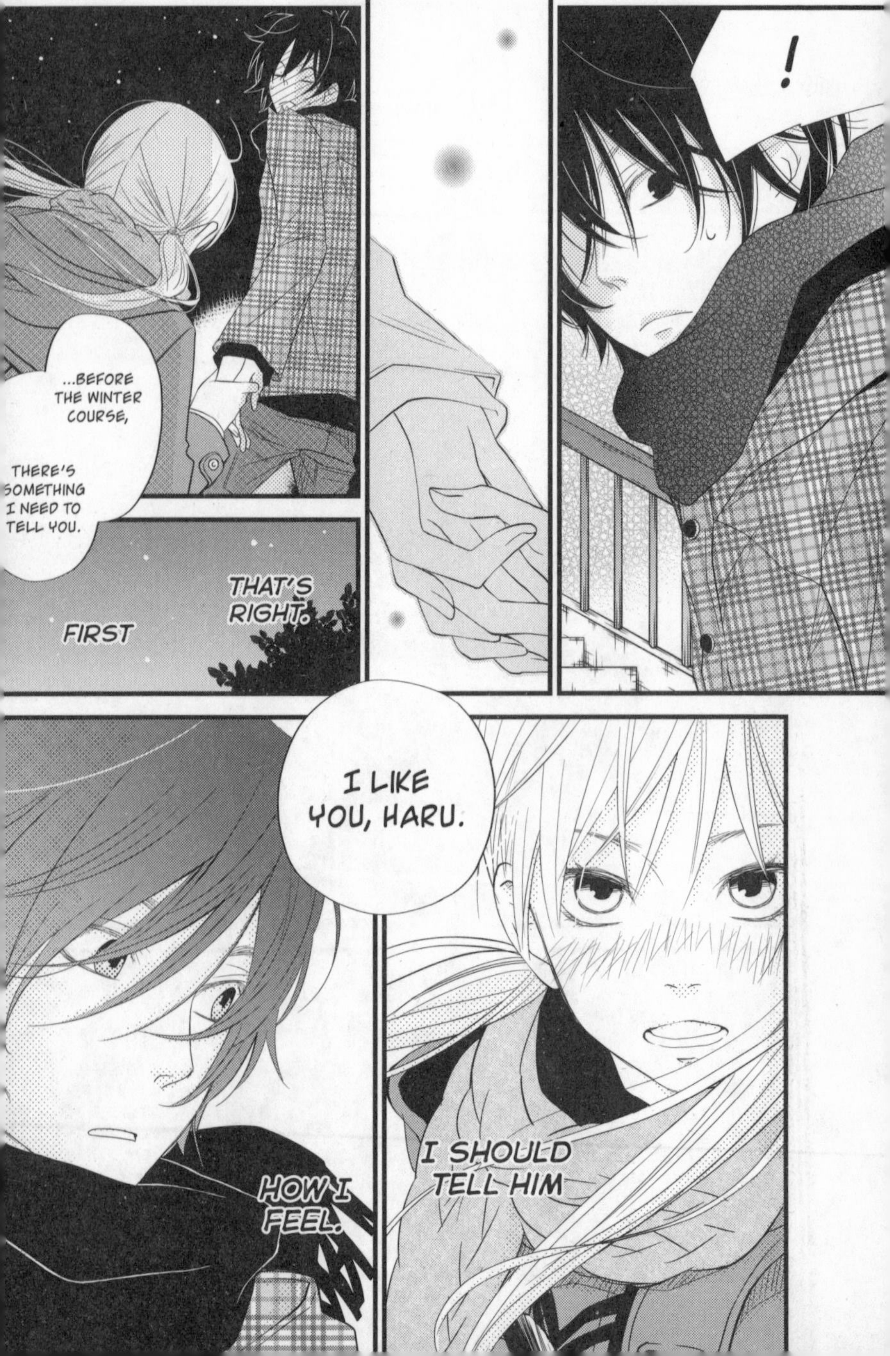
!
...BEFORE THE WINTER COURSE,
THERE'S SOMETHING I NEED TO TELL YOU.
THAT'S RIGHT.
FIRST
I LIKE YOU, HARU.
I SHOULD TELL HIM
HOW I FEEL.

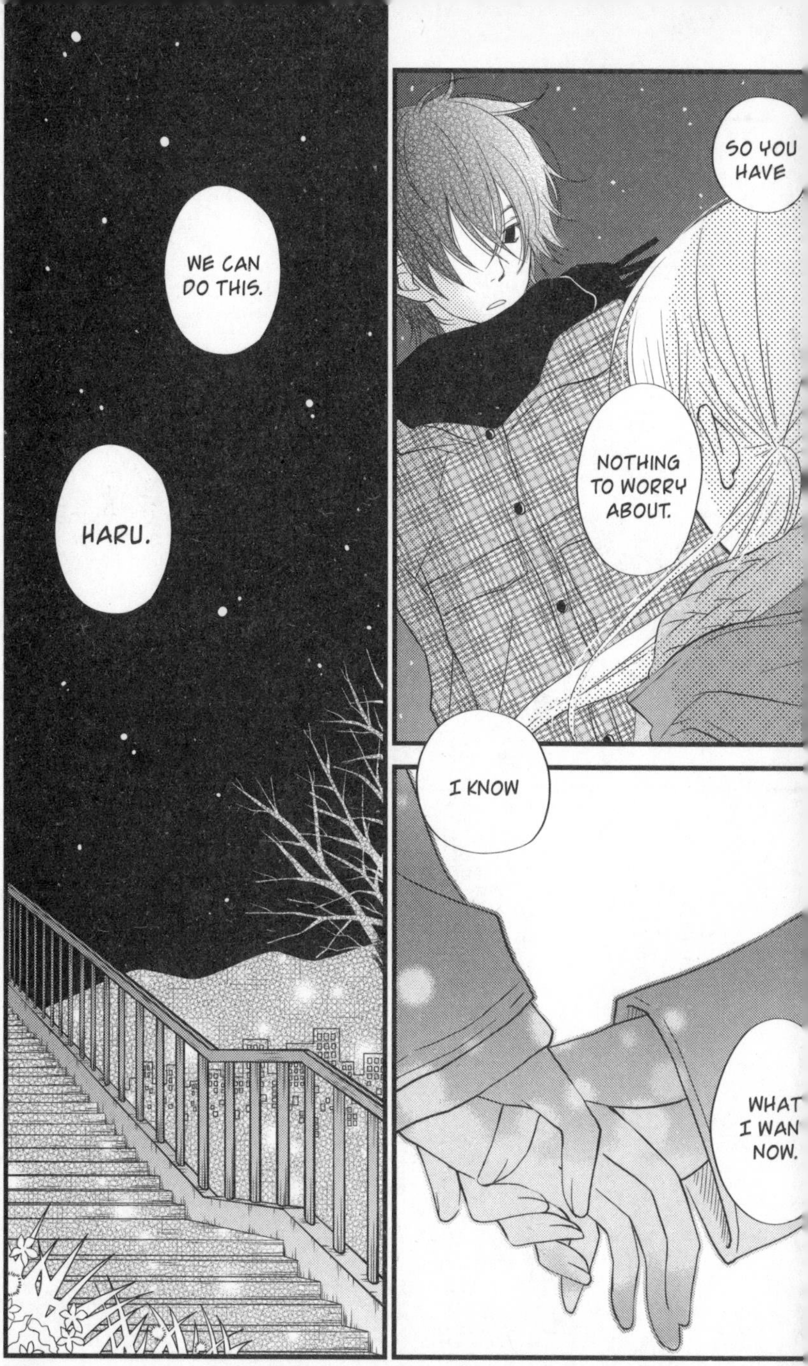
SO YOU HAVE
NOTHING TO WORRY ABOUT.
I KNOW
WHAT I WAN NOW.
WE CAN DO THIS.
HARU.

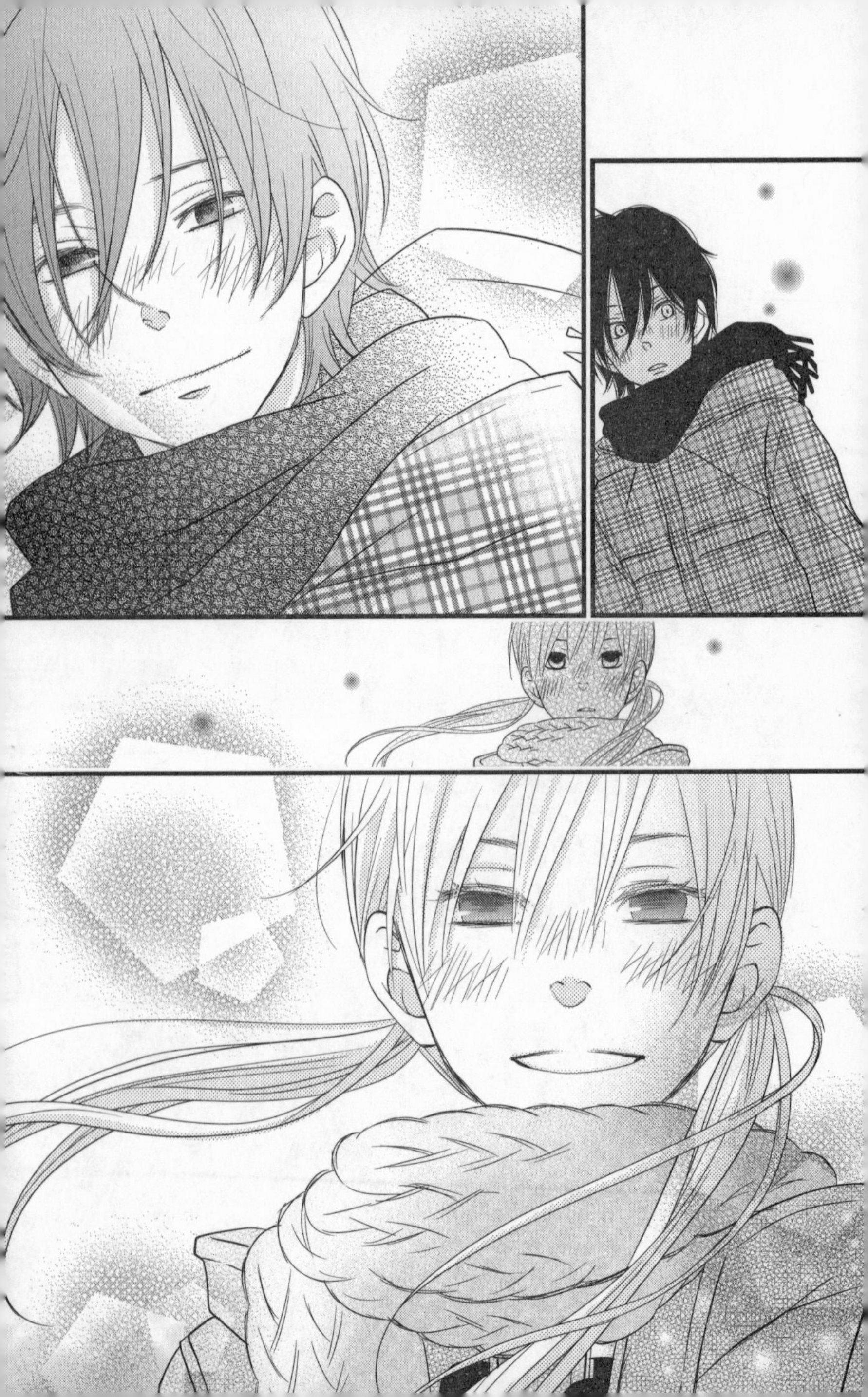

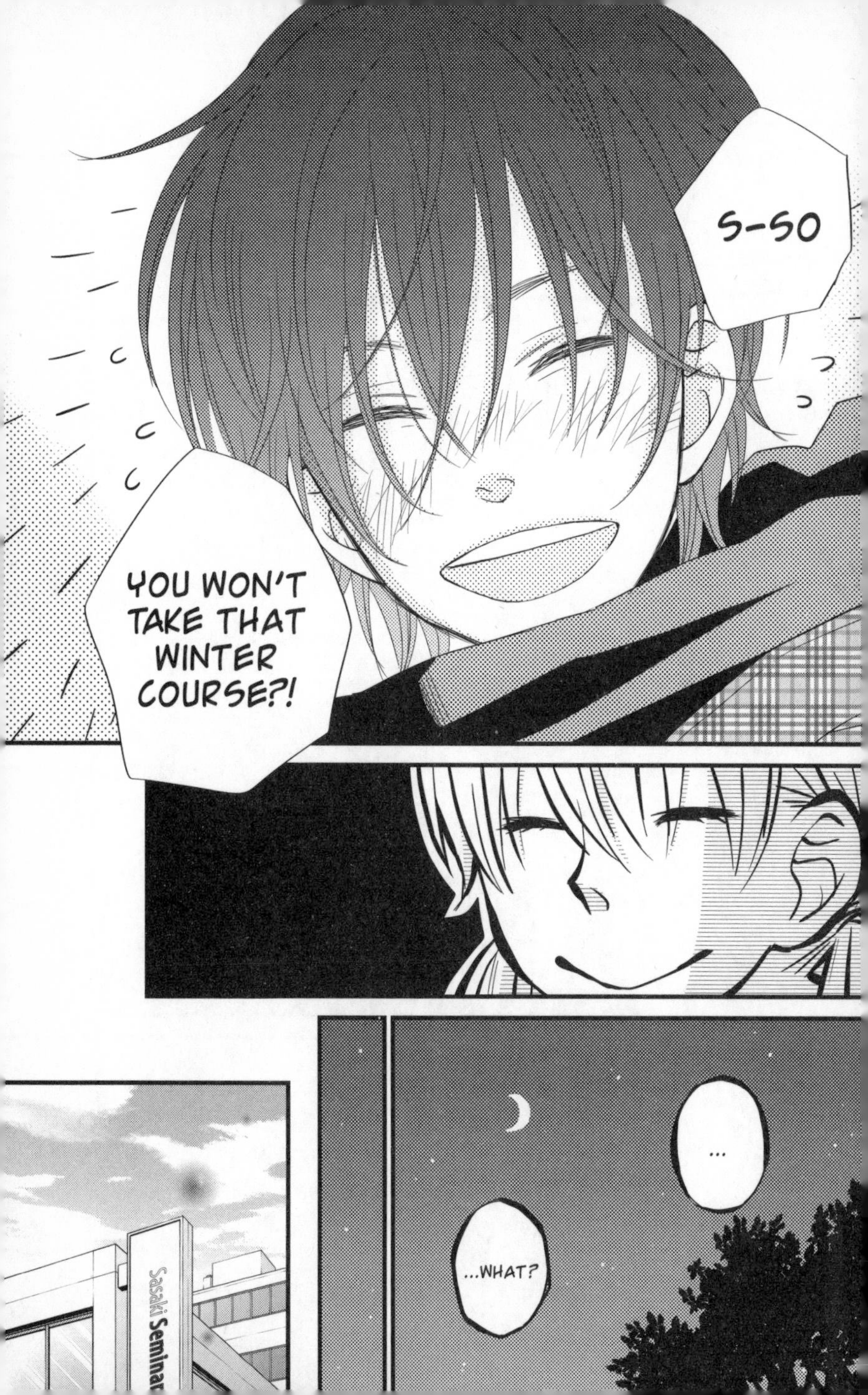
S-SO
YOU WON'T TAKE THAT WINTER COURSE?!
...
...WHAT?
Sasaki Seminar

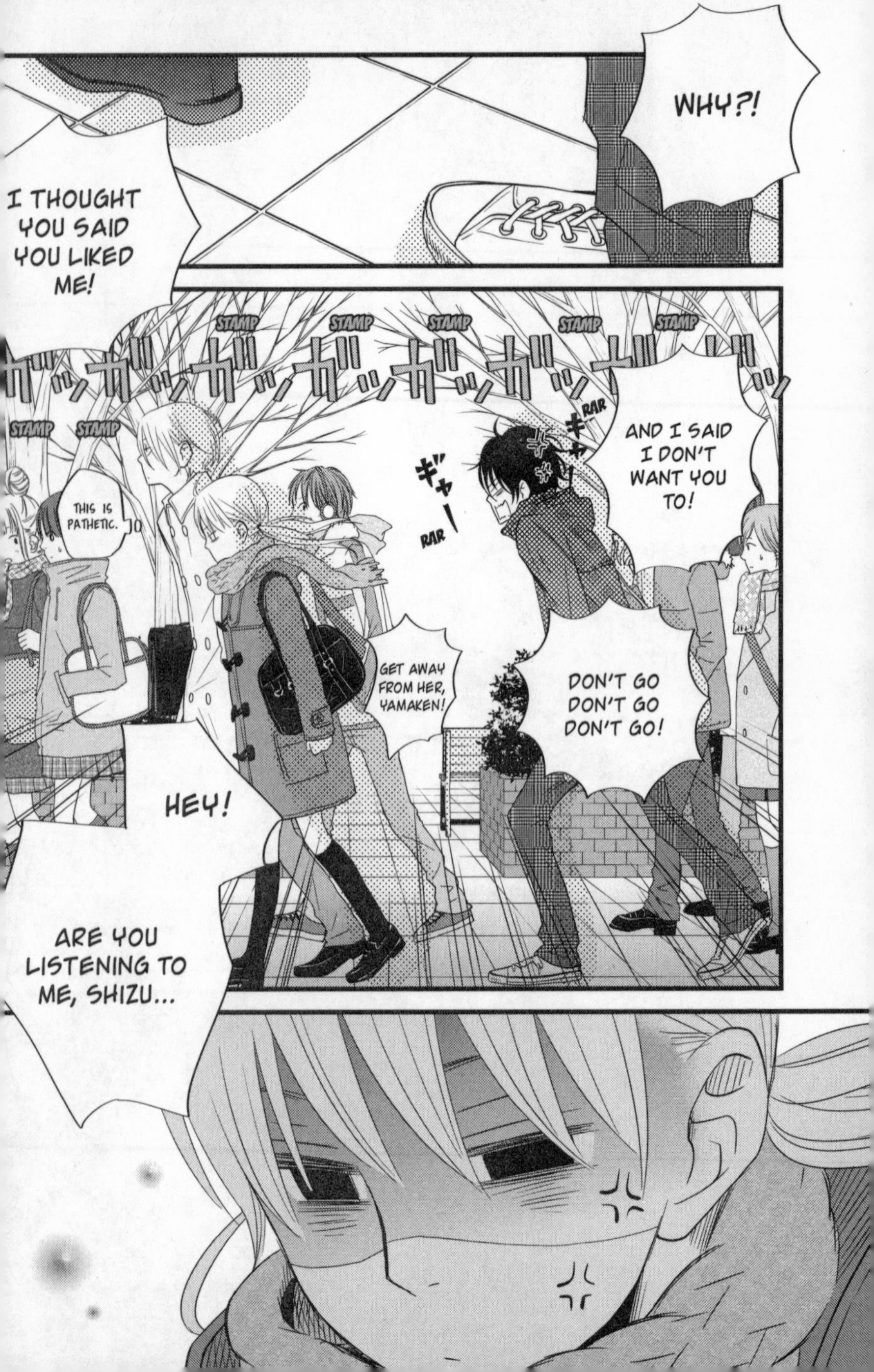
WHY?!
I THOUGHT YOU SAID YOU LIKED ME!
STAMP STAMP STAMP STAMP STAMP STAMP STAMP
AND I SAID I DON'T WANT YOU TO!
RAR
ギャー
RAR
DON'T GO DON'T GO DON'T GO!
GET AWAY FROM HER, YAMAKEN!
THIS IS PATHETIC.
HEY!
ARE YOU LISTENING TO ME, SHIZU...

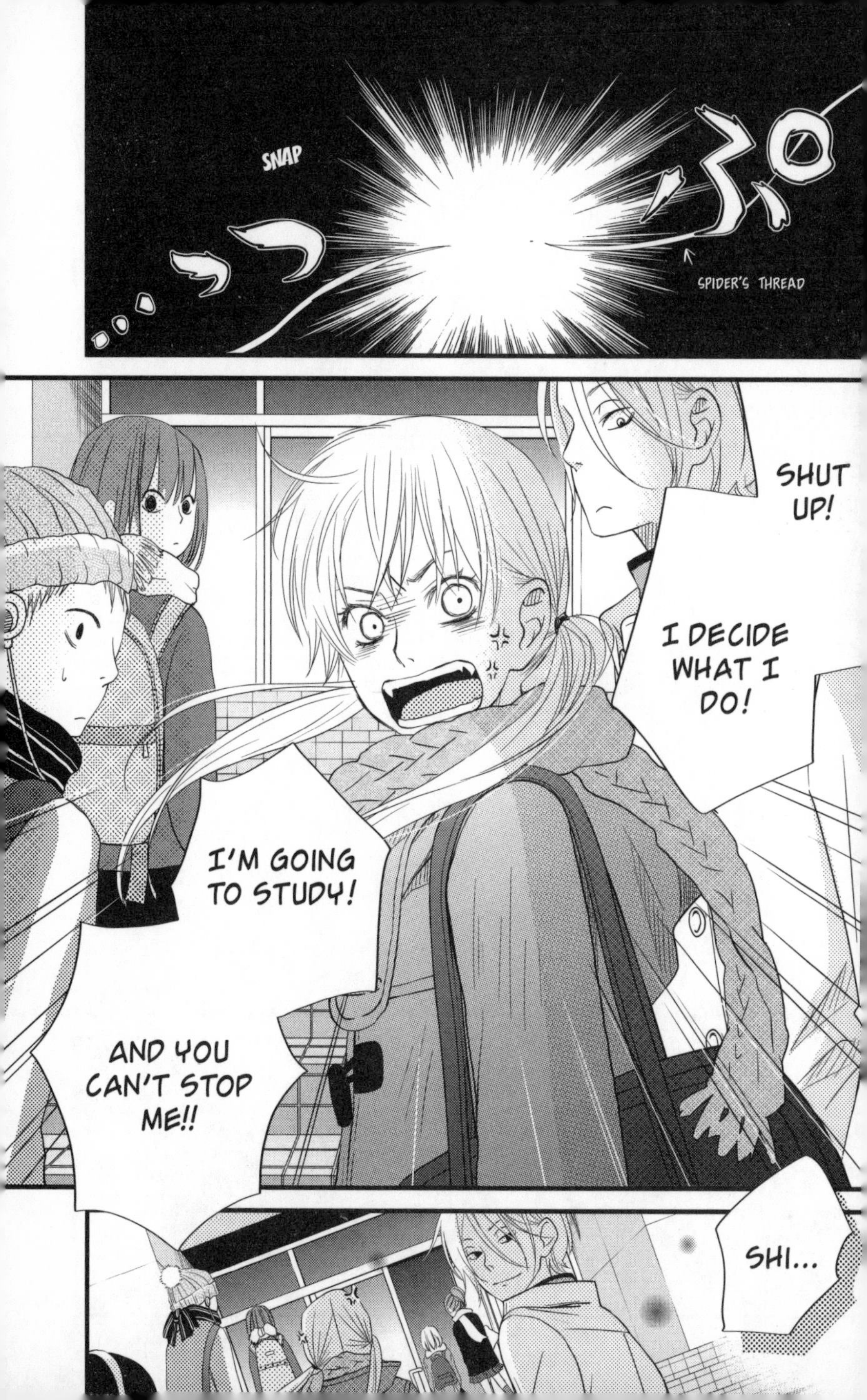
SPIDER'S THREAD
SNAP
SHUT UP!
I DECIDE WHAT I DO!
I'M GOING TO STUDY!
AND YOU CAN'T STOP ME!!
SHI...

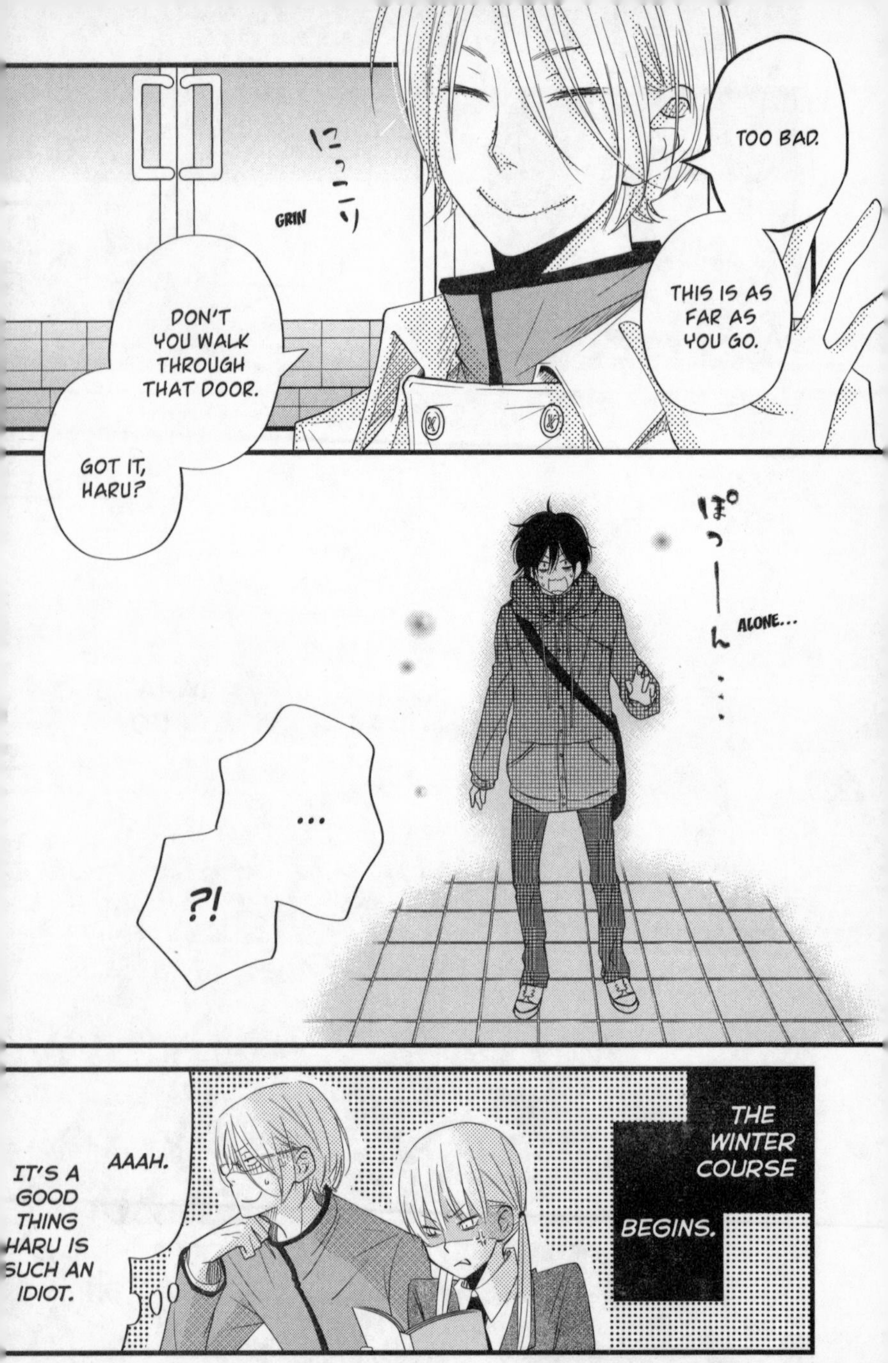
TOO BAD.
にっこり
GRIN
THIS IS AS FAR AS YOU GO.
DON'T YOU WALK THROUGH THAT DOOR.
GOT IT, HARU?
ぽつーん…
ALONE...
...
?!
THE WINTER COURSE BEGINS.
AAAH.
IT'S A GOOD THING HARU IS SUCH AN IDIOT.

Let's Party

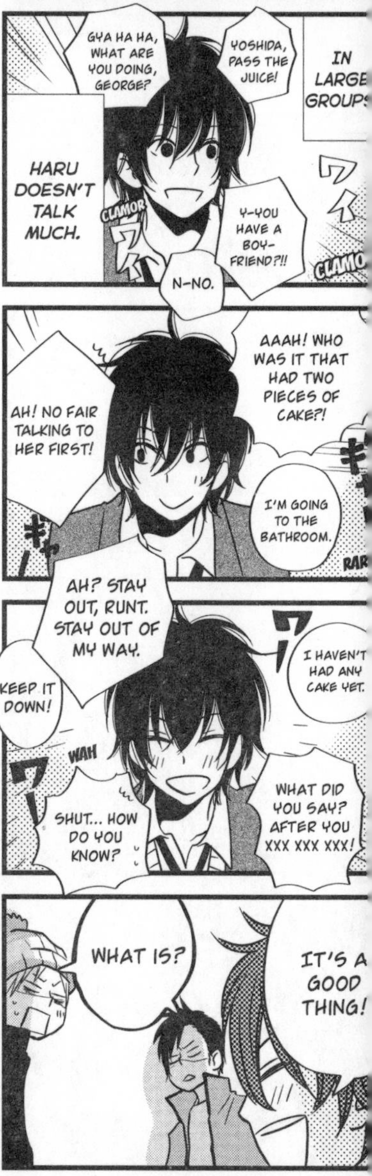
IN LARGE GROUPS
YOSHIDA, PASS THE JUICE!
GYA HA HA, WHAT ARE YOU DOING, GEORGE?
CLAMOR
Y-YOU HAVE A BOY-FRIEND?!!
HARU DOESN'T TALK MUCH.
CLAMOR
N-NO.
AAAH! WHO WAS IT THAT HAD TWO PIECES OF CAKE?!
AH! NO FAIR TALKING TO HER FIRST!
I'M GOING TO THE BATHROOM.
I HAVEN'T HAD ANY CAKE YET.
AH? STAY OUT, RUNT. STAY OUT OF MY WAY.
KEEP IT DOWN!
WAH
WHAT DID YOU SAY? AFTER YOU XXX XXX XXX!
SHUT... HOW DO YOU KNOW?
IT'S A GOOD THING!
WHAT IS?

Gestalt Collapse

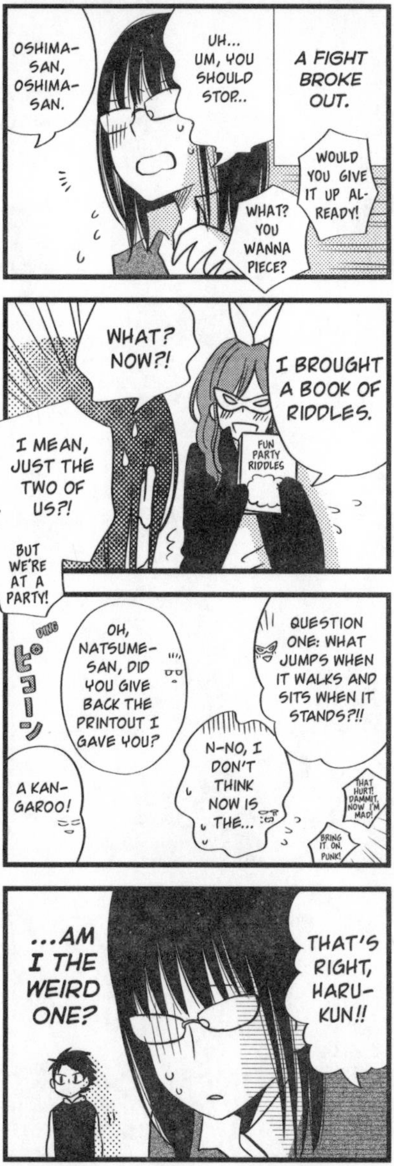
A FIGHT BROKE OUT.
UH... UM, YOU SHOULD STOP...
OSHIMA-SAN, OSHIMA-SAN.
WOULD YOU GIVE IT UP AL-READY!
WHAT? YOU WANNA PIECE?
I BROUGHT A BOOK OF RIDDLES.
WHAT? NOW?!
FUN PARTY RIDDLES
I MEAN, JUST THE TWO OF US?!
BUT WE'RE AT A PARTY!
QUESTION ONE: WHAT JUMPS WHEN IT WALKS AND SITS WHEN IT STANDS?!!
OH, NATSUME-SAN, DID YOU GIVE BACK THE PRINTOUT I GAVE YOU?
DING
N-NO, I DON'T THINK NOW IS THE...
THAT HURT! DAMMIT, NOW I'M MAD!
BRING IT ON, PUNK!
A KAN-GAROO!
THAT'S RIGHT, HARU-KUN!!
...AM I THE WEIRD ONE?

Normal

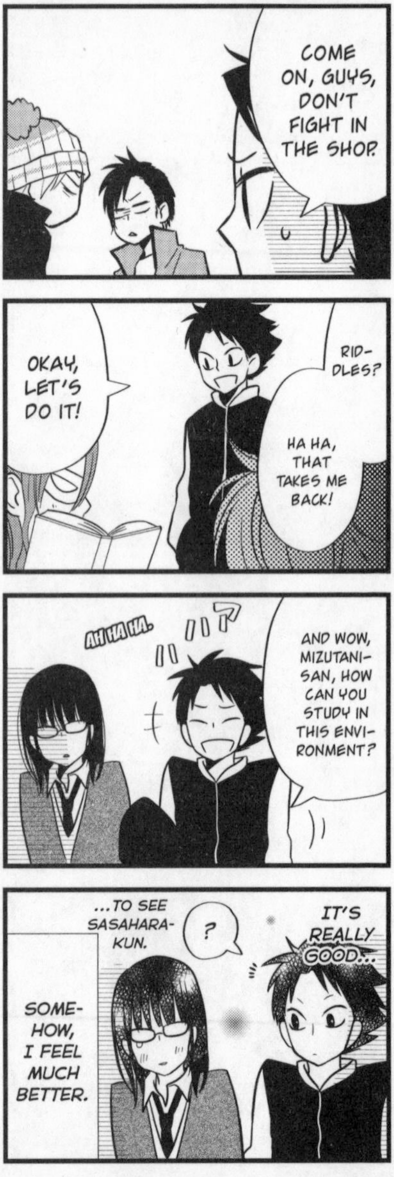
COME ON, GUYS, DON'T FIGHT IN THE SHOP.
RID-DLES?
HA HA, THAT TAKES ME BACK!
OKAY, LET'S DO IT!
AND WOW, MIZUTANI-SAN, HOW CAN YOU STUDY IN THIS ENVIRONMENT?
AH HA HA.
IT'S REALLY GOOD...
...TO SEE SASAHARA-KUN.
?
SOME-HOW, I FEEL MUCH BETTER.

Mitchan's Anti-Haru Lecture

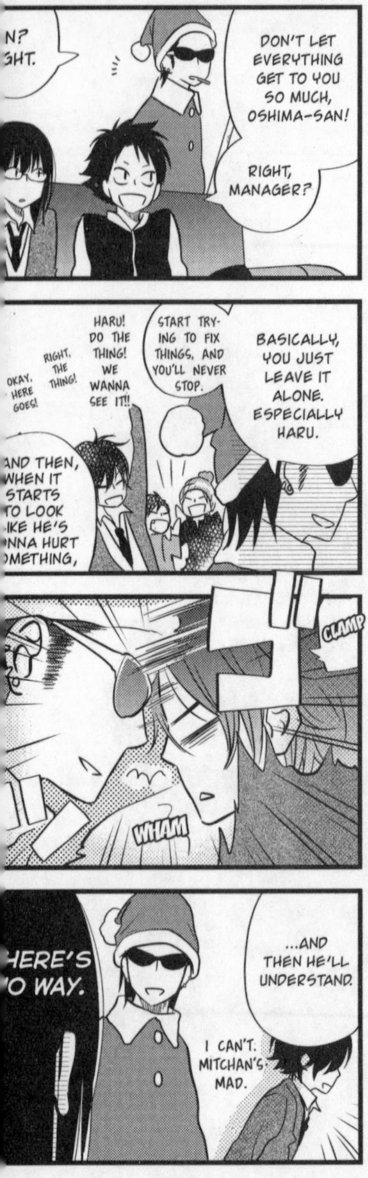
DON'T LET EVERYTHING GET TO YOU SO MUCH, OSHIMA-SAN!
RIGHT, MANAGER?
N? GHT.
BASICALLY, YOU JUST LEAVE IT ALONE. ESPECIALLY HARU.
START TRY-ING TO FIX THINGS, AND YOU'LL NEVER STOP.
HARU! DO THE THING! WE WANNA SEE IT!!
RIGHT, THE THING!
OKAY, HERE GOES!
AND THEN, WHEN IT STARTS TO LOOK IKE HE'S NNA HURT OMETHING,
CLAMP
WHAM
...AND THEN HE'LL UNDERSTAND.
I CAN'T. MITCHAN'S MAD.
HERE'S O WAY.

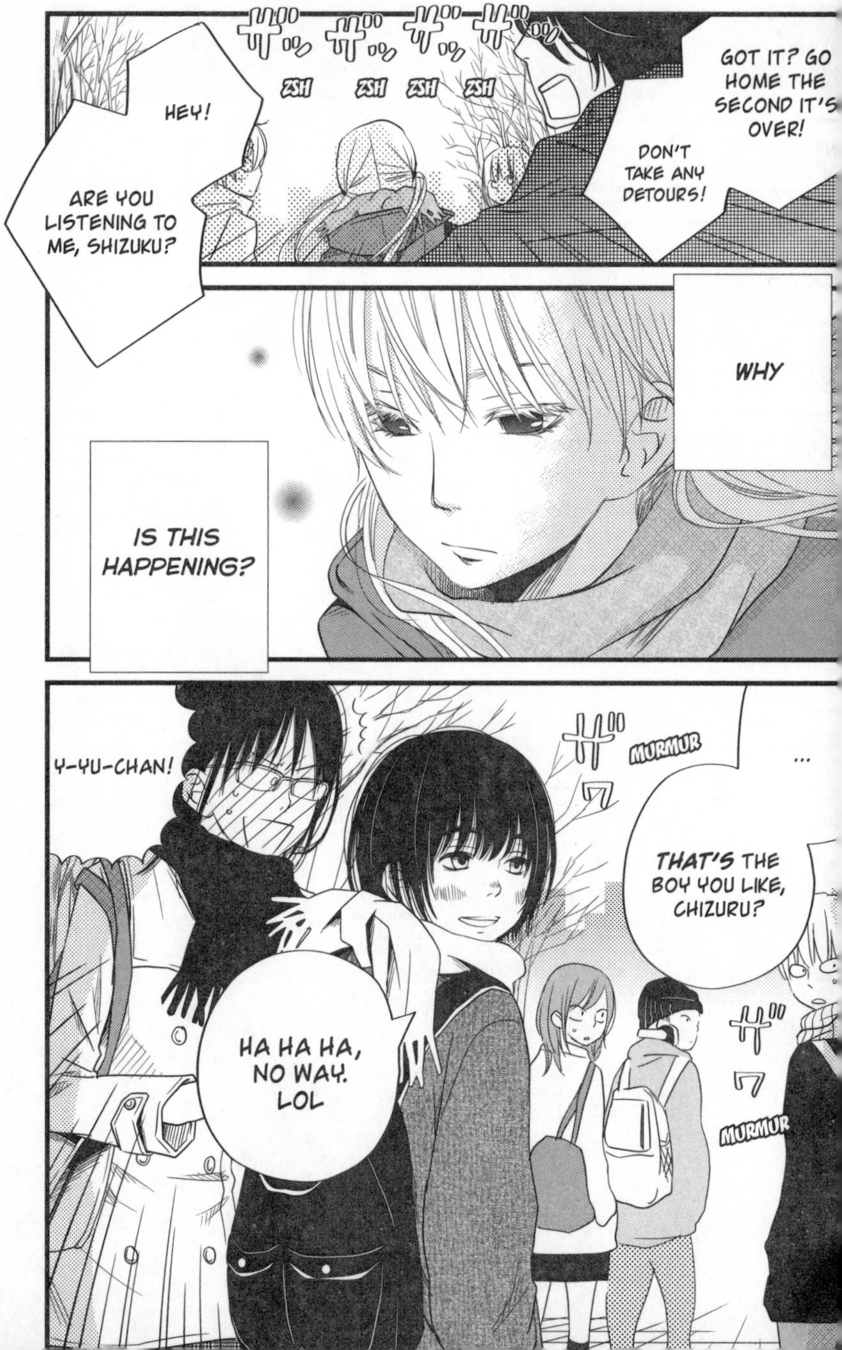
GOT IT? GO HOME THE SECOND IT'S OVER!
DON'T TAKE ANY DETOURS!
ZSH ZSH ZSH ZSH
HEY!
ARE YOU LISTENING TO ME, SHIZUKU?
WHY
IS THIS HAPPENING?
...
THAT'S THE BOY YOU LIKE, CHIZURU?
MURMUR
MURMUR
HA HA HA, NO WAY. LOL
Y-YU-CHAN!

Chapter 15 Kenji-kun, the Yamaguchis' Boy

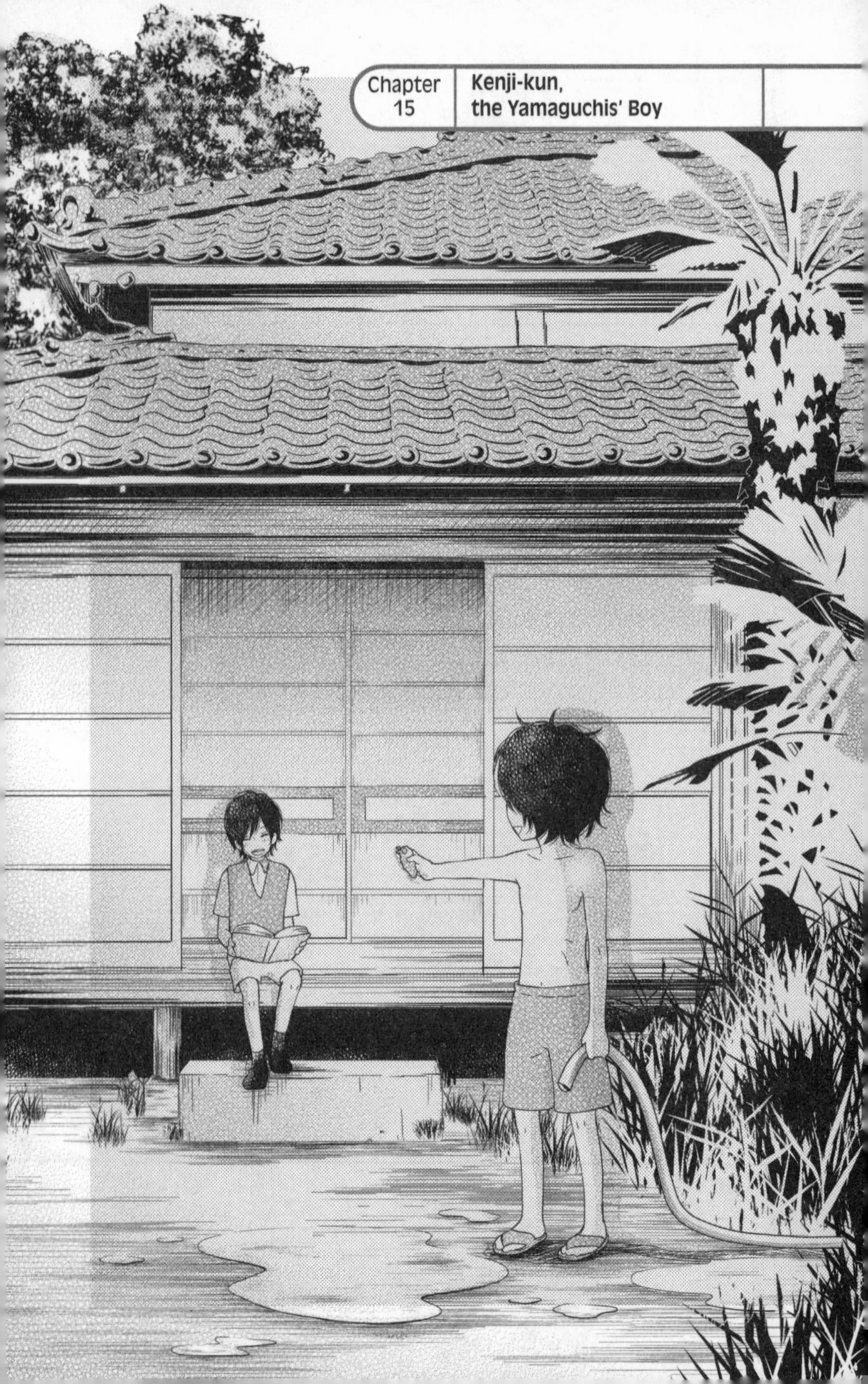

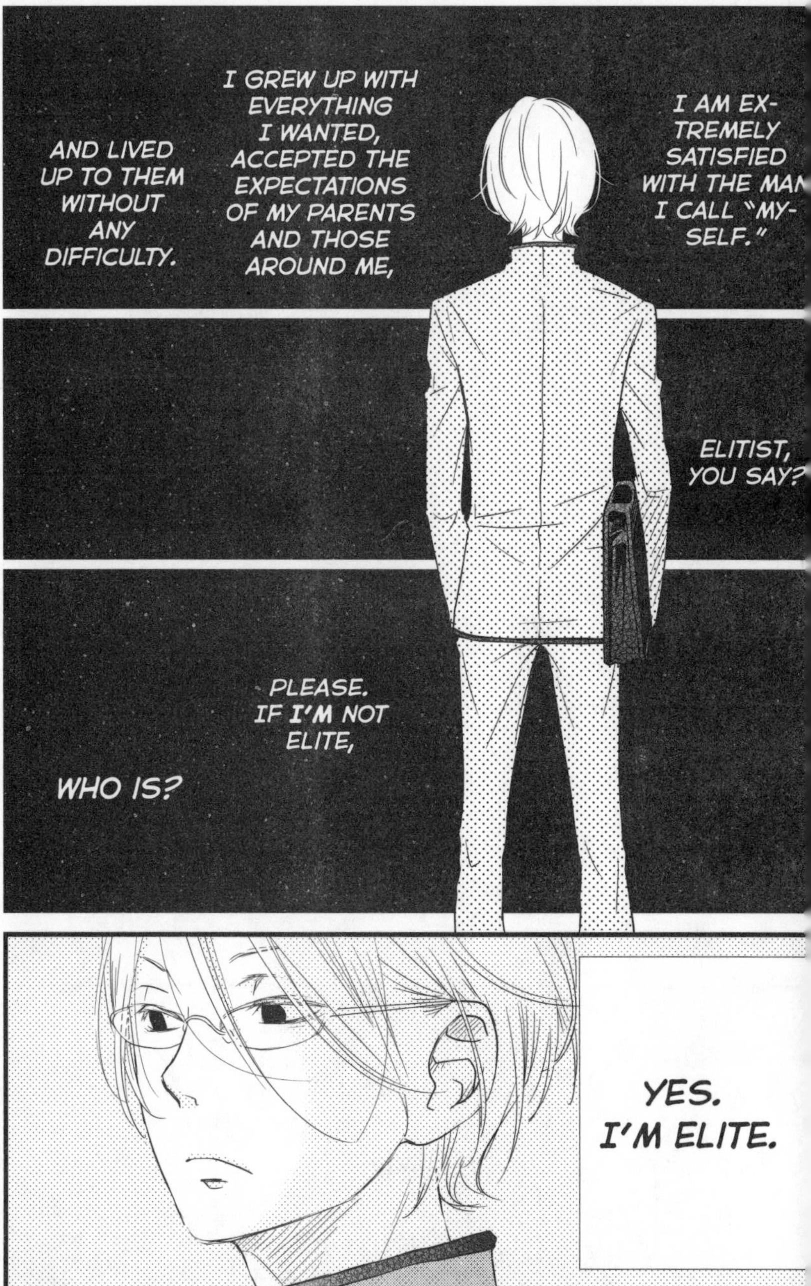
I AM EXTREMELY SATISFIED WITH THE MAN I CALL "MYSELF."
I GREW UP WITH EVERYTHING I WANTED, ACCEPTED THE EXPECTATIONS OF MY PARENTS AND THOSE AROUND ME,
AND LIVED UP TO THEM WITHOUT ANY DIFFICULTY.
ELITIST, YOU SAY?
PLEASE. IF **I'M** NOT ELITE,
WHO IS?
YES. I'M ELITE.

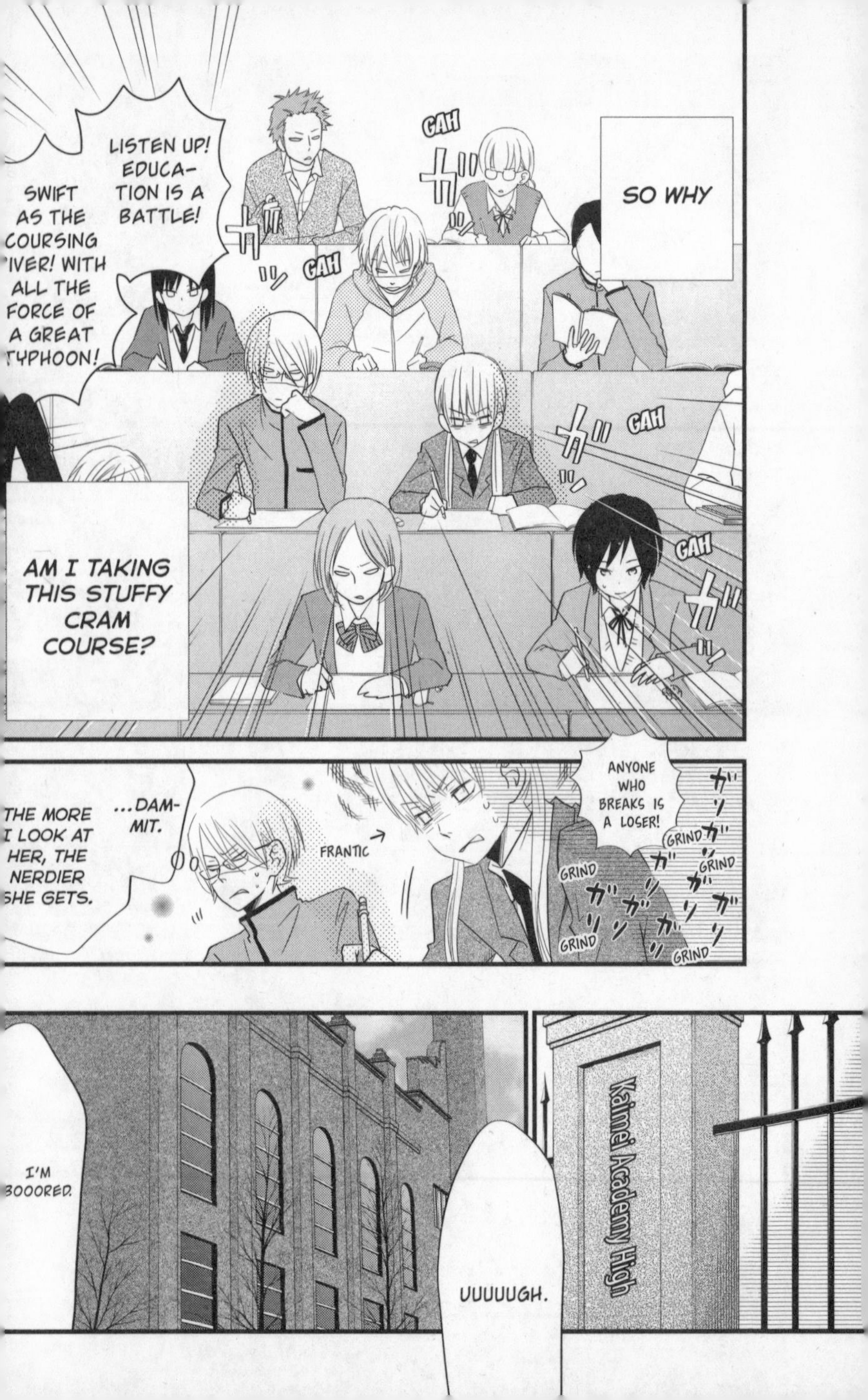
SO WHY
GAH
GAH
LISTEN UP! EDUCATION IS A BATTLE!
SWIFT AS THE COURSING IVER! WITH ALL THE FORCE OF A GREAT TYPHOON!
GAH
GAH
GAH
AM I TAKING THIS STUFFY CRAM COURSE?
ANYONE WHO BREAKS IS A LOSER!
GRIND
GRIND
GRIND
GRIND
GRIND
FRANTIC
...DAMMIT.
THE MORE I LOOK AT HER, THE NERDIER SHE GETS.
Kaimei Academy High
UUUUUGH.
I'M BOOORED.

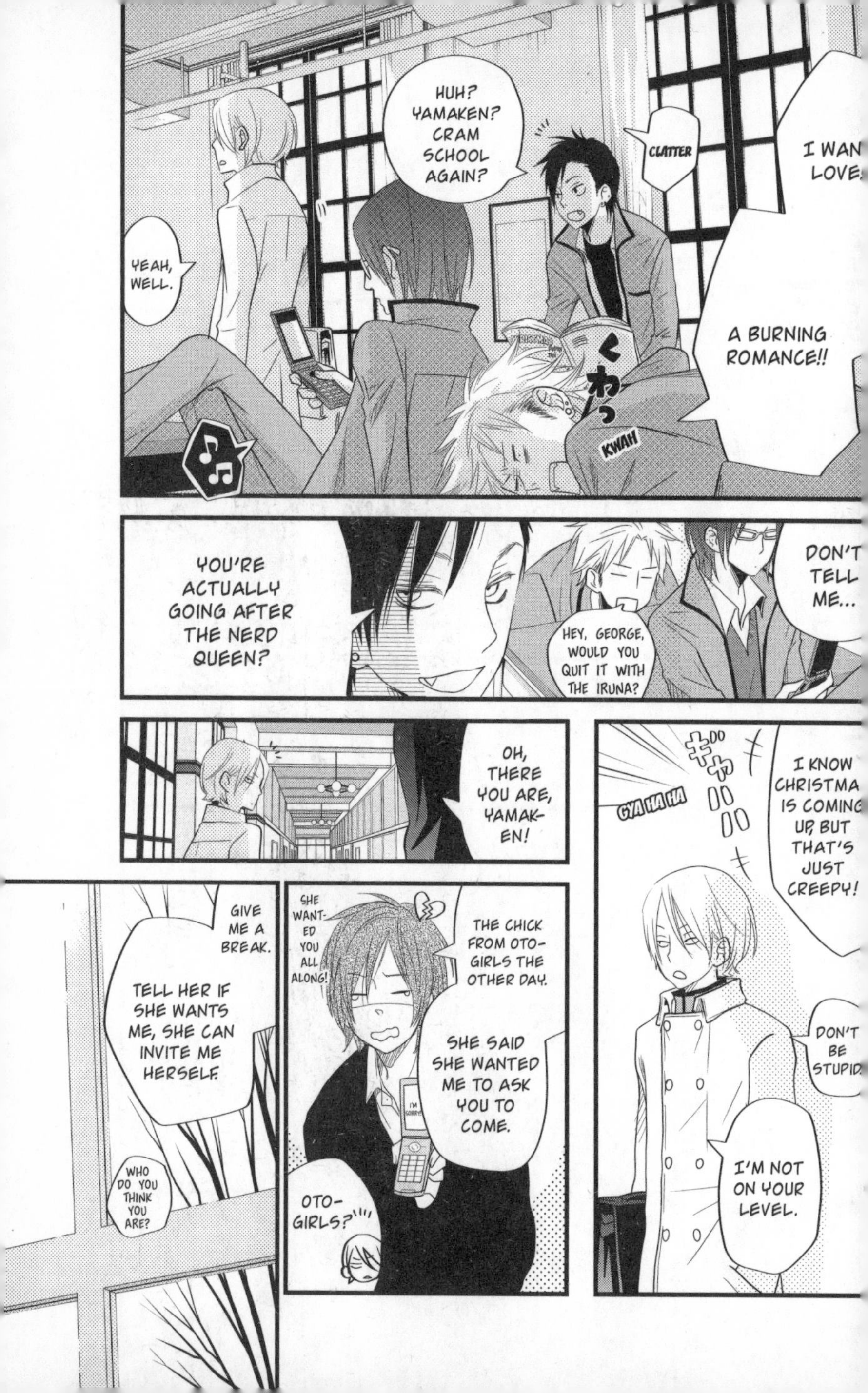
I WAN
LOVE.
A BURNING ROMANCE!!
CLATTER
くわっ
KWAH
HUH? YAMAKEN? CRAM SCHOOL AGAIN?
YEAH, WELL.
DON'T TELL ME...
HEY, GEORGE, WOULD YOU QUIT IT WITH THE IRUNA?
YOU'RE ACTUALLY GOING AFTER THE NERD QUEEN?
I KNOW CHRISTMA IS COMING UP, BUT THAT'S JUST CREEPY!
GYA HA HA
DON'T BE STUPID
I'M NOT ON YOUR LEVEL.
OH, THERE YOU ARE, YAMAKEN!
THE CHICK FROM OTO-GIRLS THE OTHER DAY.
SHE WANTED YOU ALL ALONG!
SHE SAID SHE WANTED ME TO ASK YOU TO COME.
I'M SORRY
OTO-GIRLS?
GIVE ME A BREAK.
TELL HER IF SHE WANTS ME, SHE CAN INVITE ME HERSELF.
WHO DO YOU THINK YOU ARE?

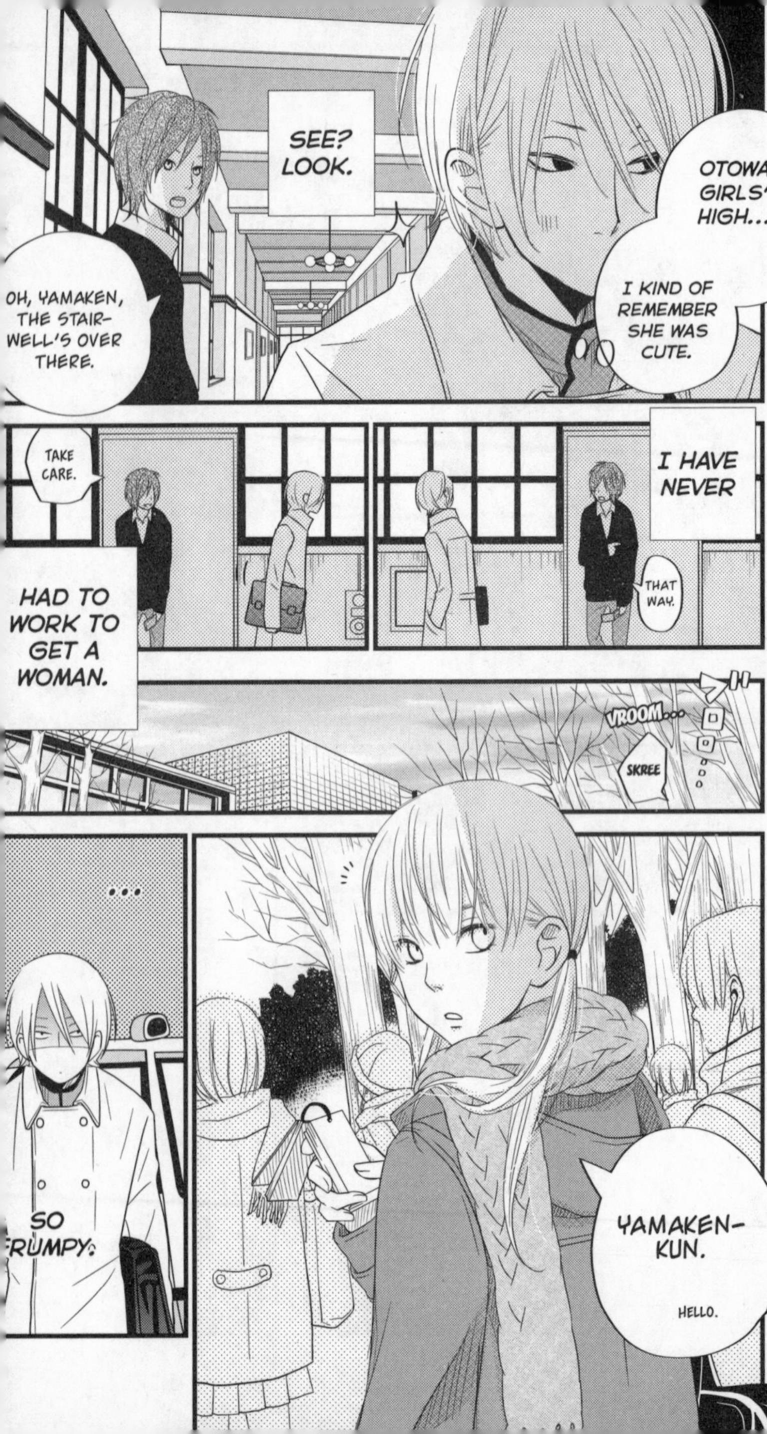
OTOWA GIRLS' HIGH...
I KIND OF REMEMBER SHE WAS CUTE.
SEE? LOOK.
OH, YAMAKEN, THE STAIR-WELL'S OVER THERE.
I HAVE NEVER
THAT WAY.
TAKE CARE.
HAD TO WORK TO GET A WOMAN.
VROOM...
SKREE
YAMAKEN-KUN.
HELLO.
...
SO FRUMPY.

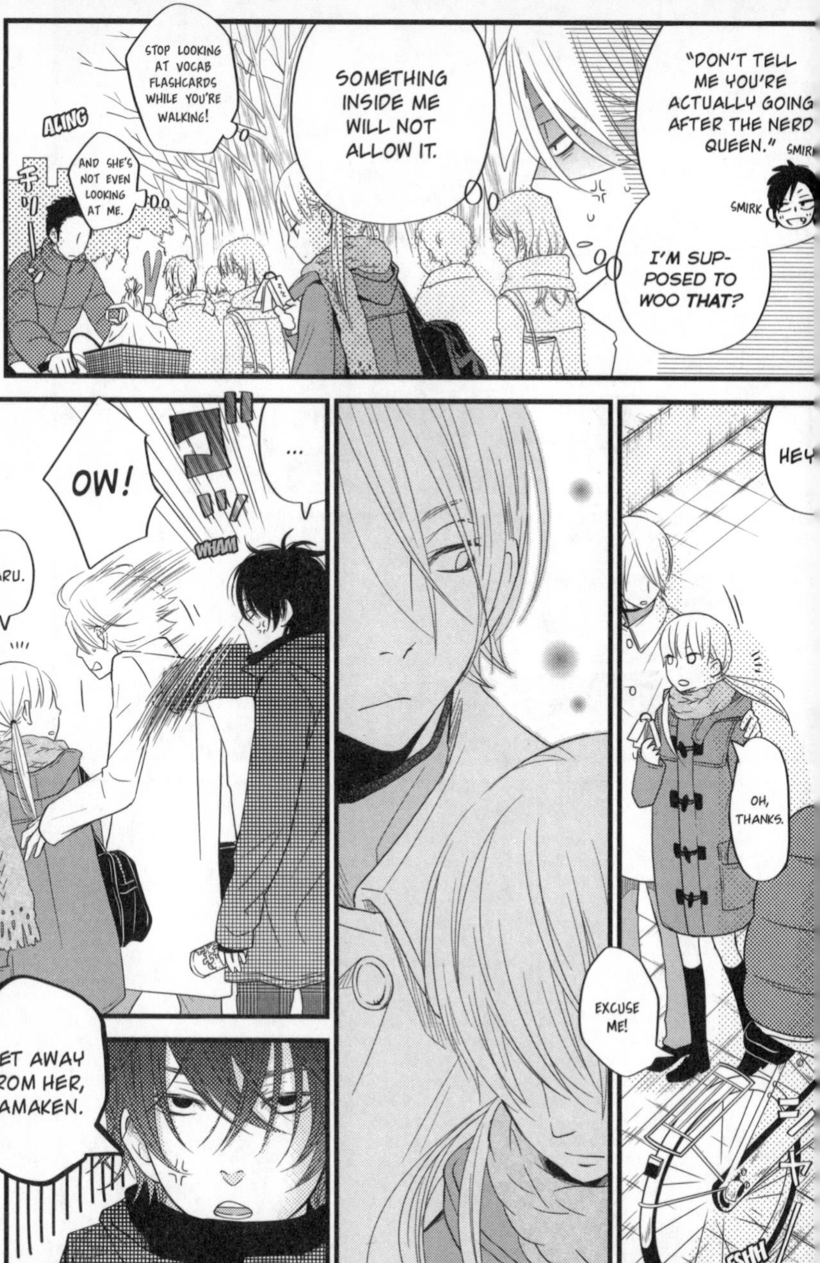
"DON'T TELL ME YOU'RE ACTUALLY GOING AFTER THE NERD QUEEN."
SMIR
SMIRK
I'M SUP-POSED TO WOO THAT?
SOMETHING INSIDE ME WILL NOT ALLOW IT.
STOP LOOKING AT VOCAB FLASHCARDS WHILE YOU'RE WALKING!
AND SHE'S NOT EVEN LOOKING AT ME.
ALING
HEY
OH, THANKS.
EXCUSE ME!
FSHH
...
WHAM
OW!
HARU.
GET AWAY FROM HER, YAMAKEN.

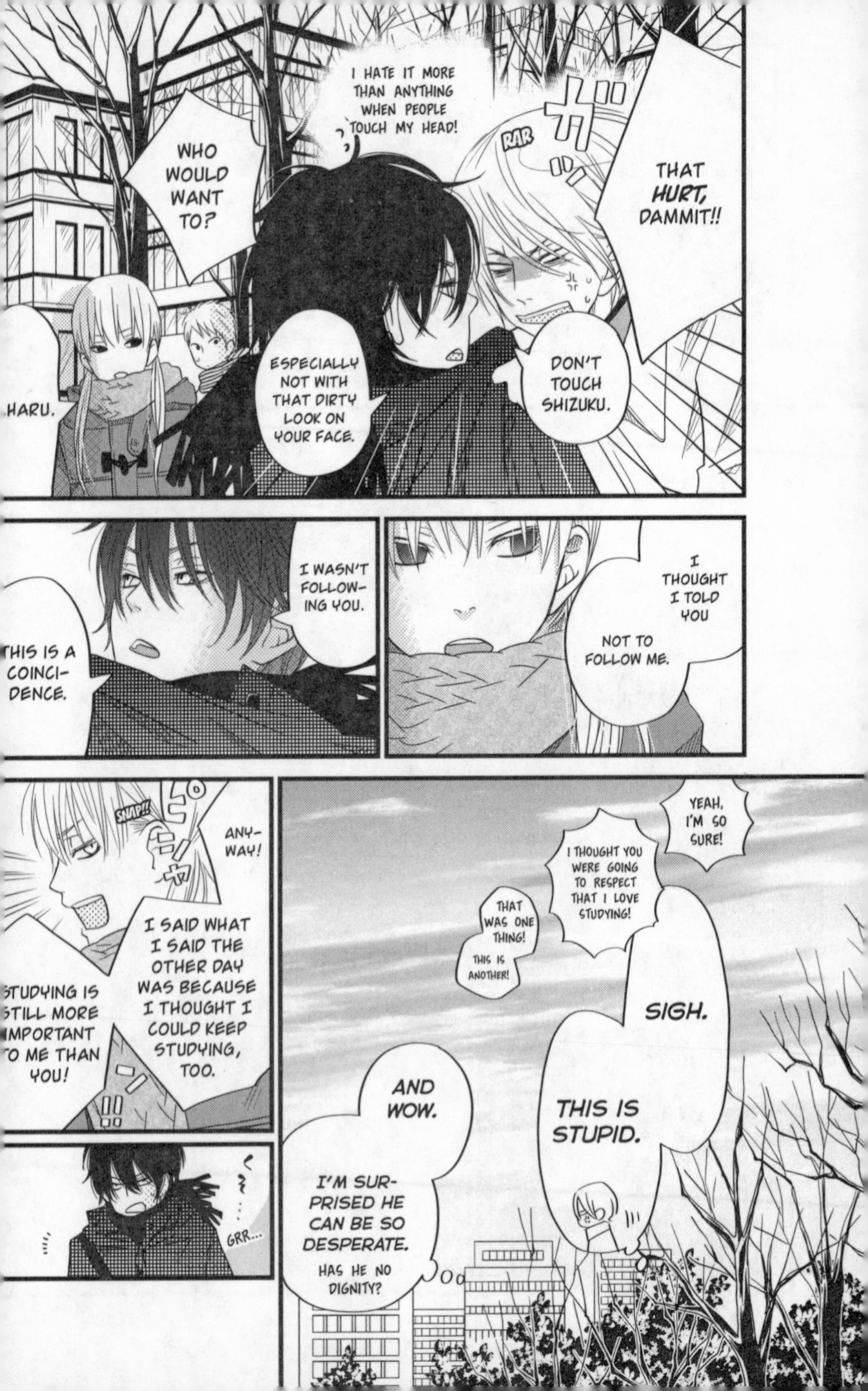
THAT HURT, DAMMIT!!
RAR
I HATE IT MORE THAN ANYTHING WHEN PEOPLE TOUCH MY HEAD!
WHO WOULD WANT TO?
DON'T TOUCH SHIZUKU.
ESPECIALLY NOT WITH THAT DIRTY LOOK ON YOUR FACE.
HARU.
I THOUGHT I TOLD YOU
NOT TO FOLLOW ME.
I WASN'T FOLLOWING YOU.
THIS IS A COINCIDENCE.
YEAH, I'M SO SURE!
I THOUGHT YOU WERE GOING TO RESPECT THAT I LOVE STUDYING!
THAT WAS ONE THING!
THIS IS ANOTHER!
SIGH.
THIS IS STUPID.
AND WOW.
I'M SURPRISED HE CAN BE SO DESPERATE.
HAS HE NO DIGNITY?
SNAP!!
ANYWAY!
I SAID WHAT I SAID THE OTHER DAY WAS BECAUSE I THOUGHT I COULD KEEP STUDYING, TOO.
STUDYING IS STILL MORE IMPORTANT TO ME THAN YOU!
GRR...

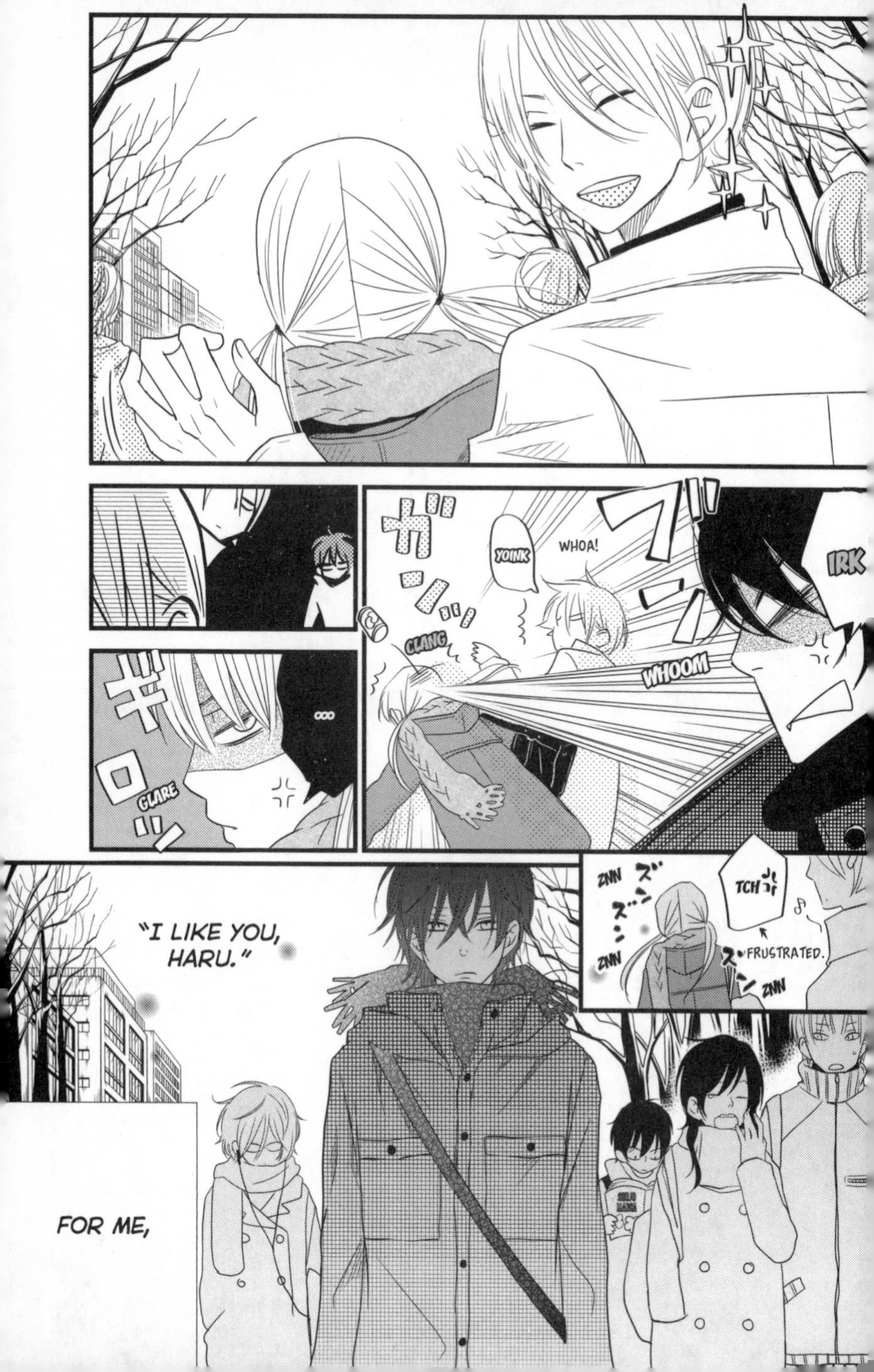
YOINK
WHOA!
IRK
CLANG
WHOOM
GLARE
...
TCH
ZNN
ZNN
FRUSTRATED.
ZNN
"I LIKE YOU, HARU."
FOR ME,

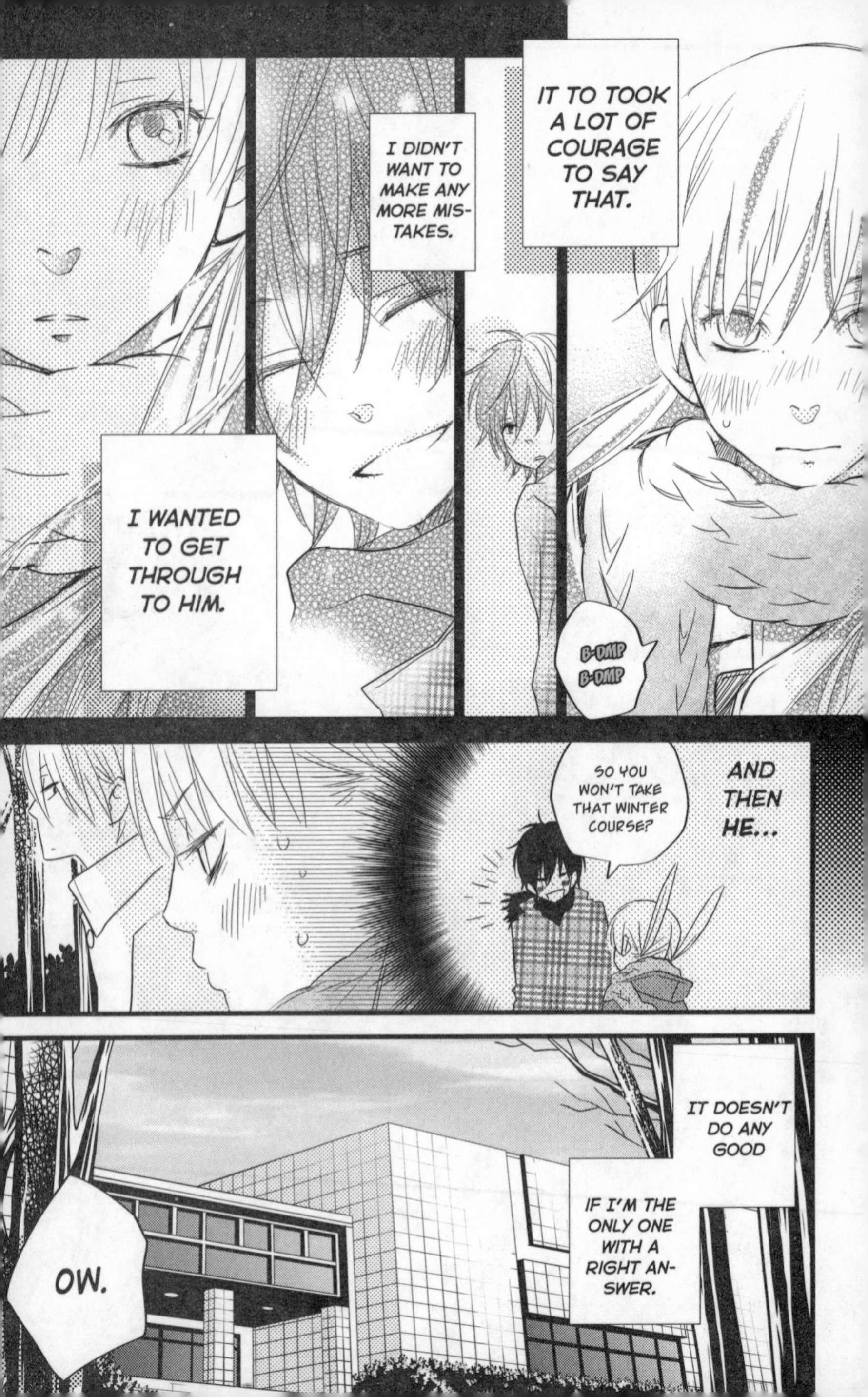
IT TO TOOK A LOT OF COURAGE TO SAY THAT.
B-DMP B-DMP
I DIDN'T WANT TO MAKE ANY MORE MIS-TAKES.
I WANTED TO GET THROUGH TO HIM.
AND THEN HE...
SO YOU WON'T TAKE THAT WINTER COURSE?
IT DOESN'T DO ANY GOOD
IF I'M THE ONLY ONE WITH A RIGHT AN-SWER.
OW.

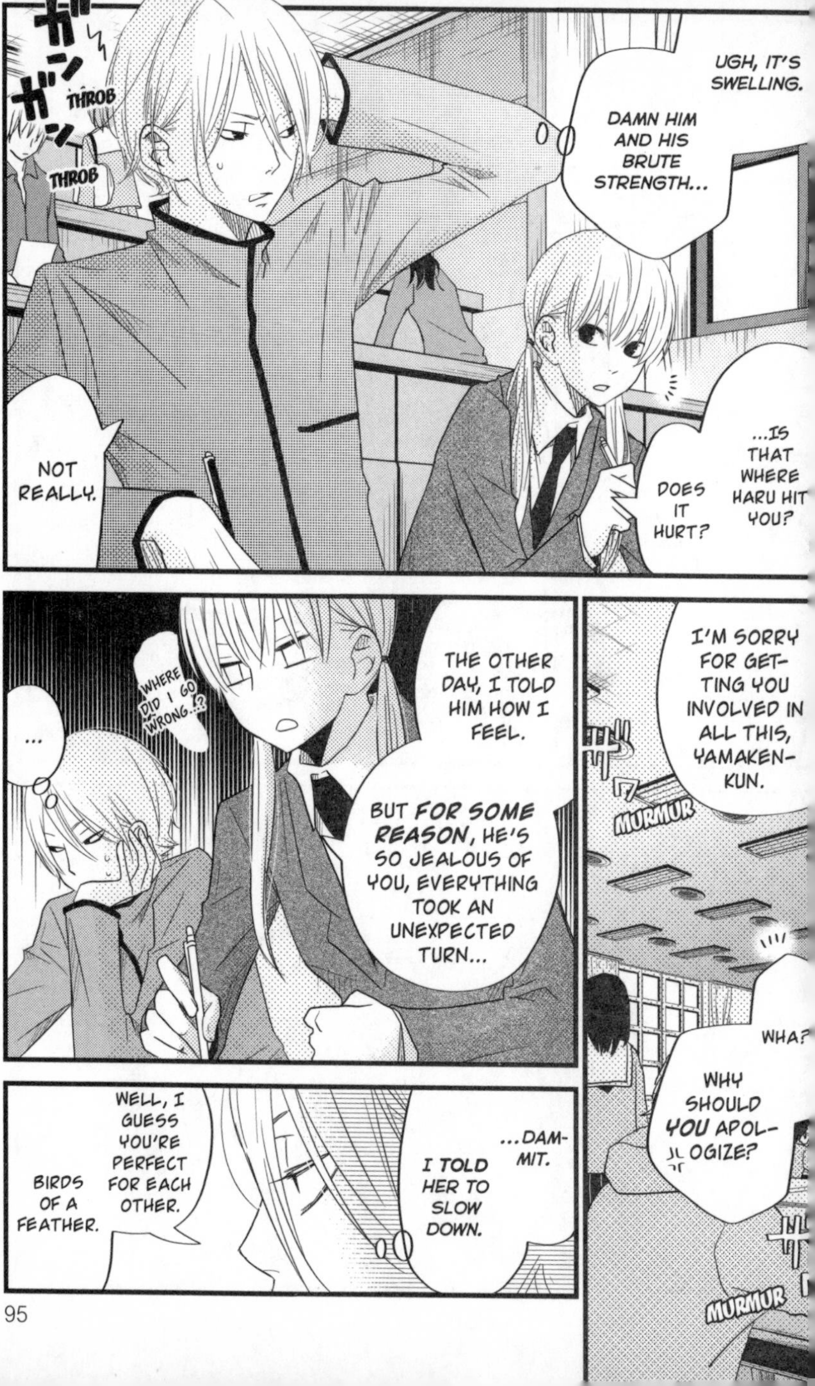
UGH, IT'S SWELLING.
DAMN HIM AND HIS BRUTE STRENGTH...
THROB
THROB
...IS THAT WHERE HARU HIT YOU?
DOES IT HURT?
NOT REALLY.
I'M SORRY FOR GETTING YOU INVOLVED IN ALL THIS, YAMAKEN-KUN.
MURMUR
WHA?
WHY SHOULD YOU APOLOGIZE?
MURMUR
THE OTHER DAY, I TOLD HIM HOW I FEEL.
BUT FOR SOME REASON, HE'S SO JEALOUS OF YOU, EVERYTHING TOOK AN UNEXPECTED TURN...
WHERE DID I GO WRONG..!?
...
...DAMMIT.
I TOLD HER TO SLOW DOWN.
WELL, I GUESS YOU'RE PERFECT FOR EACH OTHER.
BIRDS OF A FEATHER.

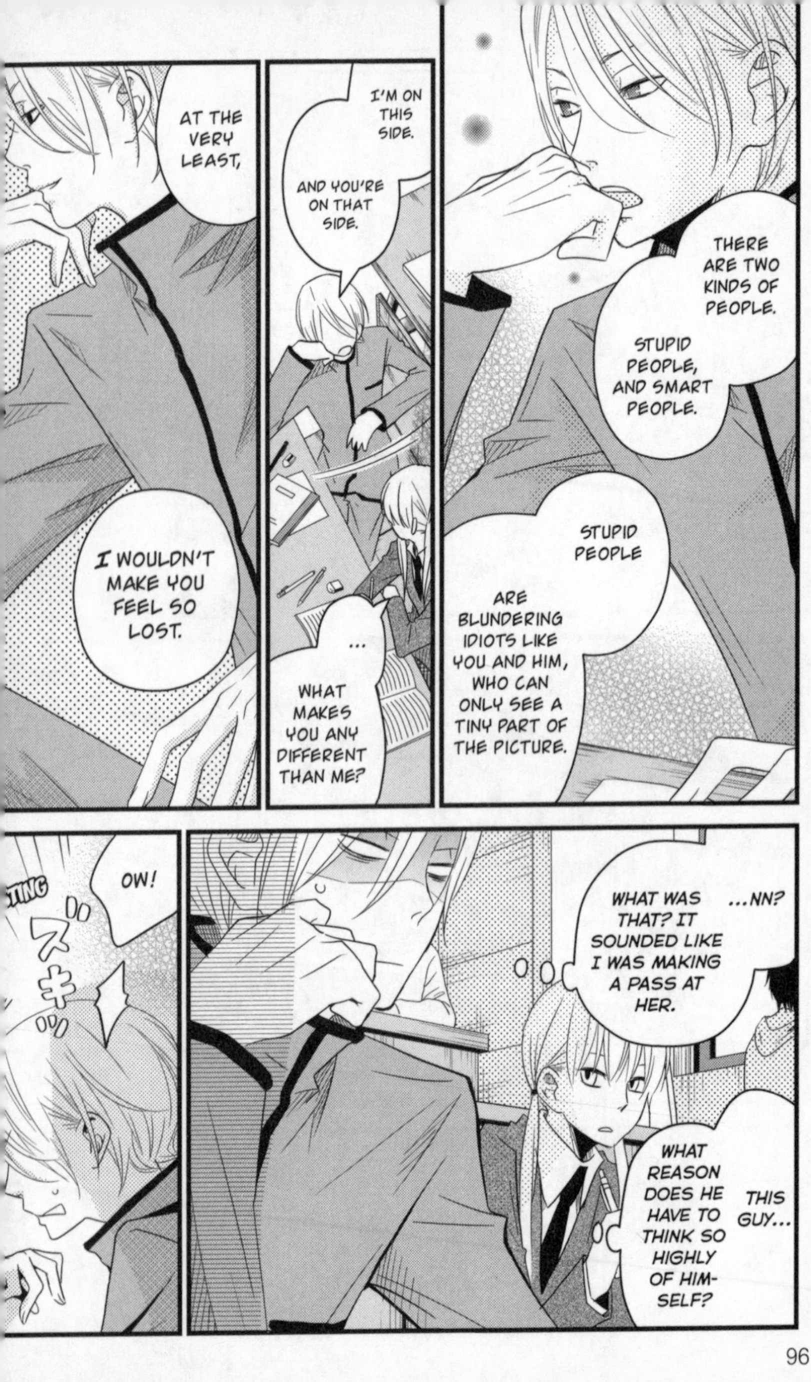
THERE ARE TWO KINDS OF PEOPLE.
STUPID PEOPLE, AND SMART PEOPLE.
STUPID PEOPLE
ARE BLUNDERING IDIOTS LIKE YOU AND HIM, WHO CAN ONLY SEE A TINY PART OF THE PICTURE.
I'M ON THIS SIDE.
AND YOU'RE ON THAT SIDE.
...
WHAT MAKES YOU ANY DIFFERENT THAN ME?
AT THE VERY LEAST,
I WOULDN'T MAKE YOU FEEL SO LOST.
...NN?
WHAT WAS THAT? IT SOUNDED LIKE I WAS MAKING A PASS AT HER.
THIS GUY...
WHAT REASON DOES HE HAVE TO THINK SO HIGHLY OF HIM-SELF?
OW!
ズキ

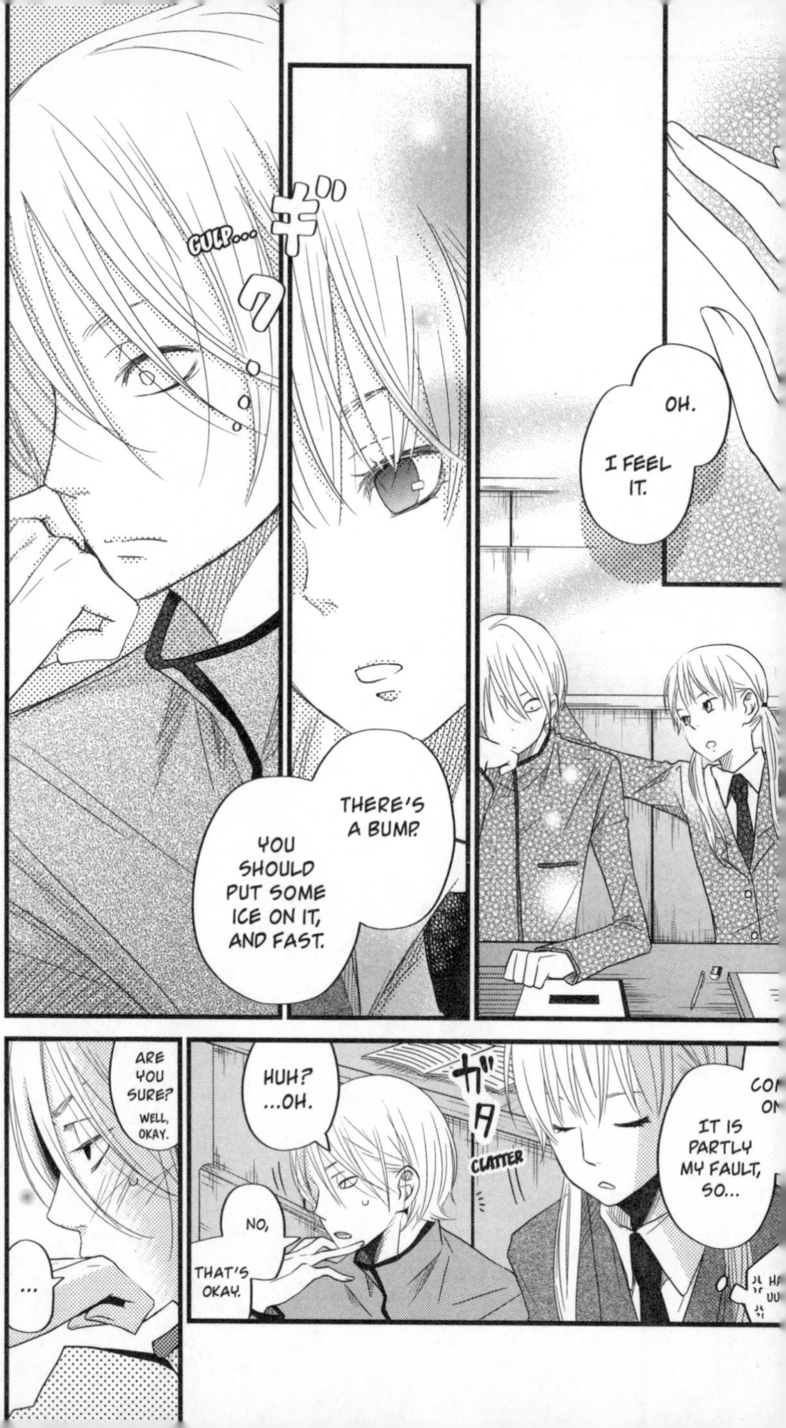
OH.
I FEEL IT.
THERE'S A BUMP.
YOU SHOULD PUT SOME ICE ON IT, AND FAST.
GULP...
IT IS PARTLY MY FAULT, SO...
CLATTER
HUH? ...OH.
NO, THAT'S OKAY.
ARE YOU SURE?
WELL, OKAY.
...

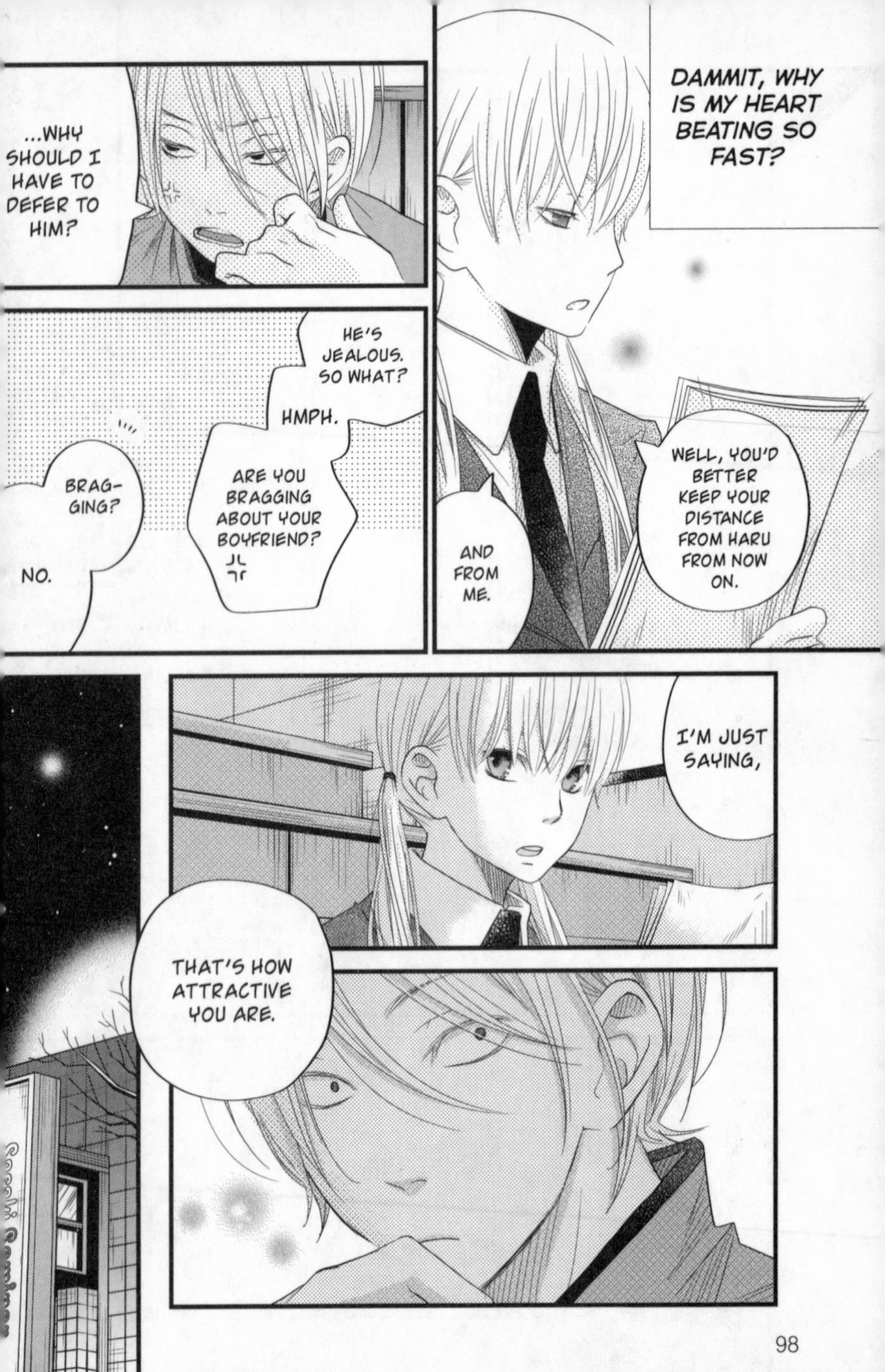
DAMMIT, WHY IS MY HEART BEATING SO FAST?
WELL, YOU'D BETTER KEEP YOUR DISTANCE FROM HARU FROM NOW ON.
AND FROM ME.
...WHY SHOULD I HAVE TO DEFER TO HIM?
HE'S JEALOUS. SO WHAT?
HMPH.
ARE YOU BRAGGING ABOUT YOUR BOYFRIEND?
BRAG-GING?
NO.
I'M JUST SAYING,
THAT'S HOW ATTRACTIVE YOU ARE.

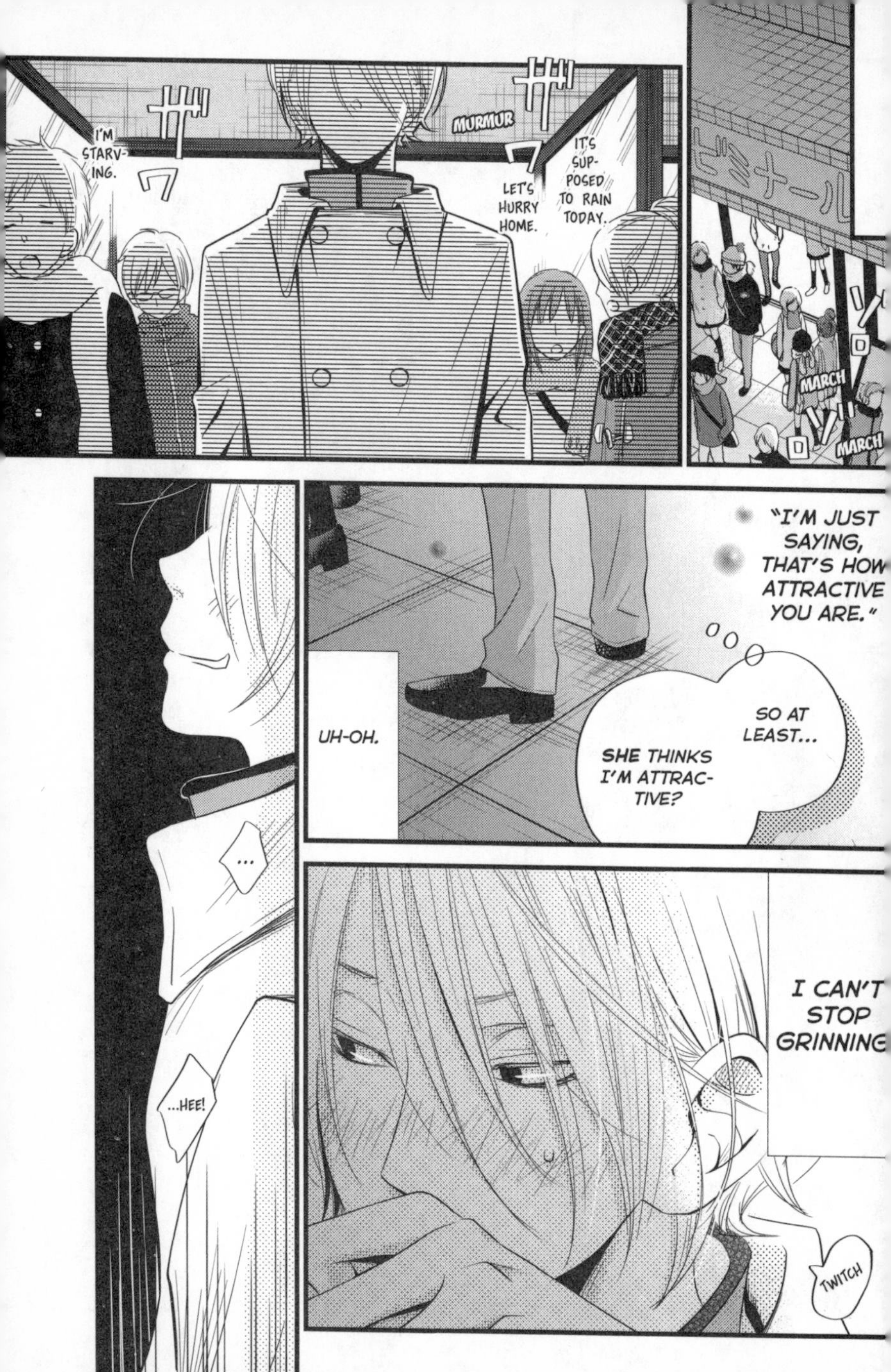
MARCH
MARCH
IT'S SUPPOSED TO RAIN TODAY.
LET'S HURRY HOME.
MURMUR
I'M STARVING.
"I'M JUST SAYING, THAT'S HOW ATTRACTIVE YOU ARE."
SO AT LEAST...
SHE THINKS I'M ATTRACTIVE?
UH-OH.
I CAN'T STOP GRINNING
TWITCH
...
...HEE!

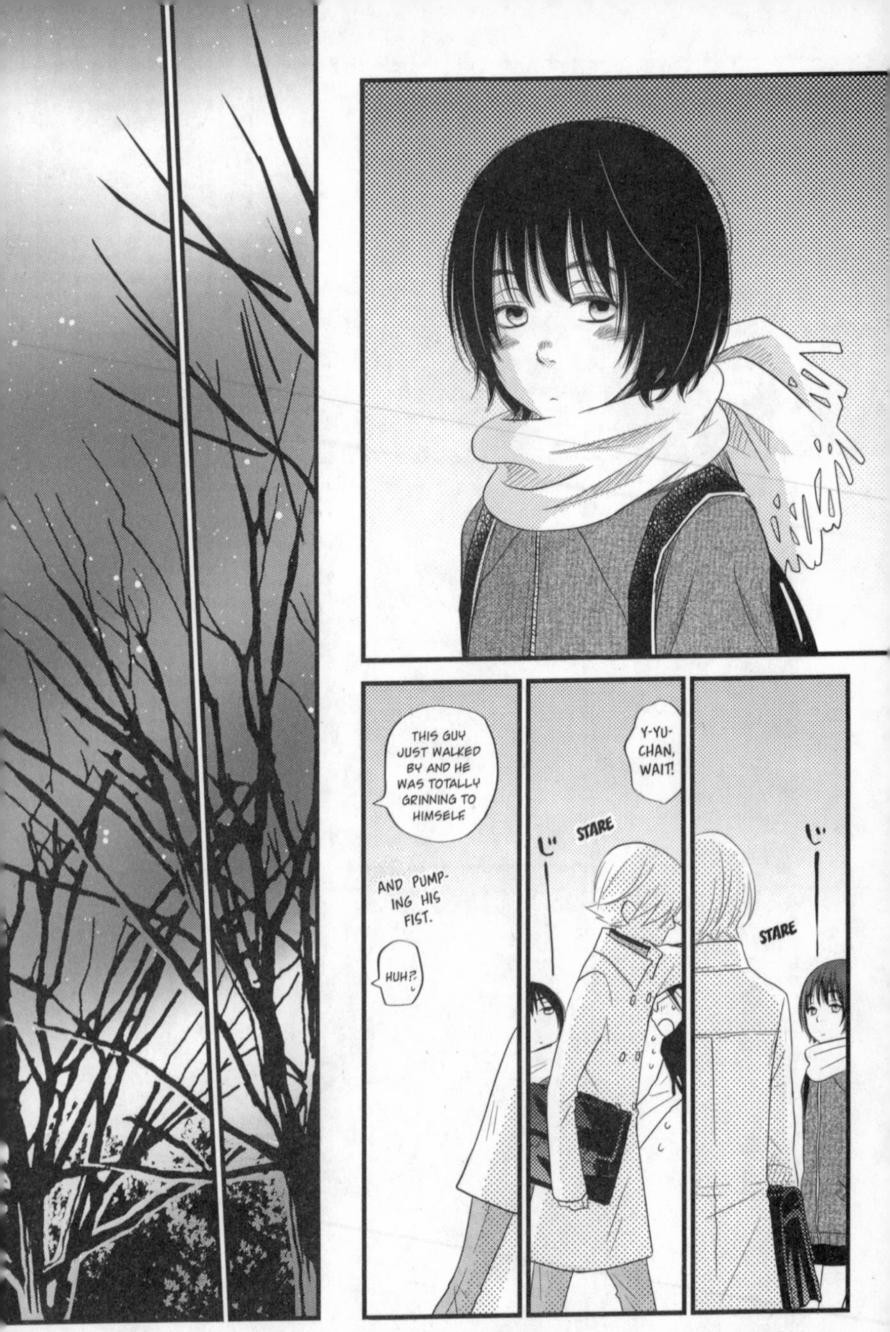
STARE
じー
Y-YU-CHAN, WAIT!
じー
STARE
THIS GUY JUST WALKED BY AND HE WAS TOTALLY GRINNING TO HIMSELF
AND PUMPING HIS FIST.
HUH?!

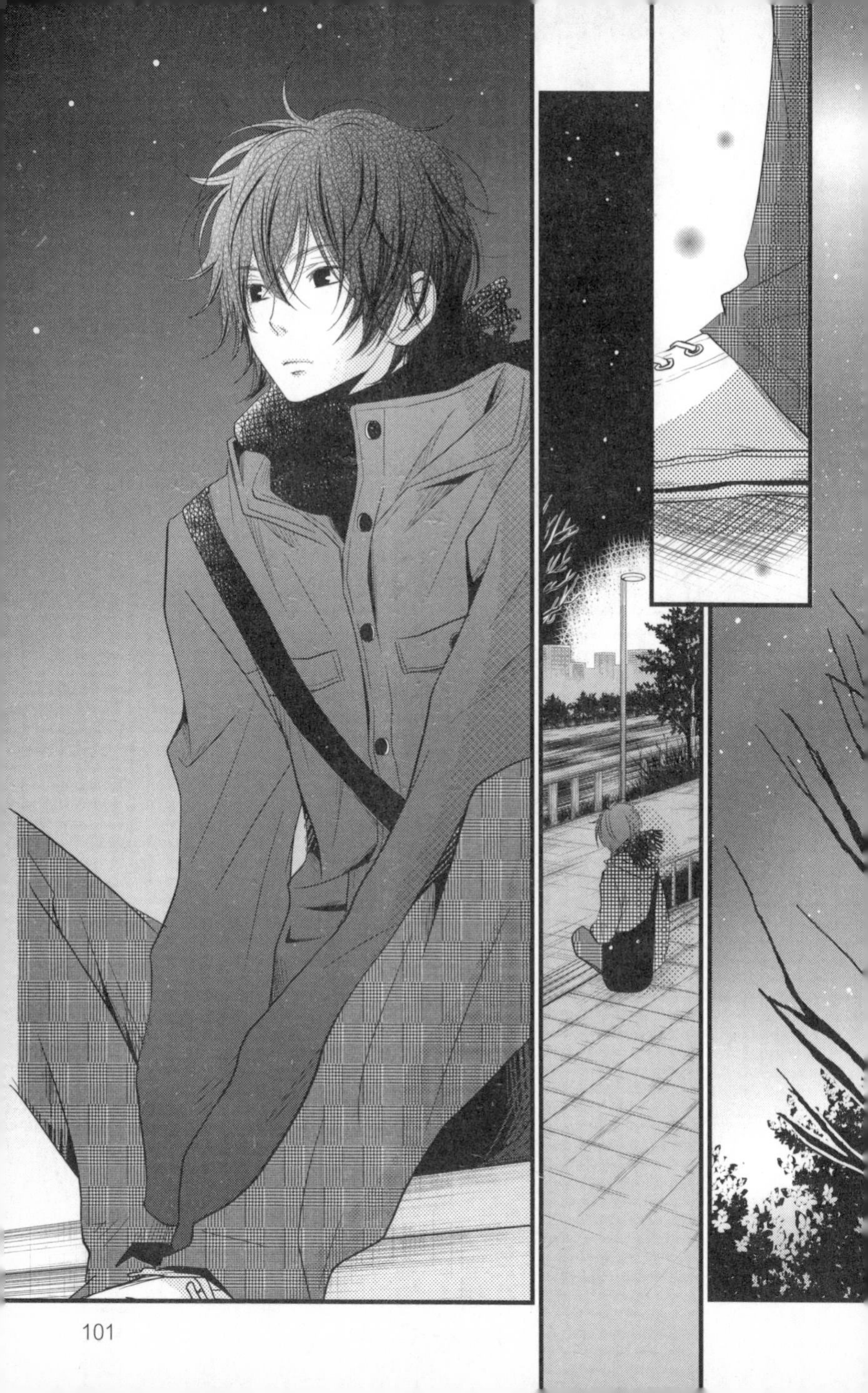

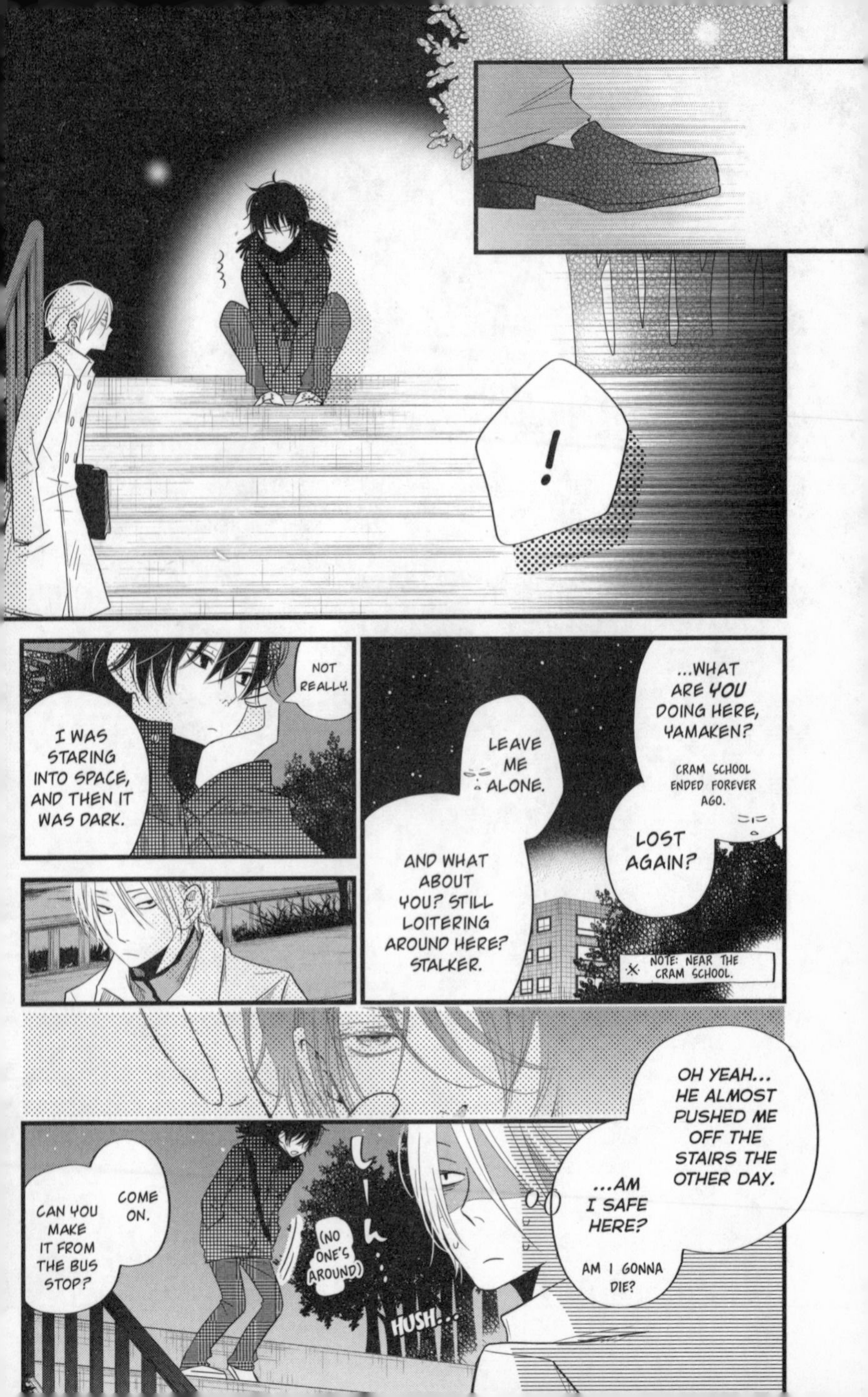
!
...WHAT ARE YOU DOING HERE, YAMAKEN?
CRAM SCHOOL ENDED FOREVER AGO.
LOST AGAIN?
LEAVE ME ALONE.
※ NOTE: NEAR THE CRAM SCHOOL.
AND WHAT ABOUT YOU? STILL LOITERING AROUND HERE? STALKER.
NOT REALLY.
I WAS STARING INTO SPACE, AND THEN IT WAS DARK.
OH YEAH... HE ALMOST PUSHED ME OFF THE STAIRS THE OTHER DAY.
...AM I SAFE HERE?
AM I GONNA DIE?
HUSH...
(NO ONE'S AROUND)
COME ON.
CAN YOU MAKE IT FROM THE BUS STOP?

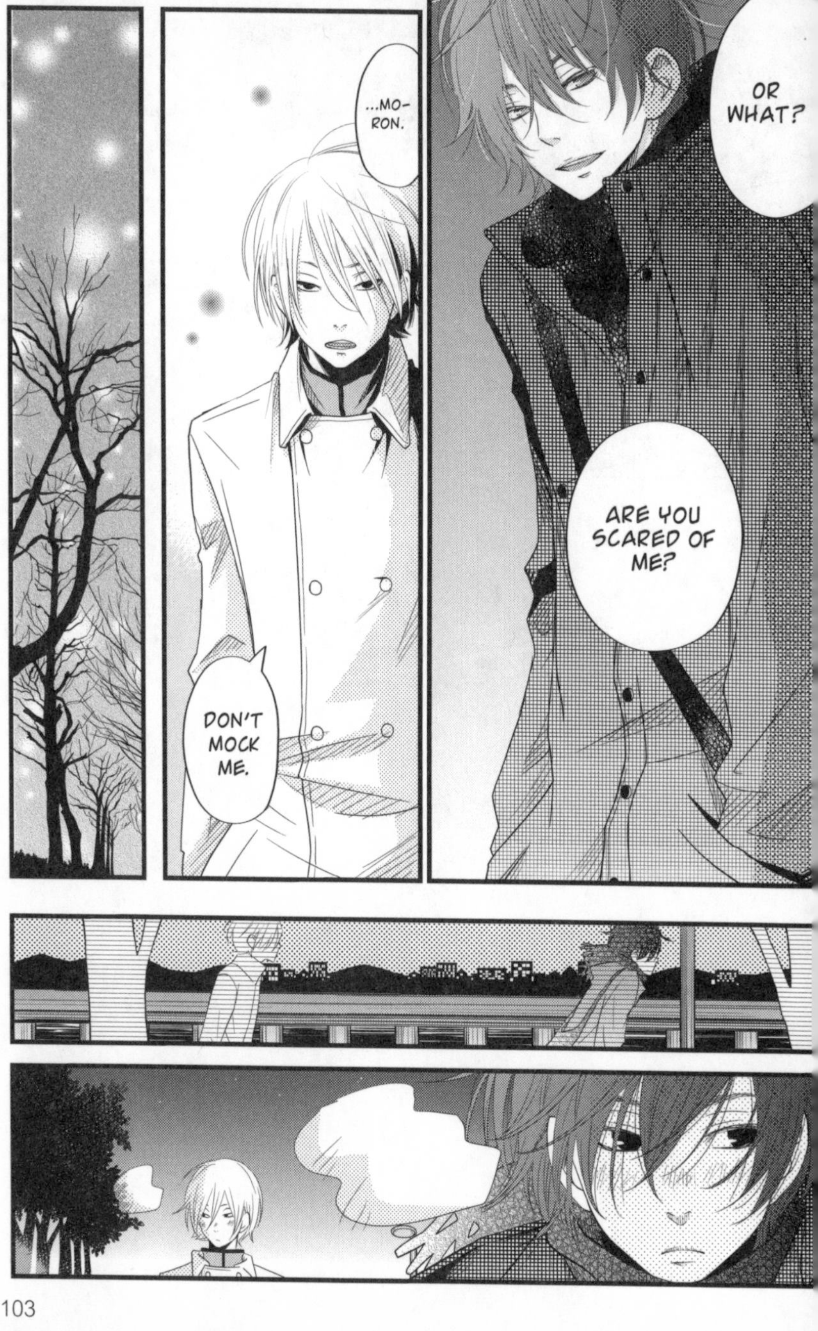
OR WHAT?
ARE YOU SCARED OF ME?
...MO-RON.
DON'T MOCK ME.

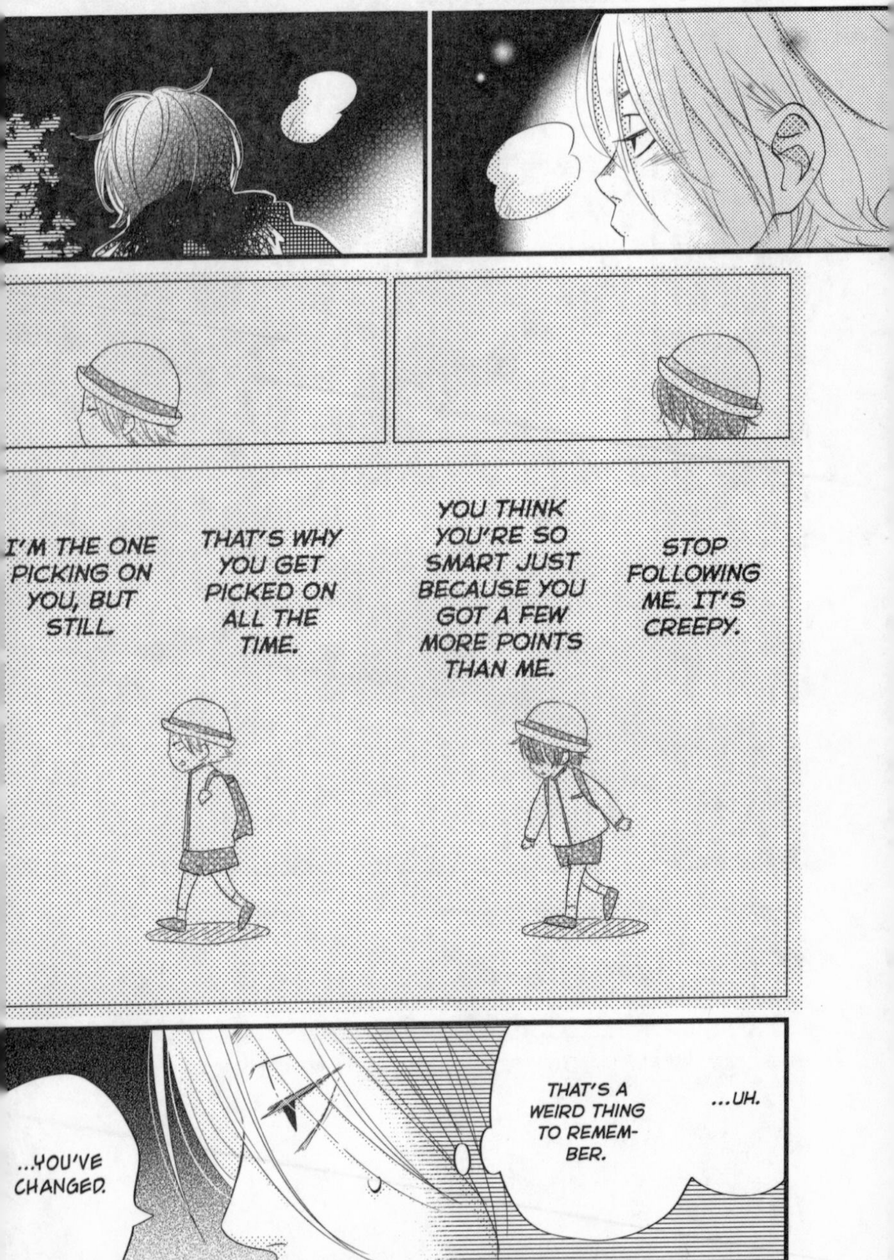
STOP FOLLOWING ME. IT'S CREEPY.
YOU THINK YOU'RE SO SMART JUST BECAUSE YOU GOT A FEW MORE POINTS THAN ME.
THAT'S WHY YOU GET PICKED ON ALL THE TIME.
I'M THE ONE PICKING ON YOU, BUT STILL.
...UH.
THAT'S A WEIRD THING TO REMEMBER.
...YOU'VE CHANGED.

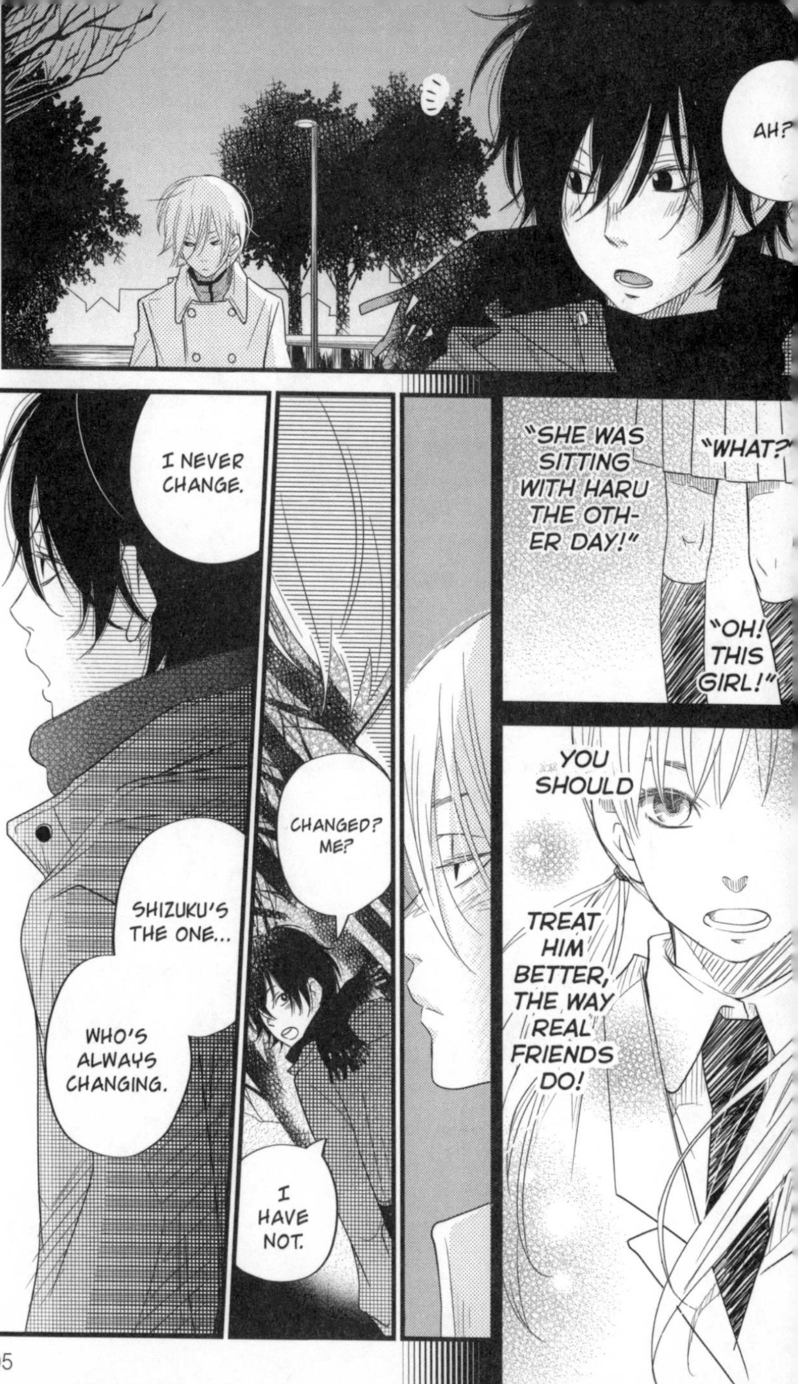
AH?
"WHAT?"
"SHE WAS SITTING WITH HARU THE OTH-ER DAY!"
"OH! THIS GIRL!"
YOU SHOULD
TREAT HIM BETTER, THE WAY REAL FRIENDS DO!
CHANGED? ME?
I HAVE NOT.
I NEVER CHANGE.
SHIZUKU'S THE ONE...
WHO'S ALWAYS CHANGING.

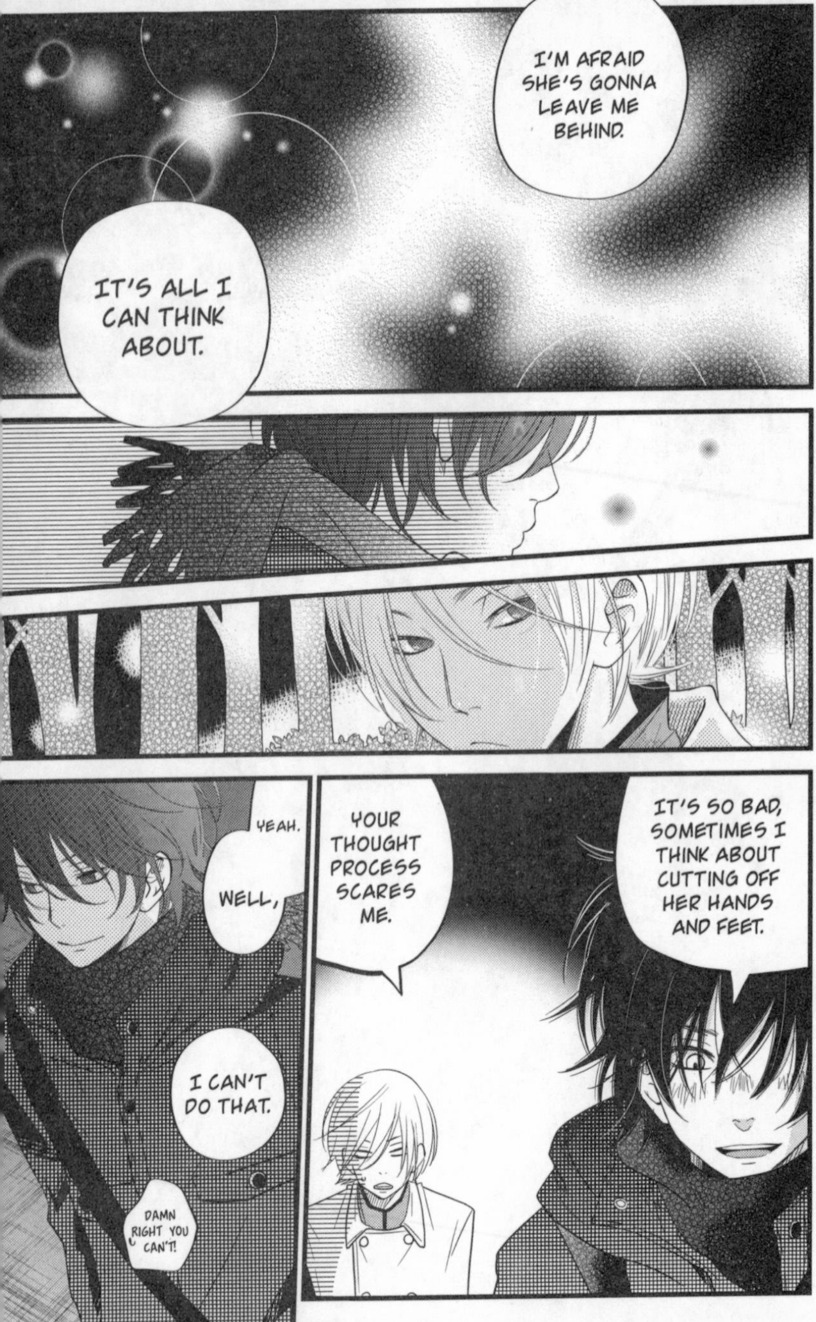
I'M AFRAID SHE'S GONNA LEAVE ME BEHIND.
IT'S ALL I CAN THINK ABOUT.
IT'S SO BAD, SOMETIMES I THINK ABOUT CUTTING OFF HER HANDS AND FEET.
YOUR THOUGHT PROCESS SCARES ME.
YEAH.
WELL,
I CAN'T DO THAT.
DAMN RIGHT YOU CAN'T!

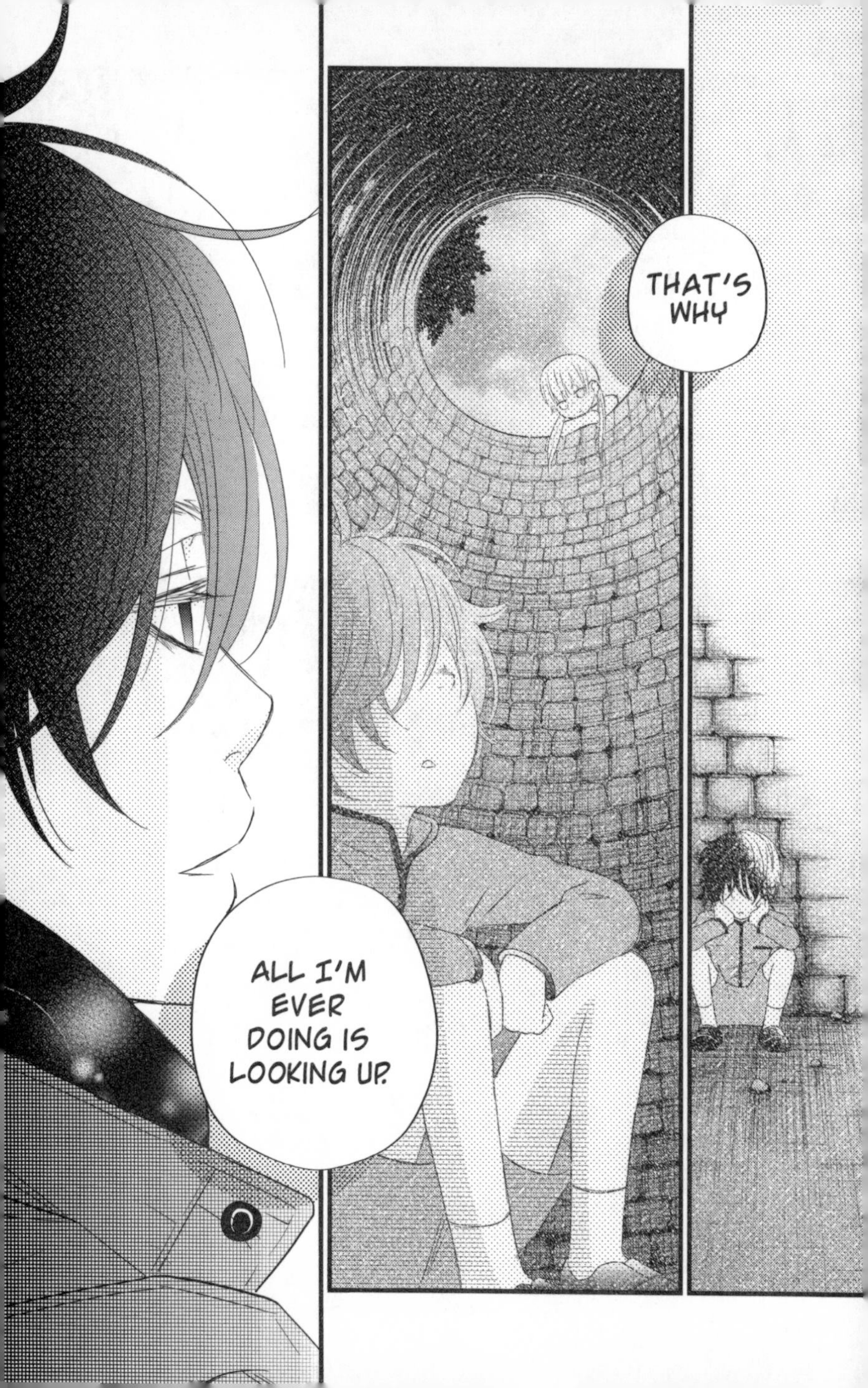
THAT'S WHY
ALL I'M EVER DOING IS LOOKING UP.

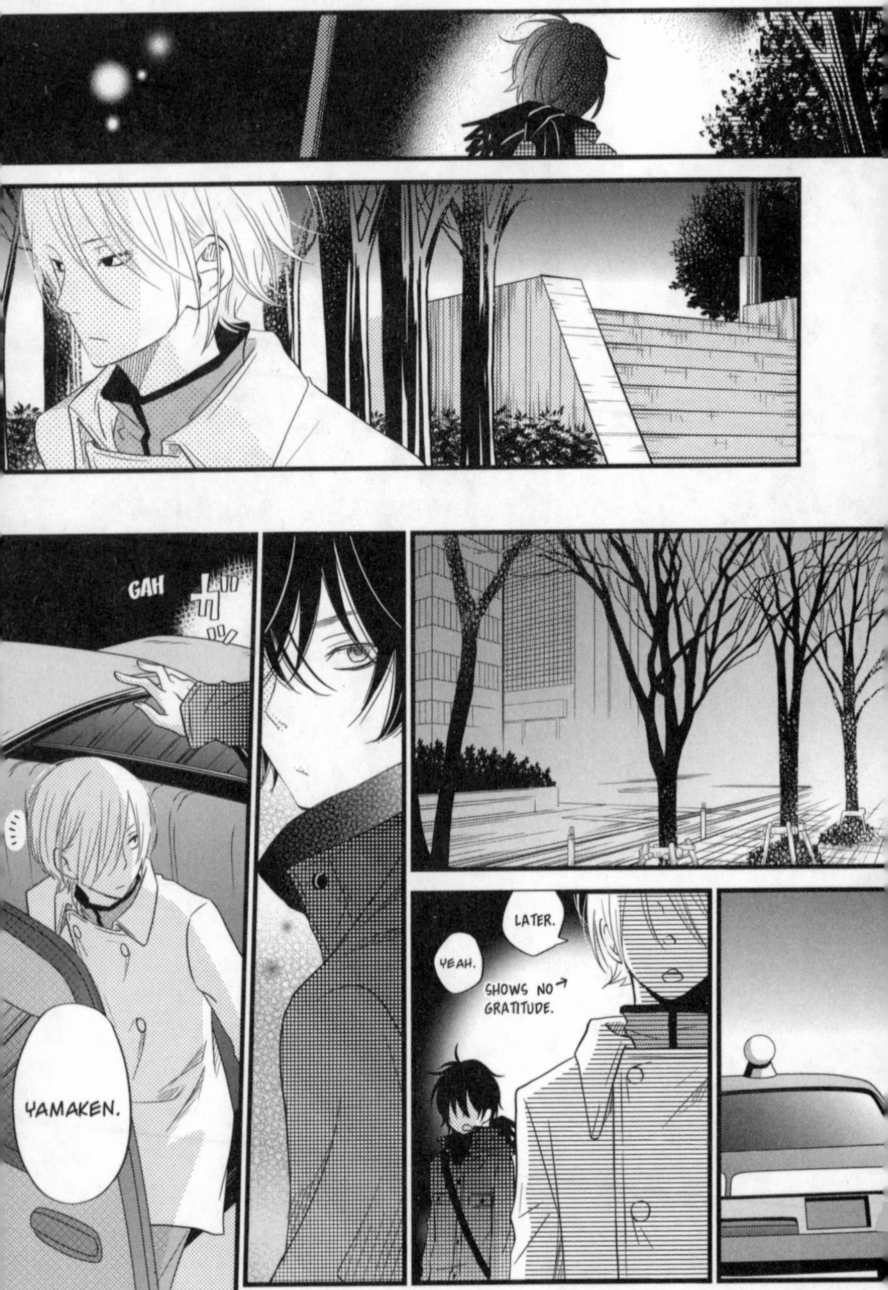
LATER.
YEAH.
SHOWS NO GRATITUDE.
GAH
YAMAKEN.

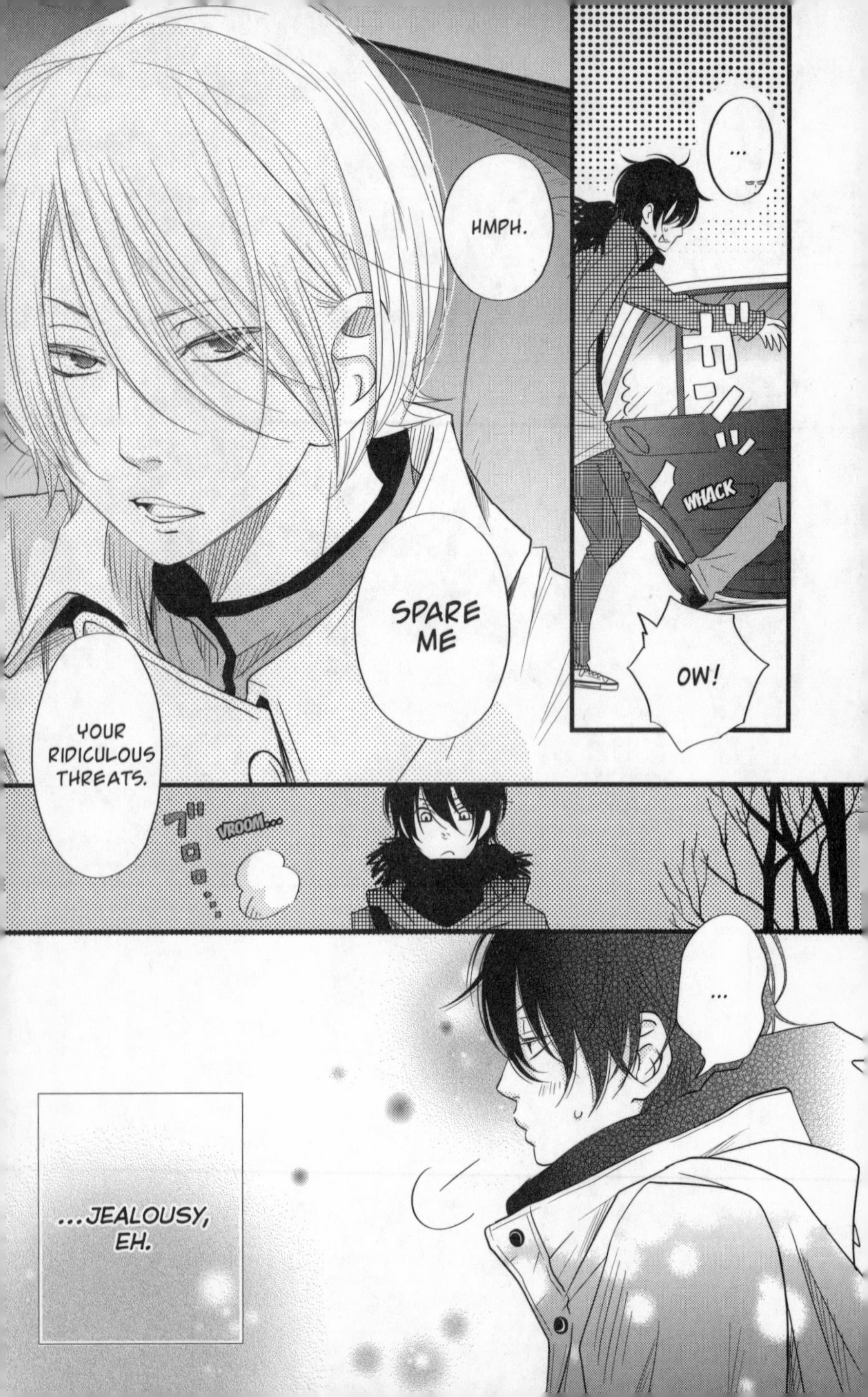
...
WHACK
OW!
HMPH.
SPARE ME
YOUR RIDICULOUS THREATS.
VROOM...
...
...JEALOUSY, EH.

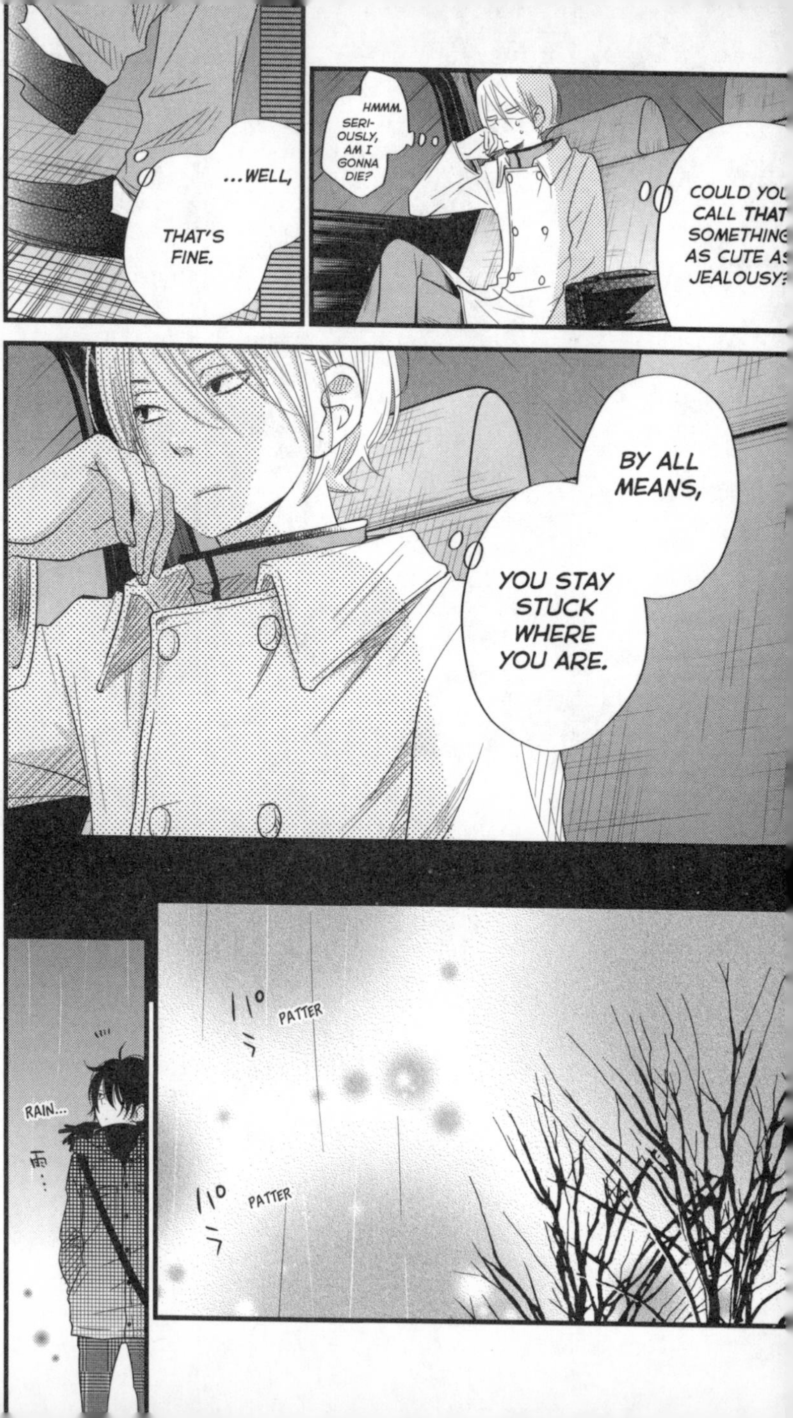
COULD YOU CALL THAT SOMETHING AS CUTE AS JEALOUSY?
HMMM. SERIOUSLY, AM I GONNA DIE?
...WELL, THAT'S FINE.
BY ALL MEANS, YOU STAY STUCK WHERE YOU ARE.
PATTER
PATTER
RAIN...
雨…

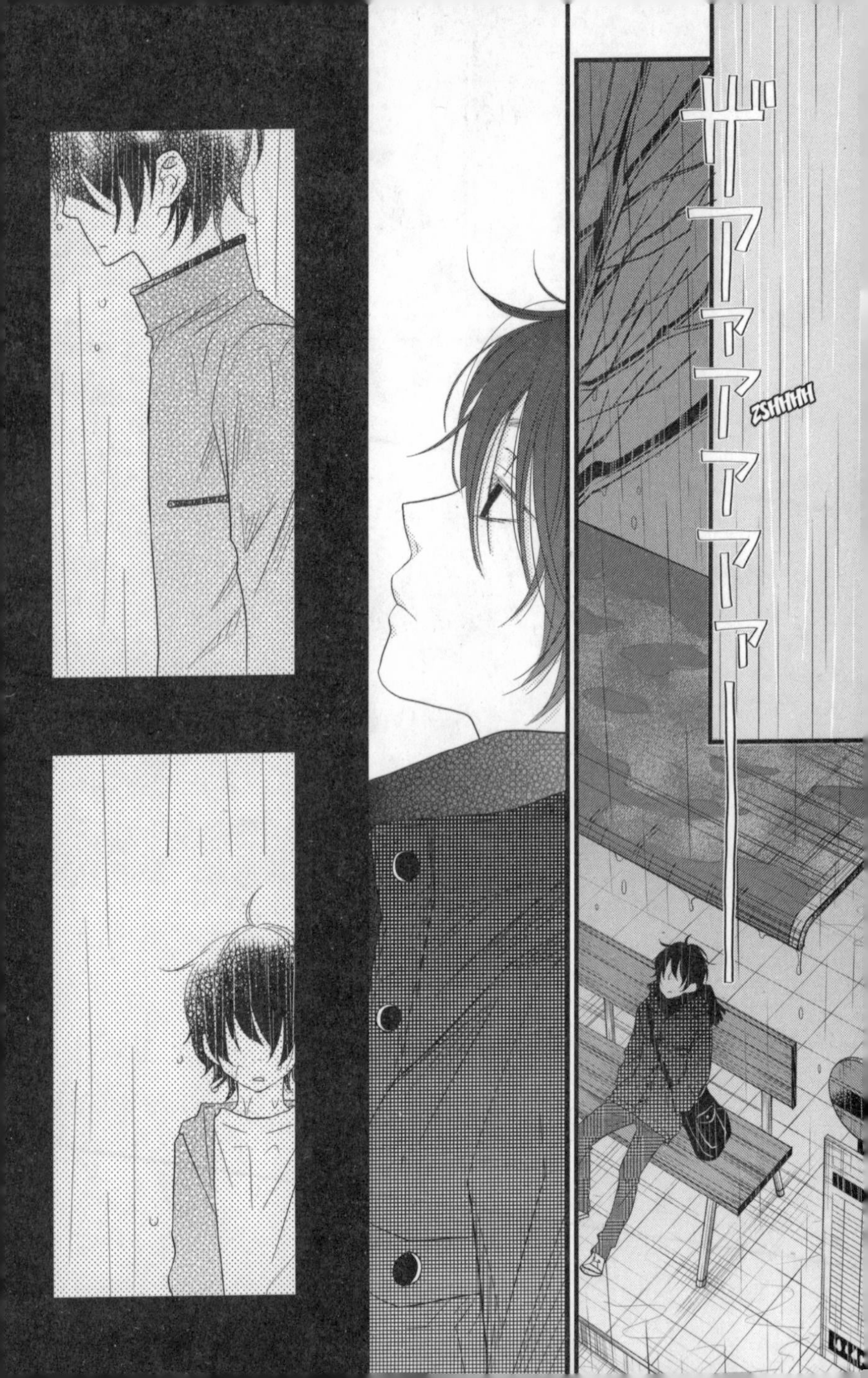
ザアアアアアアー
ZSHHHH

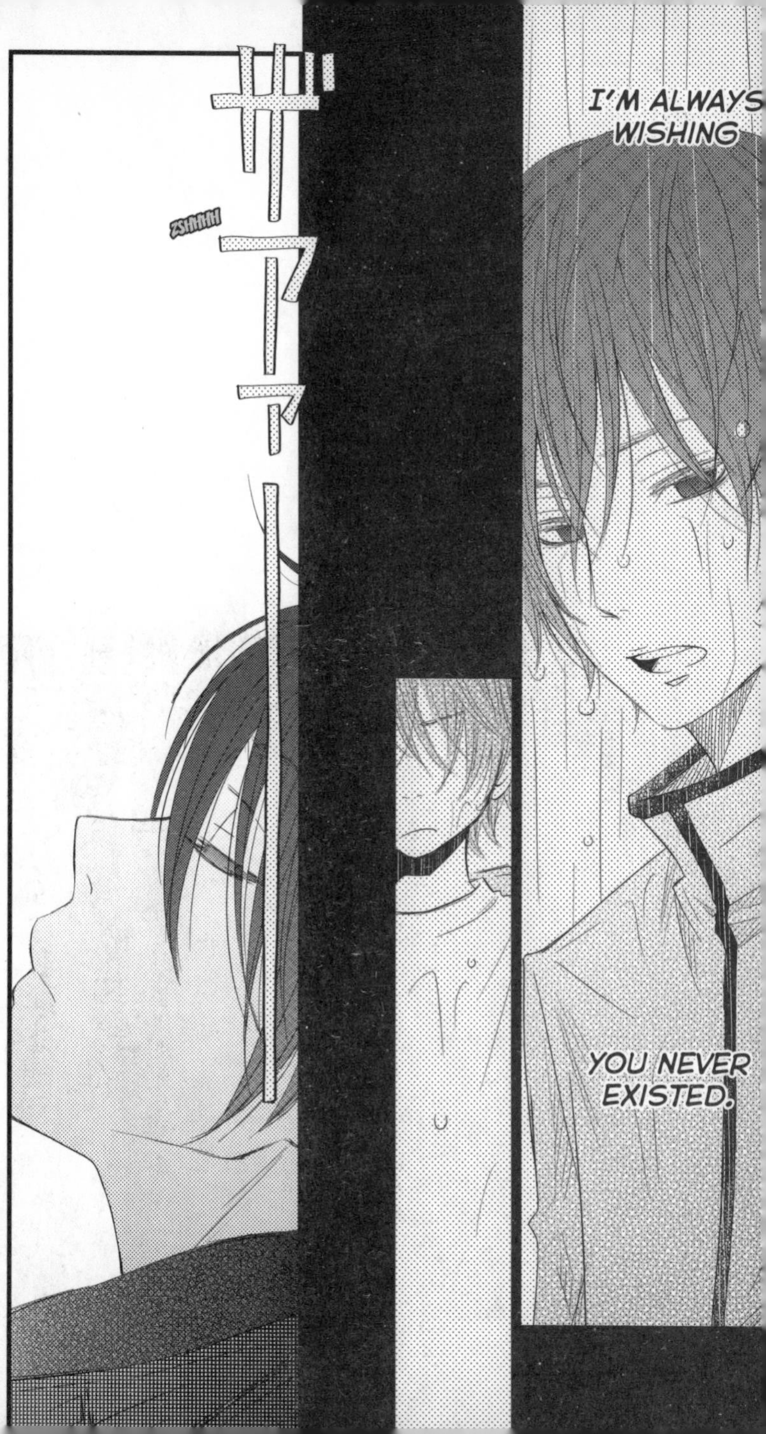
I'M ALWAYS WISHING
YOU NEVER EXISTED.
ザーァー
ZSHHHH

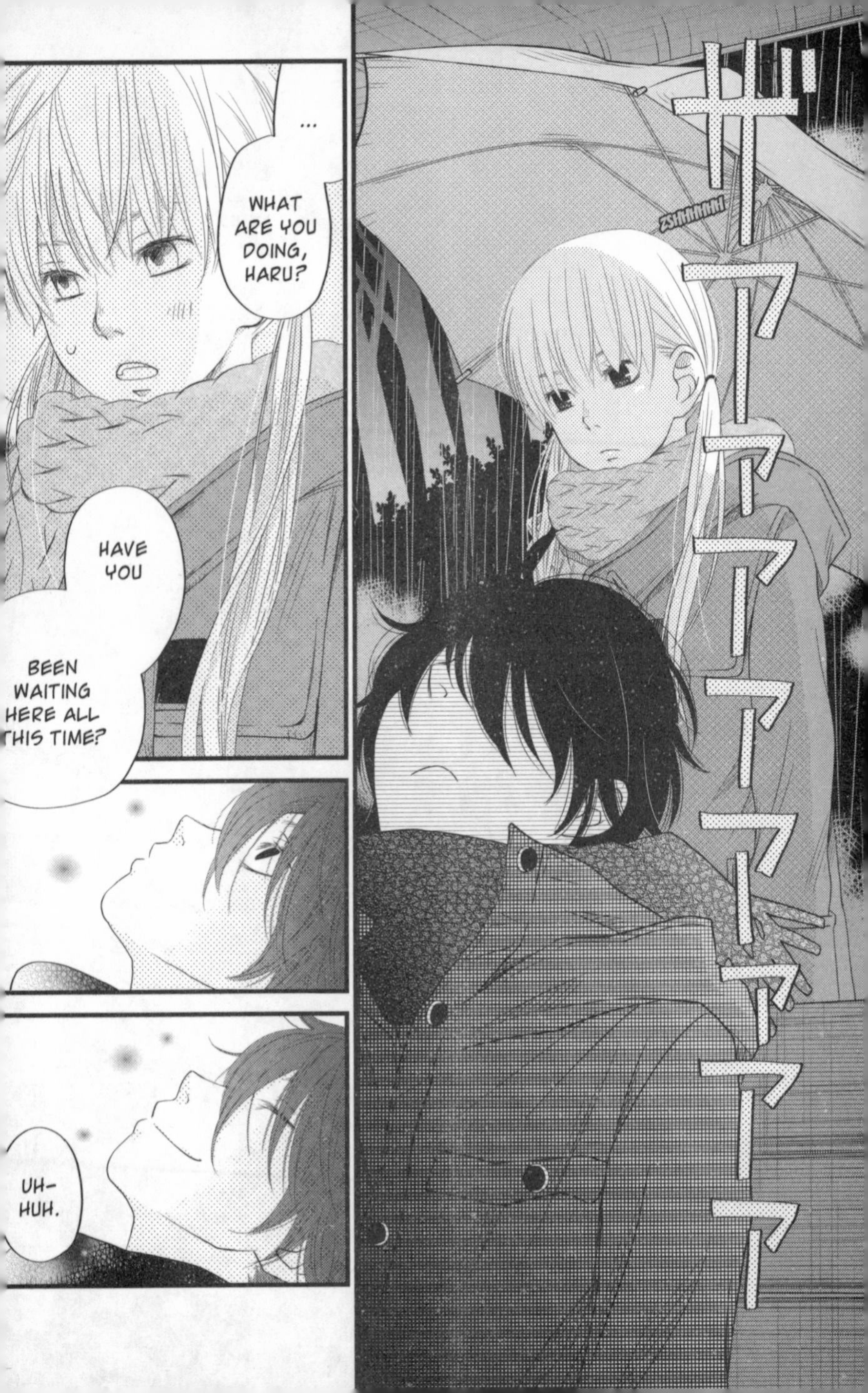
ザァァァァァァァァ
ZSHHHHHHH
...
WHAT ARE YOU DOING, HARU?
HAVE YOU
BEEN WAITING HERE ALL THIS TIME?
UH-HUH.

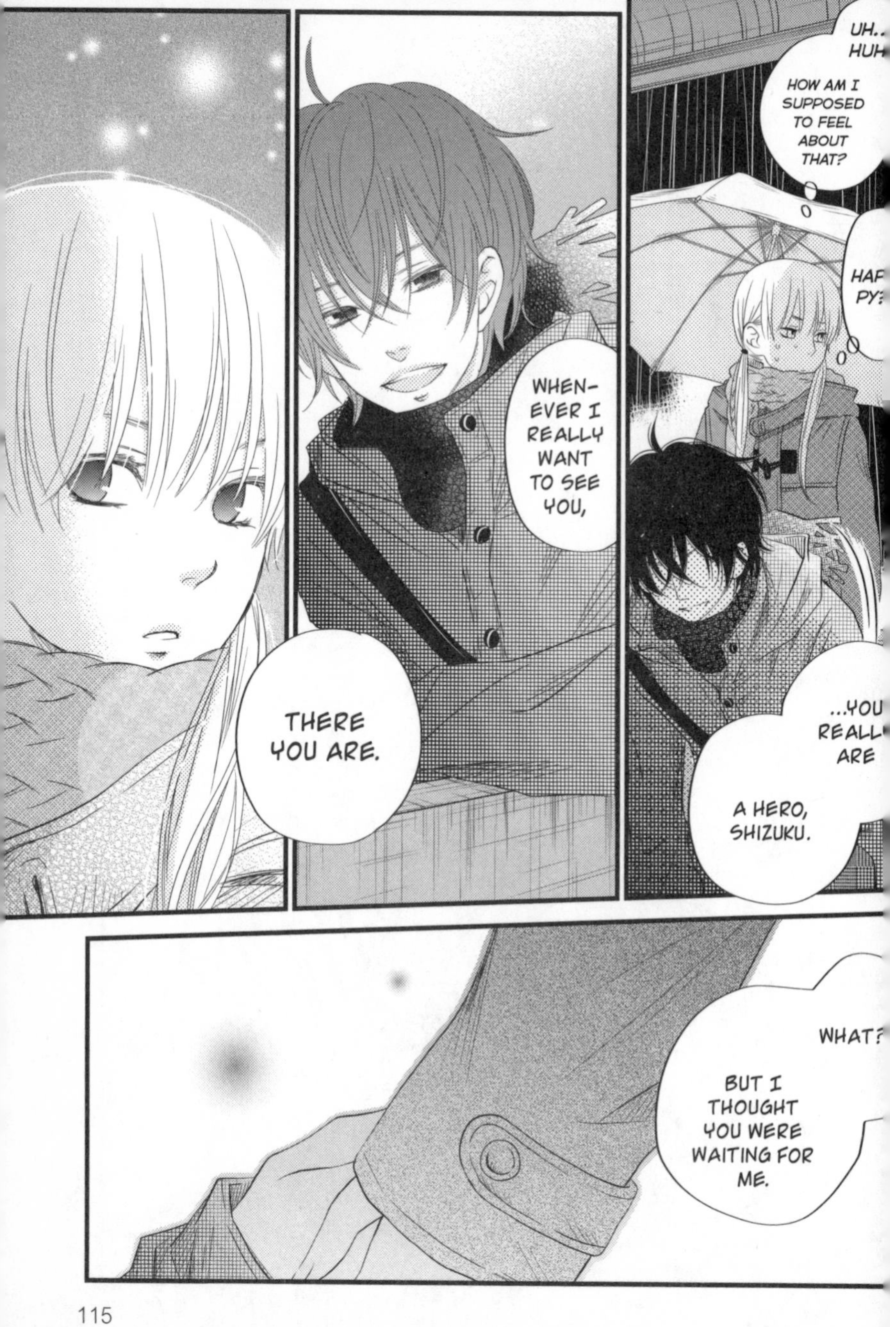
UH... HUH
HOW AM I SUPPOSED TO FEEL ABOUT THAT?
HAPPY?
...YOU REALLY ARE
A HERO, SHIZUKU.
WHENEVER I REALLY WANT TO SEE YOU,
THERE YOU ARE.
WHAT?
BUT I THOUGHT YOU WERE WAITING FOR ME.

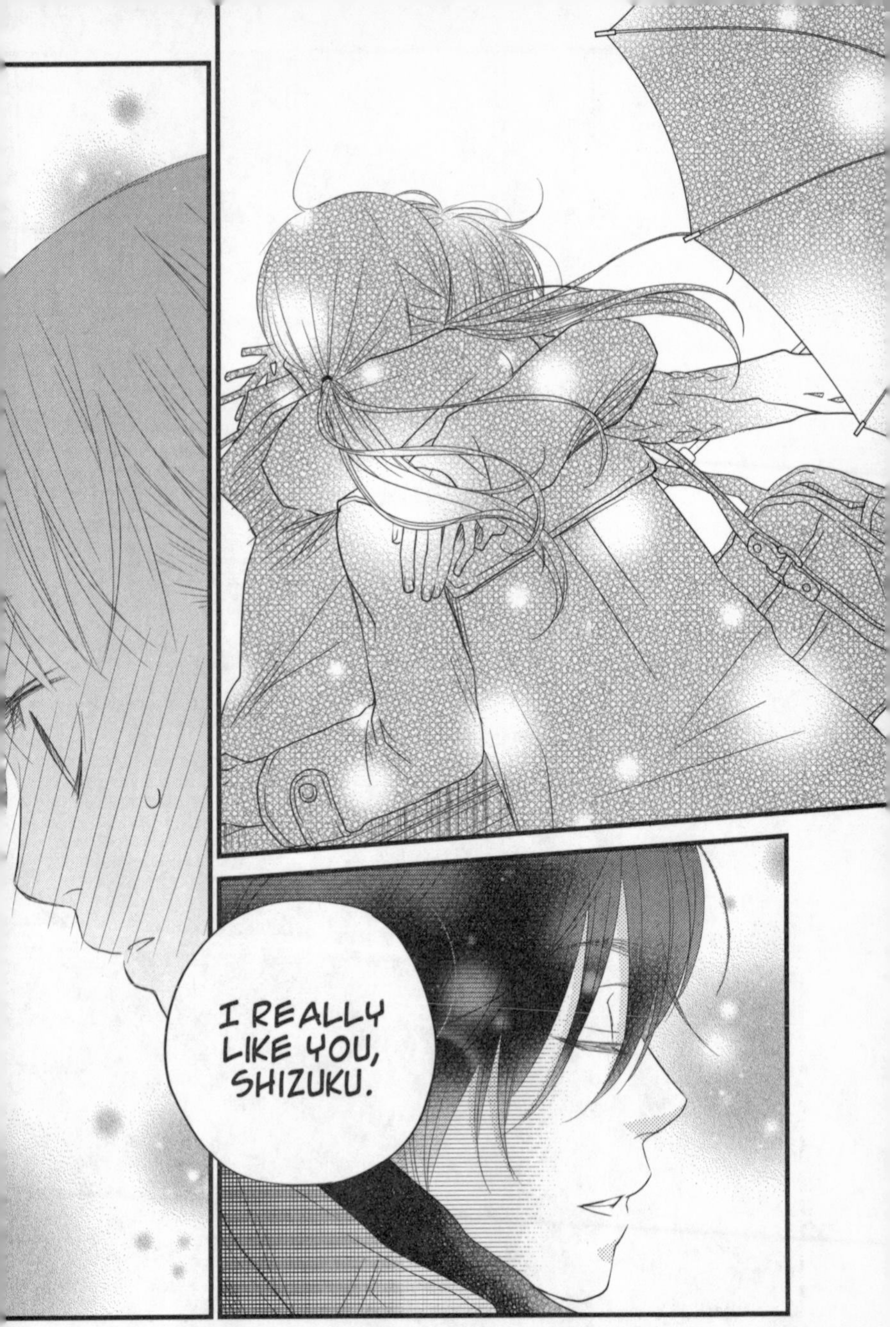
I REALLY LIKE YOU, SHIZUKU.

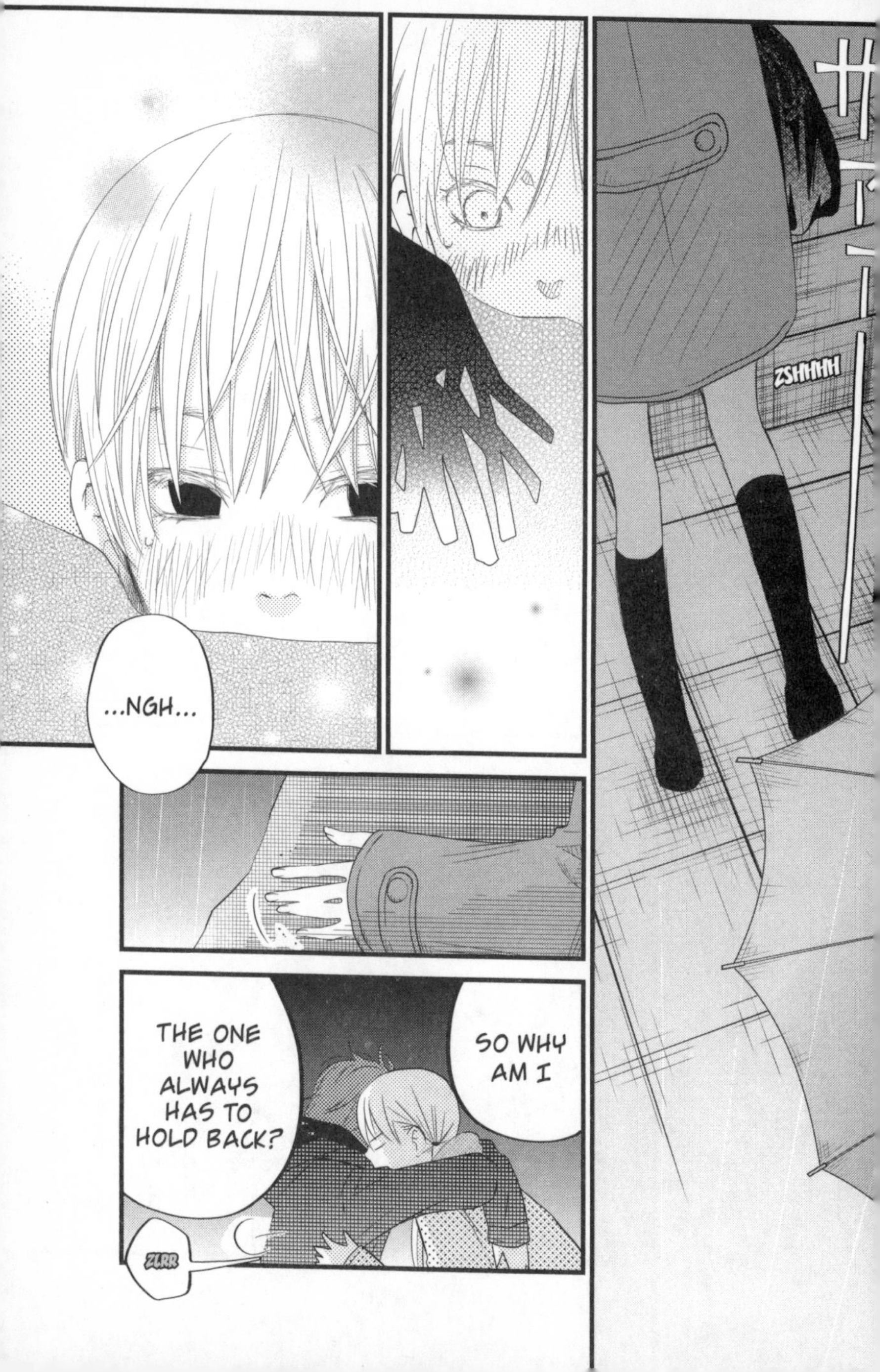
ZSHHHH
...NGH...
SO WHY AM I
THE ONE WHO ALWAYS HAS TO HOLD BACK?
ZLRR

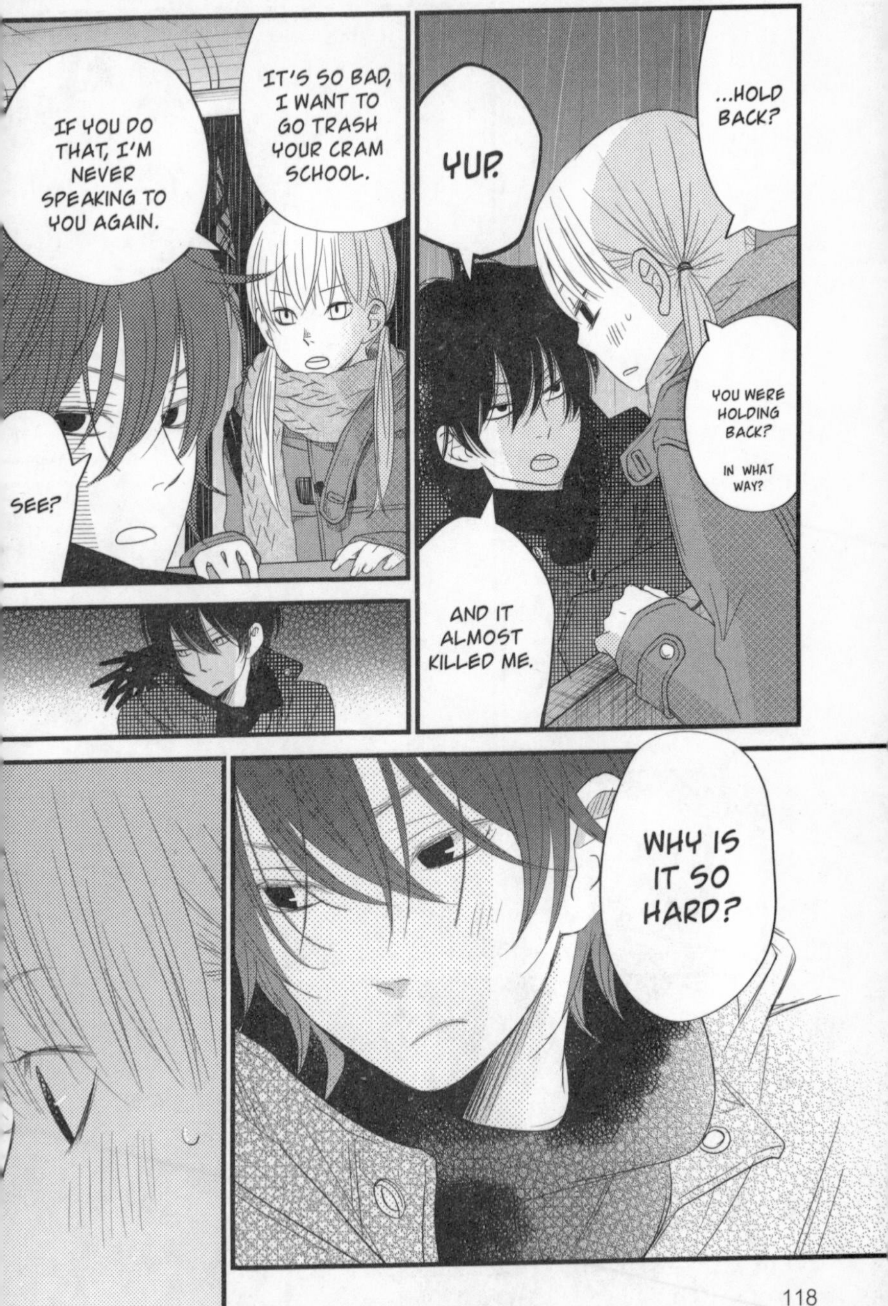
...HOLD BACK?
YUP.
YOU WERE HOLDING BACK? IN WHAT WAY?
AND IT ALMOST KILLED ME.
IT'S SO BAD, I WANT TO GO TRASH YOUR CRAM SCHOOL.
IF YOU DO THAT, I'M NEVER SPEAKING TO YOU AGAIN.
SEE?
WHY IS IT SO HARD?

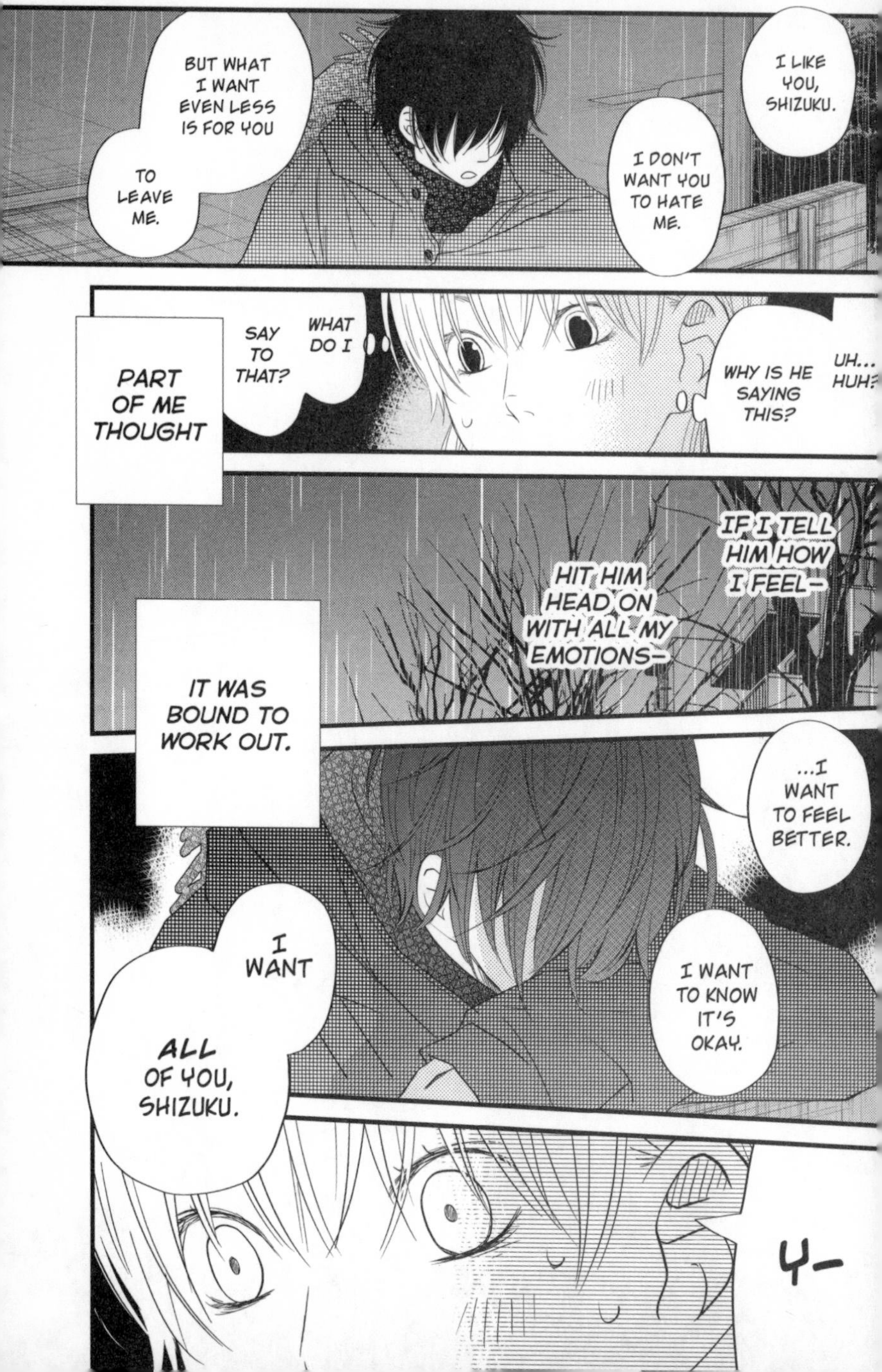

I LIKE YOU, SHIZUKU.
I DON'T WANT YOU TO HATE ME.
BUT WHAT I WANT EVEN LESS IS FOR YOU
TO LEAVE ME.
UH... HUH?
WHY IS HE SAYING THIS?
WHAT DO I SAY TO THAT?
PART OF ME THOUGHT
IF I TELL HIM HOW I FEEL–
HIT HIM HEAD ON WITH ALL MY EMOTIONS–
IT WAS BOUND TO WORK OUT.
...I WANT TO FEEL BETTER.
I WANT TO KNOW IT'S OKAY.
I WANT
ALL OF YOU, SHIZUKU.
Y–

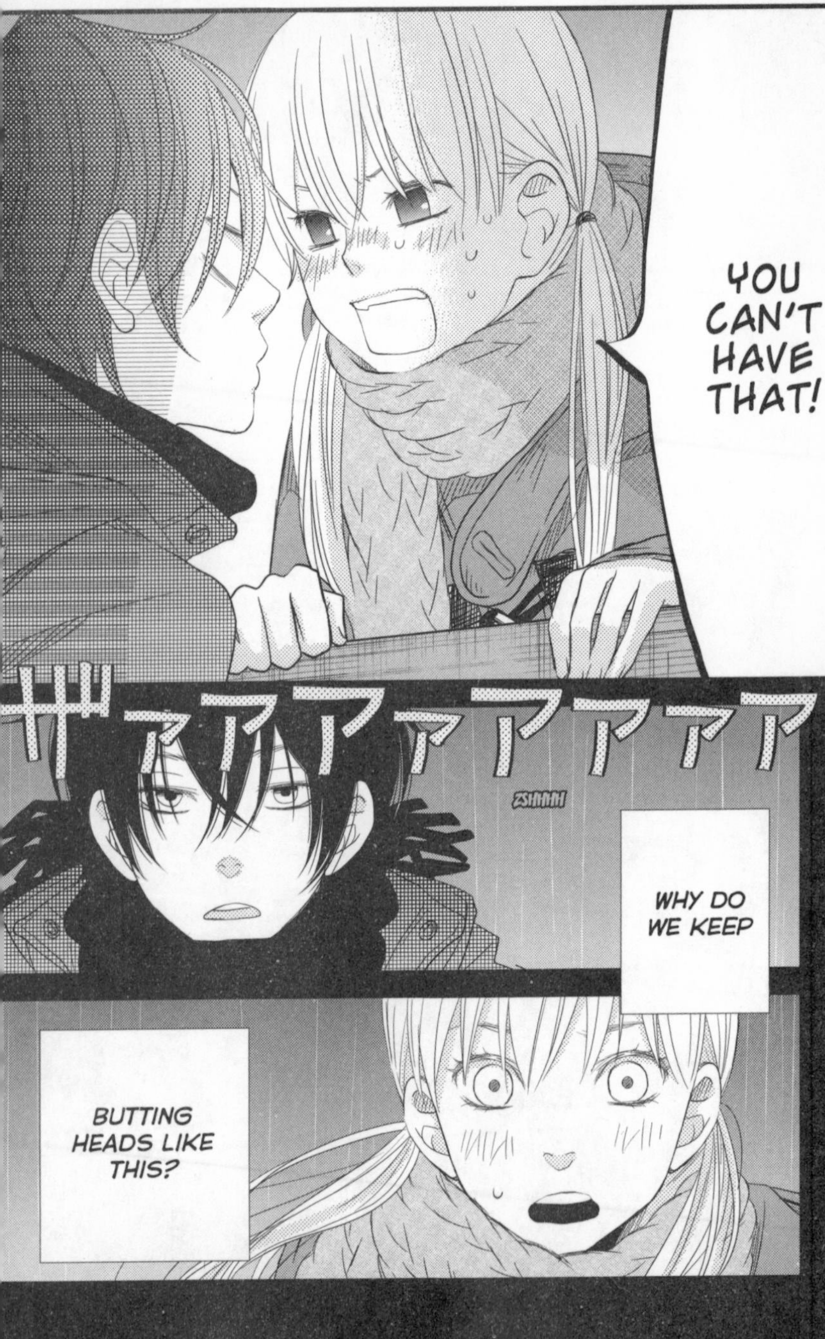
YOU CAN'T HAVE THAT!
ザァアァァアアアア
ZSHHHH
WHY DO WE KEEP
BUTTING HEADS LIKE THIS?

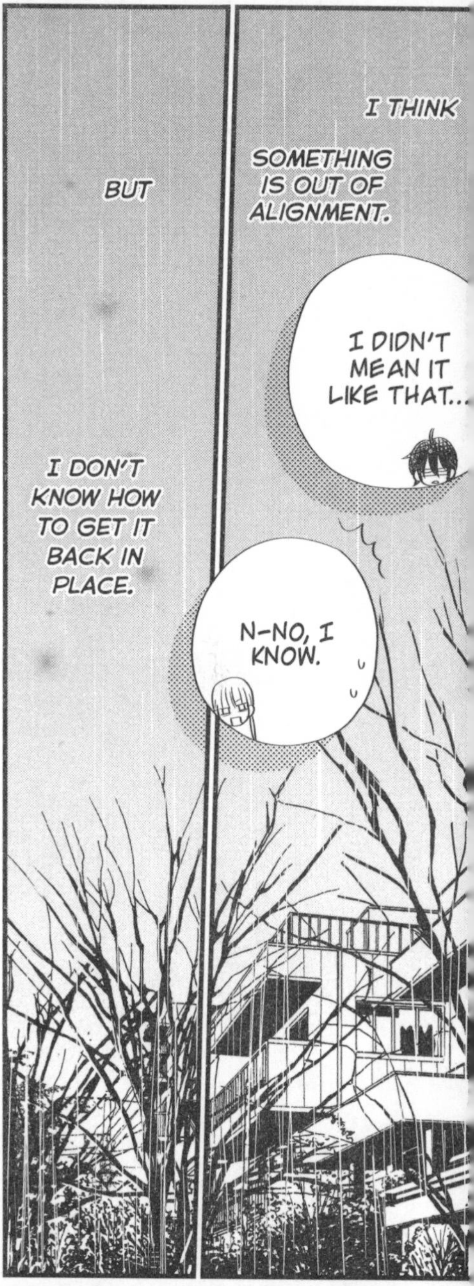
I THINK
SOMETHING IS OUT OF ALIGNMENT.
I DIDN'T MEAN IT LIKE THAT...
N-NO, I KNOW.
BUT
I DON'T KNOW HOW TO GET IT BACK IN PLACE.
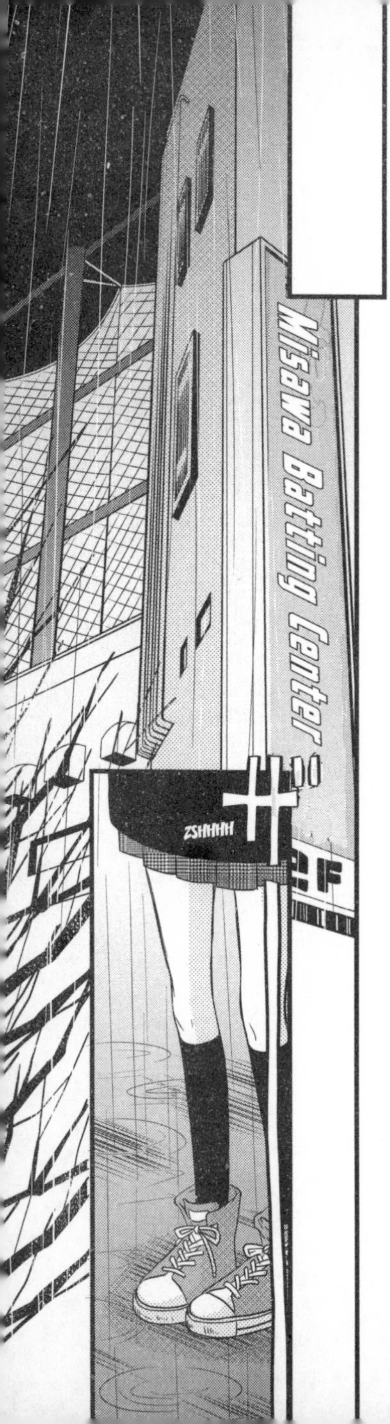
Misawa Batting Center
ZSHHHH
2F

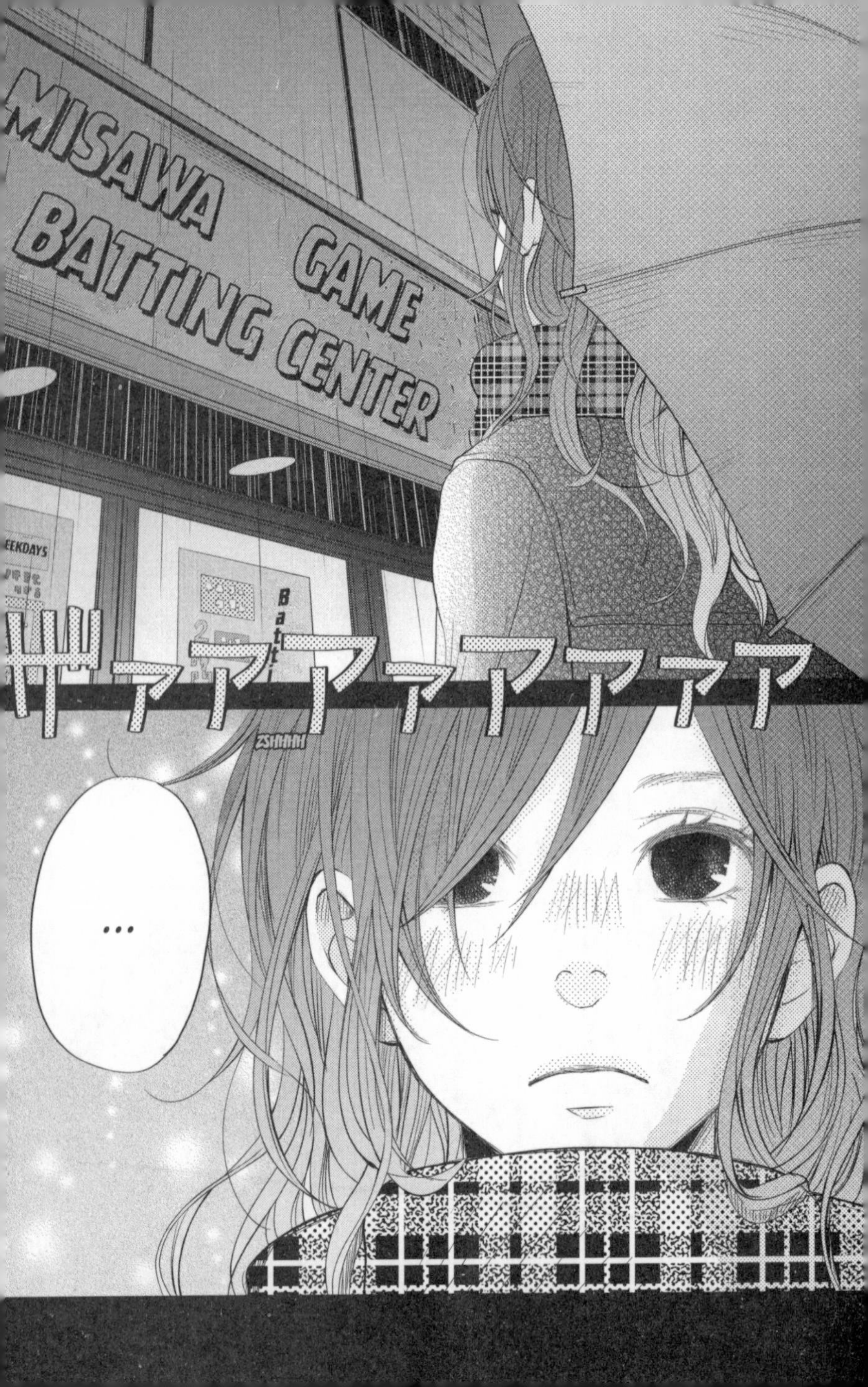
MISAWA GAME
BATTING CENTER
WEEKDAYS
ザァァァァァァァ
ZSHHHH
...

Underwater Battle

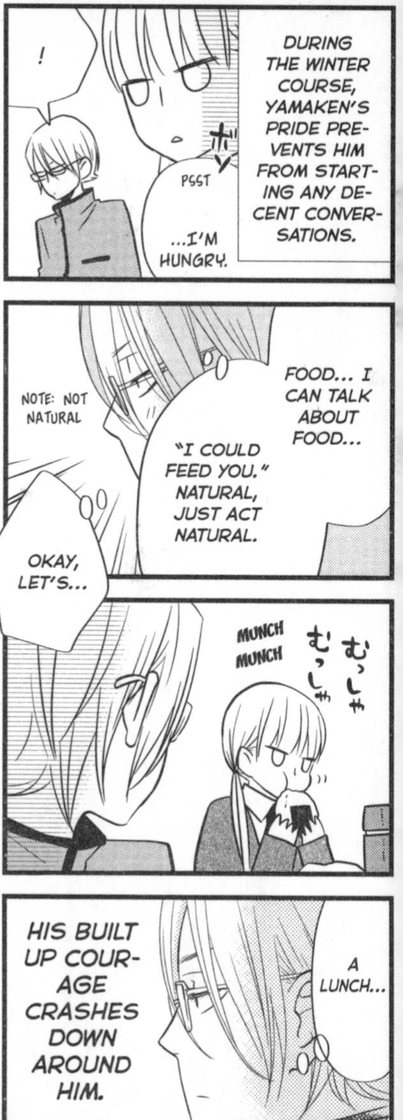

DURING THE WINTER COURSE, YAMAKEN'S PRIDE PREVENTS HIM FROM STARTING ANY DECENT CONVERSATIONS.
!
PSST
...I'M HUNGRY.
FOOD... I CAN TALK ABOUT FOOD...
"I COULD FEED YOU." NATURAL, JUST ACT NATURAL.
NOTE: NOT NATURAL
OKAY, LET'S...
むっしゃ むっしゃ
MUNCH MUNCH
A LUNCH...
HIS BUILT UP COURAGE CRASHES DOWN AROUND HIM.

Arrabbiata

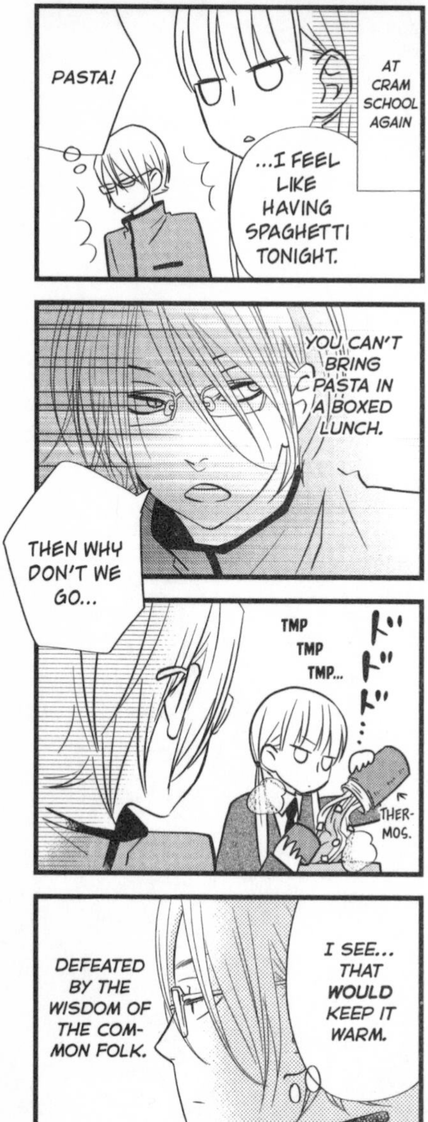

AT CRAM SCHOOL AGAIN
...I FEEL LIKE HAVING SPAGHETTI TONIGHT.
PASTA!
YOU CAN'T BRING PASTA IN A BOXED LUNCH.
THEN WHY DON'T WE GO...
ドドド...
TMP TMP TMP...
THERMOS.
I SEE... THAT WOULD KEEP IT WARM.
DEFEATED BY THE WISDOM OF THE COMMON FOLK.

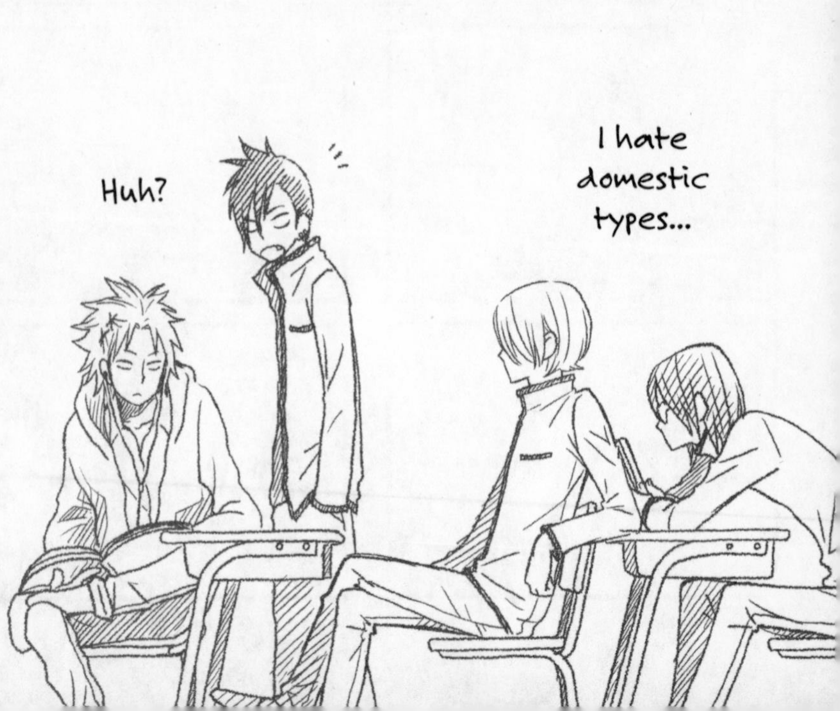
I hate domestic types...
Huh?

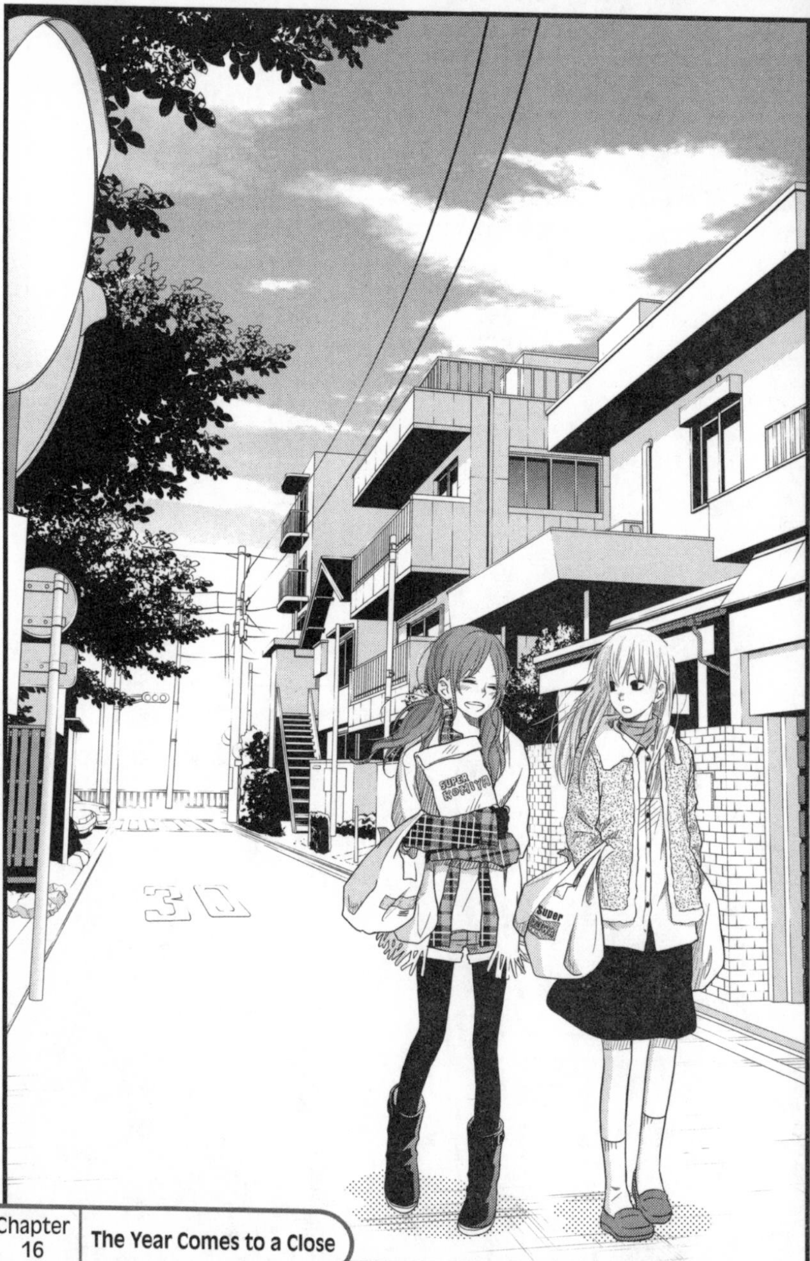
SUPER KOMIYA
30

Chapter 16 The Year Comes to a Close

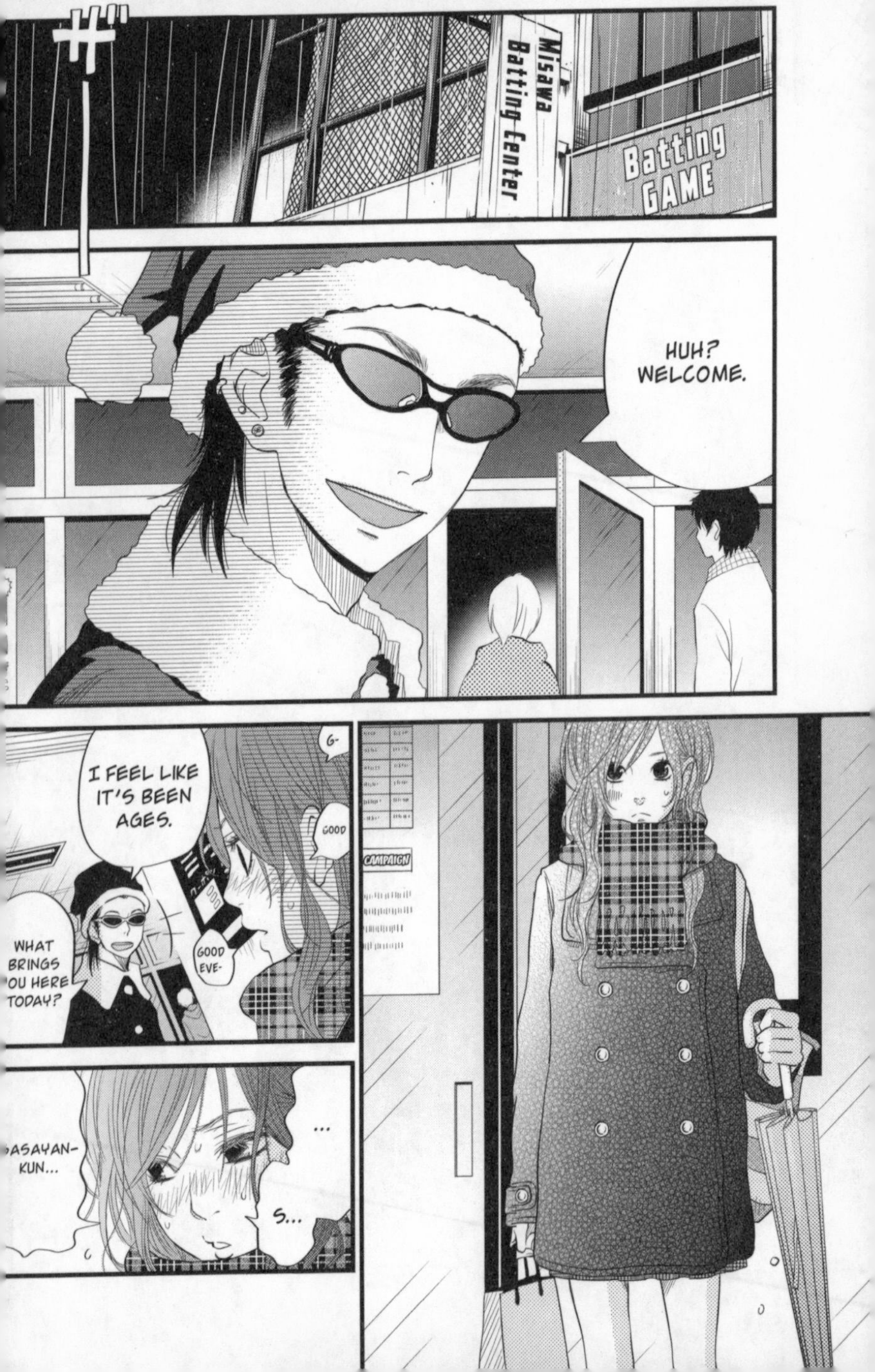
Misawa Batting Center
Batting GAME
ザ
HUH? WELCOME.
G-
I FEEL LIKE IT'S BEEN AGES.
GOOD
GOOD EVE-
WHAT BRINGS OU HERE TODAY?
...
SASAYAN-KUN...
S...

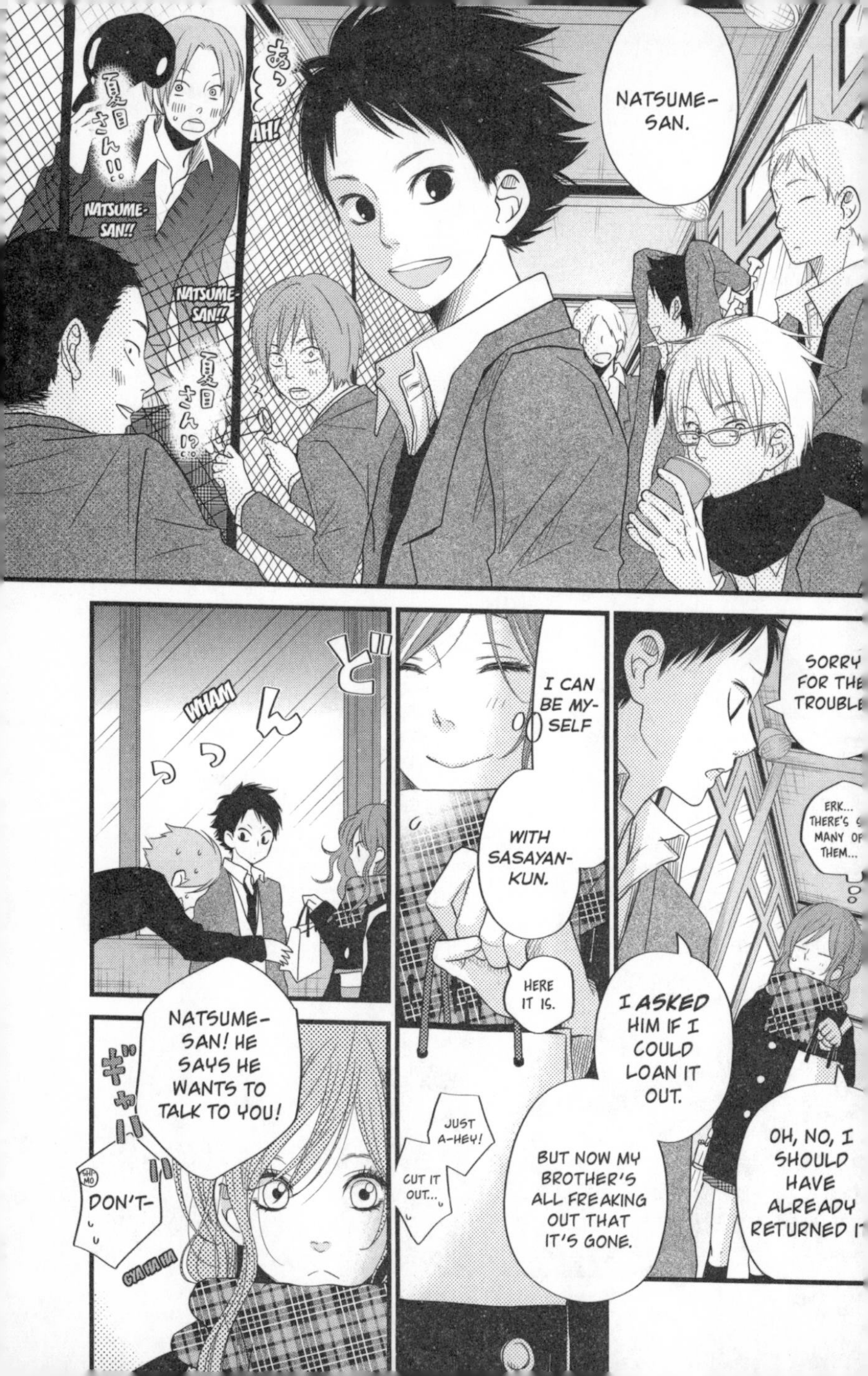
NATSUME-SAN.
あっ
AH!
夏目さん!!
NATSUME-SAN!!
NATSUME-SAN!!
夏目さん!?
SORRY FOR THE TROUBLE
ERK... THERE'S S MANY OF THEM...
I CAN BE MY-SELF
WITH SASAYAN-KUN.
どっ
WHAM
んつつ
OH, NO, I SHOULD HAVE ALREADY RETURNED IT
HERE IT IS.
I ASKED HIM IF I COULD LOAN IT OUT.
BUT NOW MY BROTHER'S ALL FREAKING OUT THAT IT'S GONE.
JUST A-HEY!
CUT IT OUT...
NATSUME-SAN! HE SAYS HE WANTS TO TALK TO YOU!
ギャハハ
GYA HA HA
SHIMO
DON'T-

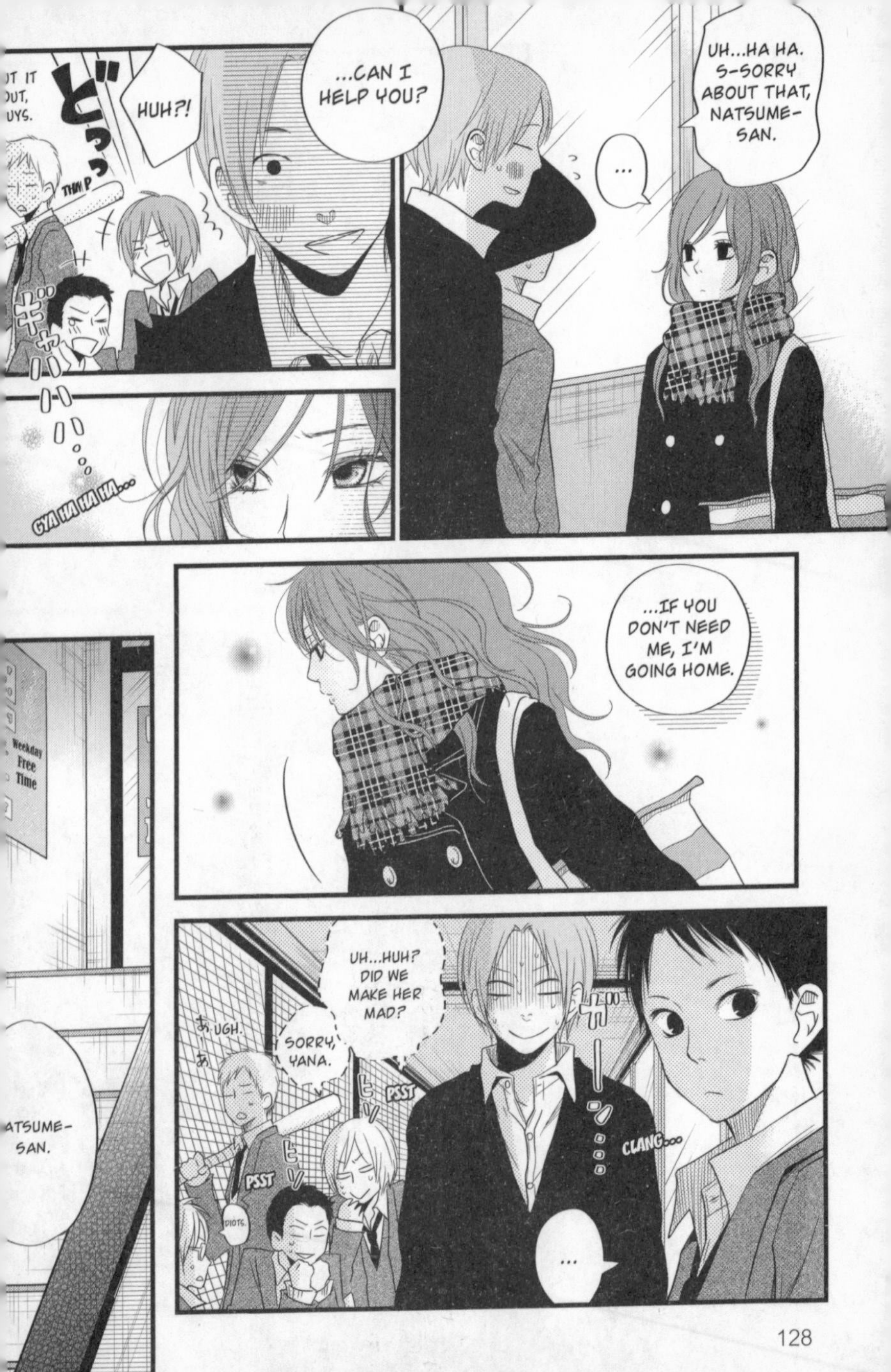

UH...HA HA. S-SORRY ABOUT THAT, NATSUME-SAN.
...
...CAN I HELP YOU?
HUH?!
UT IT OUT, UYS.
THWP
GYA HA HA HA...
...IF YOU DON'T NEED ME, I'M GOING HOME.
Weekday Free Time
ATSUME-SAN.
UH...HUH? DID WE MAKE HER MAD?
SORRY, YANA.
UGH.
PSST
PSST
IDIOTS.
CLANG...
...

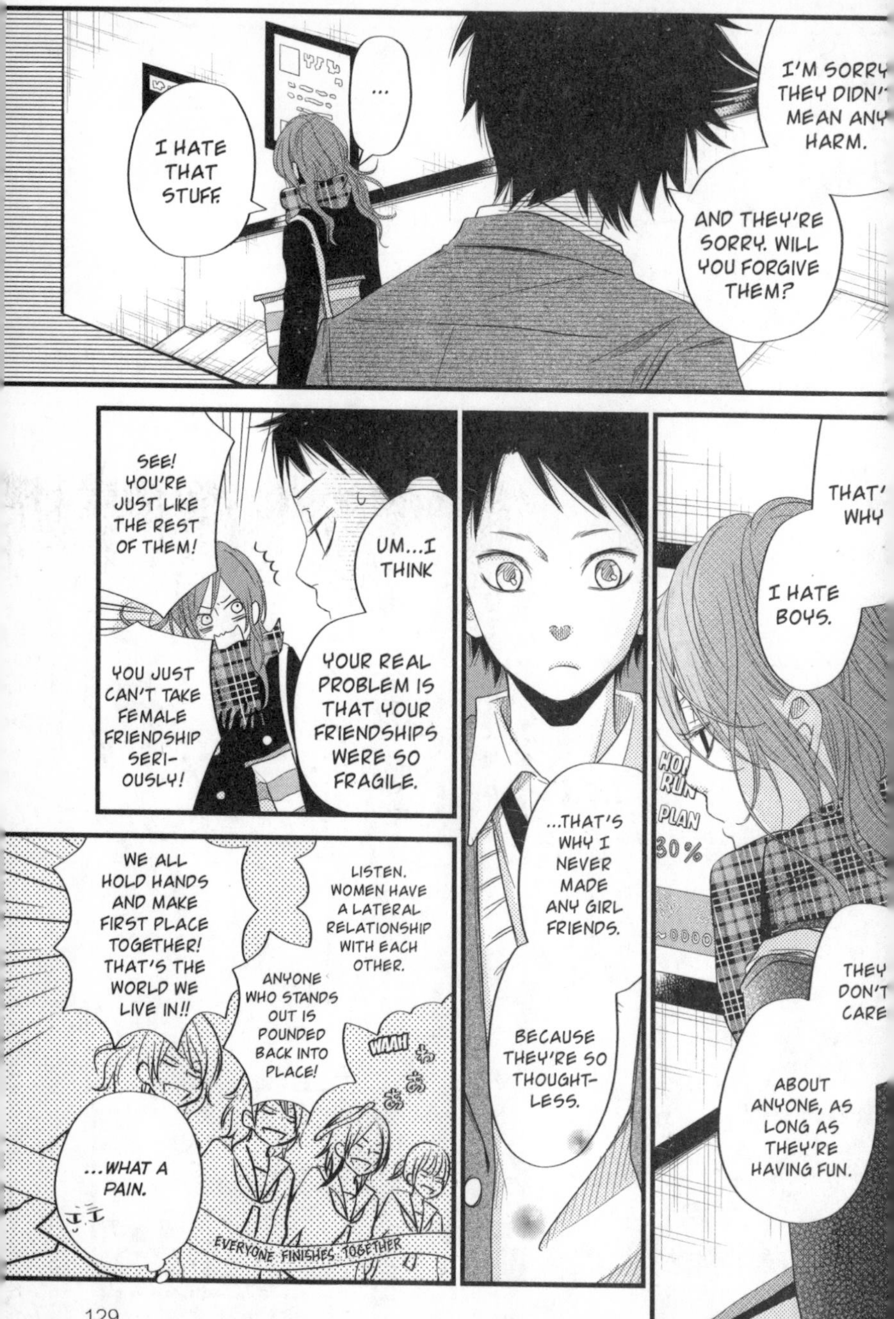
I'M SORRY THEY DIDN'T MEAN ANY HARM.
AND THEY'RE SORRY. WILL YOU FORGIVE THEM?
...
I HATE THAT STUFF.
THAT' WHY
I HATE BOYS.
THEY DON'T CARE
ABOUT ANYONE, AS LONG AS THEY'RE HAVING FUN.
PLAN
30%
...THAT'S WHY I NEVER MADE ANY GIRL FRIENDS.
BECAUSE THEY'RE SO THOUGHTLESS.
UM...I THINK
YOUR REAL PROBLEM IS THAT YOUR FRIENDSHIPS WERE SO FRAGILE.
SEE! YOU'RE JUST LIKE THE REST OF THEM!
YOU JUST CAN'T TAKE FEMALE FRIENDSHIP SERIOUSLY!
LISTEN. WOMEN HAVE A LATERAL RELATIONSHIP WITH EACH OTHER.
ANYONE WHO STANDS OUT IS POUNDED BACK INTO PLACE!
WE ALL HOLD HANDS AND MAKE FIRST PLACE TOGETHER! THAT'S THE WORLD WE LIVE IN!!
WAAH
...WHAT A PAIN.
EVERYONE FINISHES TOGETHER

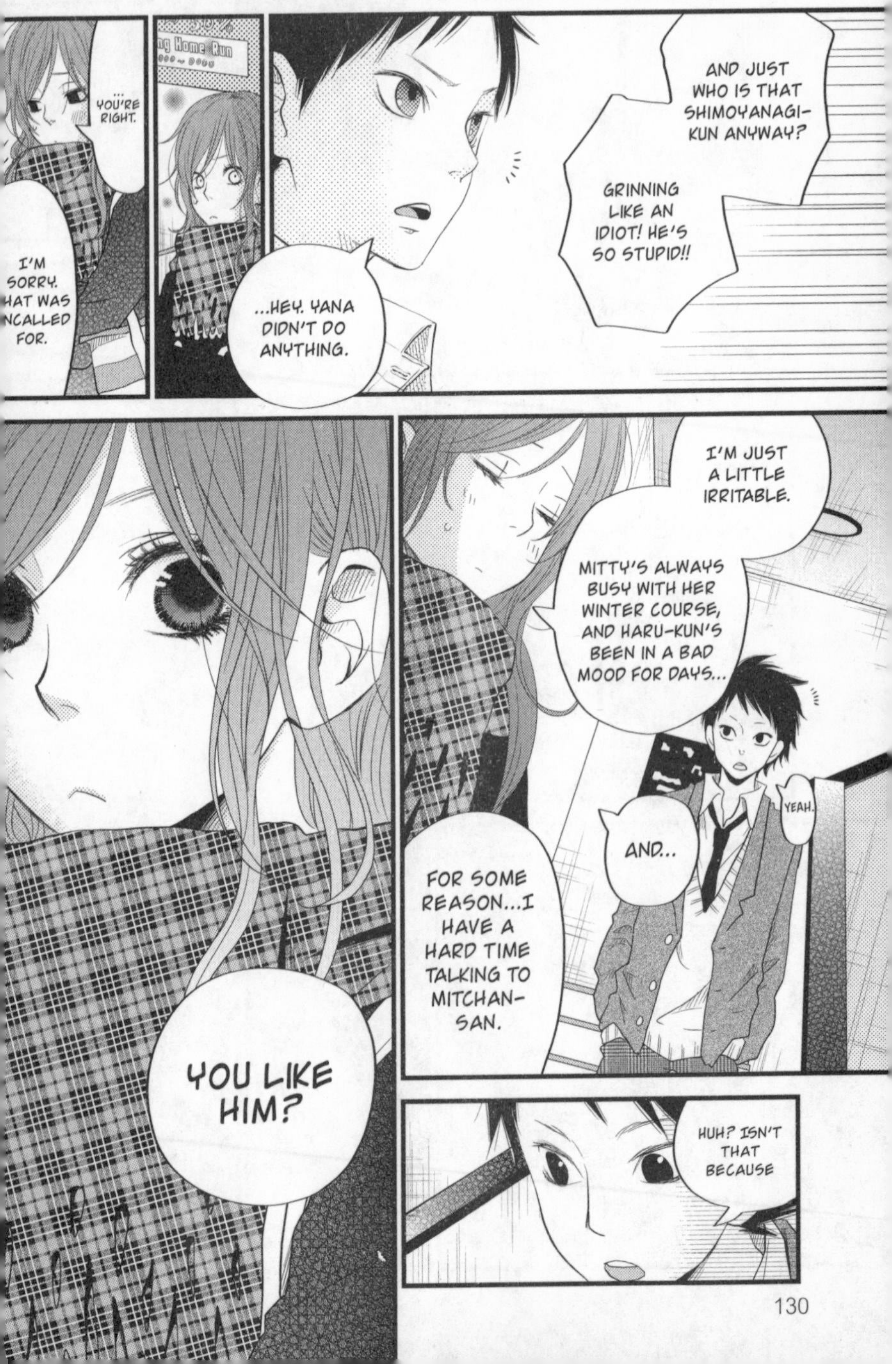
AND JUST WHO IS THAT SHIMOYANAGI-KUN ANYWAY?
GRINNING LIKE AN IDIOT! HE'S SO STUPID!!
...HEY. YANA DIDN'T DO ANYTHING.
... YOU'RE RIGHT.
I'M SORRY. HAT WAS NCALLED FOR.
I'M JUST A LITTLE IRRITABLE.
MITTY'S ALWAYS BUSY WITH HER WINTER COURSE, AND HARU-KUN'S BEEN IN A BAD MOOD FOR DAYS...
YEAH.
AND...
FOR SOME REASON...I HAVE A HARD TIME TALKING TO MITCHAN-SAN.
HUH? ISN'T THAT BECAUSE
YOU LIKE HIM?

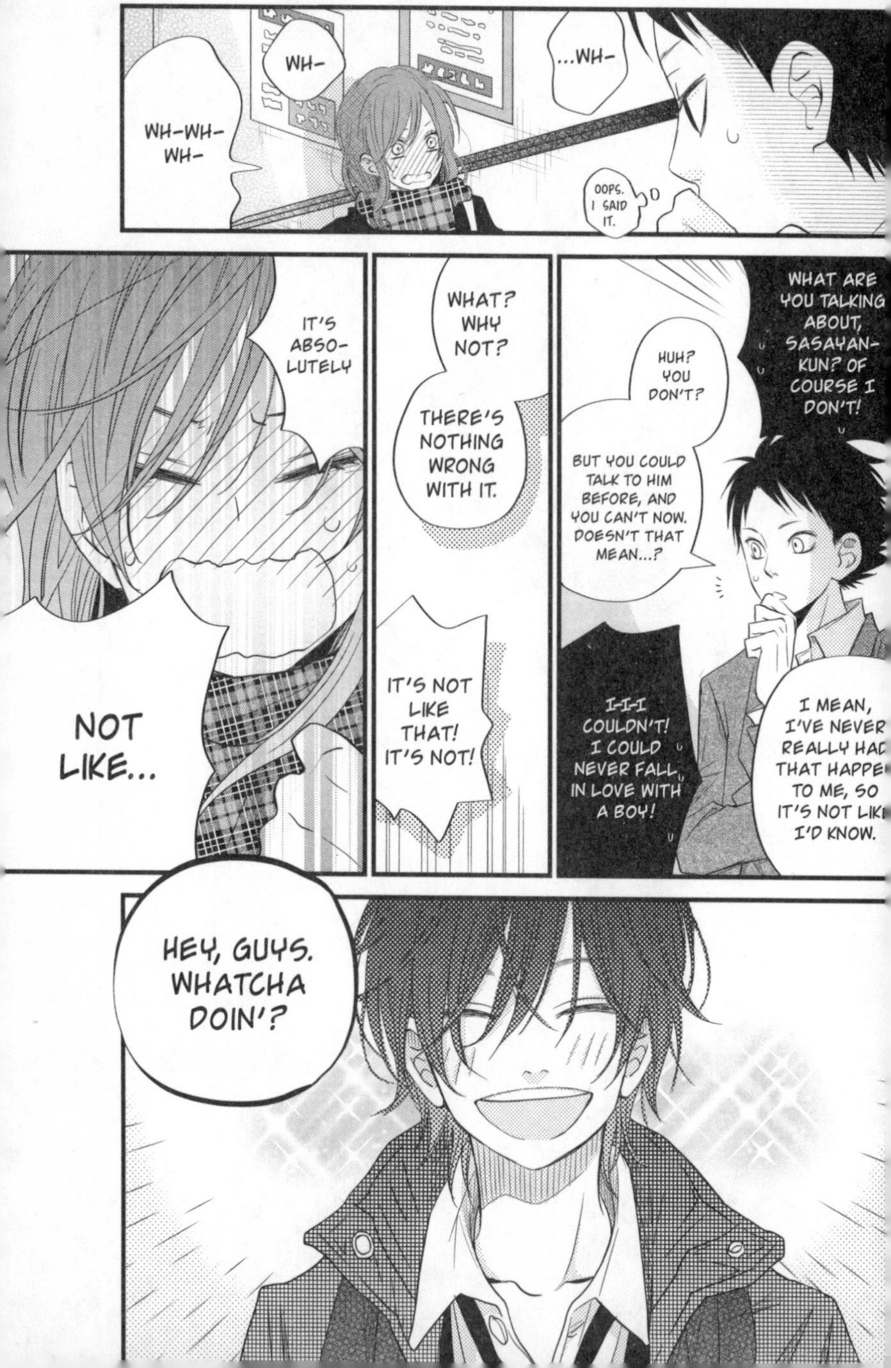
...WH-
WH-
OOPS. I SAID IT.
WH-WH-WH-
WHAT ARE YOU TALKING ABOUT, SASAYAN-KUN? OF COURSE I DON'T!
HUH? YOU DON'T?
BUT YOU COULD TALK TO HIM BEFORE, AND YOU CAN'T NOW. DOESN'T THAT MEAN...?
I MEAN, I'VE NEVER REALLY HA THAT HAPPE TO ME, SO IT'S NOT LIK I'D KNOW.
I-I-I COULDN'T! I COULD NEVER FALL IN LOVE WITH A BOY!
WHAT? WHY NOT?
THERE'S NOTHING WRONG WITH IT.
IT'S NOT LIKE THAT! IT'S NOT!
IT'S ABSO-LUTELY
NOT LIKE...
HEY, GUYS. WHATCHA DOIN'?

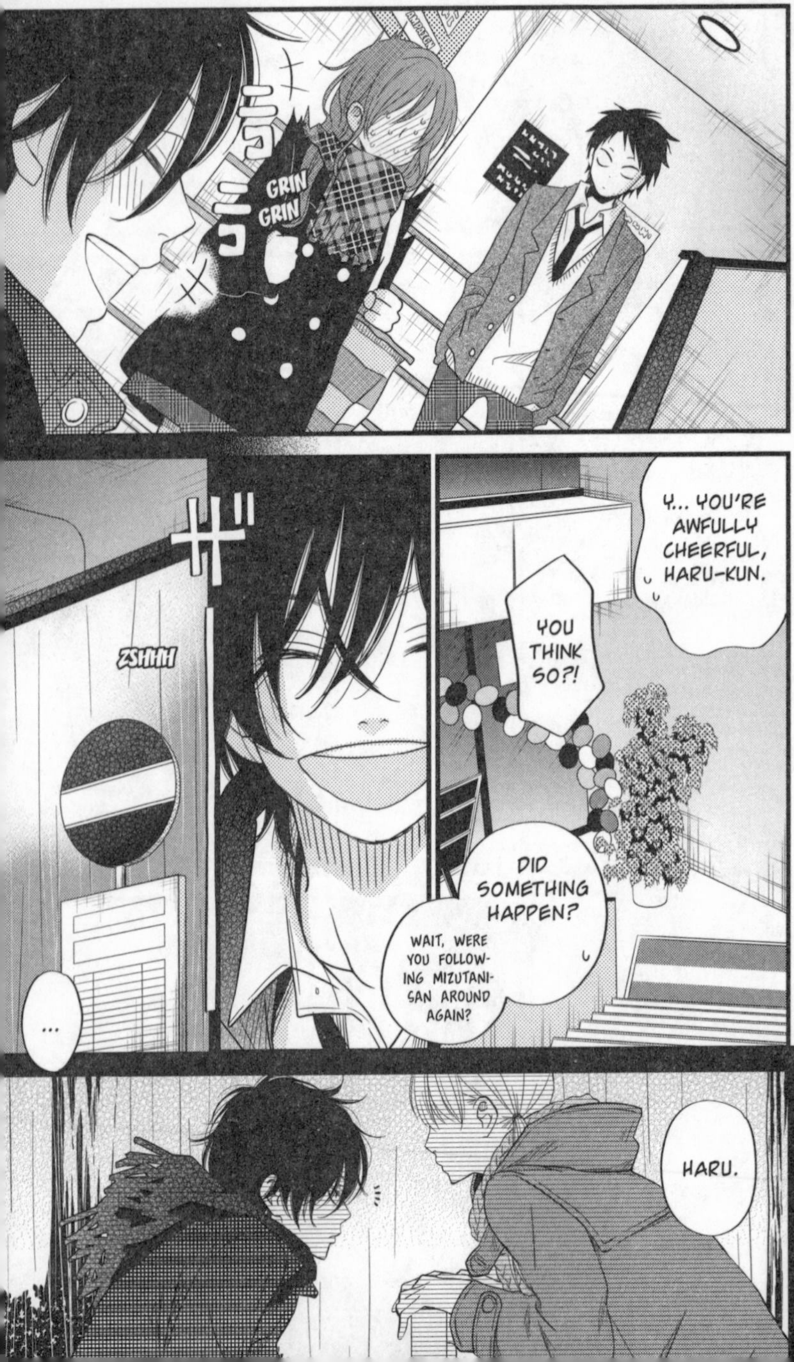
GRIN GRIN
Y... YOU'RE AWFULLY CHEERFUL, HARU-KUN.
YOU THINK SO?!
DID SOMETHING HAPPEN?
WAIT, WERE YOU FOLLOWING MIZUTANI-SAN AROUND AGAIN?
ZSHHH
...
HARU.

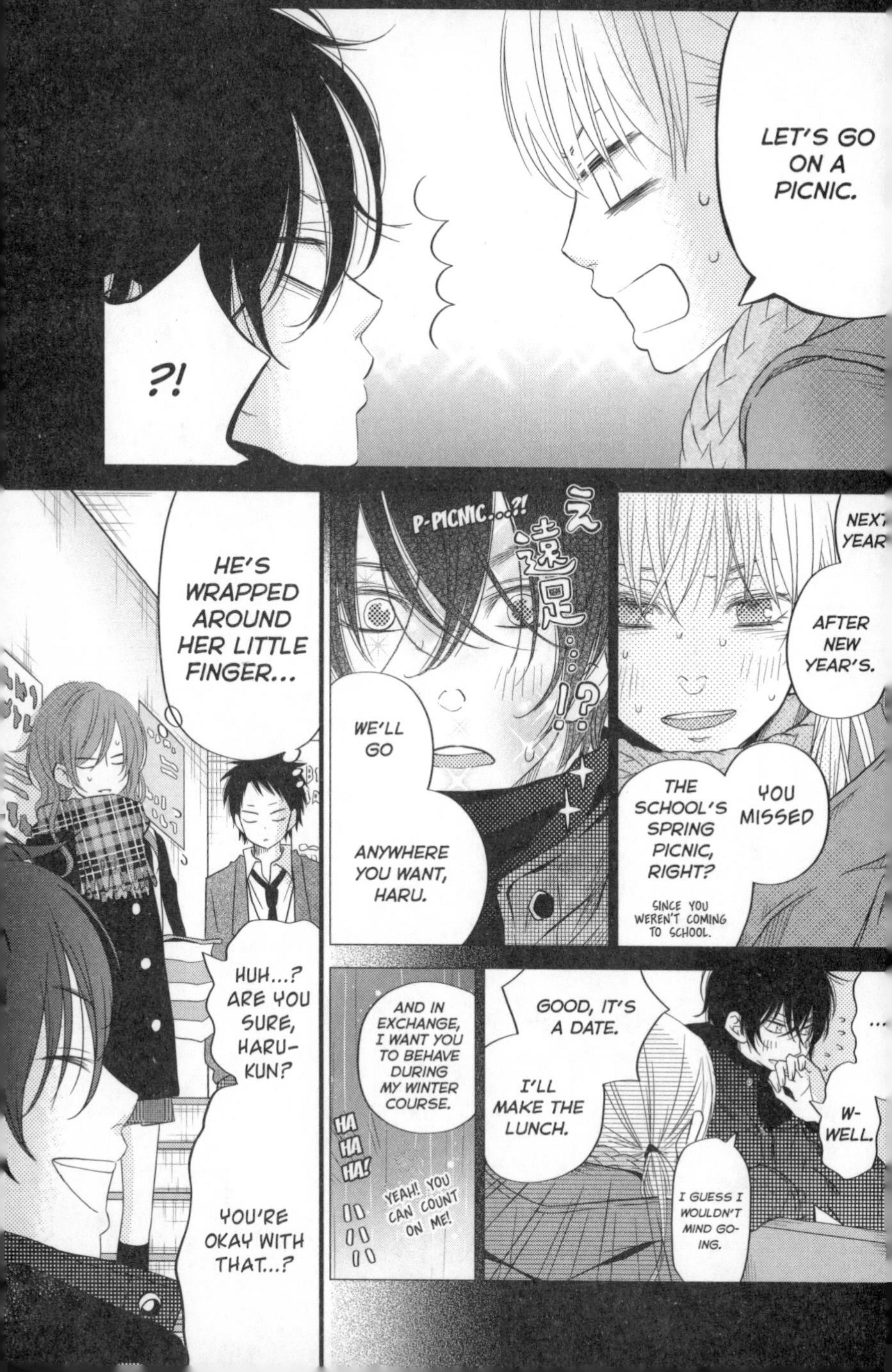
LET'S GO ON A PICNIC.
?!
NEXT YEAR
AFTER NEW YEAR'S.
YOU MISSED
THE SCHOOL'S SPRING PICNIC, RIGHT?
SINCE YOU WEREN'T COMING TO SCHOOL.
P-PICNIC...?!
え遠足…!?
WE'LL GO
ANYWHERE YOU WANT, HARU.
...
W-WELL.
I GUESS I WOULDN'T MIND GOING.
GOOD, IT'S A DATE.
I'LL MAKE THE LUNCH.
AND IN EXCHANGE, I WANT YOU TO BEHAVE DURING MY WINTER COURSE.
HA HA HA!
YEAH! YOU CAN COUNT ON ME!
HE'S WRAPPED AROUND HER LITTLE FINGER...
HUH...? ARE YOU SURE, HARU-KUN?
YOU'RE OKAY WITH THAT...?

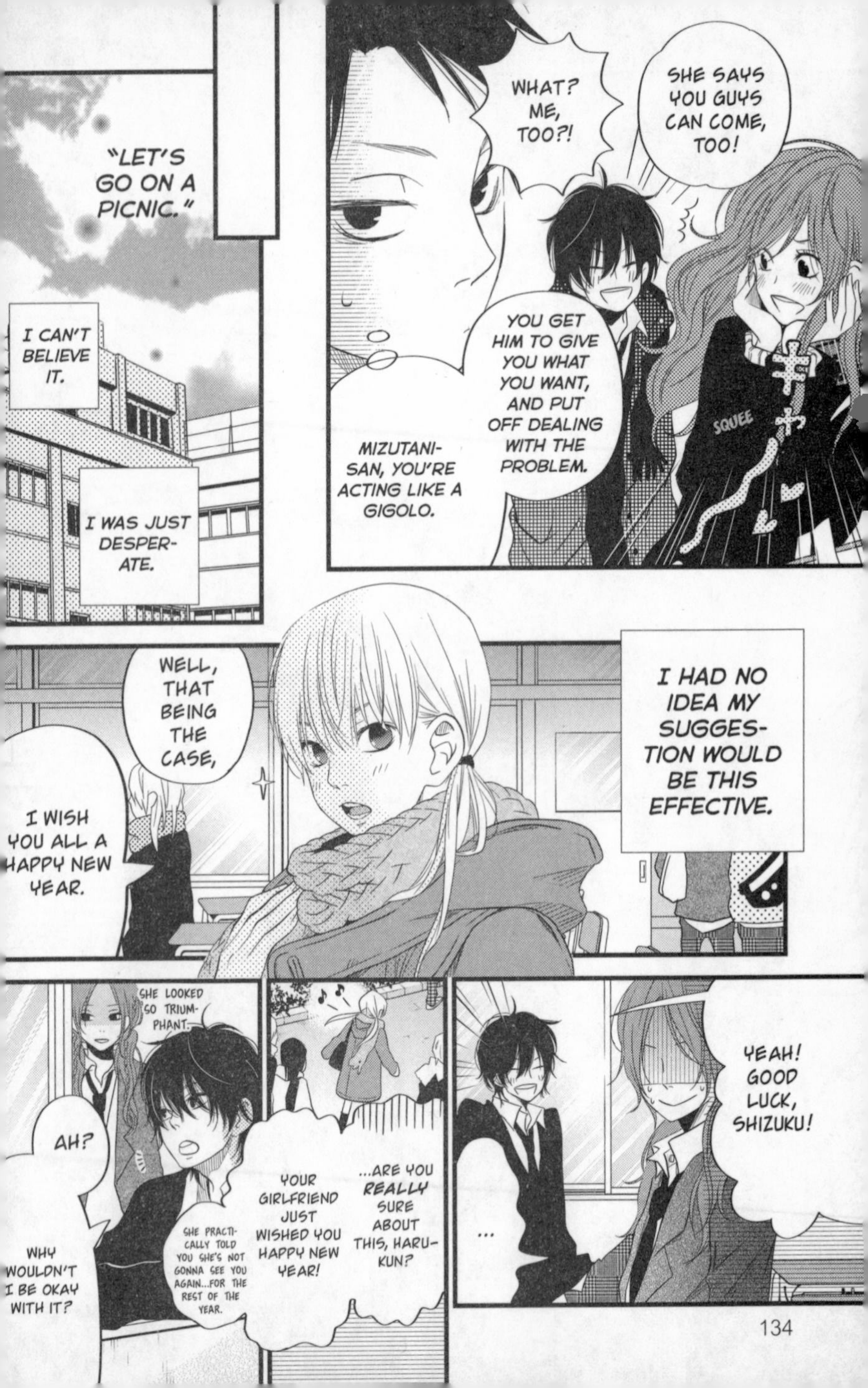
SHE SAYS YOU GUYS CAN COME, TOO!
WHAT? ME, TOO?!
SQUEE
YOU GET HIM TO GIVE YOU WHAT YOU WANT, AND PUT OFF DEALING WITH THE PROBLEM.
MIZUTANI-SAN, YOU'RE ACTING LIKE A GIGOLO.
"LET'S GO ON A PICNIC."
I CAN'T BELIEVE IT.
I WAS JUST DESPERATE.
I HAD NO IDEA MY SUGGESTION WOULD BE THIS EFFECTIVE.
WELL, THAT BEING THE CASE,
I WISH YOU ALL A HAPPY NEW YEAR.
YEAH! GOOD LUCK, SHIZUKU!
...
...ARE YOU REALLY SURE ABOUT THIS, HARU-KUN?
YOUR GIRLFRIEND JUST WISHED YOU HAPPY NEW YEAR!
SHE PRACTICALLY TOLD YOU SHE'S NOT GONNA SEE YOU AGAIN...FOR THE REST OF THE YEAR.
SHE LOOKED SO TRIUMPHANT.
AH?
WHY WOULDN'T I BE OKAY WITH IT?

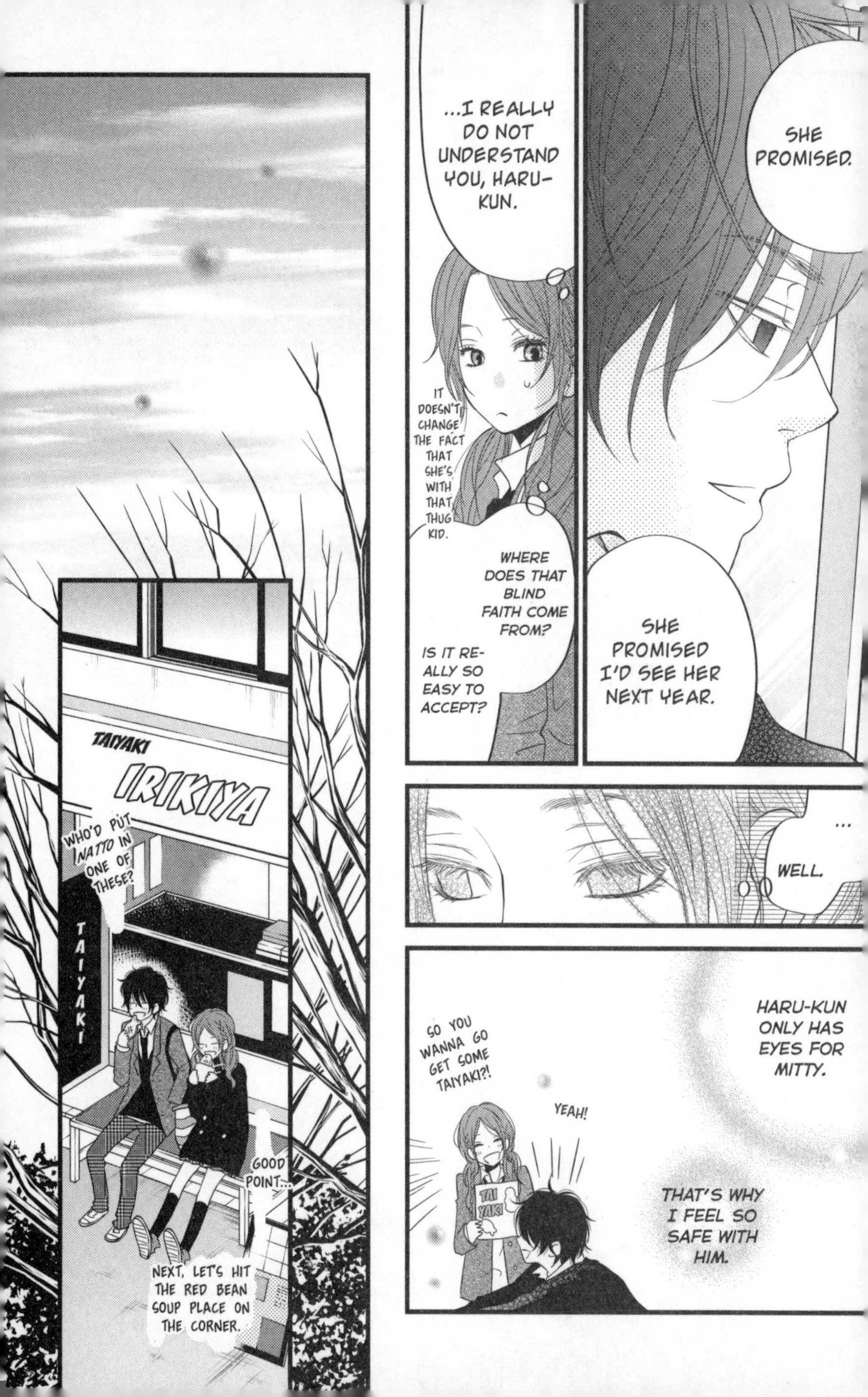
SHE PROMISED.
SHE PROMISED I'D SEE HER NEXT YEAR.
...I REALLY DO NOT UNDERSTAND YOU, HARU-KUN.
IT DOESN'T CHANGE THE FACT THAT SHE'S WITH THAT THUG KID.
WHERE DOES THAT BLIND FAITH COME FROM?
IS IT REALLY SO EASY TO ACCEPT?
...
WELL.
HARU-KUN ONLY HAS EYES FOR MITTY.
SO YOU WANNA GO GET SOME TAIYAKI?!
YEAH!
TAI YAKI
THAT'S WHY I FEEL SO SAFE WITH HIM.
TAIYAKI
IRIKIYA
TAIYAKI
WHO'D PUT NATTO IN ONE OF THESE?
GOOD POINT...
NEXT, LET'S HIT THE RED BEAN SOUP PLACE ON THE CORNER.

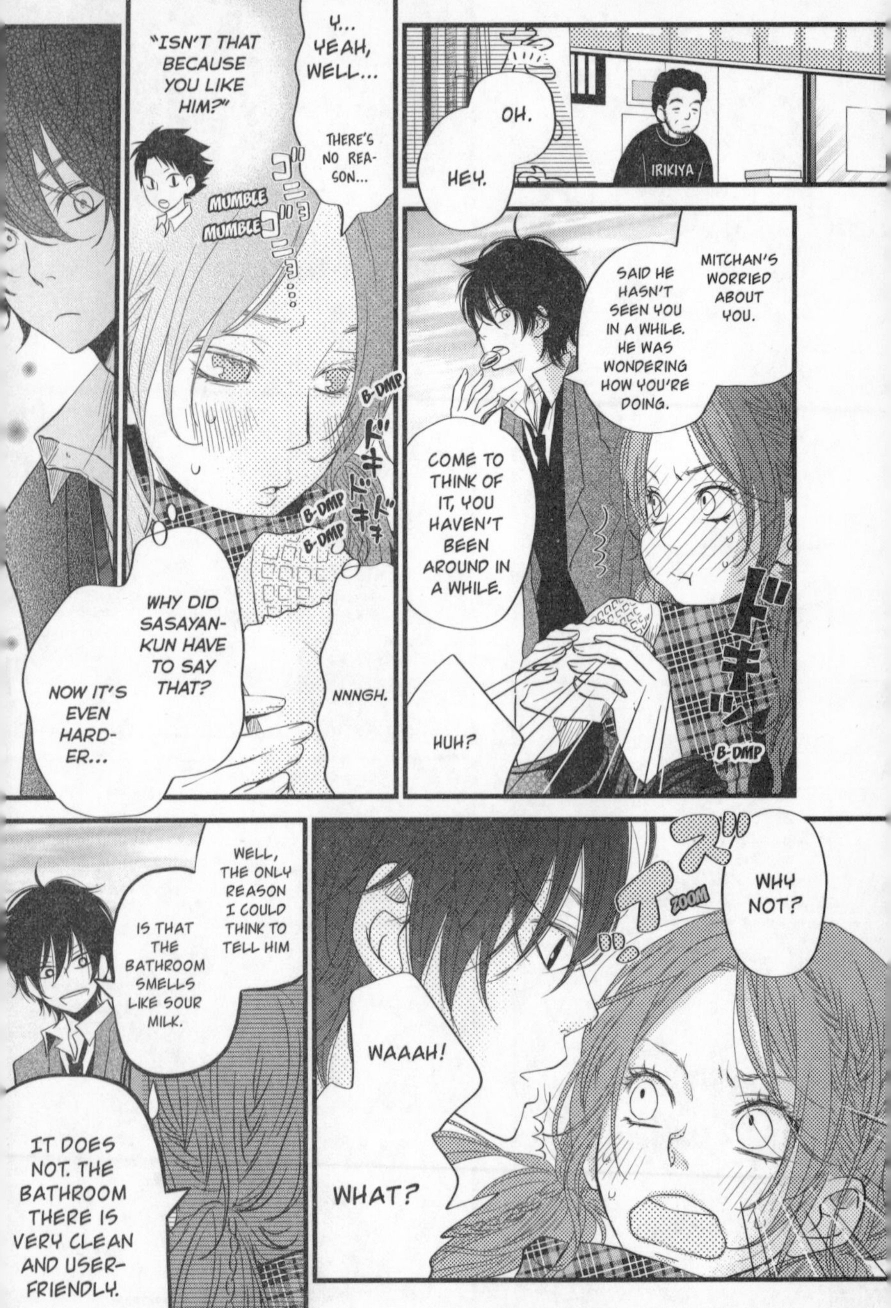
IRIKIYA
OH.
HEY.
MITCHAN'S WORRIED ABOUT YOU.
SAID HE HASN'T SEEN YOU IN A WHILE. HE WAS WONDERING HOW YOU'RE DOING.
COME TO THINK OF IT, YOU HAVEN'T BEEN AROUND IN A WHILE.
B-DMP
HUH?
Y... YEAH, WELL...
THERE'S NO REA-SON...
MUMBLE
MUMBLE
"ISN'T THAT BECAUSE YOU LIKE HIM?"
B-DMP
B-DMP
B-DMP
NNNGH.
WHY DID SASAYAN-KUN HAVE TO SAY THAT?
NOW IT'S EVEN HARD-ER...
WHY NOT?
ZOOM
WAAAH!
WHAT?
WELL, THE ONLY REASON I COULD THINK TO TELL HIM
IS THAT THE BATHROOM SMELLS LIKE SOUR MILK.
IT DOES NOT. THE BATHROOM THERE IS VERY CLEAN AND USER-FRIENDLY.

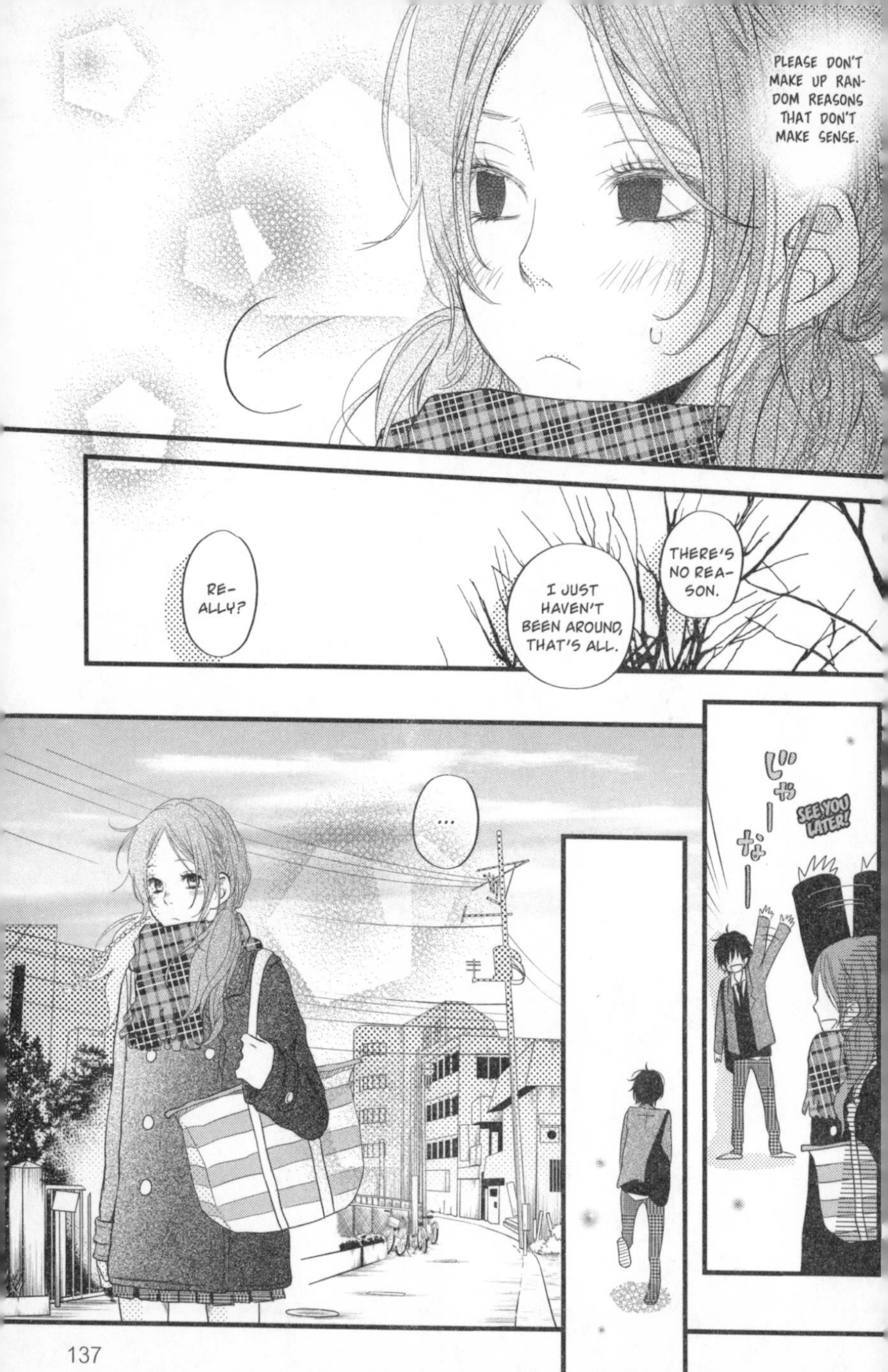
PLEASE DON'T MAKE UP RANDOM REASONS THAT DON'T MAKE SENSE.
THERE'S NO REASON.
I JUST HAVEN'T BEEN AROUND, THAT'S ALL.
REALLY?
じゃーなー
SEE YOU LATER!
...

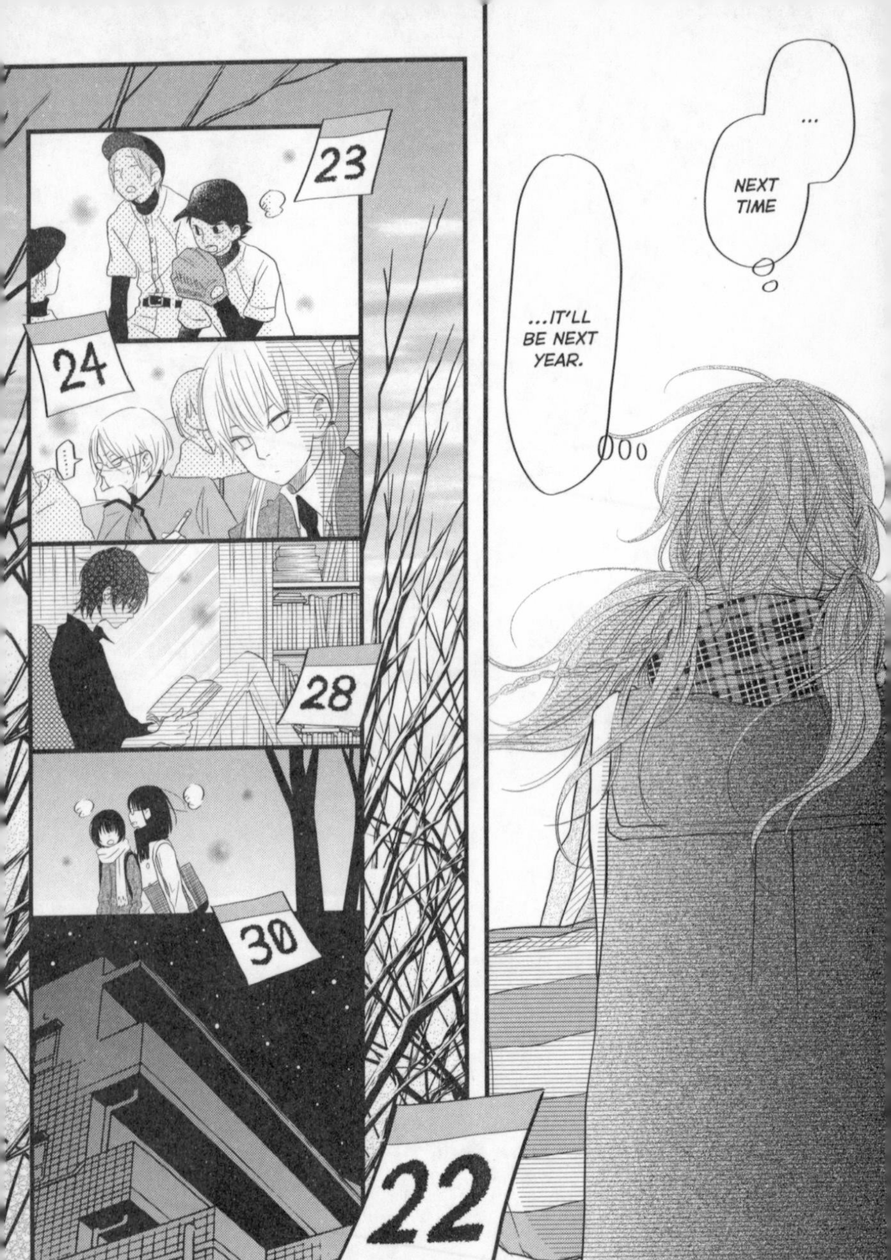
...
NEXT TIME
...IT'LL BE NEXT YEAR.
22
23
24
...
28
30

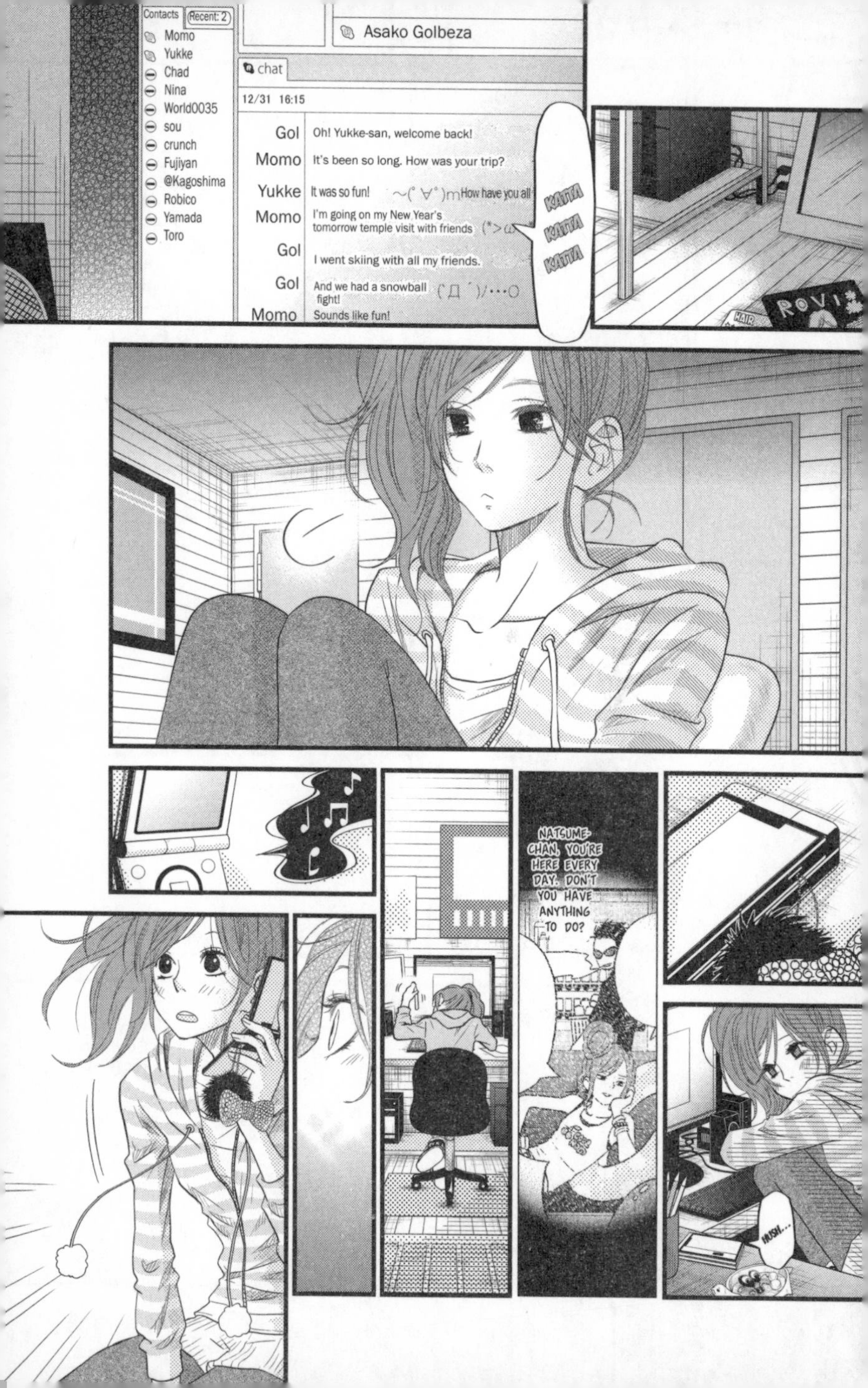
KATTA
KATTA
KATTA
HAIR
ROVI
Asako Golbeza
Contacts
Recent: 2
Momo
Yukke
Chad
Nina
World0035
sou
crunch
Fujiyan
@Kagoshima
Robico
Yamada
Toro
chat
12/31 16:15
Gol Oh! Yukke-san, welcome back!
Momo It's been so long. How was your trip?
Yukke It was so fun! ~(° ∀°)m How have you all
Momo I'm going on my New Year's tomorrow temple visit with friends (*>ω
Gol I went skiing with all my friends.
Gol And we had a snowball fight! (゚Д ゚)/…○
Momo Sounds like fun!
HUSH...
NATSUME-CHAN, YOU'RE HERE EVERY DAY. DON'T YOU HAVE ANYTHING TO DO?

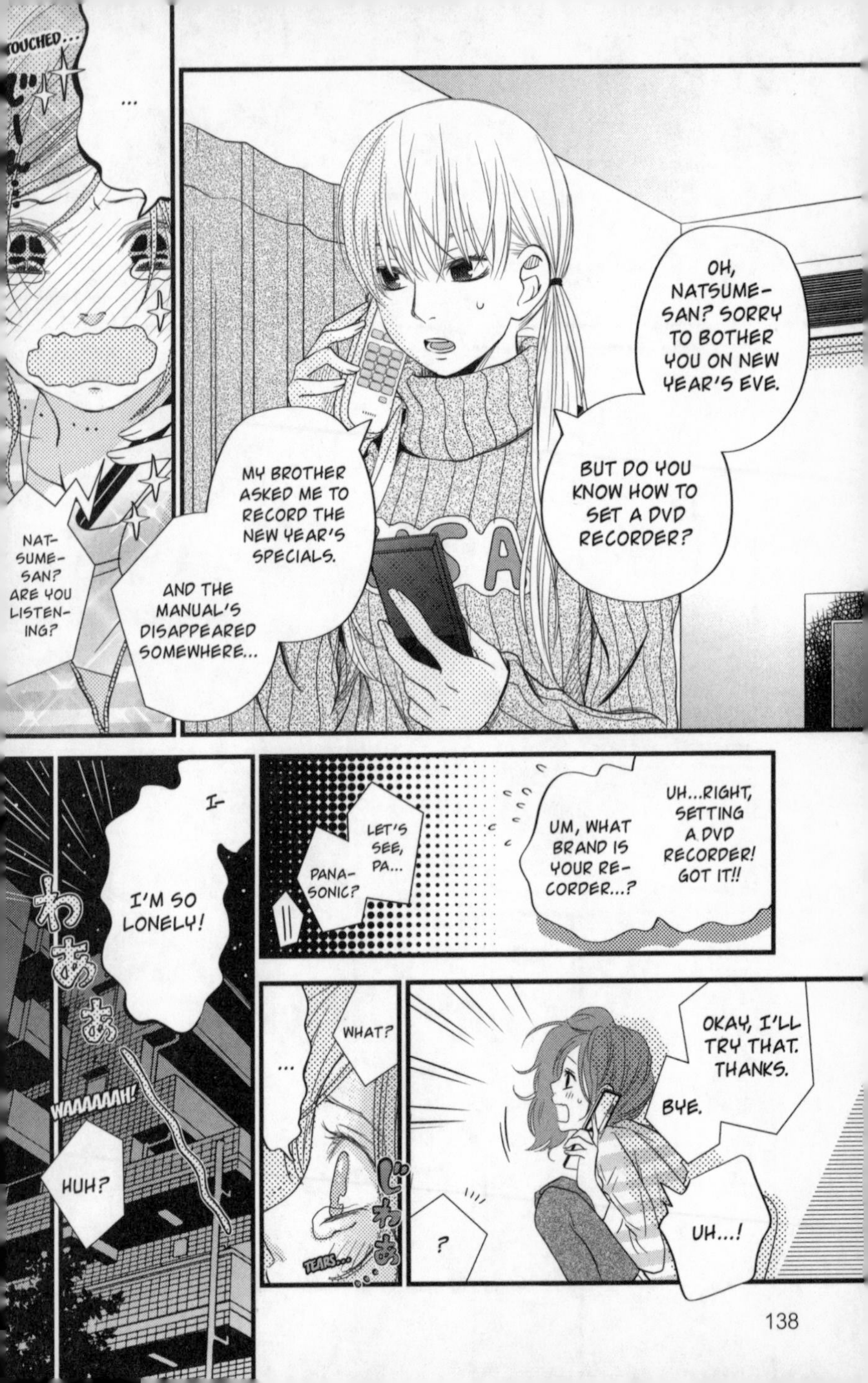
OH, NATSUME-SAN? SORRY TO BOTHER YOU ON NEW YEAR'S EVE.
BUT DO YOU KNOW HOW TO SET A DVD RECORDER?
MY BROTHER ASKED ME TO RECORD THE NEW YEAR'S SPECIALS.
AND THE MANUAL'S DISAPPEARED SOMEWHERE...
TOUCHED...
...
NAT-SUME-SAN? ARE YOU LISTEN-ING?
UH...RIGHT, SETTING A DVD RECORDER! GOT IT!!
UM, WHAT BRAND IS YOUR RE-CORDER...?
LET'S SEE, PA...
PANA-SONIC?
OKAY, I'LL TRY THAT. THANKS.
BYE.
UH...!
WHAT?
...
?
TEARS...
I-
I'M SO LONELY!
WAAAAAAH!
HUH?

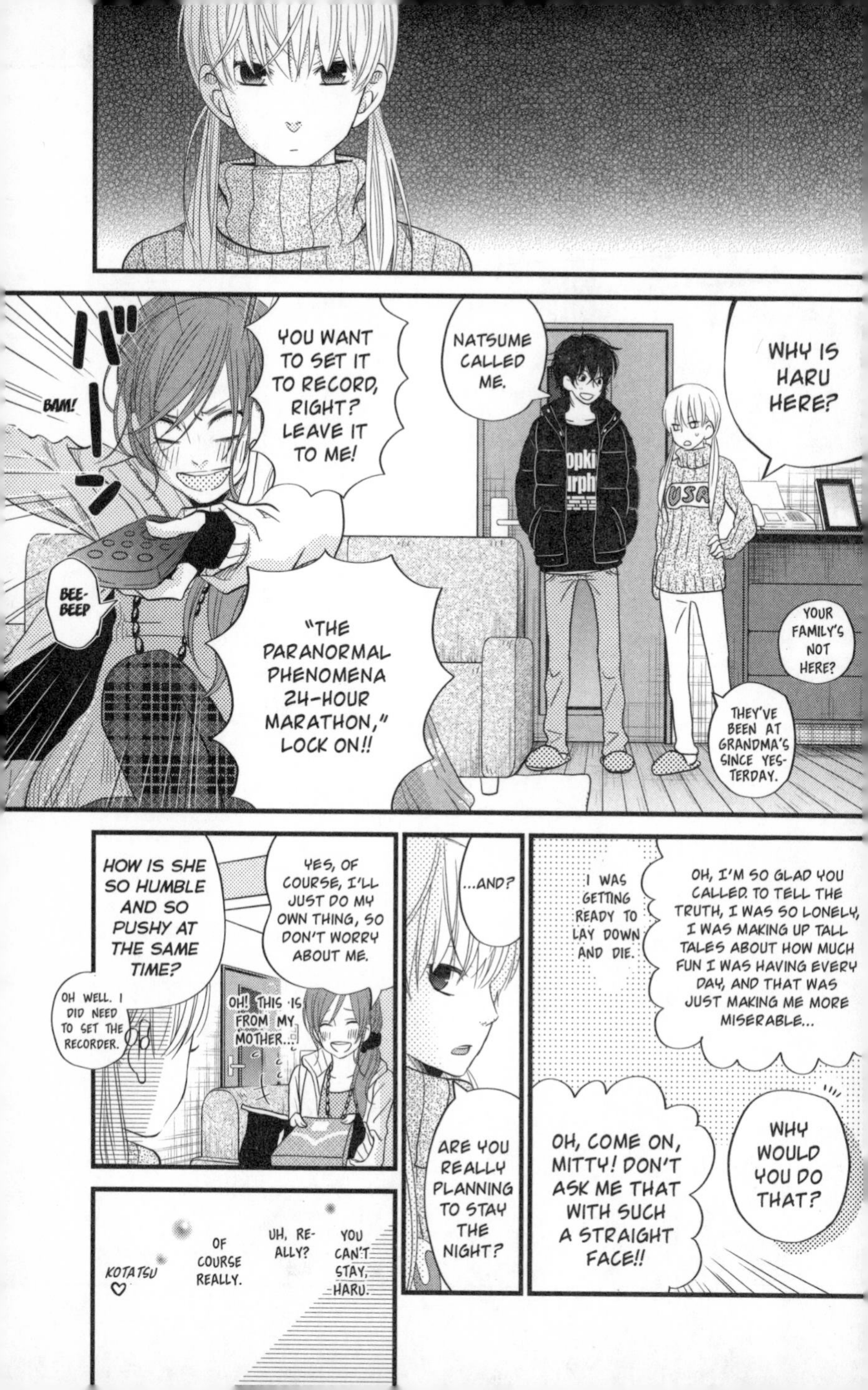
WHY IS HARU HERE?
NATSUME CALLED ME.
YOU WANT TO SET IT TO RECORD, RIGHT? LEAVE IT TO ME!
バーン
BAM!
YOUR FAMILY'S NOT HERE?
THEY'VE BEEN AT GRANDMA'S SINCE YES-TERDAY.
"THE PARANORMAL PHENOMENA 24-HOUR MARATHON," LOCK ON!!
BEE-BEEP
OH, I'M SO GLAD YOU CALLED. TO TELL THE TRUTH, I WAS SO LONELY, I WAS MAKING UP TALL TALES ABOUT HOW MUCH FUN I WAS HAVING EVERY DAY, AND THAT WAS JUST MAKING ME MORE MISERABLE...
I WAS GETTING READY TO LAY DOWN AND DIE.
WHY WOULD YOU DO THAT?
OH, COME ON, MITTY! DON'T ASK ME THAT WITH SUCH A STRAIGHT FACE!!
...AND?
ARE YOU REALLY PLANNING TO STAY THE NIGHT?
YES, OF COURSE, I'LL JUST DO MY OWN THING, SO DON'T WORRY ABOUT ME.
HOW IS SHE SO HUMBLE AND SO PUSHY AT THE SAME TIME?
OH WELL. I DID NEED TO SET THE RECORDER.
OH! THIS IS FROM MY MOTHER...
YOU CAN'T STAY, HARU.
UH, RE-ALLY?
OF COURSE REALLY.
KOTATSU ♡

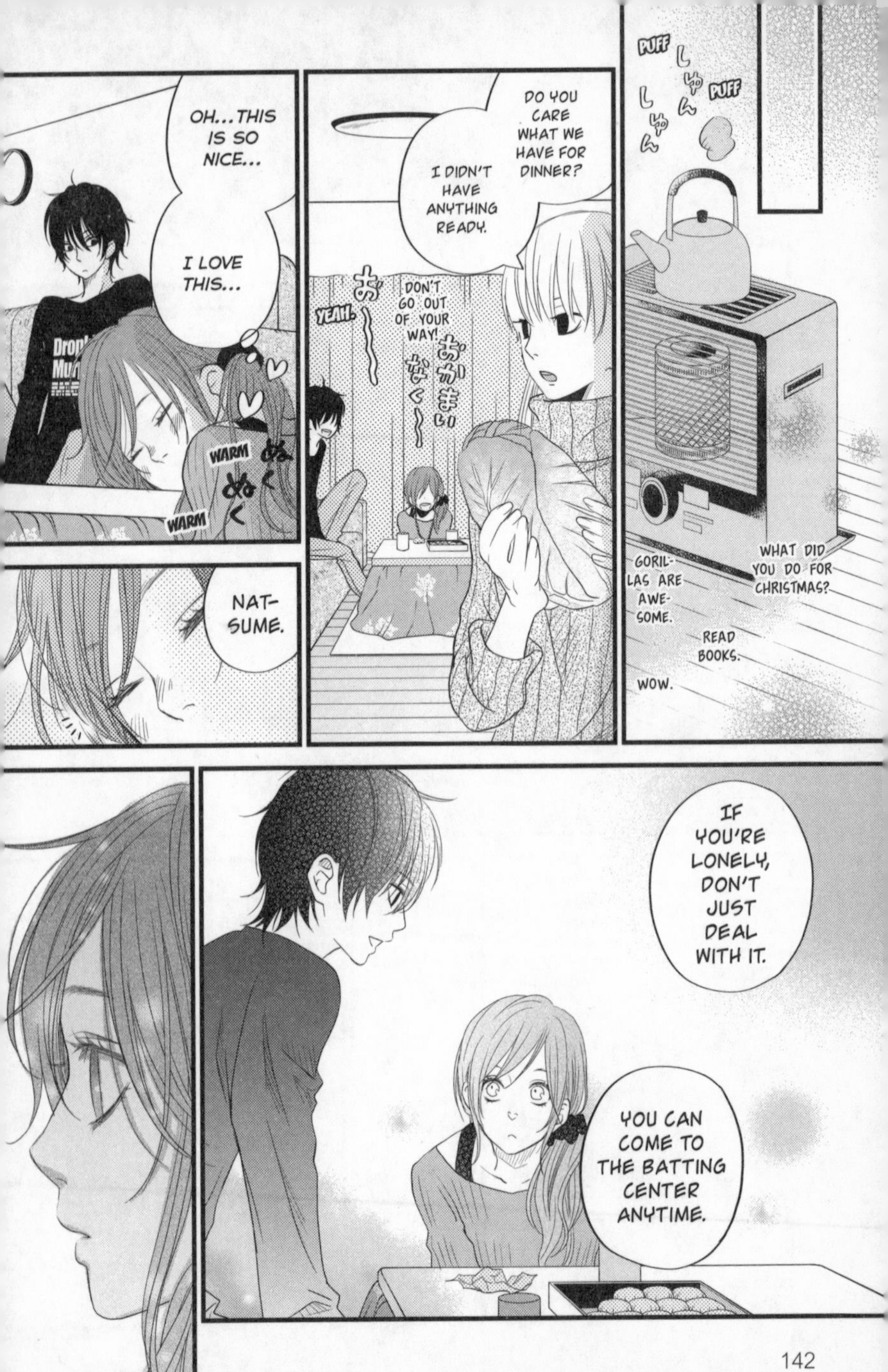
PUFF
しゅんしゅん
PUFF
WHAT DID YOU DO FOR CHRISTMAS?
GORIL-LAS ARE AWE-SOME.
READ BOOKS.
WOW.
DO YOU CARE WHAT WE HAVE FOR DINNER?
I DIDN'T HAVE ANYTHING READY.
DON'T GO OUT OF YOUR WAY!
おかまいなく~
YEAH.
あ~~
OH...THIS IS SO NICE...
I LOVE THIS...
WARM
ぬくぬく
WARM
NAT-SUME.
IF YOU'RE LONELY, DON'T JUST DEAL WITH IT.
YOU CAN COME TO THE BATTING CENTER ANYTIME.

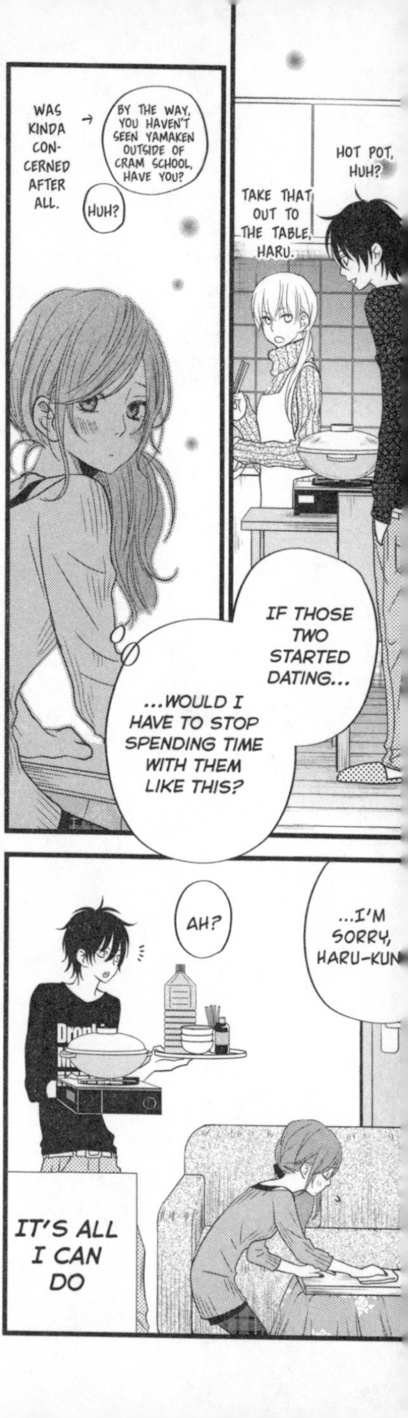
HOT POT, HUH?
TAKE THAT OUT TO THE TABLE, HARU.
IF THOSE TWO STARTED DATING...
...WOULD I HAVE TO STOP SPENDING TIME WITH THEM LIKE THIS?
BY THE WAY, YOU HAVEN'T SEEN YAMAKEN OUTSIDE OF CRAM SCHOOL, HAVE YOU?
WAS KINDA CONCERNED AFTER ALL.
HUH?
...I'M SORRY, HARU-KUN
AH?
IT'S ALL I CAN DO

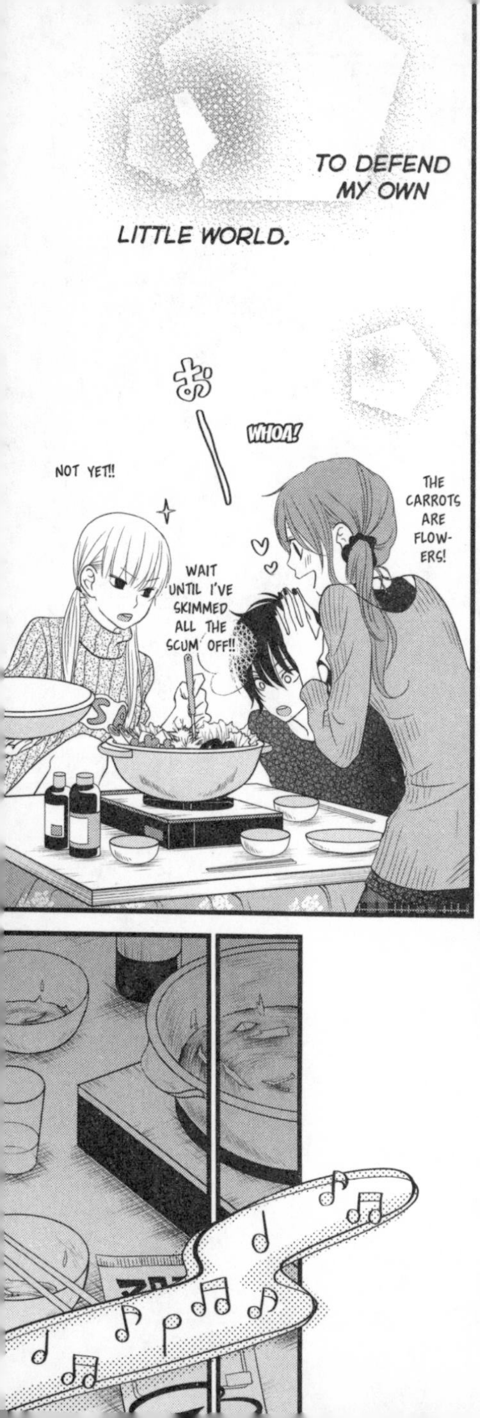
TO DEFEND MY OWN
LITTLE WORLD.
THE CARROTS ARE FLOWERS!
WHOA!
お
WAIT UNTIL I'VE SKIMMED ALL THE SCUM OFF!!
NOT YET!!

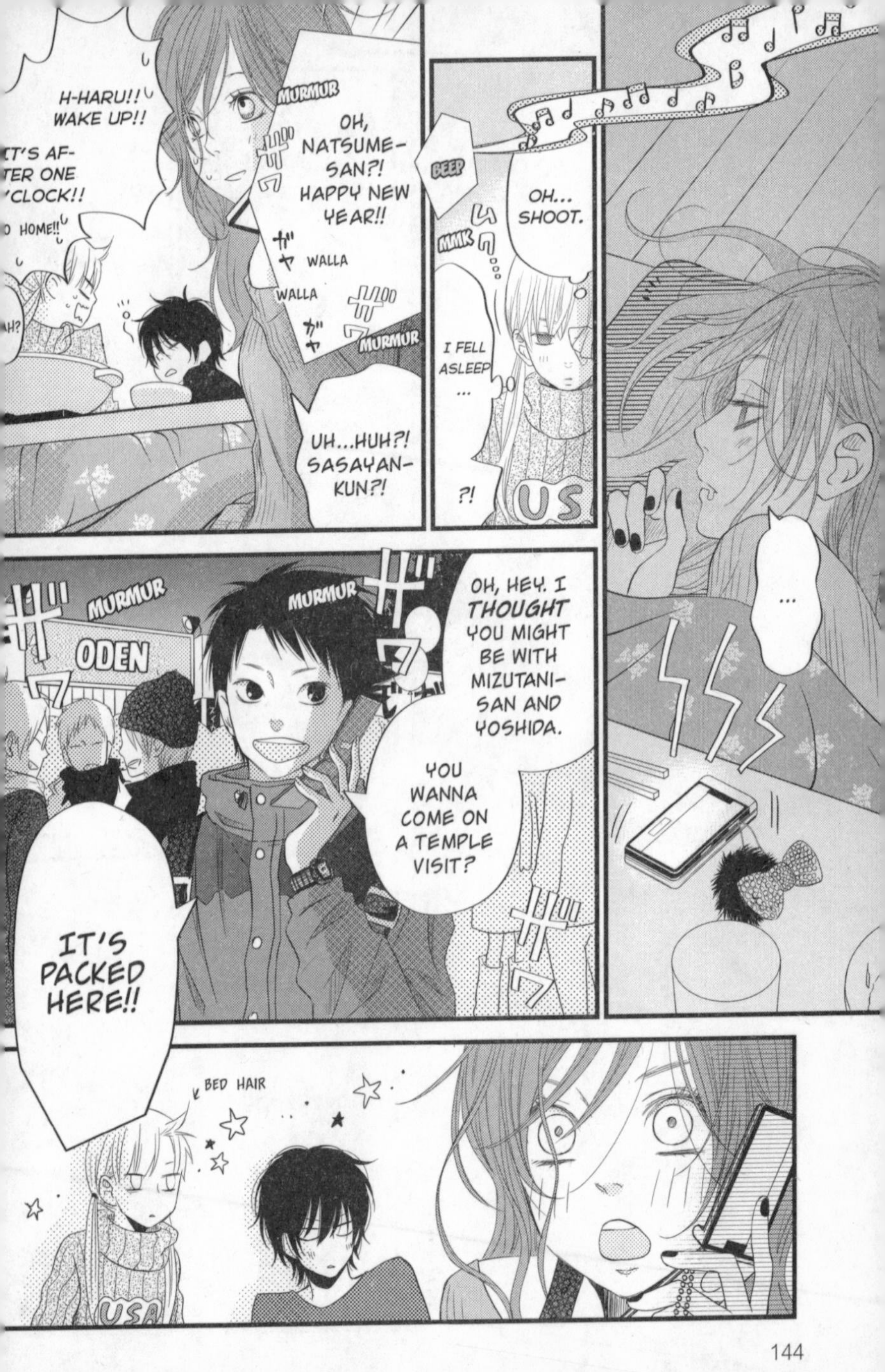
...
BEEP
OH... SHOOT.
MMK
I FELL ASLEEP ...
?!
OH, NATSUME-SAN?! HAPPY NEW YEAR!!
MURMUR
H-HARU!! WAKE UP!!
T'S AF-TER ONE 'CLOCK!!
O HOME!!
UH...HUH?! SASAYAN-KUN?!
WALLA
WALLA
MURMUR
OH, HEY. I *THOUGHT* YOU MIGHT BE WITH MIZUTANI-SAN AND YOSHIDA.
MURMUR
MURMUR
ODEN
YOU WANNA COME ON A TEMPLE VISIT?
IT'S PACKED HERE!!
BED HAIR

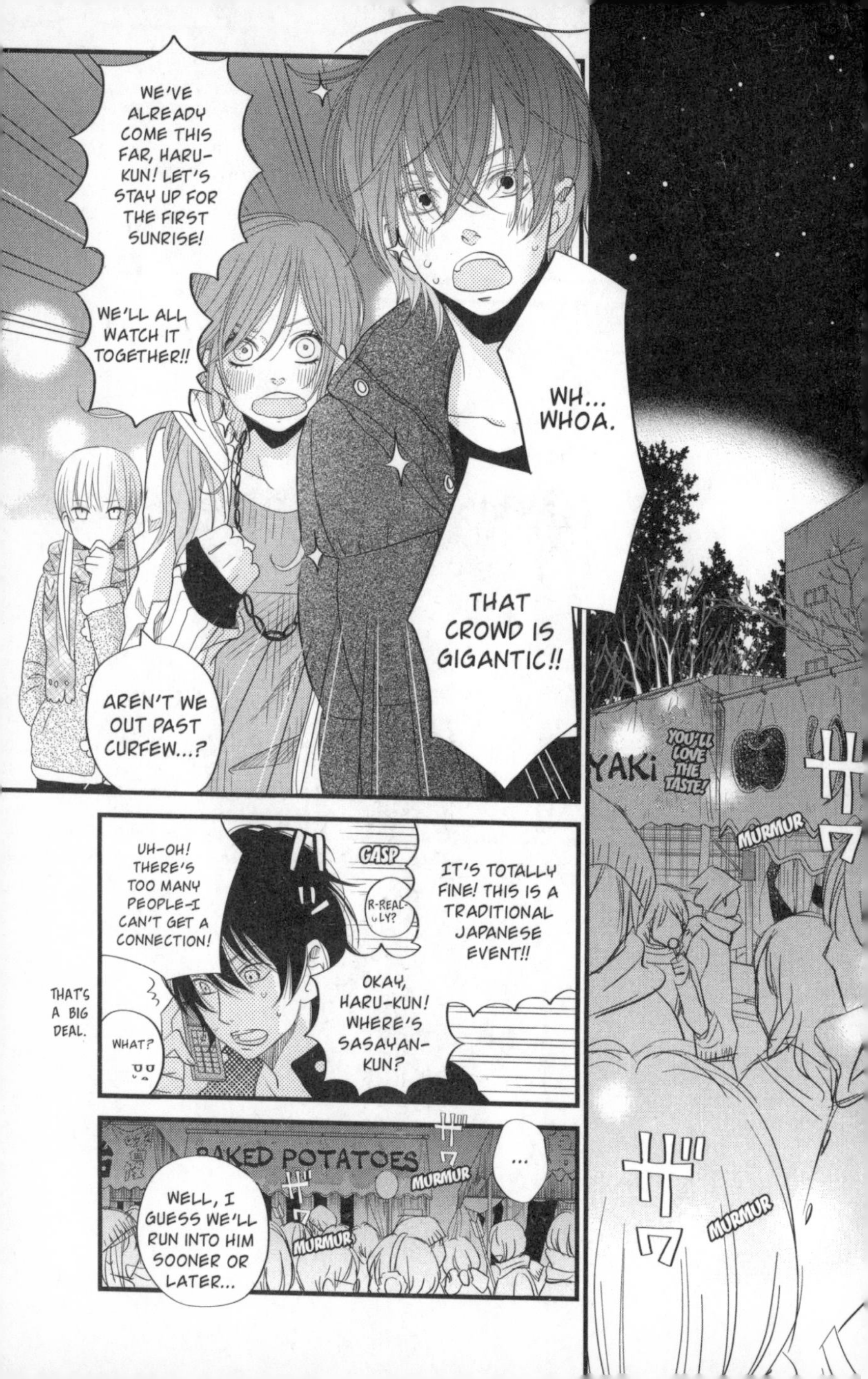
YAKi
YOU'LL LOVE THE TASTE!
ザワ
MURMUR
ザワ
MURMUR
WH... WHOA.
THAT CROWD IS GIGANTIC!!
WE'VE ALREADY COME THIS FAR, HARU-KUN! LET'S STAY UP FOR THE FIRST SUNRISE!
WE'LL ALL WATCH IT TOGETHER!!
AREN'T WE OUT PAST CURFEW...?
IT'S TOTALLY FINE! THIS IS A TRADITIONAL JAPANESE EVENT!!
R-REALLY?
GASP
UH-OH! THERE'S TOO MANY PEOPLE-I CAN'T GET A CONNECTION!
OKAY, HARU-KUN! WHERE'S SASAYAN-KUN?
WHAT?
THAT'S A BIG DEAL.
...
ザワ
MURMUR
BAKED POTATOES
ザワ
MURMUR
WELL, I GUESS WE'LL RUN INTO HIM SOONER OR LATER...

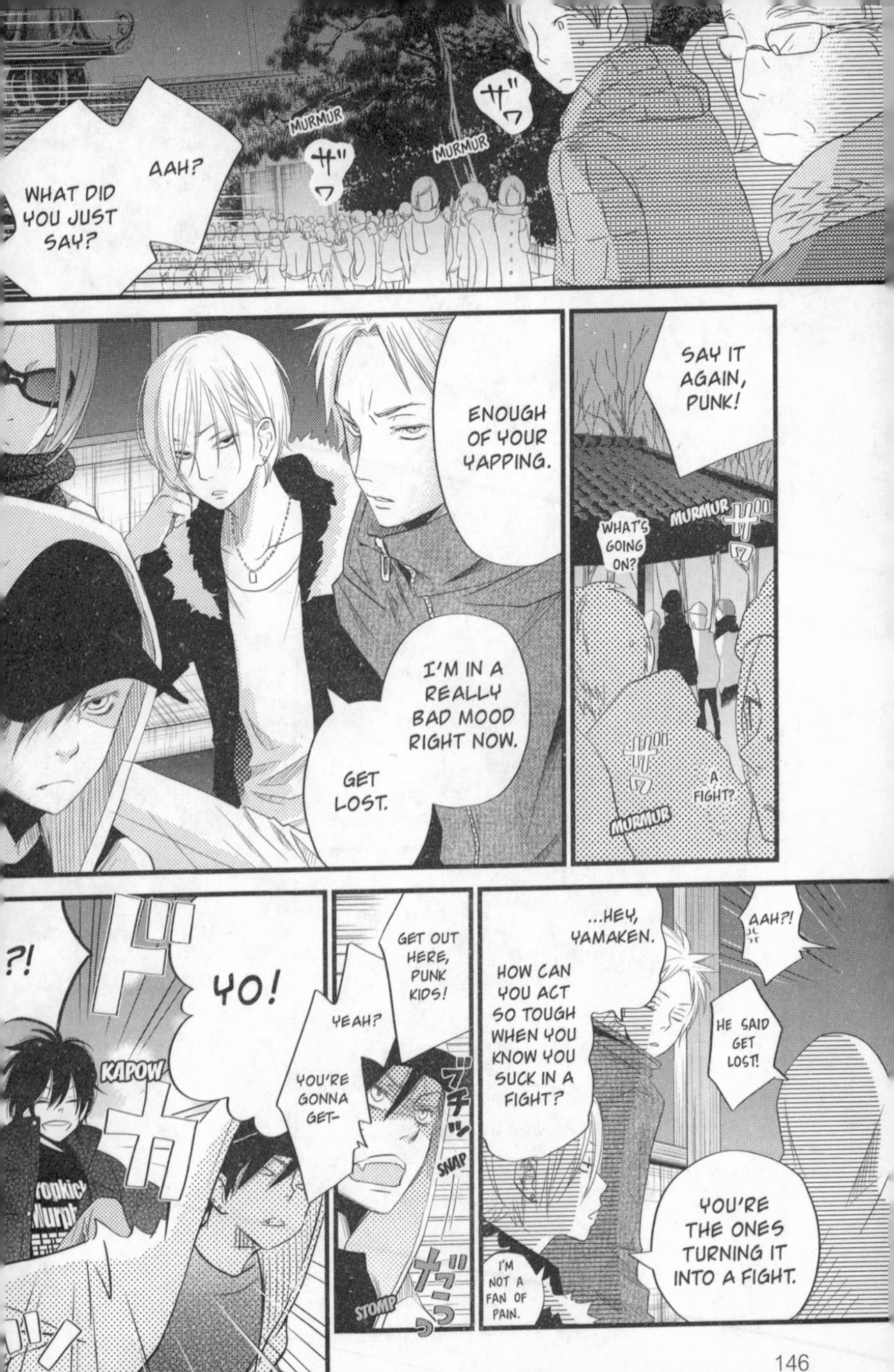
ザワ
MURMUR
MURMUR
ザワ
AAH?
WHAT DID YOU JUST SAY?
SAY IT AGAIN, PUNK!
MURMUR
ザワ
WHAT'S GOING ON?
ザワ
A FIGHT?
MURMUR
ENOUGH OF YOUR YAPPING.
I'M IN A REALLY BAD MOOD RIGHT NOW.
GET LOST.
AAH?!
HE SAID GET LOST!
...HEY, YAMAKEN.
HOW CAN YOU ACT SO TOUGH WHEN YOU KNOW YOU SUCK IN A FIGHT?
YOU'RE THE ONES TURNING IT INTO A FIGHT.
I'M NOT A FAN OF PAIN.
GET OUT HERE, PUNK KIDS!
YEAH?
YOU'RE GONNA GET-
ブチッ
SNAP
STOMP
YO!
?!
KAPOW

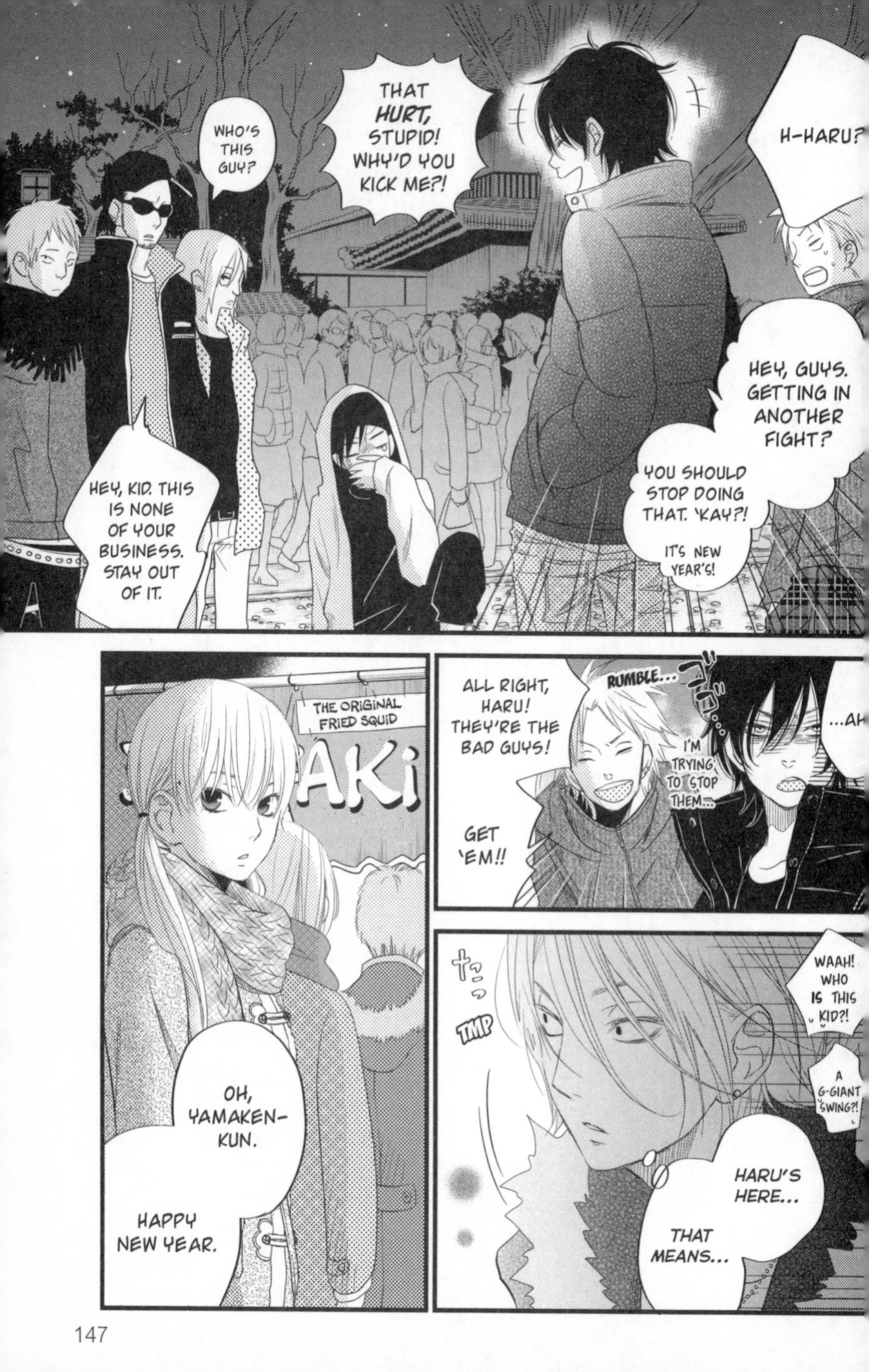
H-HARU?
THAT HURT, STUPID! WHY'D YOU KICK ME?!
WHO'S THIS GUY?
HEY, GUYS. GETTING IN ANOTHER FIGHT?
YOU SHOULD STOP DOING THAT. 'KAY?!
IT'S NEW YEAR'S!
HEY, KID. THIS IS NONE OF YOUR BUSINESS. STAY OUT OF IT.
...AH
RUMBLE...
I'M TRYING TO STOP THEM...
ALL RIGHT, HARU! THEY'RE THE BAD GUYS!
GET 'EM!!
WAAH! WHO IS THIS KID?!
A G-GIANT SWING?!
TMP
HARU'S HERE...
THAT MEANS...
THE ORIGINAL FRIED SQUID
AKi
OH, YAMAKEN-KUN.
HAPPY NEW YEAR.

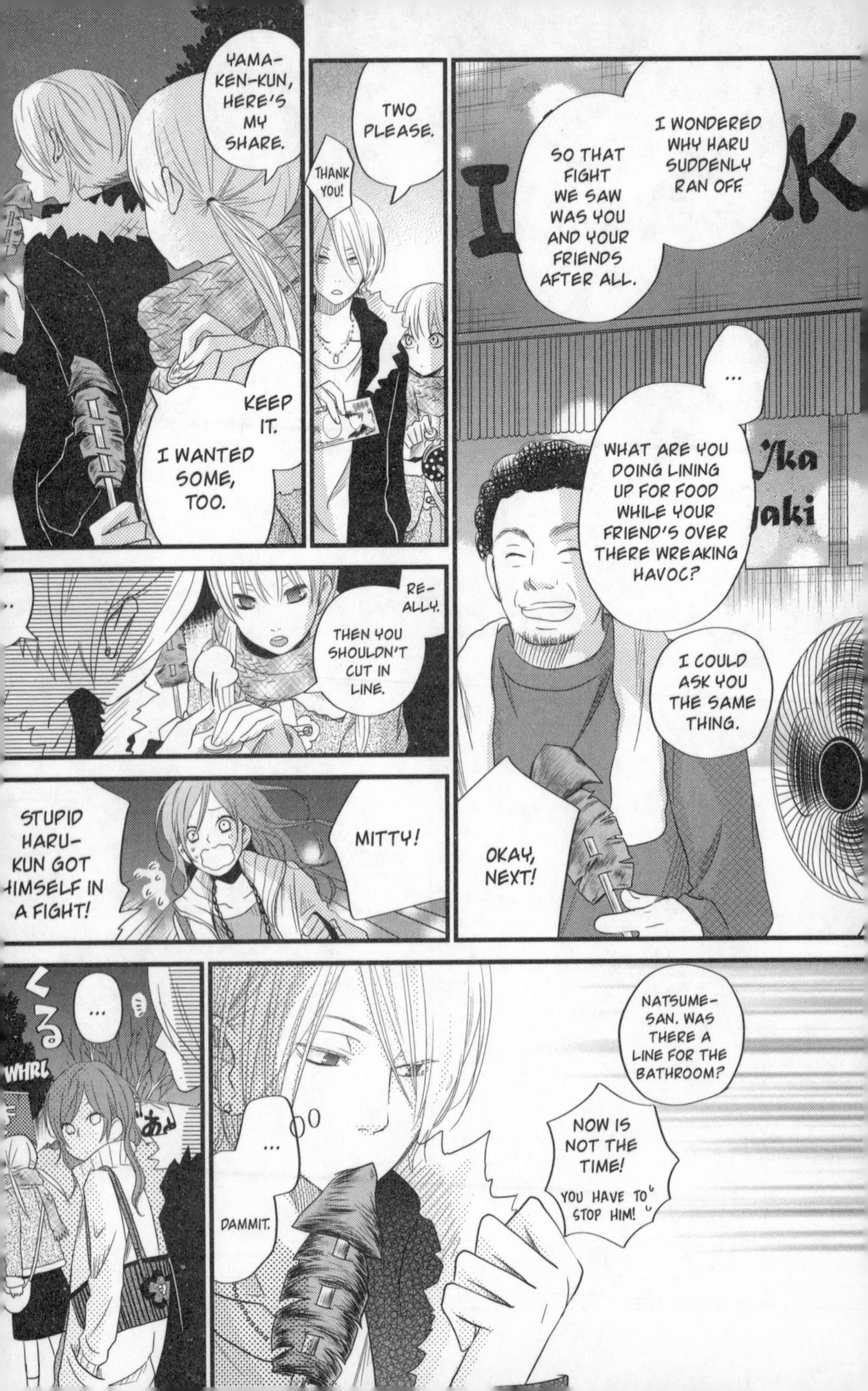
I WONDERED WHY HARU SUDDENLY RAN OFF.
SO THAT FIGHT WE SAW WAS YOU AND YOUR FRIENDS AFTER ALL.
...
WHAT ARE YOU DOING LINING UP FOR FOOD WHILE YOUR FRIEND'S OVER THERE WREAKING HAVOC?
I COULD ASK YOU THE SAME THING.
OKAY, NEXT!
TWO PLEASE.
THANK YOU!
YAMA-KEN-KUN, HERE'S MY SHARE.
KEEP IT.
I WANTED SOME, TOO.
RE-ALLY.
THEN YOU SHOULDN'T CUT IN LINE.
MITTY!
STUPID HARU-KUN GOT HIMSELF IN A FIGHT!
NATSUME-SAN. WAS THERE A LINE FOR THE BATHROOM?
NOW IS NOT THE TIME!
YOU HAVE TO STOP HIM!
...
DAMMIT.
...
くる
WHIRL

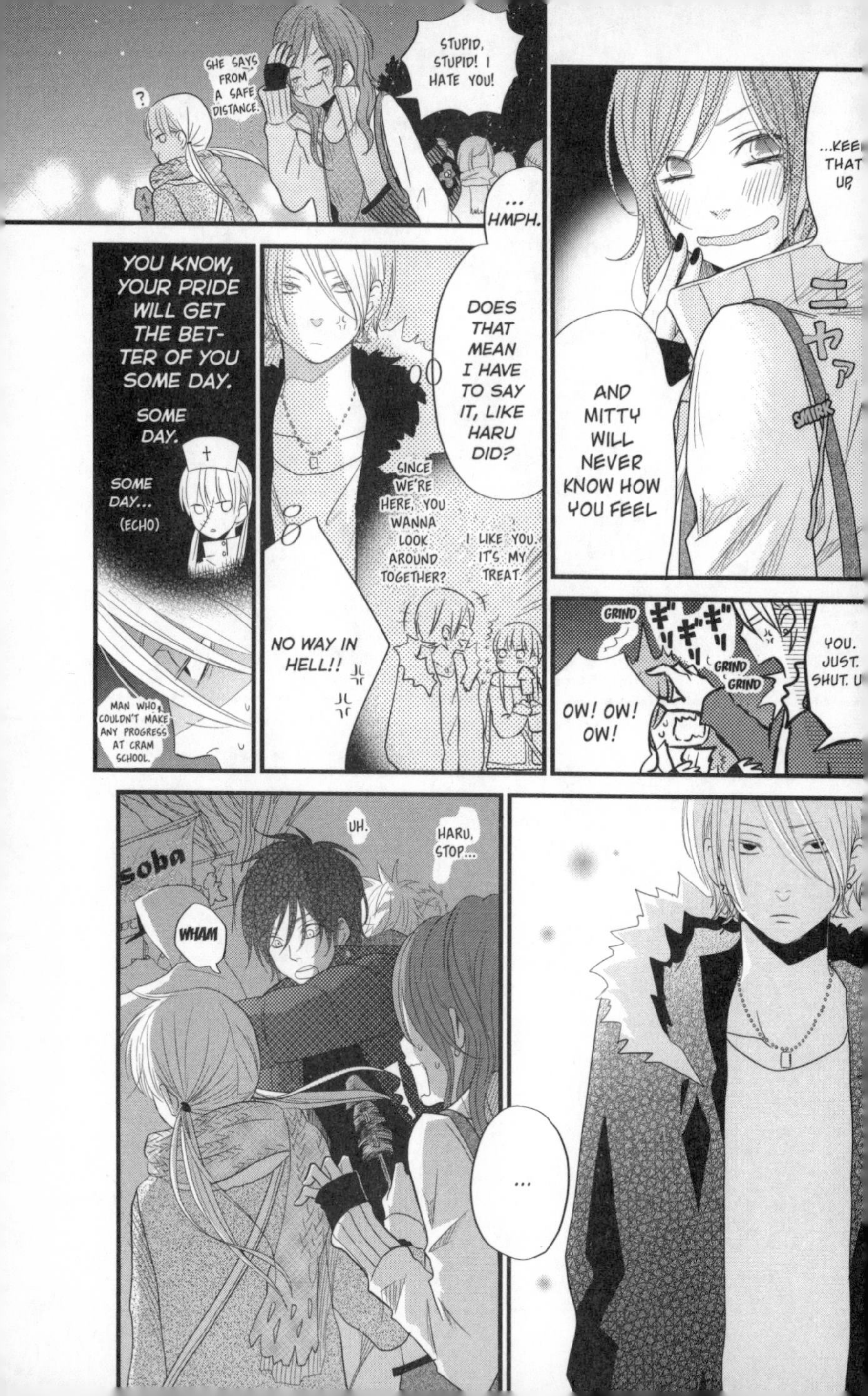
STUPID, STUPID! I HATE YOU!
SHE SAYS FROM A SAFE DISTANCE.
?
...HMPH.
...KEE THAT UP,
AND MITTY WILL NEVER KNOW HOW YOU FEEL
SMIRK
YOU. JUST. SHUT. U
GRIND
GRIND
GRIND
OW! OW! OW!
DOES THAT MEAN I HAVE TO SAY IT, LIKE HARU DID?
SINCE WE'RE HERE, YOU WANNA LOOK AROUND TOGETHER?
I LIKE YOU. IT'S MY TREAT.
NO WAY IN HELL!!
YOU KNOW, YOUR PRIDE WILL GET THE BETTER OF YOU SOME DAY.
SOME DAY.
SOME DAY...
(ECHO)
MAN WHO COULDN'T MAKE ANY PROGRESS AT CRAM SCHOOL.
...
HARU, STOP...
UH.
soba
WHAM

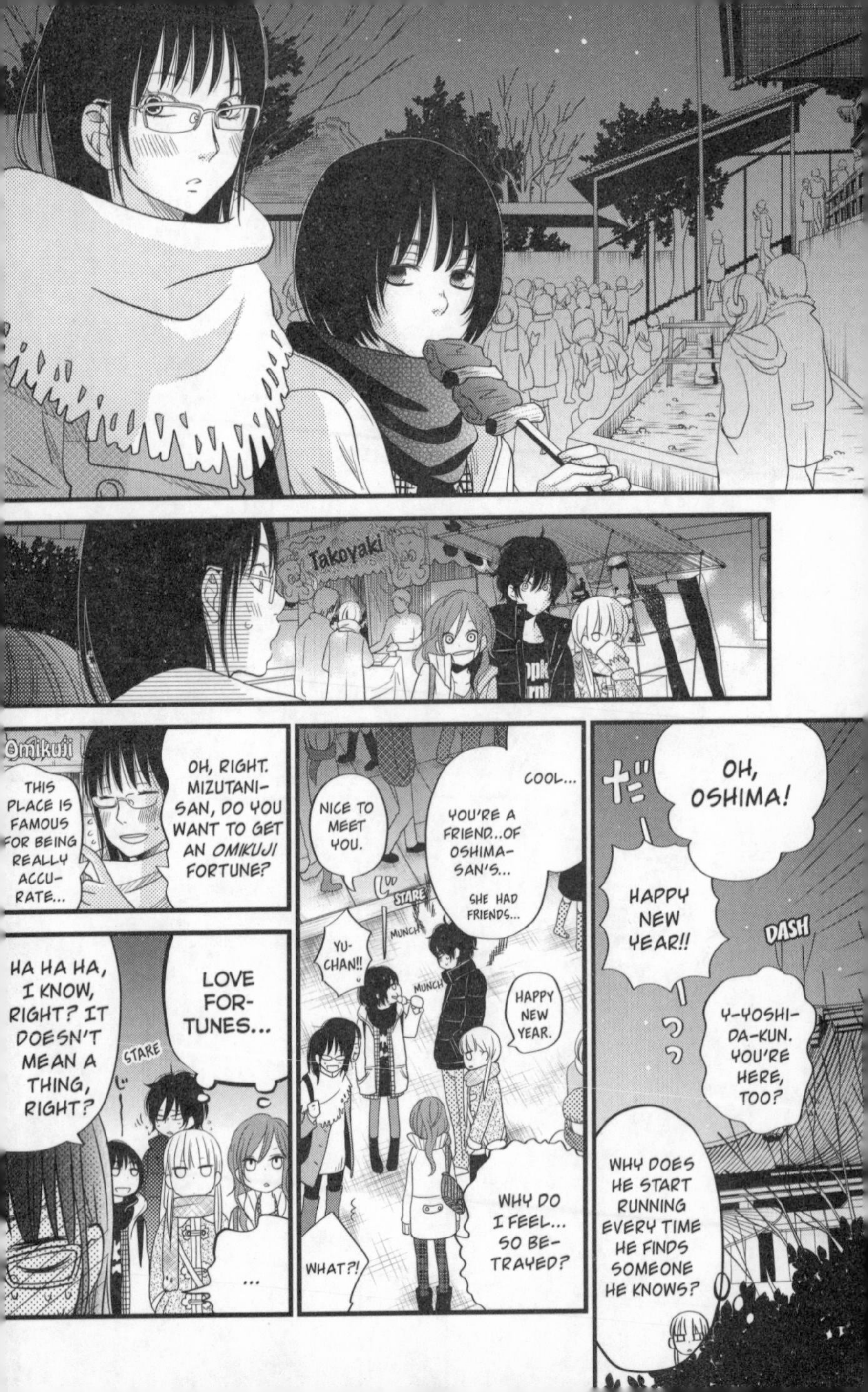
Takoyaki
OH, OSHIMA!
HAPPY NEW YEAR!!
DASH
Y-YOSHIDA-KUN. YOU'RE HERE, TOO?
WHY DOES HE START RUNNING EVERY TIME HE FINDS SOMEONE HE KNOWS?
COOL...
YOU'RE A FRIEND...OF OSHIMA-SAN'S...
SHE HAD FRIENDS...
NICE TO MEET YOU.
STARE
YU-CHAN!!
MUNCH
MUNCH
HAPPY NEW YEAR.
WHY DO I FEEL... SO BE-TRAYED?
WHAT?!
Omikuji
OH, RIGHT. MIZUTANI-SAN, DO YOU WANT TO GET AN OMIKUJI FORTUNE?
THIS PLACE IS FAMOUS FOR BEING REALLY ACCU-RATE...
LOVE FOR-TUNES...
HA HA HA, I KNOW, RIGHT? IT DOESN'T MEAN A THING, RIGHT?
STARE
...

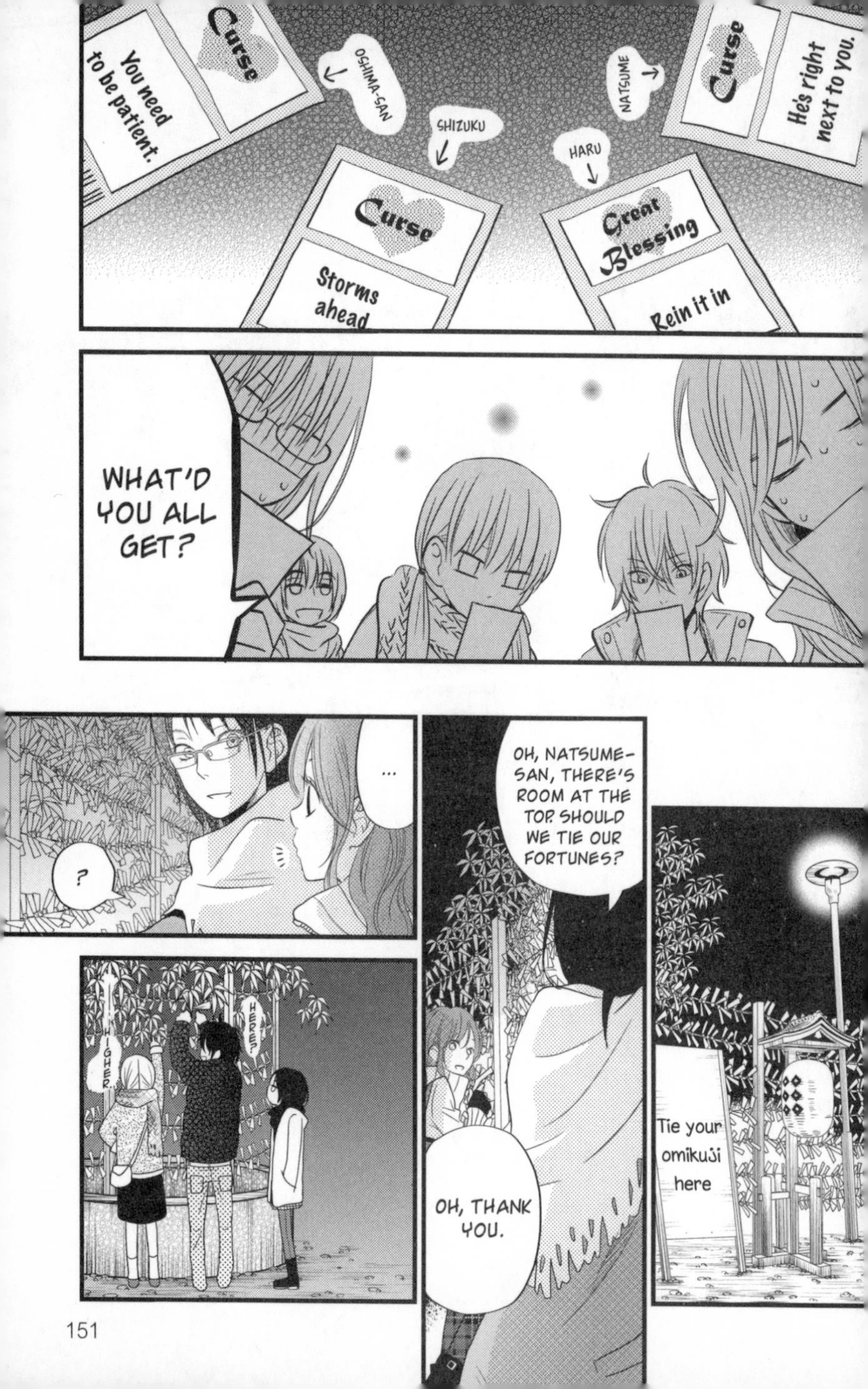
NATSUME
Curse
He's right next to you.
HARU
Great Blessing
Rein it in
SHIZUKU
Curse
Storms ahead
OSHIMA-SAN
Curse
You need to be patient.
WHAT'D YOU ALL GET?
Tie your omikuji here
OH, NATSUME-SAN, THERE'S ROOM AT THE TOP. SHOULD WE TIE OUR FORTUNES?
OH, THANK YOU.
...
?
HERE?
HIGHER.

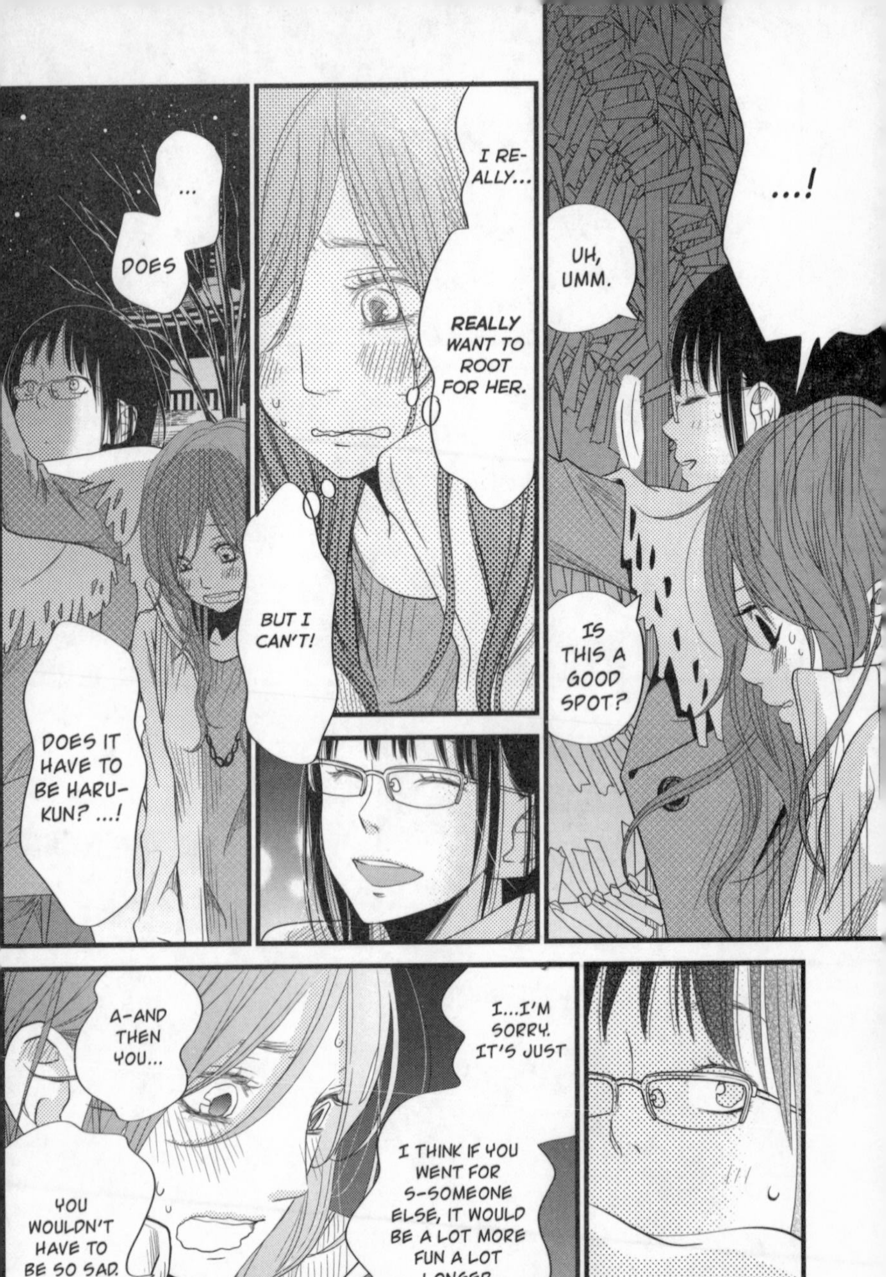
...!
UH, UMM.
IS THIS A GOOD SPOT?
I RE-ALLY...
REALLY WANT TO ROOT FOR HER.
BUT I CAN'T!
...
DOES
DOES IT HAVE TO BE HARU-KUN? ...!
I...I'M SORRY. IT'S JUST
A-AND THEN YOU...
I THINK IF YOU WENT FOR S-SOMEONE ELSE, IT WOULD BE A LOT MORE FUN A LOT LONGER.
YOU WOULDN'T HAVE TO BE SO SAD.

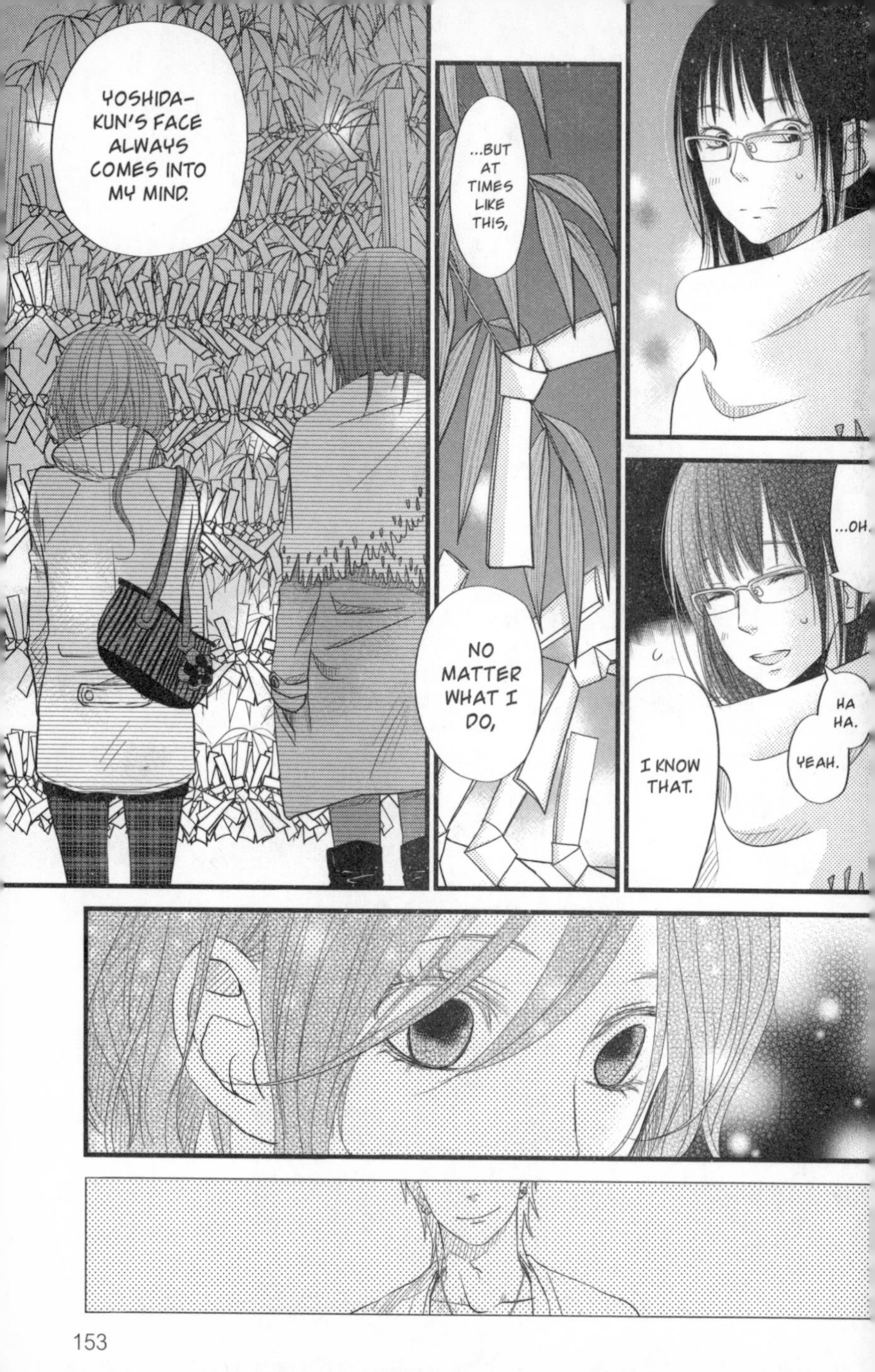
...OH.
HA HA.
YEAH.
I KNOW THAT.
...BUT AT TIMES LIKE THIS,
NO MATTER WHAT I DO,
YOSHIDA-KUN'S FACE ALWAYS COMES INTO MY MIND.

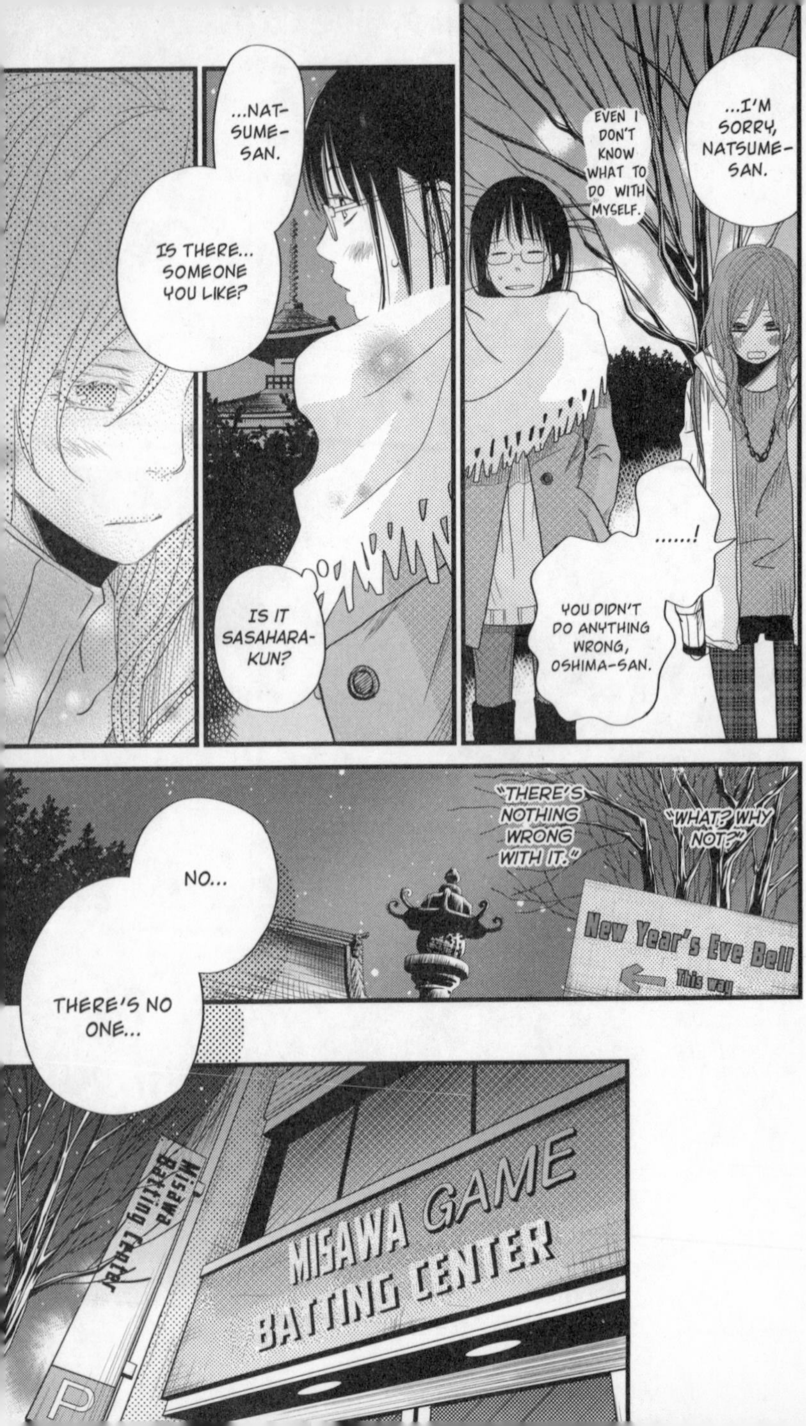
...I'M SORRY, NATSUME-SAN.
EVEN I DON'T KNOW WHAT TO DO WITH MYSELF.
......!
YOU DIDN'T DO ANYTHING WRONG, OSHIMA-SAN.
...NAT-SUME-SAN.
IS THERE... SOMEONE YOU LIKE?
IS IT SASAHARA-KUN?
"WHAT? WHY NOT?"
"THERE'S NOTHING WRONG WITH IT."
New Year's Eve Bell
This way
NO...
THERE'S NO ONE...
MISAWA GAME
BATTING CENTER
Misawa Batting Center
P

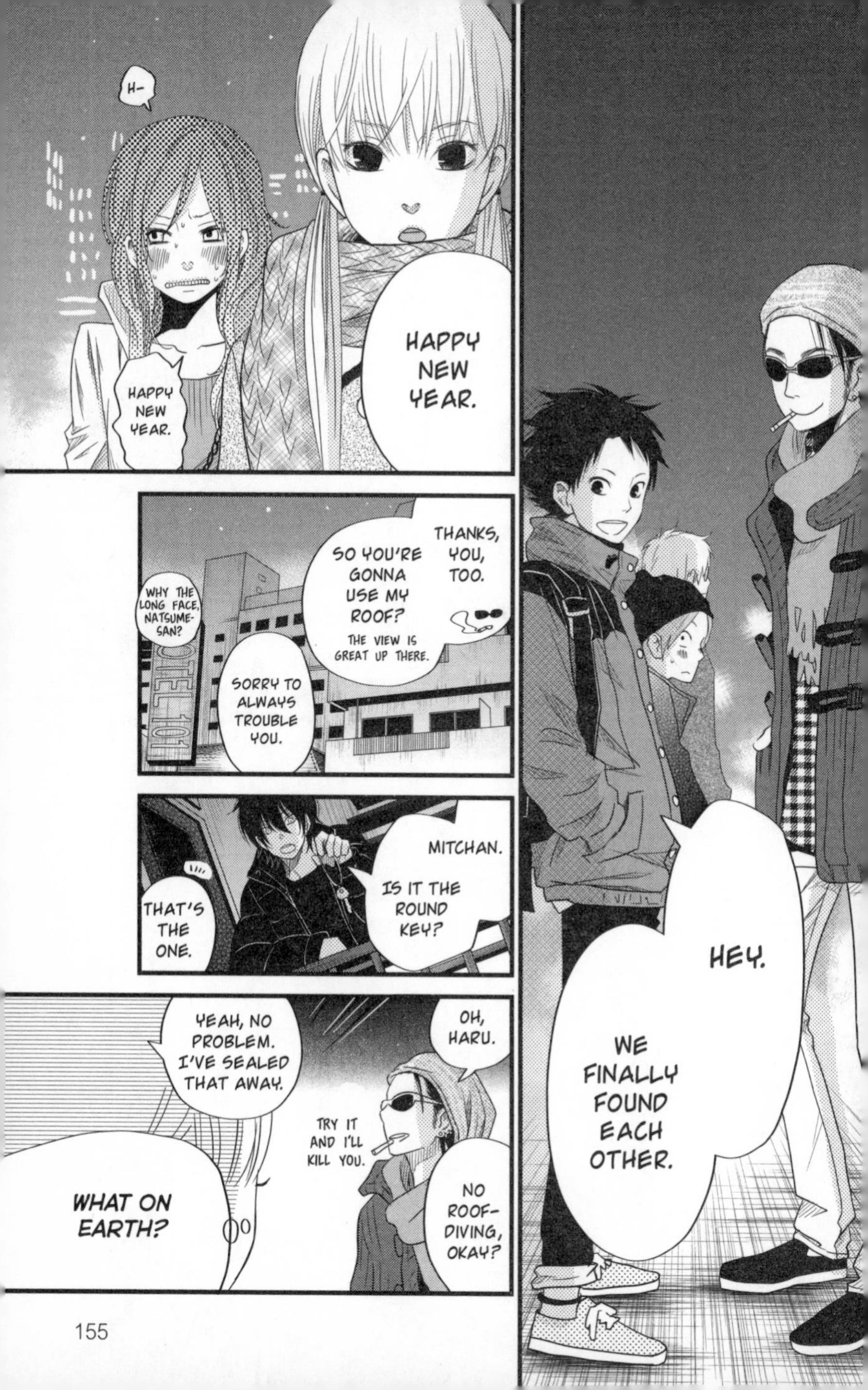
HEY.
WE FINALLY FOUND EACH OTHER.
HAPPY NEW YEAR.
H-
HAPPY NEW YEAR.
THANKS, YOU, TOO.
SO YOU'RE GONNA USE MY ROOF?
THE VIEW IS GREAT UP THERE.
WHY THE LONG FACE, NATSUME-SAN?
SORRY TO ALWAYS TROUBLE YOU.
MITCHAN.
IS IT THE ROUND KEY?
THAT'S THE ONE.
OH, HARU.
NO ROOF-DIVING, OKAY?
YEAH, NO PROBLEM. I'VE SEALED THAT AWAY.
TRY IT AND I'LL KILL YOU.
WHAT ON EARTH?

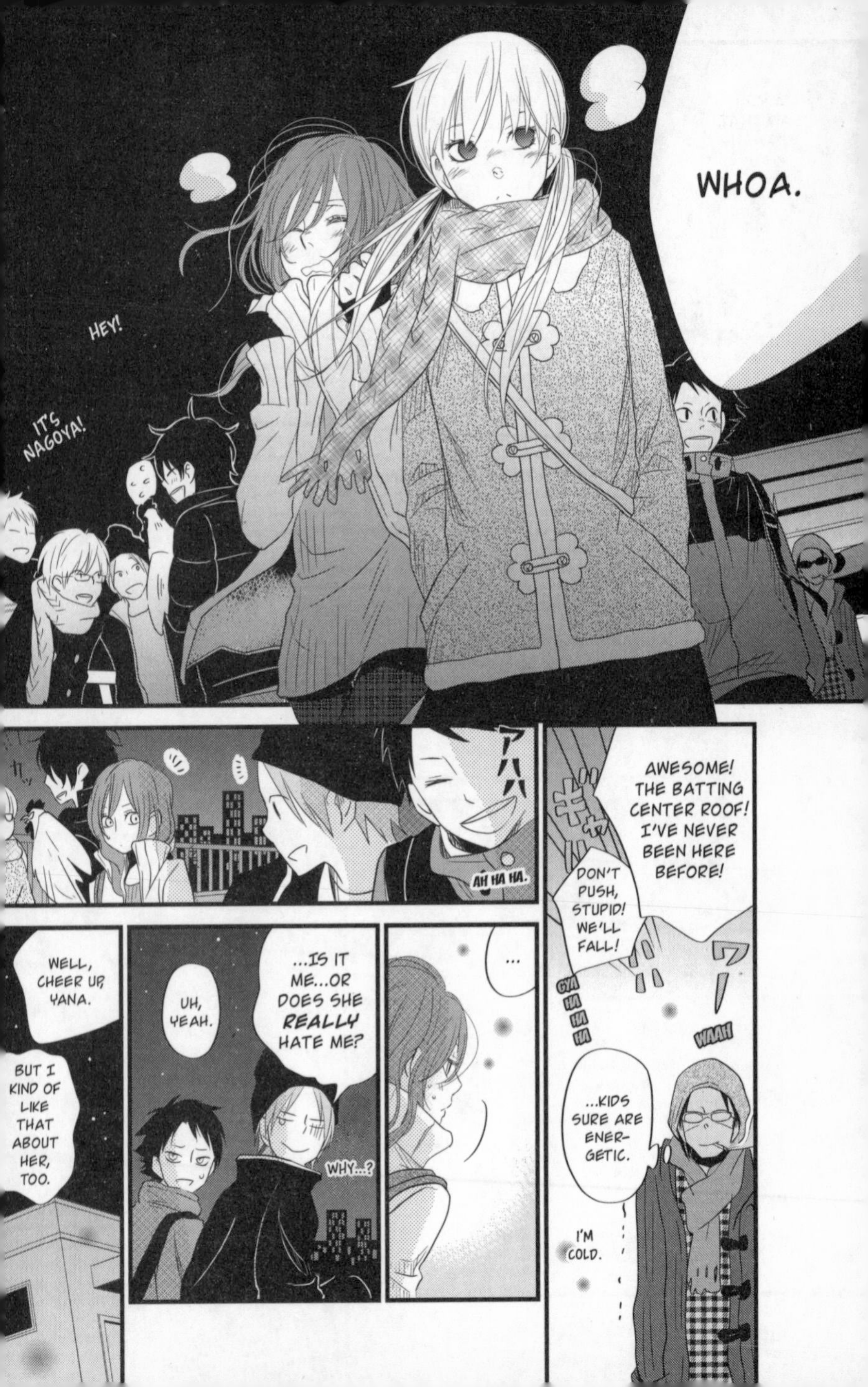

WHOA.
HEY!
IT'S NAGOYA!
AWESOME! THE BATTING CENTER ROOF! I'VE NEVER BEEN HERE BEFORE!
DON'T PUSH, STUPID! WE'LL FALL!
WAAH
CYA HA HA HA
...KIDS SURE ARE ENER-GETIC.
I'M COLD.
AH HA HA.
...
...IS IT ME...OR DOES SHE ***REALLY*** HATE ME?
UH, YEAH.
WHY...?
WELL, CHEER UP, YANA.
BUT I KIND OF LIKE THAT ABOUT HER, TOO.

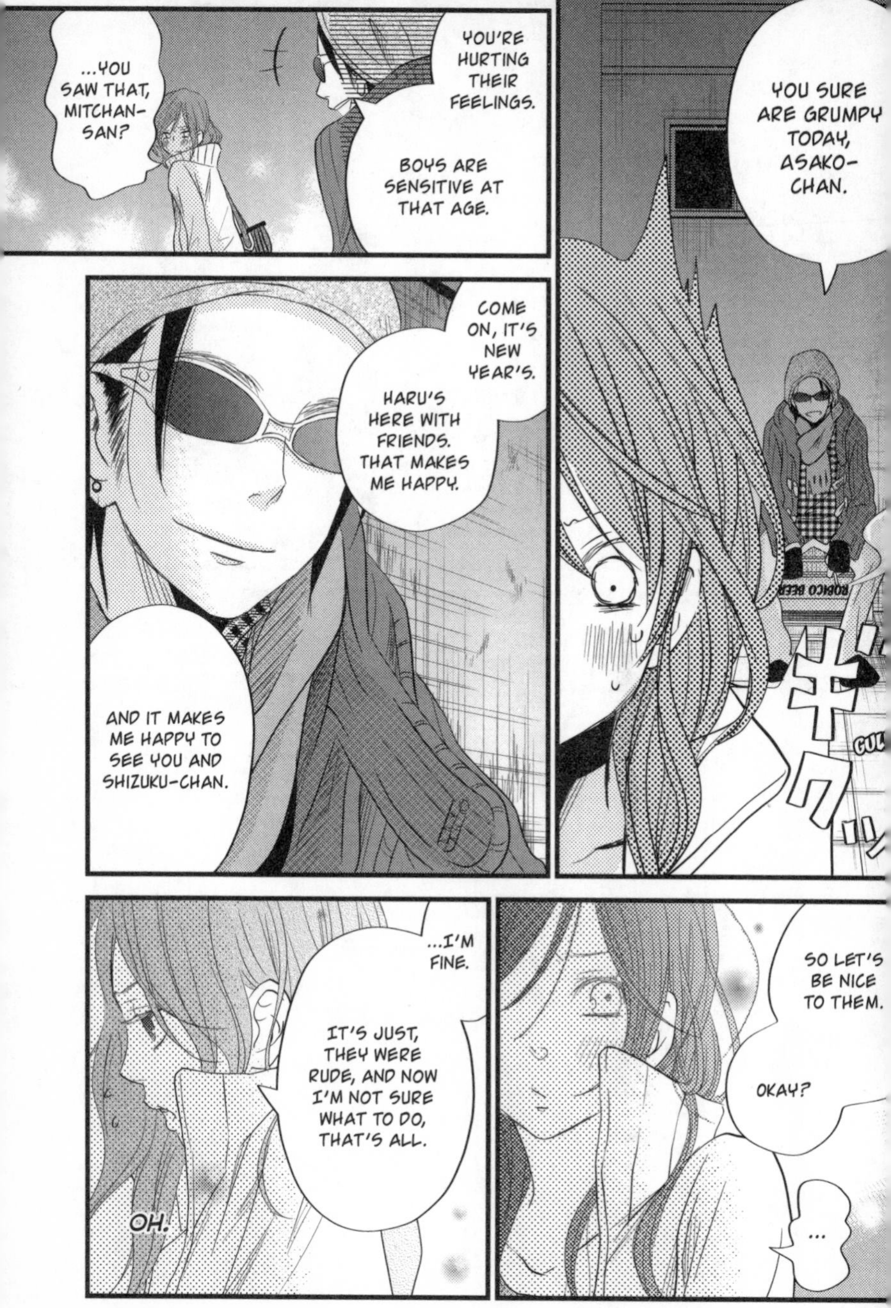
YOU SURE ARE GRUMPY TODAY, ASAKO-CHAN.
GUL
YOU'RE HURTING THEIR FEELINGS.
BOYS ARE SENSITIVE AT THAT AGE.
...YOU SAW THAT, MITCHAN-SAN?
COME ON, IT'S NEW YEAR'S.
HARU'S HERE WITH FRIENDS. THAT MAKES ME HAPPY.
AND IT MAKES ME HAPPY TO SEE YOU AND SHIZUKU-CHAN.
SO LET'S BE NICE TO THEM.
OKAY?
...
...I'M FINE.
IT'S JUST, THEY WERE RUDE, AND NOW I'M NOT SURE WHAT TO DO, THAT'S ALL.
OH.

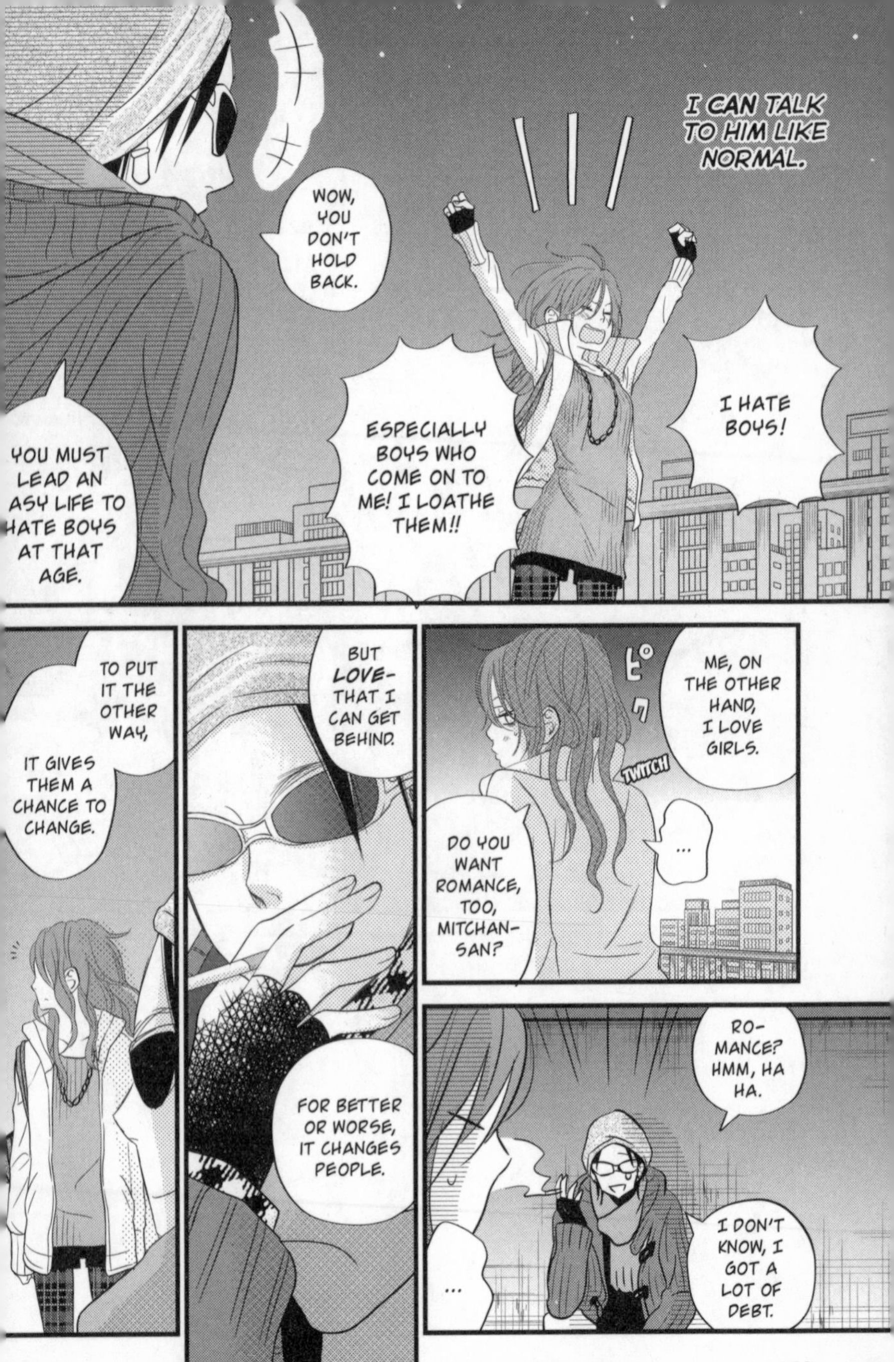
I CAN TALK TO HIM LIKE NORMAL.
I HATE BOYS!
ESPECIALLY BOYS WHO COME ON TO ME! I LOATHE THEM!!
WOW, YOU DON'T HOLD BACK.
YOU MUST LEAD AN ASY LIFE TO HATE BOYS AT THAT AGE.
ME, ON THE OTHER HAND, I LOVE GIRLS.
ピク
TWITCH
...
DO YOU WANT ROMANCE, TOO, MITCHAN-SAN?
ROMANCE? HMM, HA HA.
I DON'T KNOW, I GOT A LOT OF DEBT.
...
BUT LOVE-THAT I CAN GET BEHIND.
FOR BETTER OR WORSE, IT CHANGES PEOPLE.
TO PUT IT THE OTHER WAY,
IT GIVES THEM A CHANCE TO CHANGE.

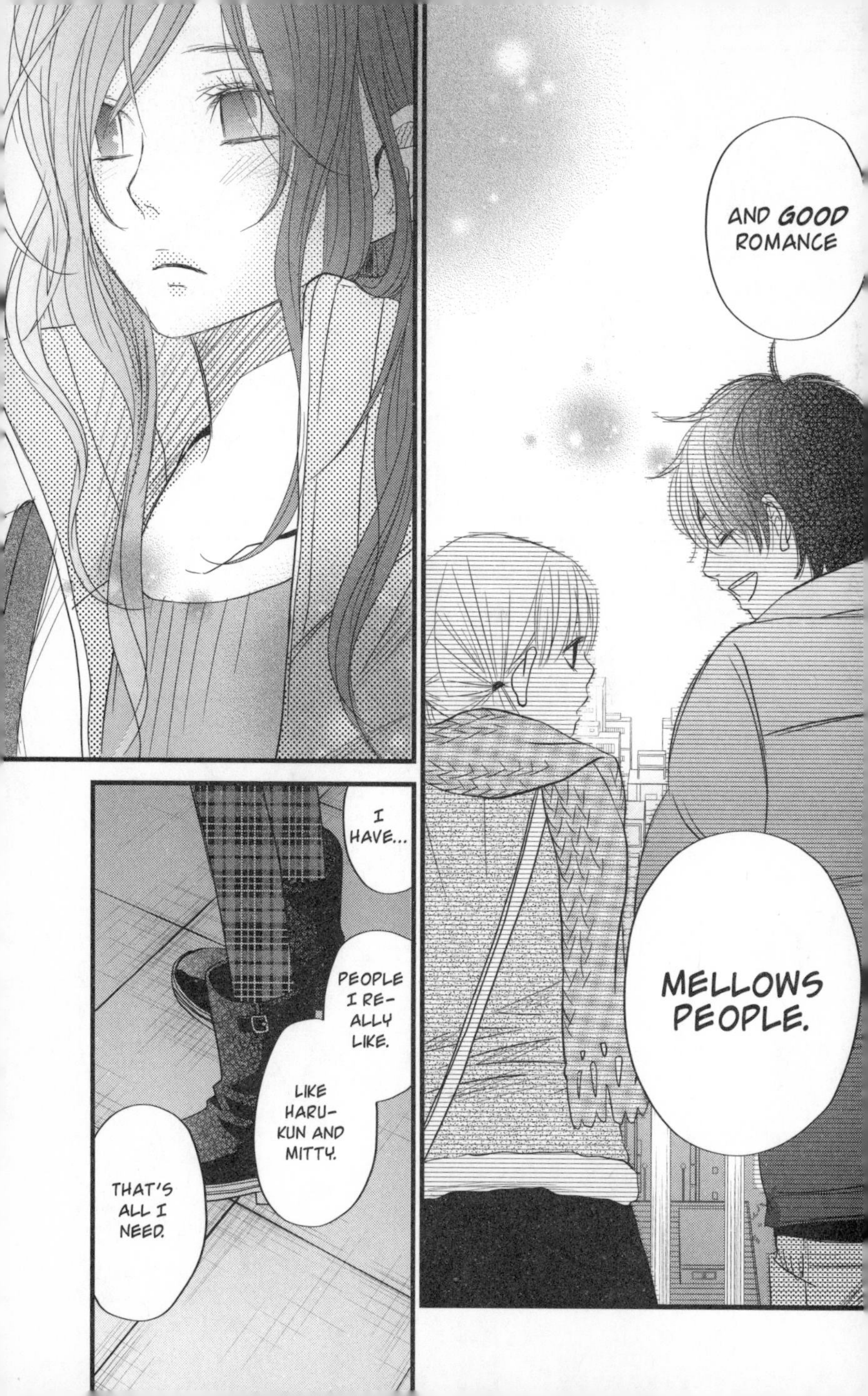
AND GOOD ROMANCE
MELLOWS PEOPLE.
I HAVE...
PEOPLE I RE-ALLY LIKE.
LIKE HARU-KUN AND MITTY.
THAT'S ALL I NEED.

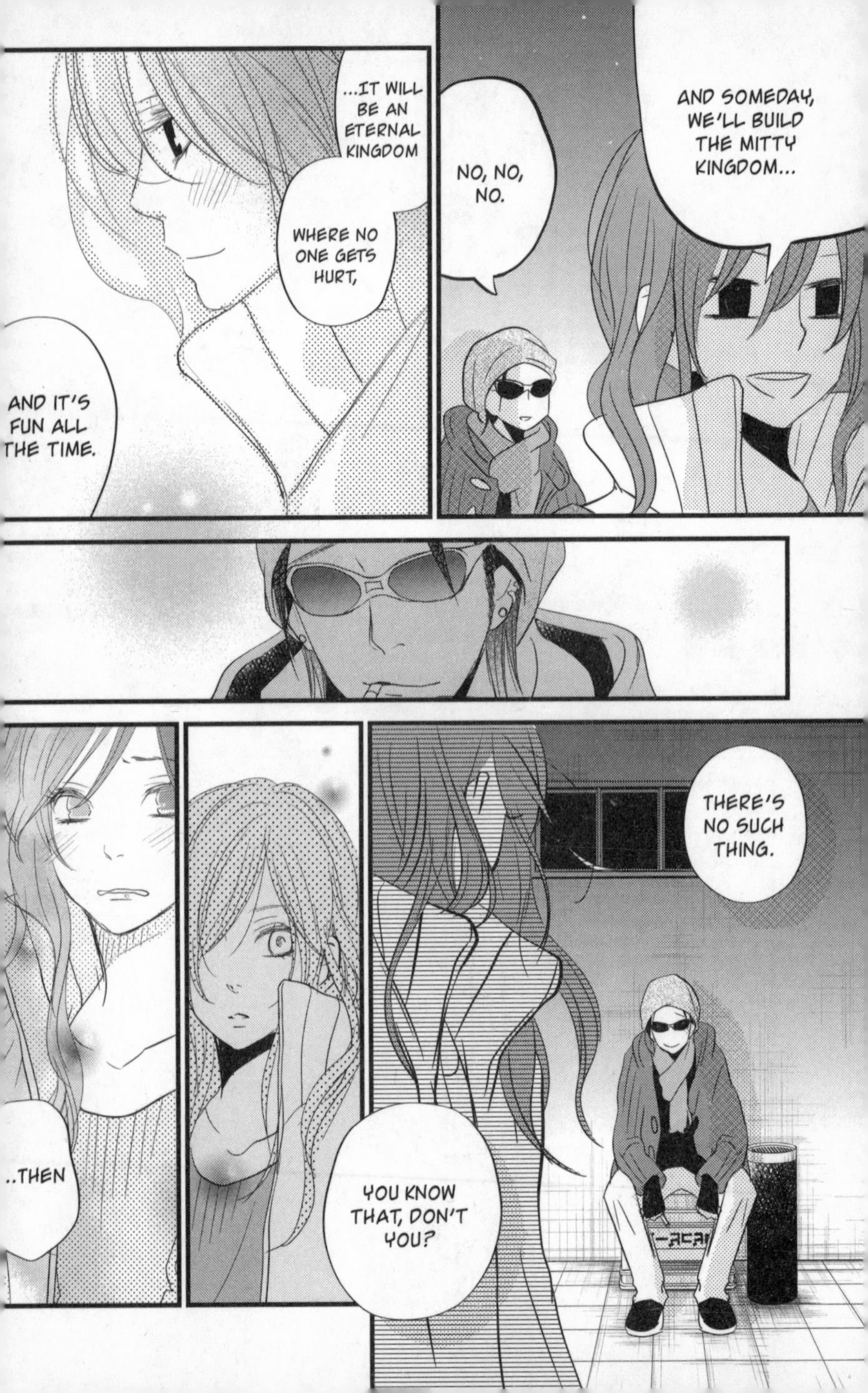
AND SOMEDAY, WE'LL BUILD THE MITTY KINGDOM...
NO, NO, NO.
...IT WILL BE AN ETERNAL KINGDOM
WHERE NO ONE GETS HURT,
AND IT'S FUN ALL THE TIME.
THERE'S NO SUCH THING.
YOU KNOW THAT, DON'T YOU?
..THEN

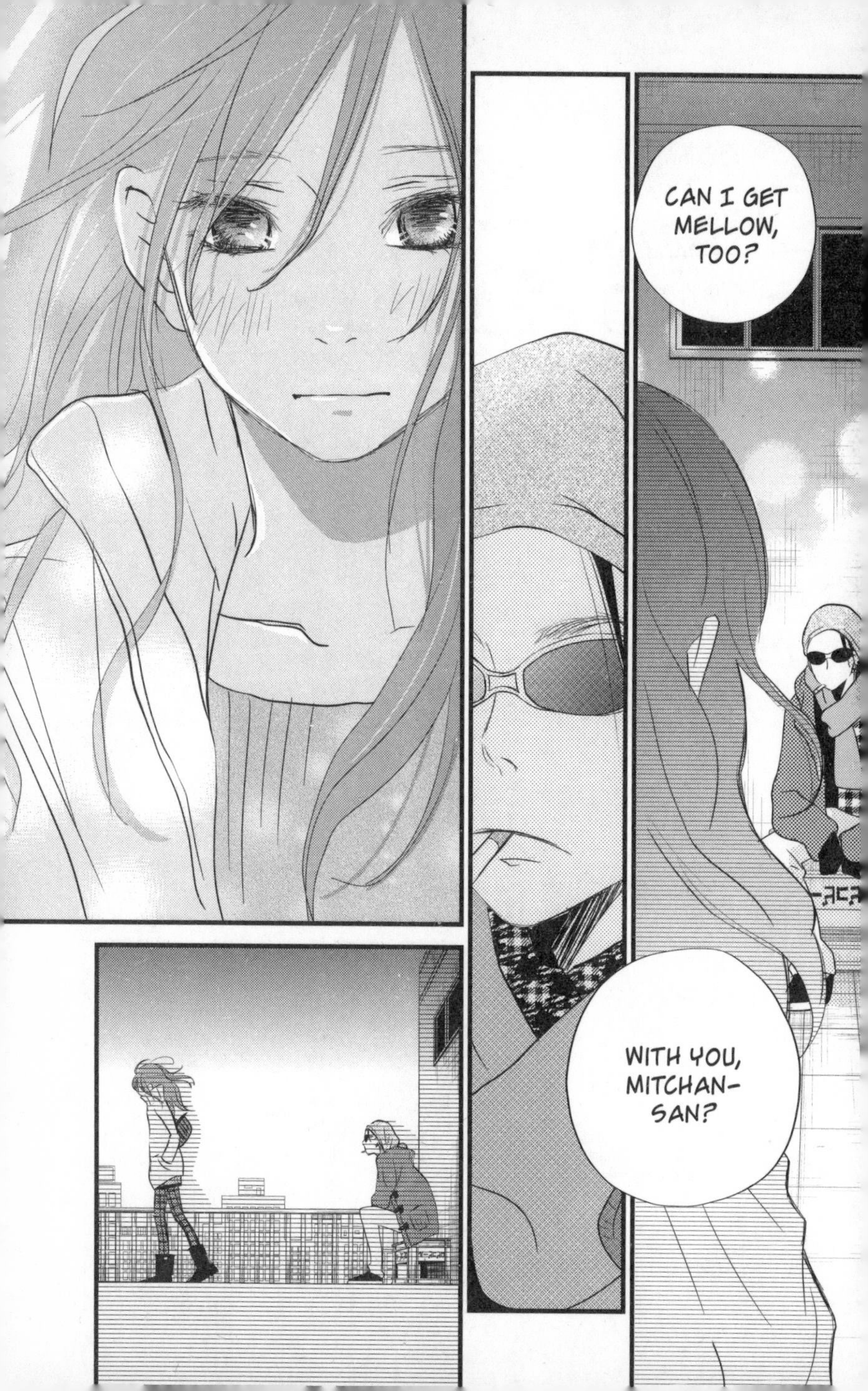

CAN I GET MELLOW, TOO?
WITH YOU, MITCHAN-SAN?

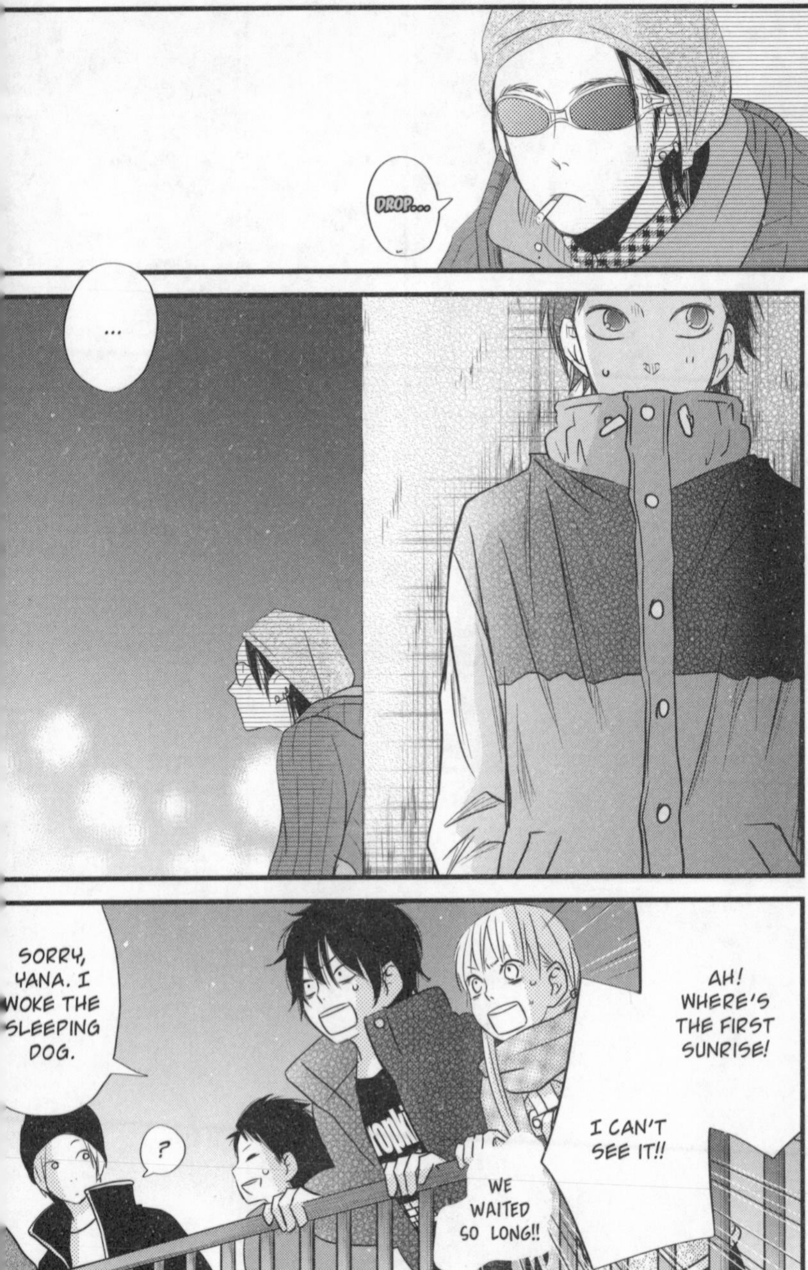
DROP...
...
AH! WHERE'S THE FIRST SUNRISE!
I CAN'T SEE IT!!
WE WAITED SO LONG!!
?
SORRY, YANA. I WOKE THE SLEEPING DOG.

Continued in Volume 5!!

Amazake

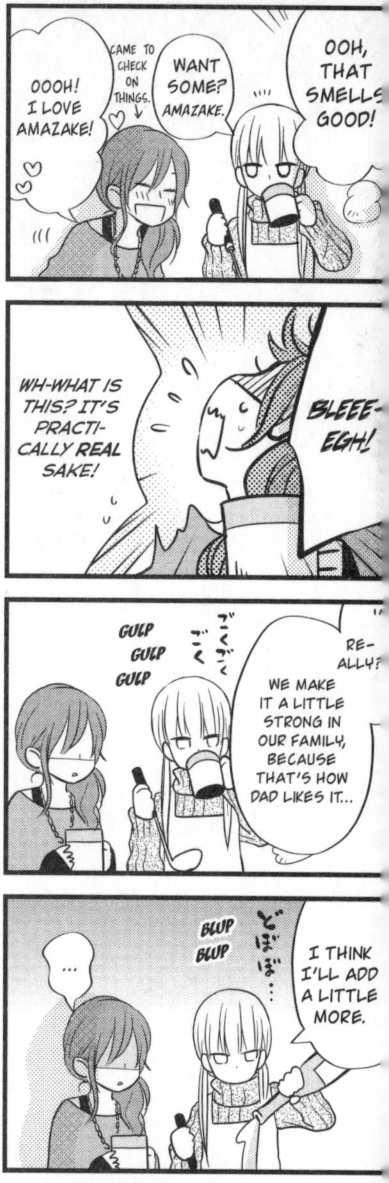
OOH, THAT SMELLS GOOD!
WANT SOME? AMAZAKE.
CAME TO CHECK ON THINGS.
OOOH! I LOVE AMAZAKE!
BLEEE-EGH!
WH-WHAT IS THIS? IT'S PRACTI-CALLY REAL SAKE!
RE-ALLY?
WE MAKE IT A LITTLE STRONG IN OUR FAMILY, BECAUSE THAT'S HOW DAD LIKES IT...
ごくごく
GULP GULP GULP
I THINK I'LL ADD A LITTLE MORE.
どぼぼ…
BLUP BLUP
...

Defeated

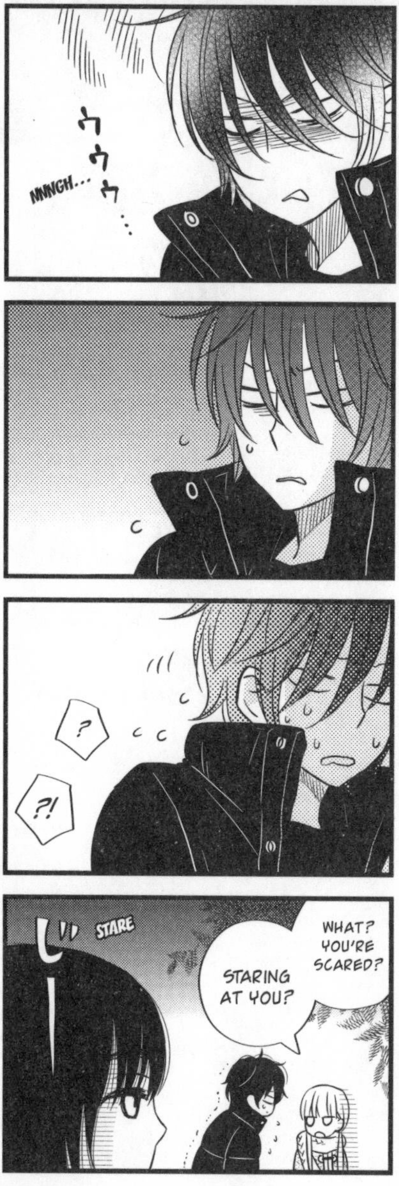
ウウウ…
NNNGH...
?
?!
WHAT? YOU'RE SCARED?
STARING AT YOU?
じー
STARE

Chapter 16.5 | When the New Year's Bell Stops Ringing

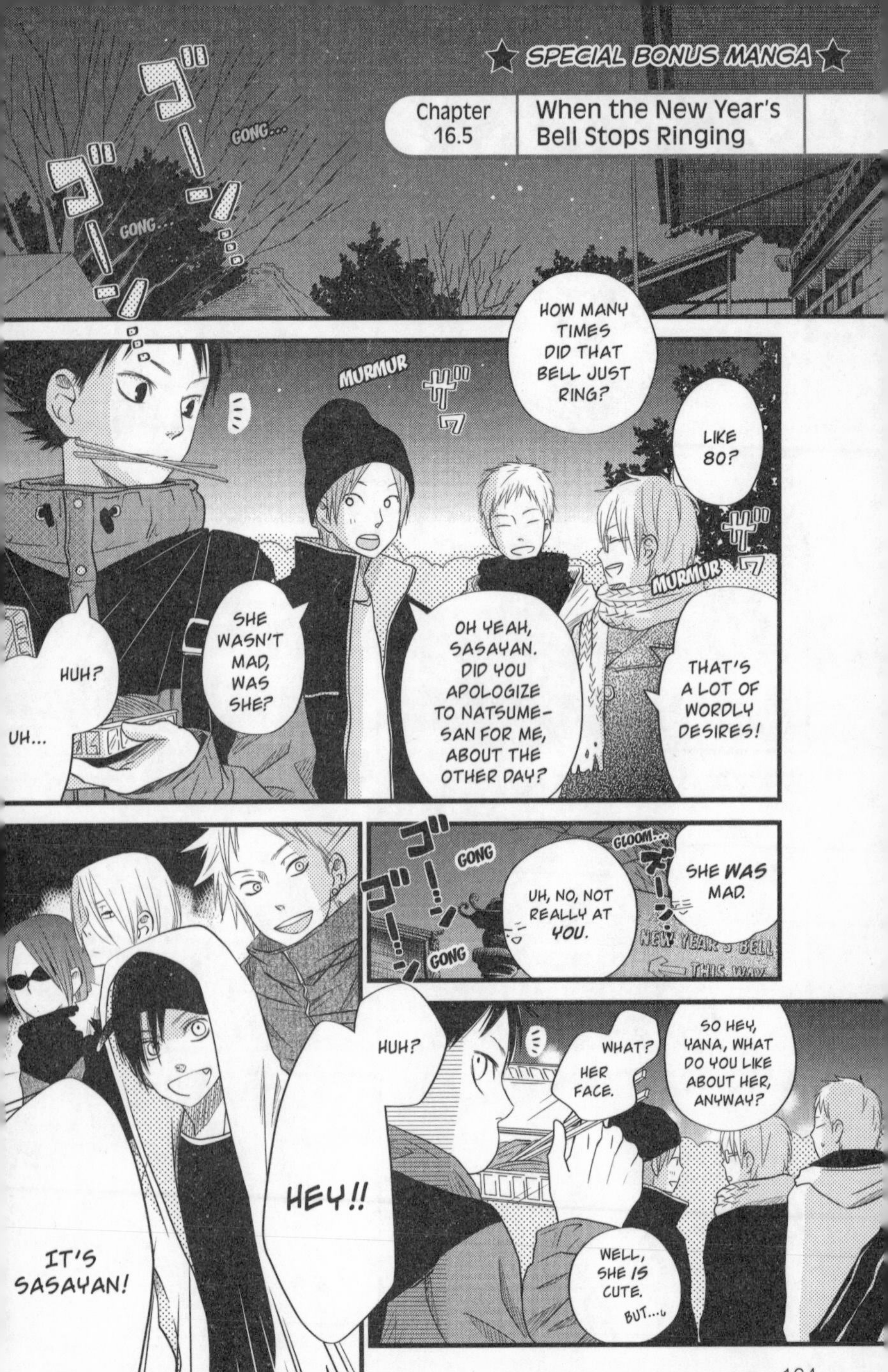
GONG...
GONG...
HOW MANY TIMES DID THAT BELL JUST RING?
LIKE 80?
THAT'S A LOT OF WORDLY DESIRES!
MURMUR
OH YEAH, SASAYAN. DID YOU APOLOGIZE TO NATSUME-SAN FOR ME, ABOUT THE OTHER DAY?
SHE WASN'T MAD, WAS SHE?
MURMUR
HUH?
UH...
SHE *WAS* MAD.
GLOOM...
UH, NO, NOT REALLY AT *YOU*.
GONG
GONG
NEW YEAR'S BELL
THIS WAY
SO HEY, YANA, WHAT DO YOU LIKE ABOUT HER, ANYWAY?
WHAT?
HER FACE.
WELL, SHE *IS* CUTE.
BUT...
HUH?
HEY!!
IT'S SASAYAN!

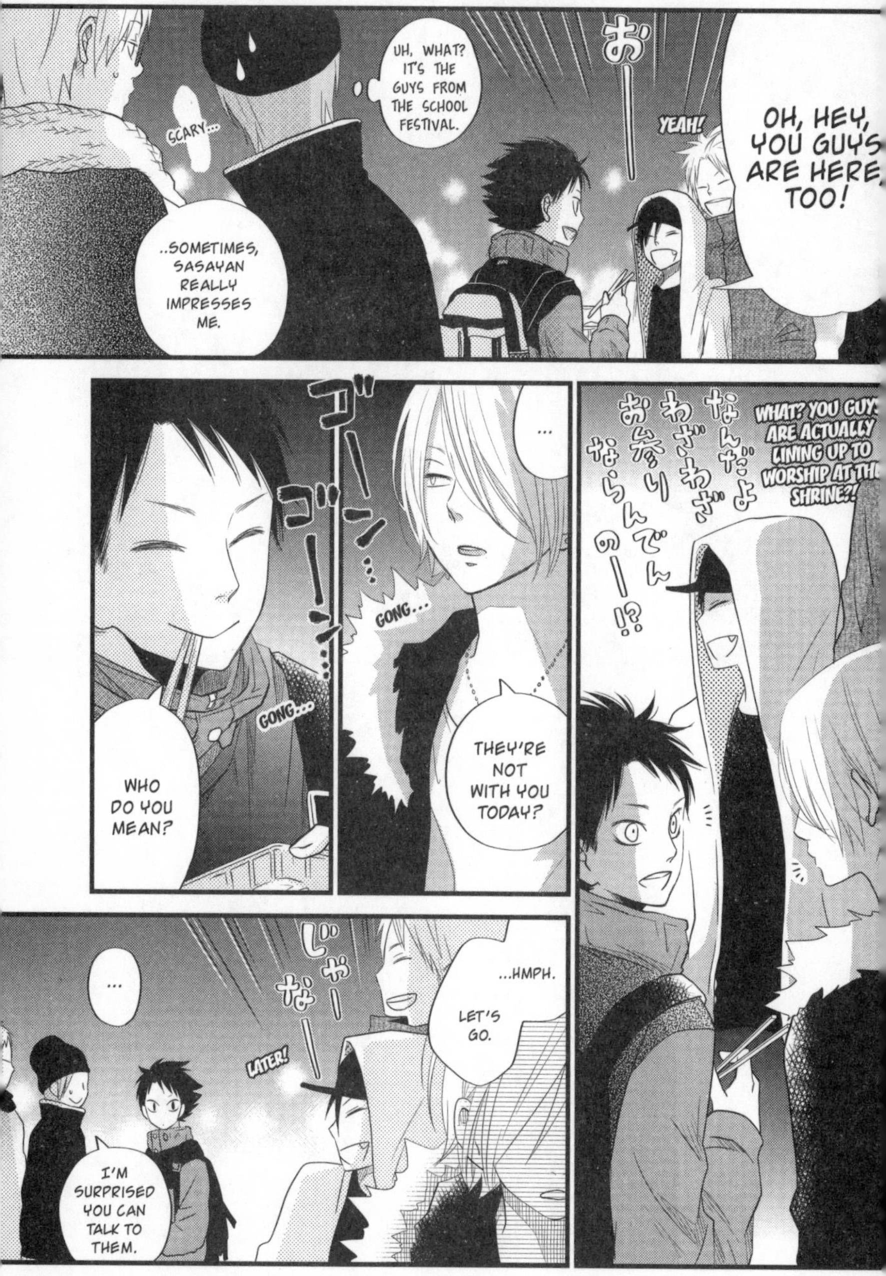
OH, HEY, YOU GUYS ARE HERE, TOO!
おーー
YEAH!
UH, WHAT? IT'S THE GUYS FROM THE SCHOOL FESTIVAL.
SCARY...
..SOMETIMES, SASAYAN REALLY IMPRESSES ME.
なんだよわざわざお参りならんでんのー!?
WHAT? YOU GUYS ARE ACTUALLY LINING UP TO WORSHIP AT THE SHRINE?!
...
THEY'RE NOT WITH YOU TODAY?
ゴーン…
GONG...
ゴーーン…
GONG...
WHO DO YOU MEAN?
...HMPH.
LET'S GO.
じゃーなー
LATER!
...
I'M SURPRISED YOU CAN TALK TO THEM.

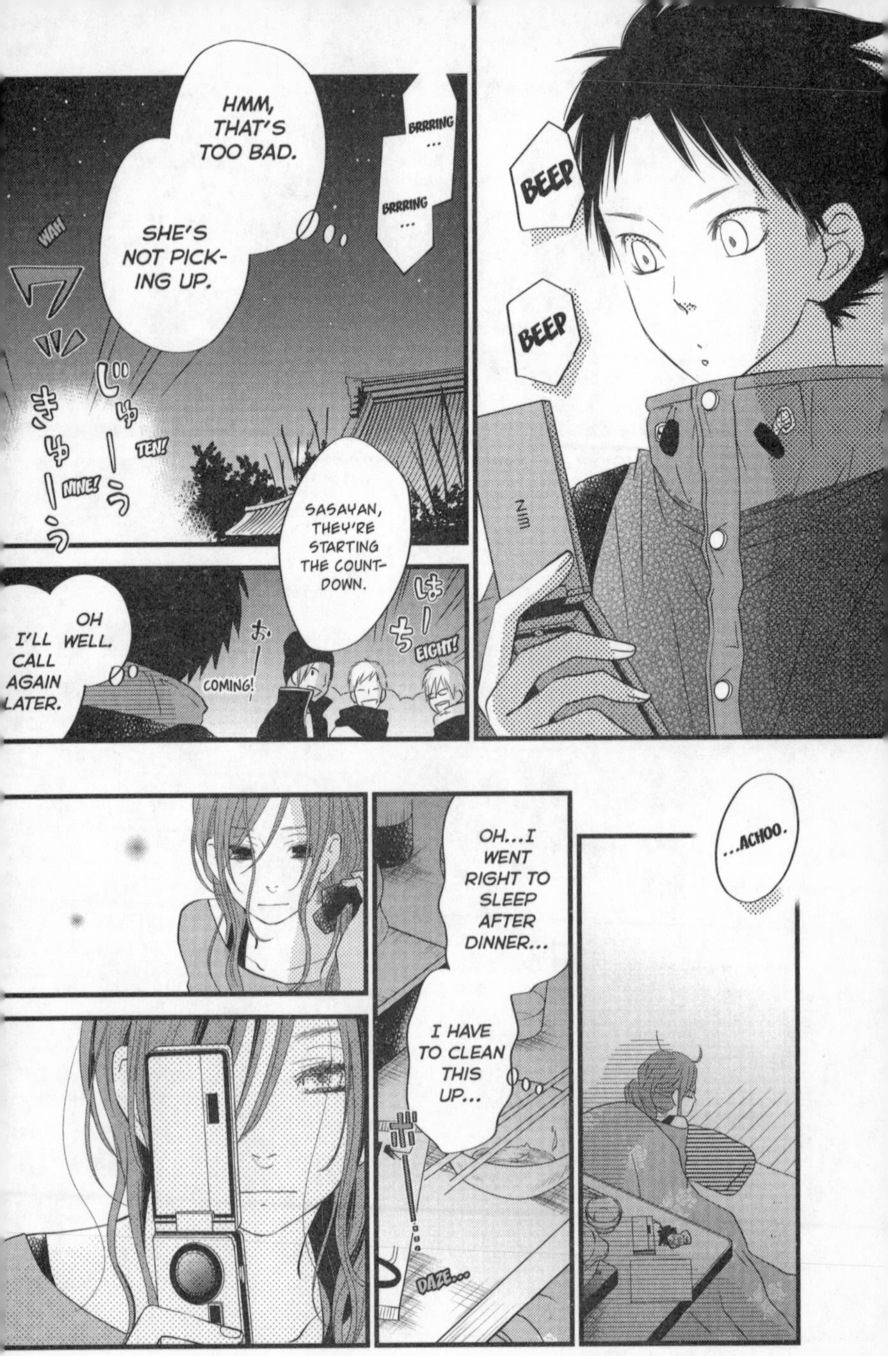

BEEP
BEEP
BRRRING...
BRRRING...
HMM, THAT'S TOO BAD.
SHE'S NOT PICK-ING UP.
じゅーう
TEN!
ワッきゅーう
NINE!
WAH
SASAYAN, THEY'RE STARTING THE COUNT-DOWN.
はーち
EIGHT!
おー
COMING!
OH WELL. I'LL CALL AGAIN LATER.
...ACHOO.
OH...I WENT RIGHT TO SLEEP AFTER DINNER...
I HAVE TO CLEAN THIS UP...
DAZE...

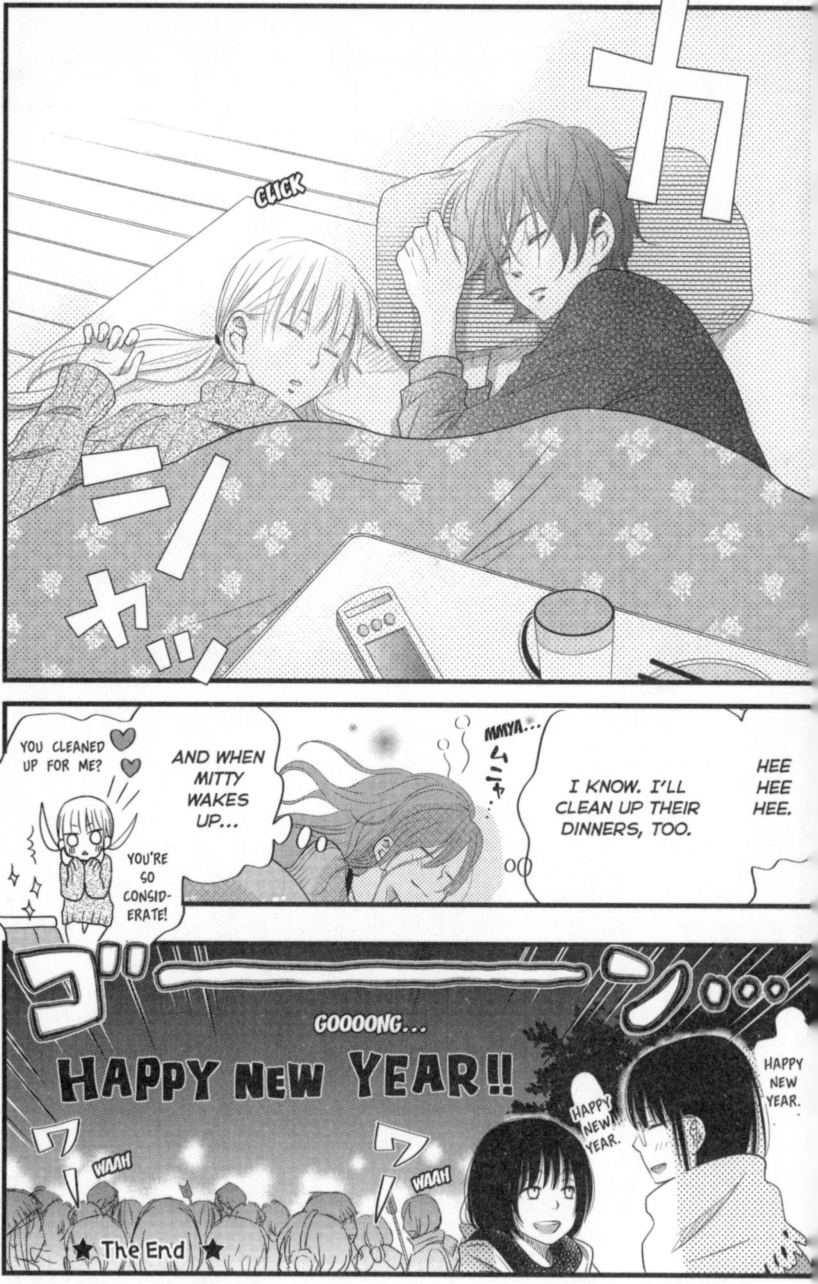
CLICK
HEE HEE HEE.
I KNOW. I'LL CLEAN UP THEIR DINNERS, TOO.
MMYA...
ムニャ…
AND WHEN MITTY WAKES UP...
YOU CLEANED UP FOR ME?
YOU'RE SO CONSID-ERATE!
GOOOONG...
HAPPY NEW YEAR!!
HAPPY NEW YEAR.
HAPPY NEW YEAR.
WAAH
WAAH
★ The End ★

Translation Notes

Japanese is a tricky language for most Westerners, and translation is often more art than science. For your edificaiton and reading pleasure, here are notes on some of the places where we could have gone in a different direction with our translation of this book, or where a Japanese cultural reference is used.

The Dog of Flanders, page 12

The Dog of Flanders is an anime film based on the book, *A Dog of Flanders*. It's a very sad story about the life of an orphan boy.

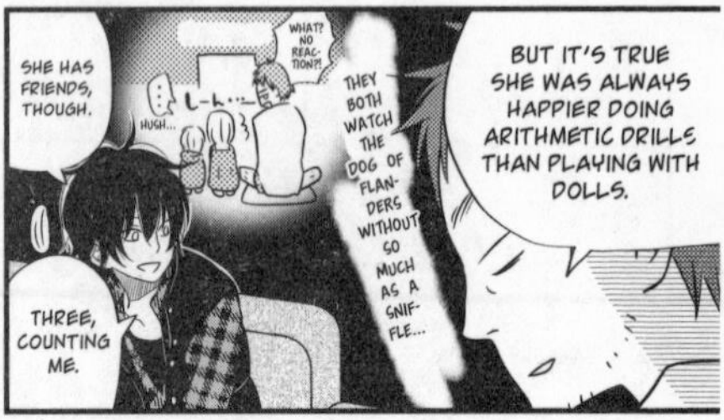
BUT IT'S TRUE SHE WAS ALWAYS HAPPIER DOING ARITHMETIC DRILLS THAN PLAYING WITH DOLLS.
THEY BOTH WATCH THE DOG OF FLANDERS WITHOUT SO MUCH AS A SNIFFLE...
WHAT? NO REACTION?!
HUGH...
SHE HAS FRIENDS, THOUGH.
THREE, COUNTING ME.

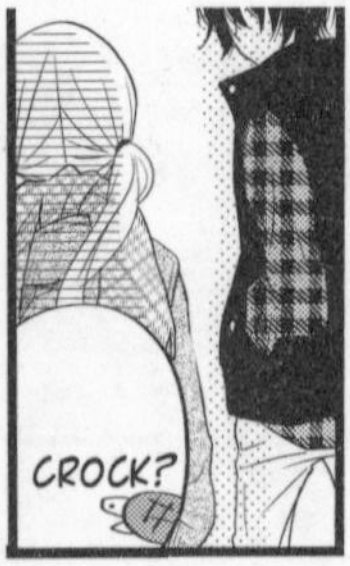
CROCK?

The crock, page 18

There's a very good reason that there's a picture of a turtle when Haru asks what Shizuku means by "crock." The word Shizuku used in Japanese was *kame*, which means "pot" or "crock," but with the right Chinese character, the word can also mean "turtle." The translators used "crock" because it was the word that worked best as far as meaning "pot" as well as somehow relating to aquatic reptiles.

The shoebox and the mysterious invitation, page 45

In Japan, it's customary to remove one's shoes before entering a building, including some public buildings such as schools. In schools where shoe removal is required, students are given little cupboards, like small lockers, to store their shoes and other small personal items. (While storing their shoes, the students wear slippers around the school.) These shoeboxes are also good places for people to leave anonymous messages such as love letters and mysterious invitations.

The invitation from Summer X is interesting to note, as it shows several hints at the mysterious character's true identity. First, there are misspellings and failed attempts at fancy Chinese kanji characters. On the original Japanese note, Summer X tried to write the kanji for "Shizuku," but it was too complicated and she gave up, instead writing the name in the simpler Japanese kana characters. Finally, the Japanese word for summer is *natsu*, and X can be used to tell people when something is *dame* (bad), or *me* for short.

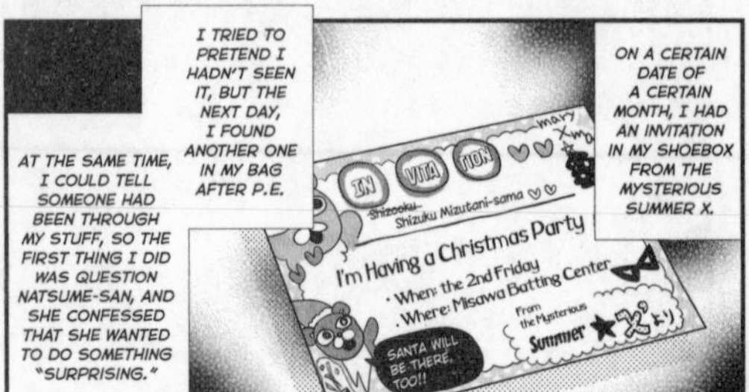
ON A CERTAIN DATE OF A CERTAIN MONTH, I HAD AN INVITATION IN MY SHOEBOX FROM THE MYSTERIOUS SUMMER X.
IN VITA TION
Shizooku Shizuku Mizutani-sama
I'm Having a Christmas Party
· When: the 2nd Friday
· Where: Misawa Batting Center
From the Mysterious Summer
SANTA WILL BE THERE, TOO!!
I TRIED TO PRETEND I HADN'T SEEN IT, BUT THE NEXT DAY, I FOUND ANOTHER ONE IN MY BAG AFTER P.E.
AT THE SAME TIME, I COULD TELL SOMEONE HAD BEEN THROUGH MY STUFF, SO THE FIRST THING I DID WAS QUESTION NATSUME-SAN, AND SHE CONFESSED THAT SHE WANTED TO DO SOMETHING "SURPRISING."

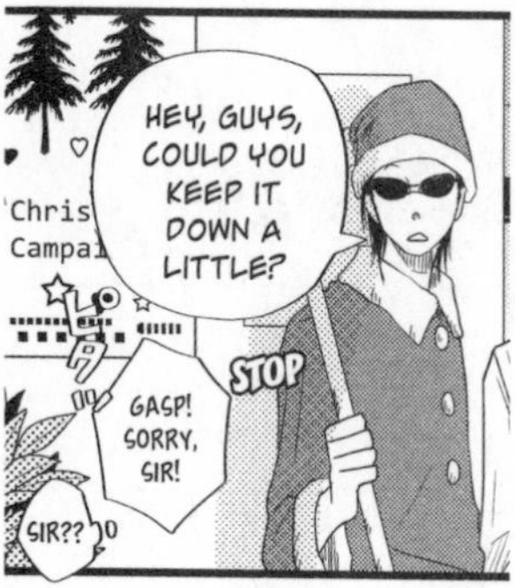
HEY, GUYS, COULD YOU KEEP IT DOWN A LITTLE?
STOP
GASP! SORRY, SIR!
SIR??

Sir, page 56

Yamaken's thug friends are trying their hardest not to offend Mitchan. In the Japanese version, when they're talking about him, they call him *ossan*, short for *oji-san*, which is how you refer to middle-aged men. But now that they're talking to him, they're trying to get into his good graces by calling him *nii-san*, which is how you refer to a younger man. It's their attempt to compliment him on his youthful appearance, whether or not they think he has one. Since the English language doesn't have such age-discriminating forms of address (at least not in modern usage), the translators indicated their excessive politeness by having the thugs call him "sir," even though that does run the risk of making the addressee feel old.

Spider's thread, page 73

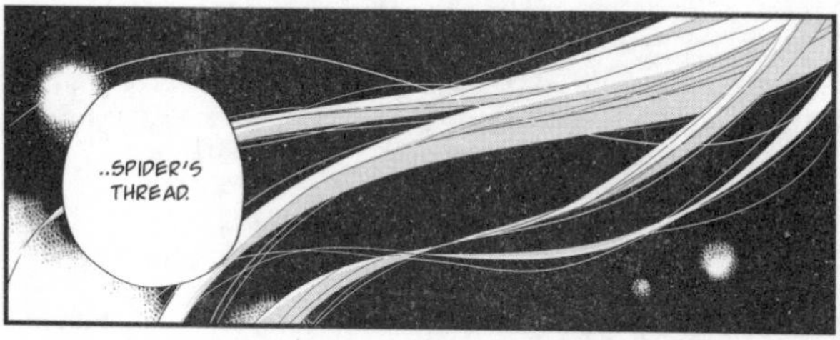
..SPIDER'S THREAD.

Haru is referencing a famous short story, "The Spider's Thread," by Ryūnosuke Akutagawa. A man guilty of various crimes finds himself in hell. The man had accomplished one good deed in life, and that was to avoid a spider instead of stepping on it. Because of this good deed, Buddha gives the criminal a chance to redeem himself by lowering a single strand of spider's thread to him, for him to climb up. As the man climbs, other convicted sinners see the way out of hell and start to climb up behind him. Concerned that their weight will cause the thread to break, the man shouts at the others to get off—the thread is his. At that point, the thread breaks, and the man had condemned himself to remain in hell by refusing to share his salvation.

Sits when it stands, page 83

For the curious, the Japanese version of the riddle was similar, but different. The question Asako can be translated to "what stands even when it's sitting?", but is a play on words. The Japanese word for "stand," tatsu, is a homonym, and can also mean "pass," as in the passage of time. Because of the way Japanese grammar works, the question could also be translated as, "What tatsus even though [someone is] sitting?" The answer: time passes even when everyone/thing is sitting around.

Swift as the coursing river, page 88

As you may have guessed, the cram school teacher here did not actually quote Disney's Mulan. Rather, he quoted a *daimyo*, or territorial lord, from the Sengoku Era of Japan, Takeda Shingen. Shingen used as his battle standard four quotations from Sun Tzu's The Art of War: "as fast as the wind," "as silent as the forest," "as fierce as the fire," "as unmovable as the mountain." In Japanese, these four quotations have been shortened to fū rin ka zan: wind, forest, fire, mountain. Kids in this particular cram school course would be expected to know exactly what the teacher is referring to with just those four words.

I know Christmas is coming up, page 89

In Japan, Christmas—and especially Christmas Eve—is a romantic holiday, and so being without a significant other can be depressing for many. Ma-bo is suggesting that Yamaken is desperate to find a Christmas Eve date.

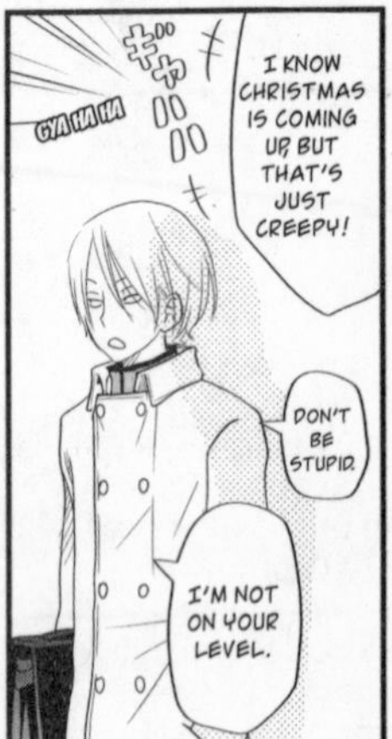
I KNOW CHRISTMAS IS COMING UP, BUT THAT'S JUST CREEPY!
GYA HA HA
DON'T BE STUPID.
I'M NOT ON YOUR LEVEL.

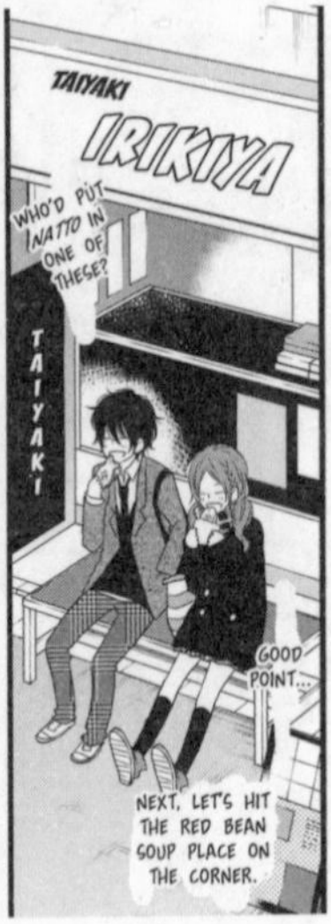
TAIYAKI
IRIKIYA
WHO'D PUT NATTO IN ONE OF THESE?
TAIYAKI
GOOD POINT...
NEXT, LET'S HIT THE RED BEAN SOUP PLACE ON THE CORNER.

Taiyaki, page 135

Taiyaki is a kind of cake made with pancake or waffle batter, and stuffed with any kind of filling you can think of, most commonly red bean paste, although of course there are some fillings that are likely to be avoided, such as *natto*—fermented soy beans. The cake is baked (*yaki*) in the shape of a kind of fish (sea bream, or *tai*), hence the name, *taiyaki*.

Kotatsu, page 141

In Japanese homes, central heating isn't always a feature. Instead, everyone sits around a kotatsu, which is a kind of table that has a heater under it.

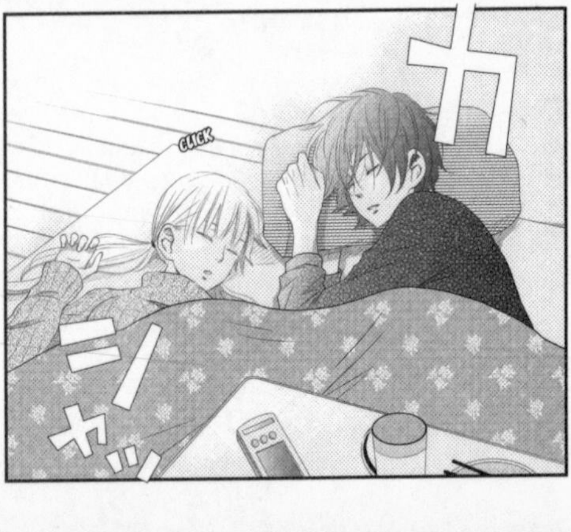
CLICK

Omikuji fortunes, page 150

An omikuji is a little strip of paper with a fortune written on it, kind of like what you find in a fortune cookie, obtained at Japanese Buddhist and Shinto shrines by making an offering and choosing one at random. Each strip lists the amount of luck the chooser is going to have, ranging from dai-kichi (great blessing, great luck), through lesser degrees of luck and on through the degrees of curses of bad luck. If you get a bad luck fortune, you can dispel the curse by tying the omikuji strip of paper to a tree or a designated wire provided by the shrine or temple.

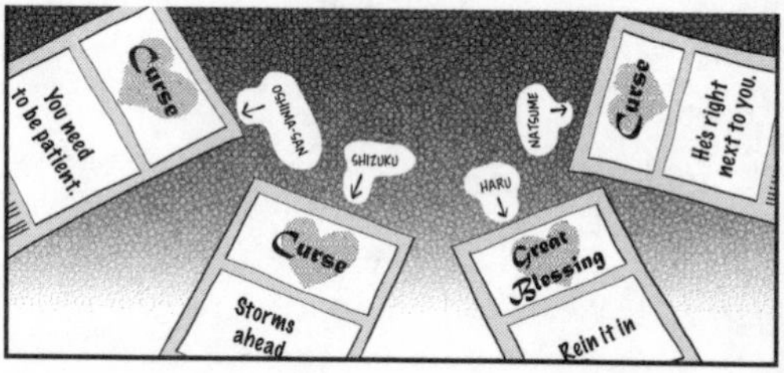
NATSUME
Curse
He's right next to you.
HARU
Great Blessing
Rein it in
SHIZUKU
Curse
Storms ahead
OSHIMA-SAN
Curse
You need to be patient.

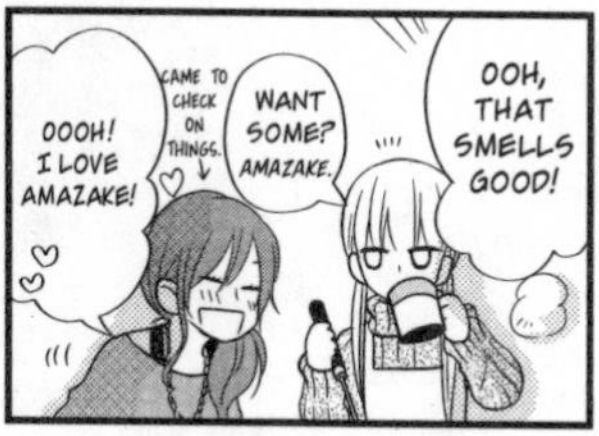
OOH, THAT SMELLS GOOD!
WANT SOME? AMAZAKE.
CAME TO CHECK ON THINGS.
OOOH! I LOVE AMAZAKE!

Amazake, page 163

Amazake means "sweet sake," and is a sweet rice wine. It is usually non-alcoholic, but sometimes it does have a small amount of alcohol, apparently more alcohol than usual in the Mizutani household.

New Year's Bell, page 164

Traditionally, the New Year's Bell is rung 108 times, around midnight. One theory as to why this is, is that the number 108 represents the types of worldly desires that exist in the world, and hearing the bell ring can purify your heart of those worldly desires that had built up over the last year. However, the number of rings can vary from temple to temple, sometimes ringing more than 200 times.

Mei Tachibana has no friends — and says she doesn't need them!

But everything changes when she accidentally roundhouse kicks the most popular boy in school! However, Yamato Kurosawa isn't angry in the slightest—in fact, he thinks his ordinary life could use an unusual girl like Mei. But winning Mei's trust will be a tough task. How long will she refuse to say, "I love you"?

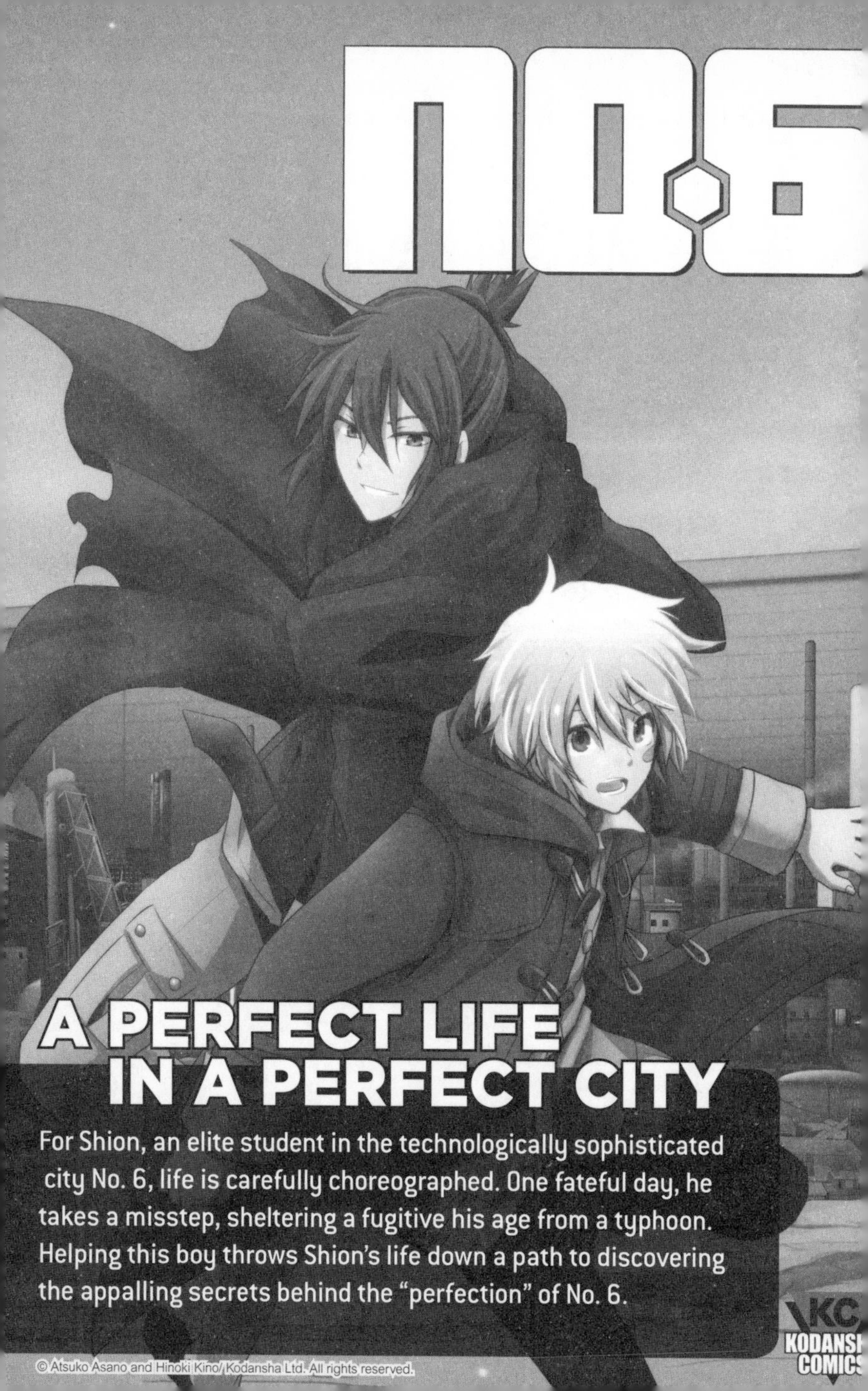
NO.6
A PERFECT LIFE
IN A PERFECT CITY
For Shion, an elite student in the technologically sophisticated city No. 6, life is carefully choreographed. One fateful day, he takes a misstep, sheltering a fugitive his age from a typhoon. Helping this boy throws Shion's life down a path to discovering the appalling secrets behind the "perfection" of No. 6.
KC
KODANSHA COMICS
© Atsuko Asano and Hinoki Kino/Kodansha Ltd. All rights reserved.

The Pretty Guardians are back!

★

Kodansha Comics is proud to present *Sailor Moon* with all new translations.

For more information, go to **www.kodanshacomics.com**

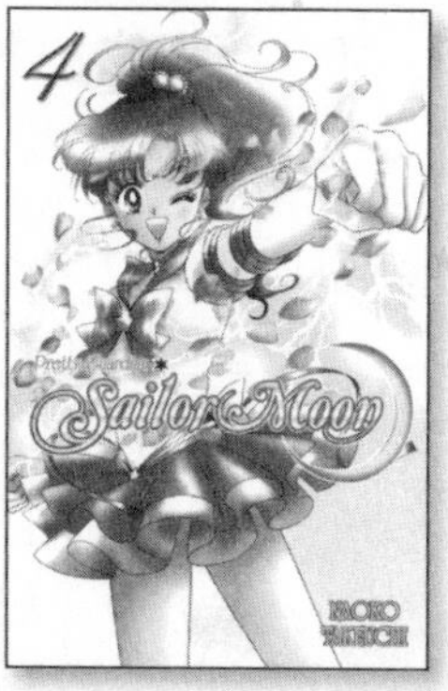
4
Pretty Guardian
Sailor Moon
NAOKO TAKEUCHI
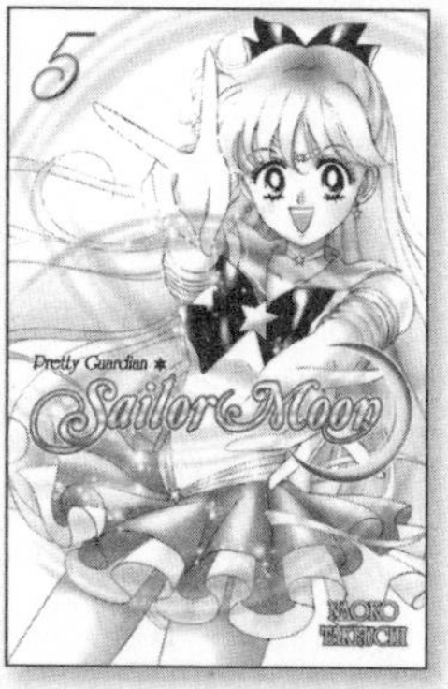
5
Pretty Guardian
Sailor Moon
NAOKO TAKEUCHI
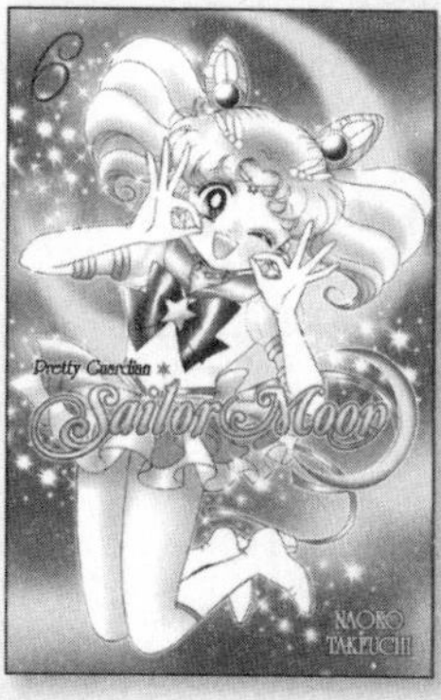
6
Pretty Guardian
Sailor Moon
NAOKO TAKEUCHI
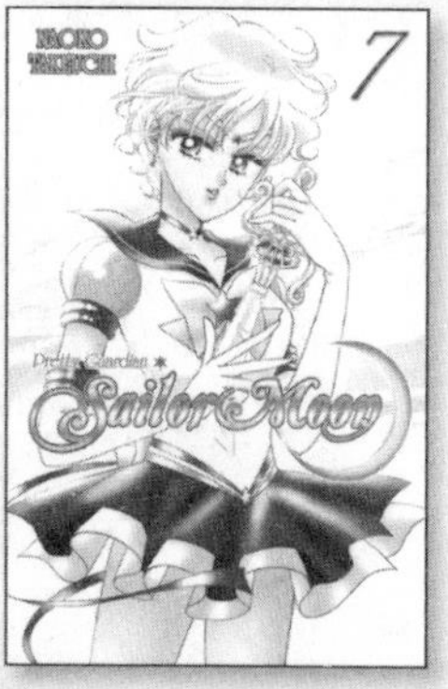
NAOKO TAKEUCHI
7
Pretty Guardian
Sailor Moon
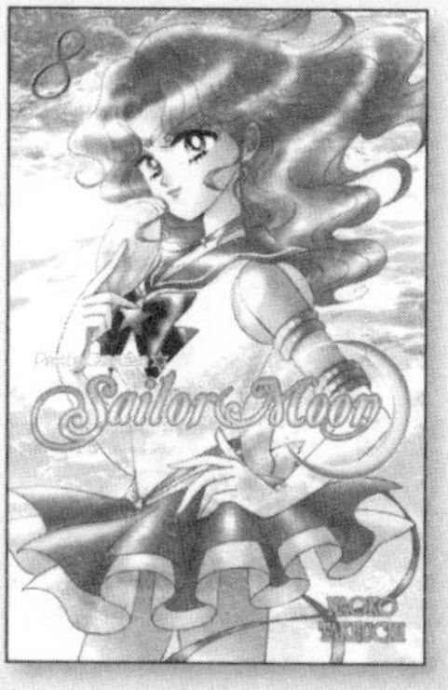
8
Sailor Moon
NAOKO TAKEUCHI
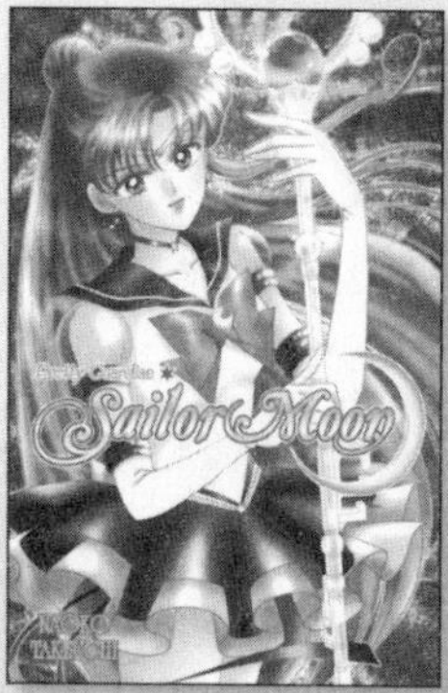
Sailor Moon
NAOKO TAKEUCHI
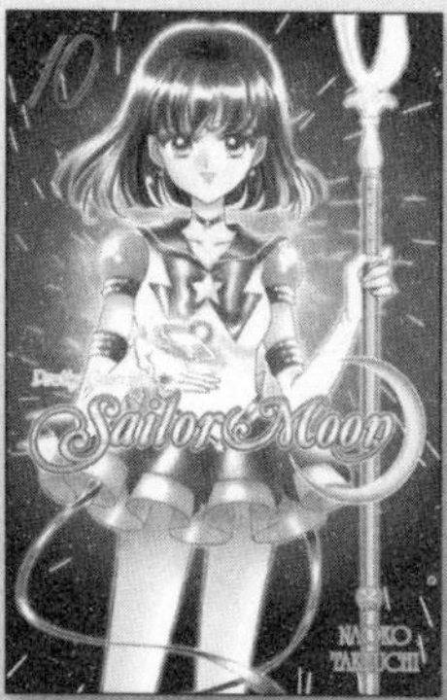
10
Sailor Moon
NAOKO TAKEUCHI
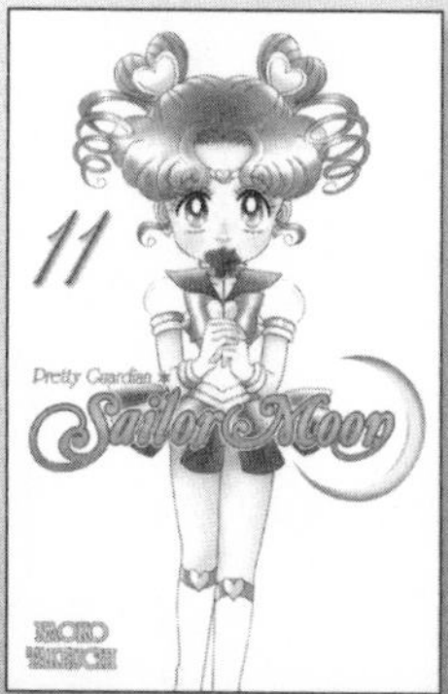
11
Pretty Guardian
Sailor Moon
NAOKO TAKEUCHI
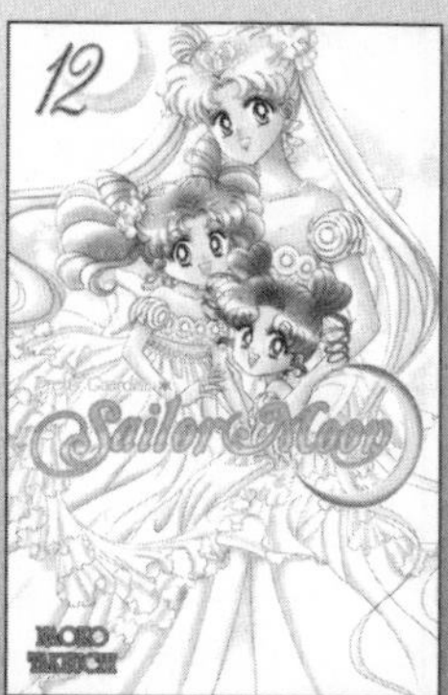
12
Sailor Moon
NAOKO TAKEUCHI

KC
KODANSHA COMICS

A Kodansha Comics Trade Paperback Original.

My Little Monster volume 4 copyright © 2010 Robico
English translation copyright © 2014 Robico

All rights reserved.

Published in the United States by Kodansha Comics, an imprint of Kodansha USA Publishing, LLC, New York.

Publication rights for this English edition arranged through Kodansha Ltd., Tokyo.

First published in Japan in 2010 by Kodansha Ltd., Tokyo, as *Tonari no Kaibutsu-kun*, volume 4.

ISBN 978-1-61262-600-0

Printed in the United States of America.

www.kodanshacomics.com

9 8 7 6 5 4 3

Translator: Alethea Nibley & Athena Nibley
Lettering: Kiyoko Shiromasa